PLAYBOY

BARTENDER'S GUIDE

PLAYBOY

BARTENDER'S
GUIDE

Thomas Mario

Illustrations by LeRoy Neiman

BARNES
& NOBLE
BOOKS
NEW YORK

A BARNES & NOBLE BOOK

This edition 2003 by Michael Friedman Publishing Group under
license from Playboy Enterprises International, Inc.

©1971, 1979 by Thomas Mario

The present work is based in part on Thomas Mario's
Playboy's New Host and Bar Book (Chicago: Playboy Press, 1979)

Playboy and Rabbit Head design are trademarks of
Playboy Enterprises International, Inc.

Library of Congress Cataloging-in-Publication Data available upon request.

ISBN 0-7607-4202-2

Editors: Betsy Beier and Rosy Ngo
Art Director: Jeff Batzli
Designer: Kevin Baier
Production Manager: Michael Vagnetti
Digital Imaging Specialist: Daniel J. Rutkowski

Femlin illustrations by LeRoy Neiman
Additional illustrations by Daniel Lish

Digitally reproduced and printed in USA by Quebecor World–Kingsport

3 5 7 9 10 8 6 4

Contents

Introduction

Drinking, like so many of the finer things in life, changes with the times but never goes out of style. So, while the ancient Teutonic custom of quaffing beer out of vessels made from the skulls of your enemies might raise a few eyebrows at a keg party today, the old proverb still applies: *Essen und Trinken hält Leib und Seele zusammen* ("Eating and drinking holds body and soul together"). And we've come a long way since the days of Prohibition, when it was definitively proven that not even outlawing alcohol with a Constitutional Amendment could keep Americans from drinking the stuff with abandon. Indeed, in the span of thirty years since Playboy's first bartender's guide, *Playboy's Bar Guide*, was published, the popularity and availability of different wines and spirits have exploded, and new drinking habits have proliferated among the cognoscenti with positively revolutionary fervor.

Any accomplished host today knows, for example, that the once-traditional Saturday-night boozefest, featuring straight shots of anything from white-corn liquor to Peruvian pisco, has seeped into oblivion and that the two- or three-Martini business lunch has been disfranchised by the modern taste for cold, dry white wine. Twenty years ago, if someone mentioned Riesling, it brought to mind the luscious white wine of the Rhine valley;

today, magnificent Rieslings that rival the German are made not only in California and New York, but in Washington State, as well. And it's a good guess that there are as many wine drinkers in North America as there are in France familiar with the Official Classification of the Great Growths of the Gironde, Classification of 1855. Indeed, a surprising number of those superb French premiers crus, at one time available only in Madison Avenue wine shops, are now conspicuously displayed on supermarket shelves in those states sufficiently civilized to allow supermarkets to sell wine.

The Jamaican may know his rums, the Frenchman his Cognacs, and the Scot his single malts, but the American host in the last three decades has become expert in judging the entire worldwide range of bibulous pleasures, from Campari to Courvoisier, Tanqueray to Trockenbeerenauslese. Once unceremoniously downed in shots with little more adornment than lemon and salt, the tequilas available now are as smooth as the finest Cognacs and are enjoyed in much the same way. As for the fine rums available today, you wouldn't dream of mixing them with Coke—or even ice, for that matter.

This isn't to imply that brandy, gin, vodka, and whiskey have gone out of style. But instead of serving shots of stiff, straight liquor at the highest possible proof, today's hosts are featuring refined liquors regardless of proof and turning to easy-sail entertaining with mixed drinks. At today's tailgates, you'll be offered anything from Stingers to sparkling Spanish cavas. And at the beach or the pool, the number of tall coolers proffered has grown exponentially. In tune with these trends, Playboy's NEW *Bartender's Guide* has expanded its recipes for mixed drinks from approximately 1,000 to 1,400.

For those Americans new to the fine art of hosting, endless avenues have been opened now that the United States distills some of the best spirits and makes some of the finest wines in the world. The nation is also the world's largest clearinghouse for potations shipped from every corner of the earth. Obviously, in order to navigate this growing network of choices, a road atlas is crucial. But in stocking your cellar or liquor cabinet, you hardly need one of those encyclopedic tomes describing in painstaking detail the chemistry of distillation and the yearly rainfall in the world's vineyards.

What is helpful is a down-to-earth guide such as this one that provides practical information about spirits and cocktail preparation: when age is important and when it is not; how to store and pour; which drinking vessel is appropriate; and whether drinks should be chilled, mixed, stirred, shaken, frappéed, garnished, blended in a pitcher, or brewed in a bowl.

Serving fine food and drink has evolved from the isolated hobby of a few to become the foundation of every host's education, and it is our hope to build upon that foundation with this completely up-to-date revision of the classic guide to entertaining. The *Playboy Bartender's Guide* is offered in the belief that whenever two or more people touch glasses, it isn't just the liquor stirring up fun—it's the appetite for life and the excitement felt at the many ways of satisfying that appetite. Encouraging this *joie de vivre* is not only Playboy's primary mission, it is also the raison d'être for this book.

A votre santé!

CHAPTER 1

☀ GLASSWARE ☀
☀ THE LONG AND SHORT OF IT ☀

Because fine glasses make drinking surprisingly more pleasurable, you should acquire those that are both functional and elegantly shaped. They should be so handsome that the mere sight of the sparkling, clear glasses on the shelf makes you want to pour liquor into them and begin quaffing. In choosing them, it isn't necessary to spend months delving into the drinking customs of Roman nobles or attempt to acquire gilt-decorated goblets made by Venetian glassmakers in the seventeenth century. It is helpful, however, to understand crystal and lime glass.

> CRYSTAL is glassware that contains lead, and the lead gives it weight, a bell-like tone, magnificent luster, and also a magnificent price.

> LIME GLASS (or soda-lime glass) lacks lead as one of its components and, while comparatively inexpensive, lacks the brilliance of crystal.

Crystal made in Europe is about 25 percent lead. In the United States the lead content may fall below 20 percent, and such crystal is sometimes called "half-lead" glassware. For fine entertaining, for displaying the rich color of a fine wine, crystal drinking vessels and the liquid poured into them are mutually flattering. For more casual entertaining, lime glassware not only costs less but also in some cases is more durable than its elegant cousin.

A label that says "hand-blown" or "mouth-blown" is usually the guide to the handsomest of all glassware. "Hand-blown" simply refers to the method wherein the glassmaker dips a long tube into a pot of molten glass, picks up a blob at one end of his pipe, and then, with his lips and breath as tools, blows until the bowl takes shape. He twists, turns, rubs, and paddles the blown bubble until it reaches its final perfect curve. Blown glassware is similar but made by machine. Pressed glassware—the least expensive—is made by pouring molten glass into molds from which it takes its shape. Today you can find drinkware of pressed glass with heavenly lines and limpid forms. Finally, there's "cut" glass—that is, glass cut or engraved and polished to reflect as much prismatic light as possible—the darling of conservative drinkers and very impressive when used for an Old-Fashioned cocktail or Whiskey and Soda.

Regardless of the quality of glassware you decide on, you'll find it available in three basic shapes.

1. *TUMBLERS* Glasses of cylindrical shape, sometimes with a heavy or "sham" bottom, which adds stability

2. *FOOTED GLASSES* Glasses of cylindrical or bowl shape that rest on a round pedestal or foot but with no stem

3. *STEMWARE* Glasses with a bowl, stem, and foot

Stemware not only is gracious to the eye but can be held in the hand without warming the contents of the bowl, and it is easier on furniture because condensation on the cold glass rarely makes its way down to the base or foot. Tumblers are less formal, more secure, and usually less expensive than the other two types, although some cut-glass tumblers are in the Rolls-Royce category.

If you want to limit yourself to only two kinds of glasses, the first one to buy is the on-the-rocks (also known as the lowball) glass. It's simply an old-fashioned cocktail glass, with or without a short stem. In our time it has become the bearer for any potable from ale to Zinfandel. It's practical not only for cocktails but also for whiskey, rum, gin, and vodka, and every now and then—to everyone's intense surprise—it is used for the Old-Fashioned cocktail of bourbon or Scotch, the drink for which it was originally designed. The other most sought-after glass is the tulip-shaped wineglass, holding from 8 to 11 ounces, allowing ample space for swirling and releasing the wine's bouquet. It, too, has leaped beyond its birthright and is now the vehicle for any liquid from champagne to stout. Oddball hosts, game for anything, have even been known to pour water into it.

You'll want to supplement your glass supply with such specialized vessels as sour glasses, steins and Pilsners, highball glasses, ponies, jiggers, and hollow-stemmed champagne glasses (see the glassware illustrations beginning on page 17), but it's no longer necessary to stock an infinite variety of glassware. Although it was once customary for the proper host to set out an assortment of glasses at the dinner table in anticipation of the wines that were offered with each course, now, even at black-tie dinners, you'll seldom see more than two or three different kinds of wineglasses on the table. Often there will be just one all-purpose glass for one carefully chosen wine. If a Sauternes or champagne is passed with the dessert or if port follows the demitasse, the appropriate glass can be brought out at that time.

It's also unnecessary to have all your glassware in the same pattern. Matching beverageware should be used at the dining table, but before or after dinner the patterns may vary. Dry sherry on the rocks can be poured on your patio in lightweight old-fashioned glasses, Whiskey and Soda by the hearth in stately, heavy-bottomed highball glasses.

How many glasses should you own? It depends on the maximum number of people your pad can comfortably contain at any one time. Double that number to account for drop-ins and for normal glassware breakage. Thus, if you usually invite eight for a party, stock sixteen of each kind of glass that you'd be most likely to use.

BUYING TIPS

When stocking your bar glassware for the first time or replenishing the odd or incomplete assortment of glasses you may now own, keep the following guides in mind.

- Ask if the glass is crystal or lime glass; no reputable shop will represent a glass as crystal if it is not genuine.

- Ask if it is hand-blown or machine-made; the former is more expensive although not necessarily more suitable for your needs.

- When selecting crystal, you cannot analyze a glass for its lead content. Look instead for its clarity and brilliance; hold it up to the light—there should be no bubbles, wavy lines, uneven edges, or other obvious imperfections.

- Test crystal for its bell-like tone. Using a pencil, tap the top of the glass near the edge; crystal glasses of slightly different shape from the same manufacturer will give off tones of different pitches. When you tap lime glass, the sound will be flat and edgy.

- Ask if the glass is open stock, that is, a standard product continuously available for a reasonable period of time, so that replacements can be made to keep a full set. Some bargain lines of imported glassware available during the midwinter holidays are onetime offerings, and cannot be replaced; even some American open-stock items aren't available indefinitely, and you may be frustrated if you try to replace several glasses from a set you bought five years ago.

- If you are selecting cut-crystal glassware, check to see that the cut edges of the design are distinct and uniform and that the glass, when held to the light, has a sparkling prismatic effect.

•Consider the glasses you are buying in relation to your table, linen, and china to make sure they are compatible or complementary.

•Hold the glass you are considering to be sure it has a balanced feel and that the stem is comfortable. If it is a glass with a narrow top—such as a dock glass (or the larger brandy snifter) for sherry or port—make sure it is adequate for "nosing" the wine.

•Ask if the glassware is dishwasher-safe; some extremely expensive glasses of gossamer weight, or glasses with a gold band, must be washed by hand.

The higher mathematics of whether a drinking glass should hold 6 or 8½ or 10⅝ ounces isn't important if you're pouring punch from a bowl or beer from a bottle or keg—you merely pour until you have what your thirst says is a reasonable amount and then stop. But if you're concocting a particular cocktail following a particular recipe, and the ingredients are designed to fill a 4½-ounce cocktail glass and your glass holds a miserly 3 ounces, you'll find yourself with more drinks than you intended, or with seconds that slosh around with ice until they're too weak to serve. If you're buying champagne for a party and you don't know whether your glasses hold 5½ ounces or 7 ounces, you can miscalculate badly. For special concoctions and for mass drinking, you really should know the capacity of the drinking vessels you own. If necessary, fill them with water and pour the contents into a measuring glass or beaker from the chem lab. Make a note of their capacity and use it as a guide for the next party.

Among offbeat drinking vessels you may want to consider are special glasses emblazoned with hens, tomatoes, or oranges designed for hosts who respectively specialize in Bullshots, Bloody Marys, and Screwdrivers. For the aquatic cocktail hour, there are swimming pool glasses that float. Glacier tumblers with walls that retain the cold can be prechilled in the freezer for long, icy Gin and Tonics, Cuba Libres, etc. Moscow Mule copper cups are available for husky drafts of ginger beer and vodka. The Irish Coffee goblet with a thick stem is designed for comfortably grasping the hot brew of coffee, Irish whiskey, and cream. For warm wassail in the wintertime, you'll need capacious beverage mugs with handles that stay cool. Finally, for extra-large parties of fifty to a hundred people, particularly outdoor bashes, you'll probably want the disposable, well-designed, very thin plastic drinkware with no fear of insufficient glasses or cleanup problems. The kinds of specialized beverageware you'll need depends entirely on your lifestyle.

TAKING CARE OF GLASSWARE

Whether you use a bartender at a party or do your own pouring, there are a few practical rules for handling glassware.

- Wash glasses in warm water with detergent as soon as possible after each use. Use a dishwasher if glasses are dishwasher-safe, but stack them in the machine with special care. If glasses are expensive crystal, it may be prudent to wash them by hand no matter what the label says.

- Avoid putting cold glasses in scalding water; temperature extremes may crack them.

- Glasses that may be sticky on the bottom after being used for liqueurs should be soaked before washing.

- Cut glass sometimes shows a film on the cut areas and may have to be soaked in warm water with detergent and scrubbed with a small brush in the crevices of the design.

- Do not stack glasses in the sink or on the shelf. If by any chance glasses have been stacked and become locked, place the bottom glass in warm water and fill the top with cold; the resulting expansion and contraction should separate them safely.

•If hand-washed, dry glasses with a lint-free towel. Better yet, if thirsty guests aren't waiting for another round of drinks, let the glasses drain-dry upside down on a ridged drainboard.

•Buff with a paper towel or tissue paper to give added brilliance to crystal.

•Glasses may be stored on the shelf either right side up or upside down but, in either case, never crowd the glasses, and allow a margin of about an inch, if possible, between them.

•If glasses have been stored on the shelf for months and have been unused, they may be covered with a dusty or sticky film sometimes caused by cooking fumes; check them before party time, and wash them if necessary.

•Be sure all glasses used for wine tasting are immaculate, with no trace of detergent from previous washings.

GLASS PREPARATION

There are three basic ways to prepare glasses before serving drinks—chilling, frosting, and sugar frosting.

CHILLING GLASSES Every cocktail glass should be chilled before filled. There are three ways: (1) before drinking time, store glasses in the refrigerator or freezer until they're cold; (2) bury the glasses completely in cracked ice; or (3) fill them with cracked ice and stir the ice a few times before pouring drinks.

FROSTING GLASSES For a longer-lasting frost, dip the glasses in water and, while still dripping, place them in the freezer (at its coldest setting) for two or three hours.

SUGAR-FROSTING GLASSES Glasses for appropriate cocktails, coolers, and liqueurs can be made more fascinating to the eyes and lips by frosting their rims with sugar. To administer this fancy finishing touch, make sure, first of all, that you use superfine sugar—not the regular granulated or confectioners'. Moisten the rim of each glass, inside and out, to a depth of about ¼ inch before dipping in the sugar. There are four easy methods: (1) anoint the rim with a small wedge of lemon or orange, invert the glass to shake off extra juice, then dip into sugar; (2) rub the rim with lemon or orange peel, using the outside of the rind, then dip into sugar; (3) dip the rim in grenadine, Falernum, or any other sweet syrup—or any desired liqueur—then into sugar; or (4) moisten the rim with coffee liqueur, then dip into a mixture of 3 teaspoons superfine sugar mixed well with 1 teaspoon powdered instant coffee.

The contents of all sugar-frosted glasses, needless to add, should be sipped without benefit of a straw. For party purposes, a large number of glasses may be sugar-frosted and stored in the refrigerator or freezer until drinking time.

(Margarita glasses are often salt-frosted, which I consider a bit too much of an otherwise good thing. Some alternative suggestions are offered in chapter 10, Tequila.)

GLASSWARE
FOR THE BAR

OLD-FASHIONED, OR ON-THE-ROCKS No drinking vessel gets a bigger play these days than the old-fashioned, or on-the-rocks, glass. Over the years the old-fashioned glass has blossomed into an all-purpose glass, bearer of any drink from a Scotch Old-Fashioned to a Bourbon Mist to a Black Russian. It may have straight flared sides or be barrel-shaped or footed. Double old-fashioned glasses holding up to 15 ounces are great labor savers for hosts because demands for seconds are spaced further apart.

COCKTAIL For safe conveyance twixt dinner table and lips, the minimum-size cocktail glass should hold 4½ ounces. A larger version holds 6 ounces and is often called the California or double cocktail, excellent for oversize drinks like the Derby Daiquiri and for foamy blender cocktails.

HIGHBALL, COLLINS, AND COOLER The straight, tall, thin glass ranging in size from 8 to 12 ounces is sometimes called the shell glass, and is used not only for highballs but also for Gin and Tonics, Collins drinks, Cobblers, Daisies, Screwdrivers, Bloody Marys, beer, and other drinks. More elegant is the weighted-bottom glass. Glasses of the same tall shape that hold up to 21 ounces are known as "coolers" and can accommodate king-size Collinses, extra-long juleps, Polynesian rum drinks, and other long summer libations.

DELMONICO, OR SOUR This glass may be footed or straight-sided and varies in size from 4½ to 7 ounces. Used for Whiskey, Rum, or Brandy Sours, it doubles for fruit juice, Sherry Flips, Port Flips, and morning-after pick-me-ups.

LIQUEUR, CORDIAL, AND PONY These 1-ounce capacity glasses may be rounded or straight-sided. The latter is called a pousse-café and can hold a rainbow's spectrum of different liqueurs in layers.

WHISKEY SHOT, OR JIGGER No modern host should buy a shot glass that holds less than 1½ ounces. Used more frequently for measuring than drinking, it's the proper glass for a Boilermaker (straight whiskey followed by beer). The heavy-bottomed type provides stability; the extra-long sham bottom sometimes seen in public bars is out of place in your pad.

BRANDY AND BRANDY SNIFTER These glasses have a rounded bowl for retaining their liquor's rich, volatile fragrance. Glasses range in size from 2 ounces to a sensible 8-ounce size, comfortable for holding as well as nosing, to large balloon styles holding up to 25 ounces, which are considered completely affected by professional brandymen.

 ALL-PURPOSE WINE The tulip shape is designed for trapping the wine's bouquet and enables you to comfortably eye the wine's color, swirl the wine, and nose it. Volumes range from 8 to 11 ounces; the glass is never more than half-filled. Used for both red and white table wines as well as champagne.

 *BURGUNDY AND RHINE WINE* For most Dionysian delights, the all-purpose wineglass will be very satisfying. But the host who makes a continuing avocation of buying wines for his own cellar and laying down vintage wines for later years may also like to own the balloon-shaped red-wine glass, beloved by Burgundians, or the graceful, tall-stemmed glass for Rhine wines or Moselles.

 *PORT AND SHERRY* Although port in both England and the United States is frequently sipped from the squat port glass and sherry from the Y-shaped glass, neither of these glasses is as satisfying as the dock glass, which can be used for either port or sherry and is favored by both

sherrymen in Spain and port connoisseurs in Oporto. For Madeira, too, the dock glass is recommended.

CHAMPAGNE The glass that is the darling of most enlightened champagne drinkers is a slightly narrower version of the all-purpose wineglass but with a taller stem. It is never more than half-filled. Saucer champagne glasses allow a somewhat faster release of bubbles and are customarily used for champagne cocktails. The long throat of the hollow-stemmed champagne glass is designed to show continuing life in bubbly; it's also used for sparkling Burgundy.

BEER The trumpet-shaped Pilsner glass retains cold and fizz as long as possible and is the proper glass for a Black Velvet (Guinness stout and champagne). The heavy glass stein is a perfect suds container at bull sessions and bachelor parties. The glass tankard with graceful lines is made with a weighted bottom. The silver or pewter tankard with glass bottom is in the best English tradition for leisurely sipping ale or stout.

OTHER TOOLS
OF THE TRADE

Before any host drops a single silver onion into a Gibson or decorates a tall glass with a long orange horse's neck or pulls the cork from his favorite bottle of Bordeaux, he should scan the assortment of small hand tools now available for serving spirits and wine. Below is a tableau of bar gadgetry showing some of the most useful implements for the conveniences and pleasures of party drinking.

Long tongs snugly grip ice cubes, although in many wet circles of society, hands are de rigueur for picking up rocks from an ice bucket.

A cork bottle-stopper with a no-drip pouring end is useful for dispensing anything from créme de cassis to vermouth.

A coil-rimmed strainer for the cocktail mixing glass is a good trap against ice floes tumbling into the cocktail glass.

A small glass compote dish is a convenient vessel for cherries, olives, and onions.

A long-handled bar spoon/stirrer is used either in a cocktail mixing glass or as a substitute for a glass Martini stirrer, as well as for stirring all long, deep potations—coolers, pitchers, punches, and Zombies.

An ice pick may be used for chipping large ice blocks into suitable sizes for punch bowls and is also useful for unsticking ice cubes in an ice bucket.

 A jigger with ½- and 1½-ounce measures is ideal for measuring liquor.

An olive, onion, or cherry grabber will find its mark even in the most stubborn bottle.

A nutmeg grater is welcome for long, year-end partying when flips, nogs, grogs, and gloggs are flowing.

A sturdy metal bottle stopper is less likely to get lost than a common plastic disc. Keeps anything from club soda to bitter lemon sparkling from one night to the next.

Both drinking glass and drink look better when placed on an attractive coaster. The trouble with most shoddy coasters isn't that they disappear but that they don't disappear fast enough.

This stainless steel knife–cum-opener has a pronged edge for stabbing fruit and other garnishes.

A sturdy, capacious cutting board is less likely to warp than a small thin version; the board doubles as kitchen equipment.

 A heavy-duty lime or lemon squeezer is indispensable for squeezing fruit into fizzes, tonics, and tall mixtures with juniper juice.

The fang of a heavy-duty can opener sinks easily into metal.

 A set of standard measuring spoons is indispensable in formulas calling for small quantities of flavoring liqueurs, juices, or bitters.

A sharp, well-balanced French knife is best for slicing fruit.

 A folding-flat waiter's corkscrew is good for itinerant bartenders carrying pocket equipment to beaches and mountain sites for fun and games.

A bottle-cap opener of the husky type provides good leverage.

A shaker—stainless steel is preferred—is a must for making those cocktails that call for eggs, cream, heavy liqueurs or other hard-to-mix ingredients.

A wing-type corkscrew permits you to use both hands for extracting stubborn corks. (Many hosts have abandoned the conventional corkscrew in favor of the CO^2 bottle opener. A small charge of CO^2—which has no effect whatsoever on a wine's flavor—gently raises the cork out of the bottle without wrenching muscles.)

CHAPTER 2

All the *Trimmings*

The applied art of mixing alcoholic drinks depends on many things that aren't alcohol. There would be no Screwdrivers without orange juice and no Daiquiris without limes, and Irish Coffee without coffee and whipped cream would be just a glass of whiskey. Alcohol must be made tart, sweet, rich, bitter, foamy, and in countless other ways congenial to sophisticated taste buds. Frequently a drink is garnished in a manner that accents its appearance as well as its flavor and aroma, as with the olive in the Martini, the cucumber peel in the Pimm's Cup, or the strawberry in the champagne cocktail.

The number of accessories you choose to acquire for mixing will depend on whether you're going in for mass drinking or for more modest quenching. As a rule, small containers of such seasonings as bitters are less likely to lose their zest than larger bottles that hang around on the shelf too long. Large bottles of syrups like Falernum or red-currant syrup will lose their bright color and flavor if untouched for months. If this occurs, don't hesitate to discard the old stock and buy fresh replacements. Fruits and other perishables should be emphatically fresh, never brown or mealy.

The checklist that follows should be consulted not only for setting up a basic bar stock but also every time you're hosting a drinking party of sizable dimensions. Items that belong in any basic bar are marked with an asterisk to differentiate them from those less frequently used.

MIXING AIDS

ALMONDS Use them whole for Scandinavian glogg, sliced or julienne for floating on punches and tall summer drinks.

ALMOND SYRUP Called orgeat when made in France, orzata when made in Italy. Some liqueurs with a vivid almondlike flavor—such as amaretto, made from apricot pits—may be used in place of the nonalcoholic almond syrup.

APPLE JUICE Often found in congenial company with vodka. The space-saving frozen-concentrated variety is handy for parties. (See also Cider.)

APRICOTS Whole peeled canned apricots are better than the fresh for velvety blender drinks.

BANANAS They should always be speckled ripe for bar purposes. They're turned to best account in Banana Daiquiris.

*BITTER LEMON A superior mixer in high esteem among the Gin and Tonic crowd.

BITTER LEMON CONCENTRATE An essence that may be added to plain club soda in an emergency.

*BITTERS Best known is Angostura from Trinidad, but orange bitters are sometimes preferred for drinks that benefit from a soupçon of citrus. It's a good idea to keep Peychaud's bitters (obtainable in some areas only in liquor stores) on hand for making New Orleans Sazeracs.

BUTTER Use fresh sweet butter for a mellow glow in hot buttered rum.

CASSIS This black currant syrup—simpatico with vermouth—is similar to créme de cassis, except it contains no alcohol.

*CHERRIES Most common are the maraschino, with or without stems. Mint-flavored cherries provide a green decorative note; brandied pitted red cherries and pitted black cherries, with or without rum flavor, complete the cherry constellation.

CIDER In groceries, "apple cider" and "apple juice" are synonymous terms for pasteurized juice of the apple. Country cider, sold at roadside stands, is often partially fermented apple juice. Hard cider is apple juice fermented to the wine stage.

CINNAMON STICKS (OR STICK CINNAMON) Used for both stirring and flavoring hot mulled mixes. Buy the extra-long sticks for drinks in deep mugs.

CLOVES Add them whole (not ground) to hot winter wassail.

*CLUB SODA Buy it in splits for individual drinks, the 12-ounce size for several highballs, and quarts for parties or punch bowls. Most brands have good bite and can keep their fizz locked up overnight or even for several days. Generally, club soda provides more zing than seltzer water.

COCKTAIL MIXES (Not to be confused with bottled premixed cocktails.) Nonalcoholic mixes are never equal to the fresh ingredients, but many hosts like to keep them on hand as reserve ammunition. Mixes for the Bloody Mary, Daiquiri,

Mai Tai, Manhattan, Navy Grog, Scorpion, and Whiskey Sour have become standard items in many home bars. While all bottles have specific mixing directions on their labels, try varying the alcohol-mix ratio to suit your own taste.

COFFEE Brew it fresh and strong for steaming Irish Coffee.

CRANBERRY JUICE Adds brilliant color and eye-opening tartness to punches and vodka drinks.

CREAM Use heavy sweet cream for Alexanders and dessert drinks.

CURRANT SYRUP Red currants (rather than black cassis berries) go into this tart extract. It's not a substitute for grenadine but a flavoring component in its own right.

EGGS There would be no nog without them—nor a number of frothy confections such as Clover Clubs, Silver Fizzes, and the like. Use a small size for individual drinks. (Note: Raw eggs can pose a food safety hazard; if your recipe calls for raw or lightly cooked eggs, be sure to buy pasteurized eggs. Never use an egg that has a cracked shell.)

FALERNUM A delightful West Indian syrup made from almonds and spices.

*FROTHEE CREAMY HEAD A few splashes of this egg-white concentrate will give mixed drinks the creamy cap supplied otherwise by fresh egg whites; however, the head tends to disappear faster than an egg-white head.

*GINGER ALE The drier the better for modern tastes.

GINGER BEER The second-fiddle catalyst in a Moscow Mule.

GRAPEFRUIT JUICE The one fruit juice that's better canned or frozen than fresh, undoubtedly because the latter is often quite insipid and varies so much in flavor. The unsweetened variety is best for drink-making.

GRAPE JUICE One of vodka's many compatible consorts. The frozen-concentrated form is a space saver.

GRENADINE A bright-red syrup made from the pulp of pomegranates, it's used in the Jack Rose, Clover Club, Bacardi, and many other cocktails, as well as in punches and tall drinks. Unlike most additives, it can be stored on the shelf for long periods without losing its tint or tartness. Grenadine liqueur, made by Leroux, may be used in place of its non-alcoholic cousin.

GUANABANA NECTAR The luscious juice of the soursop, moderately sweetened, makes a delicious partner in rum drinks.

GUAVA JELLY Melted down to syrup, it's used for sweetening Caribbean rum drinks.

HONEY Use a light-colored honey for bar purposes. If granulation occurs, place the jar in hot water for a few minutes and then stir until the granules disappear.

LEMON JUICE The bottled juice, whether in glass or plastic containers, never equals the fresh-squeezed variety and should be kept on hand for emergency use only.

LEMONS They should be firm and green-stemmed. The size of the fruit is not too important because most recipes calling for lemon juice use ounce measurements. Before squeezing, using the palm of the hand, lean on the fruit on a cutting board, rolling it back and forth to make squeezing easier and to extract more juice.

LIME JUICE As with lemon juice, the bottled product should be used only in emergencies.

LIME JUICE, SWEETENED The best-known brand, Rose's, is actually a tart syrup rather than a substitute for fresh lime juice, and is an essential ingredient in a Gimlet.

LIMES A far from silent partner in almost all rum drinks. Choose limes with smooth green skin rather than yellow.

MANGOES OR MANGO NECTAR An exotic ingredient in some tall rum drinks.

MAPLE SYRUP Used occasionally as a drink sweetener.

MILK Essential in many brandy drinks, milk punches, and eggnogs. Use whole milk rather than skim for best results.

MINT, FRESH Mint leaves are best if taken from the mint patch directly to julep cups or glasses. When using fresh mint, choose leaves that are deep green rather than yellowed, and use small, tender leaves rather than large.

NUTMEG Used in flips, nogs, mulls, and other warmed cold-weather drinks. Buy the whole nutmeg for grating rather than the ground.

OLIVES Although the small pitted variety is a standard bar ingredient, many Martini drinkers prefer the unpitted, stuffed colossal, or supercolossal. There are also almond-, anchovy-, and onion-stuffed olives, all of which are delightful; and even pitted black olives are used in some Martini-type drinks. Be sure to store recapped jars in the refrigerator; olives should be kept in their own brine and washed just before serving. The flavor of the olives will deteriorate if stored for more than a few weeks.

ONIONS, COCKTAIL OR PEARL The sine qua non of the Gibson cocktail. Buy them in small jars and store in the refrigerator after opening. Bottled in vinegar or in vermouth and vinegar.

ORANGE FLOWER WATER A clear distillation of orange blossoms that is an essential ingredient in a Ramos Gin Fizz; sometimes labeled fleur d'orange. Available in gourmet food shops and in some liquor stores.

ORANGES Juice from fresh oranges is always better than frozen juice or the kind that comes in cartons or bottles, even though the fresh fruit varies widely in sweetness and color throughout the year. (Frozen juice also varies in quality and flavor from one brand to the next. If you must use it, say, for large blowouts, select the best brand you can find.)

ORANGE SLICES Actually wedges rather than slices, they're packed in syrup in jars. They provide a rich garnish for an Old-Fashioned.

ORGEAT (FROM FRANCE) OR ORZATA (FROM ITALY) Nonalcoholic almond syrups. (See Almond syrup.)

PAPAYA SYRUP OR NECTAR One of the tropical juices occasionally called for in Polynesian rum drinks.

PASSION FRUIT JUICE OR NECTAR A pleasantly tart mixer used in rum drinks.

PEACHES Sliced fresh in season, they make an elegant adornment for champagne, sparkling Rhine wine, and wine cups. Elbertas—frozen or canned—are best for crushed-ice blender drinks.

PINEAPPLE When buying, check for ripeness: the top-center leaves should come out easily and the fruit should have a heavy, musky pineapple aroma. Pineapple cocktail sticks in syrup are a pleasant cocktail garnish.

PINEAPPLE JUICE Best for bar purposes is the frozen-concentrated juice, followed by the canned, unsweetened variety. If canned juice is stored in the refrigerator after opening, be sure to pour it into a glass jar and cover tightly to ward off refrigerator aromas.

QUININE CONCENTRATE Used for making quinine water (commonly known as tonic) by adding to seltzer water or club soda; it's useful on boats and in other cramped bar quarters.

*QUININE WATER (A.K.A. TONIC) A staple bar item that you should keep on hand in quantity for warm-weather drinks.

RASPBERRIES Use fresh or frozen in summer wine cups, punch bowls, and blender drinks.

RASPBERRY SYRUP This bar sweetener, not as tart as grenadine, has its own distinctive fruit-with-a-punch flavor.

SALT Keep a saltcellar on hand for Bloody Marys, Bloody Marias, etc. Celery salt is widely appreciated both in the Bloody genre and in pick-me-ups. A special Margarita salt flavored with lemon is packed in wide containers for rim dipping. Also handy when applying the salt-and-lemon method to tequila shots.

SELTZER WATER Fizz from a seltzer bottle seldom has the liveliness of club soda, but it's convenient. A cartridge charge for permanent siphon equipment is a space saver, though rarely seen today.

*7-UP The most popular of all light carbonated lemon drinks, it can be mixed with almost any conceivable potable.

SOFT DRINKS Besides cola drinks and ginger ale, sodas with flavors such as pineapple, black cherry, and grapefruit are pleasant tall-drink extenders.

STRAWBERRIES Fresh berries make a colorful garnish for May wine, wine cups, fancy drinks, and summer fruit bowls. Frozen ones can be used in blender drinks with crushed ice.

STRAWBERRY SYRUP This is one of the brightest members in the family of red bar sweeteners. Be sure it's a natural, not artificial, fruit flavor—and don't keep it too long on the shelf.

*SUGAR For the bar, superfine sugar, which dissolves quickly, is preferred to plain granulated; but if kept too long after the box is opened, it will tend to lump, in which case it should be put

through a fine sieve. Do not use confectioners' sugar. Brown sugar is rarely called for except in hot mulled drinks.

SUGAR SYRUP (SIMPLE SYRUP) Some of the commercially prepared table syrups may be too thick for easy blending. Exceptions are Wuppermann's bar syrup and rock-candy syrup. Or make your own: bring 1 cup of water to a boil and stir in 1 cup of sugar; simmer 1½ minutes. The mixture should reduce to approximately 1 cup, making it possible to substitute equal amounts of syrup for sugar in any bar recipe in which it may be preferred. Pour any leftovers into a bottle or syrup container and store at room temperature. There may be some crystallization of the sugar in time, but that won't affect the syrup's usefulness.

TEA Punch bowls of colonial times often called for brewed tea as part of the liquid. Brew it for five minutes; then let it cool at room temperature to prevent the drink from clouding.

*TOMATO JUICE The base for Bloody Marys and many other pick-me-ups. Buy straight tomato juice rather than tomato-juice cocktails such as V-8, Clamato, etc. (Personal preference may vary, of course, as mentioned below in Vegetable juice.) Jars rather than cans are best for refrigerator storage.

*TONIC WATER Without this staple, there would be no Gin and Tonics. (See Quinine water.)

VEGETABLE JUICE Sometimes preferred to tomato juice in a Bloody Mary because its blend of flavors lends a somewhat livelier, more interesting flavor to the drink.

*WATER At out-of-the-way picnics and lonely beach sites, a

bottle of this offbeat ingredient is sometimes desirable as an additive to Scotch. In localities where tap water is rusty or has a pronounced taste of chlorine, use bottled spring water.

WORCESTERSHIRE SAUCE A snappy accent for Prairie Oysters, Bloody Marys, and the like.

PREPARED HORS D'OEUVRES FOR DRINKS

Besides accessories for mixing drinks, a host's larder should contain a reasonable supply of appetizers in jars, cans, or packages that can be tapped at a moment's notice. It isn't necessary to enumerate the king-size list of chips, nuggets, wafers, spreads, and other ready-to-munch snacks piled high in delis and supermarkets. But for the host who likes to offer his drop-ins something better than the old peanut-and-potato-chip alms and who doesn't have time for the preparation of his own freshly made hors d'oeuvres, there are distinguished delicacies, many of them imported, that one can store in the pantry. Most of them require no refrigeration. They are cited in the checklist below.

ANCHOVIES Flat fillets in oil or rolled with capers, pimientos, or nuts

ANCHOVY PASTE A concentrated puree used for mixing with butter, cream cheese, etc.

ARTICHOKE HEARTS Tiny, in olive oil

CAVIAR The best and most expensive is giant-grain fresh beluga, followed by sevruga and pressed caviar. Fresh caviars must be refrigerated; others in hermetically sealed jars may be kept on pantry shelves. Other, less expensive caviar from salmon, whitefish, and lumpfish is also available.

CHEESE Hard cheeses can be stored for three to four weeks and are the best type for laying in the hold and offering with drinks. Best representatives: aged farmhouse cheddar; English Cheshire; Dutch Gouda; French Mimolette and Cantal; Swiss Emmental and Gruyère; Italian provolone and pecorino; Spanish Manchego.

CLAMS Smoked in oil

CRACKERS Water table crackers, melba toasts, Japanese rice crackers, cheese sticks, etc.

DRIED FRUIT Apricots, figs, pears, banana chips, coconut chips, etc.

HERRING AND LOX In wine sauce, dill sauce, mustard sauce, cream sauce, etc.

MEATBALLS Small cocktail-size in sauce

MUSHROOMS Tiny, in olive oil; in olive oil, vinegar, and spices

MUSSELS Smoked in oil; marinated; in butter or tomato sauce

NUTS Almonds, cashews, macadamias, pistachios, roasted and salted mixed nuts,

OLIVES Oil- or brine-cured; stuffed with almonds, garlic, anchovies, red pepper, or onions

OYSTERS Smoked in oil

PÂTÉS Pâté de foie gras (goose liver); pork pâté; pâté de maison (loaf shape); pâtés (purees for spreading) of anchovies, chicken livers, game, goose, sardines, smoked rainbow trout, smoked salmon, and smoked sturgeon

SALAMI Narrow hard types, such as salamini alla cacciatora and pepperoni, unsliced

SALMON, SMOKED OR CURED Sliced in oil, canned, or vacuum-sealed

SARDINES Boneless and skinless, in olive oil, tomato sauce, or mustard

SAUSAGES Small cocktail-size

SPREADS Sun-dried tomato, artichoke, roasted red pepper, etc., in jars; prepared hummus, baba ganouj, etc.

CHAPTER 3

Barmanship

G iven a choice selection of spirits, fresh and flavorful mixing ingredients, and attractive glassware, the host at home is still several steps away from the professional bartender's finesse, an art that is public property for every drinker astride a barstool to behold. It looks deceptively easy, especially to the eye that has been mellowed by two or three dry Martinis. But there are skills, tricks of the trade, and tips in creating and serving drinks—icemanship, mixing, stirring, garnishing, and others—that can be briefly explained in the same way that a pro on the golf course can make a detailed analysis of each of the strokes and positions he's carefully mastered. Familiarize yourself with the basic barman's skills that follow and consult them for special potables, and every time you pour drinks, you'll generate among your guests the mood described superlatively by novelist Henry Fielding as "one universal grin."

ICEMANSHIP

There was a time when rocks were really rocky, when a bartender armed with an ice pick hacked away at his block of ice until it eventually disappeared. On a summer's day you'd ask for a Gin Rickey and it would come to you with one or two tottering crags of ice. It looked cool, but it couldn't possibly stand up to a contemporary Gin Rickey, because of a simple undisputed fact: ice is now much colder than it once was. Frozen water may be 32°F or, just as possible these days,–32°F. Most of today's ice cubes range from 0° to –10°F. Needless to say, for fast cooler-offers, the colder the ice, the better. Crushed ice or cracked ice is chillier in a bar glass than the cubed variety because more cooling ice surfaces come into intimate contact with the drink.

The variety of muscle-powered as well as plug-in ice crushers seems to have kept pace with the population explosion. There are ice-crusher blender attachments or settings that can reduce a tray of ice cubes to crushed ice or snow ice in twenty to thirty seconds. Even simple ice trays are now designed not only for cubes but also for ice slices, thirty-eight to a tray, and, perhaps most useful of all, for cracked ice. Lacking this equipment, however, a host needn't find the technique for cracking or crushing ice too difficult. Simply place the ice cubes in a canvas bag designed for this purpose or in a large, clean kitchen towel (wrap the towel around the ice so that there is a double thickness of cloth); then, on a carving board, bang the bag or towel with a mallet or the smooth side of a meat tenderizer. Keep your banging somewhat restrained if you want fair-size pieces of cracked ice; for crushed ice, whack away with abandon.

Every barman—amateur or pro—should insist that his ice is clean, hard, and dry, and he should make each drink or batch of drinks with fresh ice. Hoard your ice in the freezer until you actually need it. Use ice buckets with vacuum sides and lids; plastic-foam ice tubs are convenient for throwaway service. When you empty your ice trays, don't run water over them unless it's absolutely necessary to spring the ice free—the water will cause them to stick together after they're put in the bucket. Or you may have a refrigerator that not only makes ice cubes automatically but turns them out and stores them night and day—a comforting thought when one is party-planning. If the water in your fiefdom is heavily chlorinated, use bottled spring water for ice. Finally, as a host, be the most prodigal of icemen. If you're gambling on the fact that you may just possibly get by with two buckets of ice at a summer fling, don't gamble. Provide at least three or four bucketfuls for supercooling your crowd. If your ice-making equipment is somewhat limited, find out before your rumpus takes place where you can buy additional ice.

Here are three icy ideas you might want to try.

PUNCH-BOWL ICE While professional ice sculptors have for the most part replaced the commercial icehouses where you used to be able to buy a chunk of ice tailored to fit your punch bowl, you can make your own ice floe by filling a deep pot or plastic bucket with water—at least a day in advance of the party—and placing it in the freezer. The top of the ice may solidify in a hump as the water expands. When you're ready to use it, run warm water over the sides of the pot and invert it, permitting the round glacier, with its smooth bottom upright, to slide into your bowl.

AQUAVIT IN ICE At smorgasbord parties, it's a delightful custom to serve a bottle of aquavit (or sometimes straight vodka) encased in a block of ice. The job's simple: place the bottle of liquor in an empty half-gallon paper milk container with the top cut off, fill the container with water, and then set it in the freezer. The alcohol will keep the liquor from solidifying as the surrounding water freezes. Finally, tear off the paper or remove it with a knife. The long robe of ice with its rectangular sides should be partly covered with a napkin for serving and then returned to the freezer to preserve it for second skoals.

FRAPPÉED ICE CAP After-dinner frappés—refreshing alternatives to cloying desserts—are made by drizzling a liqueur or liqueurs over finely crushed ice in a saucer champagne glass. A cool and convenient variation is to make them beforehand and store them for a few hours, or even overnight, in the freezer. In time the liqueur settles to the bottom and the ice forms a solid cap on top; after you remove it from the freezer, the cap will loosen slightly, allowing the icy liqueur to be sipped from the rim of the glass sans straw.

THE MECHANICS OF
MIXING AND POURING

FILLING THE SHAKER Ice should always go into the shaker first, alcohol last. By giving ice first place, all the ingredients that follow will be cooled on their way down. Furthermore, once you acquire the habit of adding the liquor last, it's unlikely that you'll inadvertently double the spirits or, worse yet, forget them altogether, both possible errors for hosts taking jolts along with their guests. The order of ingredients between ice and alcohol follows no dogmatic ritual; whether sugar should precede the lemon juice or vice versa isn't important so far as the final drink is concerned. One useful control for drinking hosts is to put the correct number of glasses for the needed drinks in front of the shaker before adding anything—a clear reminder of how many dashes of bitters, how many spoons of this or jiggers of that are necessary. Finally, never fill a shaker to the brim; allow enough room for all ingredients to be tossed back and forth—to set up the clear, pleasant rattle of ice.

MEASURING Guests at a pour-it-yourself bar should feel free to pour as many fingers as they please, but if the host himself is preparing any kind of mixed drink, he should trust the jigger rather than his eye, just as the best professional bartenders always do. In simple drinks such as a Scotch and Soda as well as in more complicated tipples, too much liquor can be unpleasant and, in a way, as inhospitable as too little.

STIRRING To keep their icy clarity, cocktails such as Martinis, Manhattans, Rob Roys, and Gimlets should always be stirred, not shaken. (However, it's no major disaster—and sometimes a matter of preference—if you unwittingly shake rather than stir a Martini; it will turn cloudy, but only for a few minutes.) For proper dilution, stir every batch of cocktails at least twenty times. When carbonated water is added to tall drinks, stir as briefly as possible; most of the liquor rises to the top automatically, and excessive stirring only dissipates the sparkle in the water.

SHAKING Shake the shaker, not yourself. Don't just rock it—hold it well out in front of you and move it diagonally from lower left to upper right, or in any other convenient motion, with a pistonlike rhythm. In time the icy feel of the cocktail shaker will tell you that the drinks are ready for pouring. Shake one round of drinks at a time and rinse the shaker thoroughly after each use.

POURING When drinks have been shaken, pour them at once; don't let the cocktail shaker become a watery grave. If extra liquid is left in the shaker, strain it off at once; the so-called dividends left standing in ice will be weak replicas of the original drinks. Never pour drinks higher than $^1/_4$ inch from the rim of the glass. In the case of wine, a large glass should never be more than one-third to one-half full to permit swirling of the wine and the liberation of its aroma. In large brandy snifters, a $1^1/_2$-ounce drink is the maximum. When garnishes such as orange slices and pineapple sticks are being used, allow sufficient room to add them without causing the drink to overflow. When pouring more than one mixed drink, line up the glasses rim to rim, fill them half full, then pour again to the same height in each glass.

SPECIAL EFFECTS

FLOATING LIQUEURS Drinks are sometimes served with a spoonful of liqueur or 151-proof rum floating on top; usually such toppings are merely poured slowly from a spoon against the side of the glass. The Pousse-Café, on the other hand, is a multilayered after-dinner drink whose rainbow effect can be created in any one of four ways: (1) first pour the heaviest liqueur slowly against the side of the glass, following it in turn with progressively lighter liqueurs, a procedure that can be learned through trial and error or by following the drink recipes included in this book; (2) pour the liqueurs over an inverted small spoon held at the top of the glass; (3) pour the liqueurs down the side of a mixing rod held in the glass; or (4) pour the liqueurs slowly into the glass in any sequence you desire, place the glass in your refrigerator, and in time each liqueur will find its own weight level, forming distinct layers.

FLAMING LIQUORS Occasionally brandy or liqueurs are set aflame in a drink. For this bit of showmanship, the liquor should be preheated briefly—not boiled, which causes the alcohol to evaporate, but simply made hot enough so that when a flame is held to the liquor, it will begin to blaze quietly.

HOMEMADE GARNISHES

There are two kinds of garnishes. Some, like the twist of lemon in a Martini or the cucumber peel in a Pimm's Cup, actually transform the drink's aroma and savor; others are frankly adornments for bedecking the festive glass but, like neckties, which are also dispensable, should be tastefully chosen. Some of the main garnishes—like the cherry in the Manhattan—can be purchased in bottles or jars and are listed in chapter 2. The guide below tells you how to prepare your own drink garnishes and put them to best use.

ALMONDS Sliced almonds or almonds julienne are sometimes floated on tall drinks or punches. They're best if toasted beforehand and slightly cooled. Toss the almonds with a small amount of melted butter and spread in a shallow pan. Toast them in a moderate oven for ten to fifteen minutes or until light brown, stirring from time to time to avoid charring, then sprinkle generously with salt and cool before adding to drinks.

BANANAS Cut firm, ripe bananas into slices and immediately dip them into tart fruit juice to keep the fruit from darkening. Slices cut from rim to center and fastened onto the rim of a glass make a delicious adornment for Banana Daiquiris.

FRESH CHERRIES Remove the stems from fresh Bing or Royal Anne cherries; then remove the pits with a sharp-pointed paring knife or cherry pitter.

WHOLE COCONUT As with the whole pineapple, the whole coconut is sometimes used as a vessel for rum potations. The end opposite the "eyes" should be cut off. Holding the eye end in one hand, strike the opposite end a sharp blow with a heavy French knife. Pour off the liquid. Place the coconut cup in a deep dessert dish with cracked ice to keep the cup in a stable position.

CUCUMBER PEEL A cool complement to a Pimm's No. 1 Cup as well as wine cups and other slayers of summer thirsts. Using a sharp paring knife or a lemon-twist cutter, slice the peel about $1/2$ inch wide, but use it sparingly; it's surprisingly pungent.

FLOWERS Edible flowers such as orchids, gardenias, nasturtiums, roses, and hibiscus blossoms not only ornament drinks, but their exotic fragrance also enhances the flavors of rum and fruit juices in tall potables as well as summer punch bowls.

LEMON, LIME, OR ORANGE SLICES Cut the fruit crosswise just before adding to your drinks. Whenever possible, place the slice on the rocks so that the nostrils almost meet the fruit when the drink is sipped. Or you may cut each slice from rim to center and affix it to the rim of the glass.

LEMON OR ORANGE PEEL These should be cut just before using to save volatile oils. Use a lemon-twist cutter or a very sharp paring knife for the job. And, if possible, avoid cutting a large amount of peel before party time.

Drink recipes sometimes call for the peel of an entire orange or lemon in one continuous spiral—called a horse's neck. To prepare it, use a small, sharp paring knife (not a lemon-twist cutter) and, starting at the stem end, cut a continuous $1/2$-inch swath around the fruit; avoid breaking the "neck" as the piece becomes longer.

MELONS Any thick, ripe melon, such as a honeydew, cantaloupe, casaba, or Crenshaw, may be cut into round balls (using a Parisienne potato cutter or a melon-baller).

MINT LEAVES You may not be able to reach out of your penthouse window and grab fresh mint leaves, but mint should be as close to garden-fresh as possible, with tender, young (rather than overgrown) leaves. The leaves may be dipped into syrup and then into superfine sugar before planting in drinks.

NUTMEG Though most spices for hot winter drinks, like cinnamon sticks, whole cloves, and whole allspice, are simply dropped into the drink, nutmeg is generally ground. You can buy it that way, but for best effect buy it whole and grate it fresh, either by using a nutmeg grater or by rubbing it over the fine side of a square metal grater.

PINEAPPLE Like coconuts, pineapples can serve both as a garnish and as a fancy substitute drinking vessel for outsize rum drinks—when the fruit is part of the drink. To prepare a whole pineapple as a drinking vessel, lop off the leafy top and cut out the deep core of fruit with a long, narrow-bladed knife or boning knife; then remove more of the interior with a grapefruit knife. Be careful not to pierce the shell, or your drink will spring a leak.

To make pineapple sticks or wedges, start by slicing off the cap with a heavy, sharp knife, then cut off and discard a bottom slice about $1/2$ inch thick. Holding the fruit upright, shave off the skin from top to bottom and make diagonal cuts with a pointed paring knife to remove the remaining "eyes," making the outside completely edible. Finally, cut it in half from top to bottom, place fruit flat side down, and cut lengthwise into equal wedges of any desired thickness; then slice off the core end of each wedge. Cut each long wedge into smaller ones—about $2 1/2$ inches to make pineapple sticks, $1/2$ inch thick to make chunks.

If the fruit is very tart, sprinkle it heavily with sugar and marinate for three to four hours, or even overnight, before using in drinks.

POMEGRANATE SEEDS In drinks made with grenadine, a few seeds of the pomegranate, from which the syrup is made, are sometimes added for their tart succulence.

STRAWBERRIES Some prize strawberries come with their own long stems, perfect for plucking from a bar glass. Strawberries may be dipped into a red syrup such as grenadine or into beaten jelly. Very large berries may be cut in half through the stem end.

TROPICAL FRUIT For rum libations, fresh mangoes or papayas may be cut into long pieces as with pineapple sticks, or into chunks about $^3/_4$ inch thick. Passion fruit, starfruit, kiwi, and guava also make tasty and attractive garnishes.

Finally, a note on retrieving fresh-fruit garnishes: no strict code of etiquette, fortunately, exists; small pieces of fruit like melon balls or strawberries may be dropped directly into a drink and later retrieved with a spoon, a cocktail spear, or, for that matter, the bare hand. But for convenience as well as eye appeal, the fruit may be affixed to a cocktail spear, which can then be placed into the end of a straw (if the drink is a tall cooler) or across the rim of the glass.

CHAPTER 4

* SAY WHEN *
A SHORT COURSE IN THE
NEW MATH OF MIXOLOGY

You don't normally use a lab beaker marked in milliliters for pouring your Tennessee sour mash into an old-fashioned glass. Nor are you likely to pull out your calculator to verify that the quart of tonic water you're chilling holds 32 ounces. But whenever a resourceful barman plans a drink party for a dozen or two dozen people rather than the couple or foursome around a cocktail table, he makes it his business to know in advance the capacity of his bottles and glasses. At one time, you could always assume that a "fifth" was a fifth of a gallon, whether it was bourbon or California brandy. Several years ago, whenever you began reading the fine print on the labels of some of the imported swig in liquor stores, you were likely to become numb with confusion before you were soothed by the swig itself. If you were selecting amaretto, you'd have noted that one bottle held 23 ounces, another 24 ounces, and a third contained 25 ounces. Not one corresponded to the traditional U.S. fifth (25.6 ounces). You'd pick up a bottle of apricot liqueur and it would be 25 ounces; a bottle of triple sec would be 24 ounces; Chartreuse turned out to be 23.6 ounces, while Cherry Marnier dipped to 22 ounces. Fortunately, however, it should no longer be necessary to play this liquid shell game.

Happily, the wine-and-spirits wheel of chance stopped spinning in 1980, when all wines and spirits sold in the United States began, by federal regulation, to be bottled in a limited set of specific sizes. Liqueurs and cordials were initially exempt from the new regulation, and the number of available bottle sizes had risen to a virtually incalculable thirty-nine! They must now conform to the new metric standard for spirits, however, and the basic standard is six sizes. Wines (except for those bottled abroad before 1979), too, are sold in six sizes, instead of the previous sixteen for American wines and twenty-seven for imports. Today, whether you buy a bottle of domestic gin or German Jägermeister, you will own a standard size from which there is no deviation.

Undoubtedly the traditional $1^1/_2$-ounce bar jigger will continue to be the standard unit for mixing or measuring individual drinks. Other units of liquid measurement from a dash to a nip, as well as old and new bottle sizes, are described below. They should help you take a recipe for a single drink and magnify it at will, or reduce a giant-size punch bowl to the desired amount of wassail.

> *DASH* For all drink recipes in this book, a dash means $\frac{1}{8}$ teaspoon; two dashes will thus fill a $\frac{1}{4}$-teaspoon measure. Theoretically, a dash is the amount of liquid that squirts out of a bottle equipped with a dash stopper. Stoppers, however, vary in size, and to different liquor dispensers a dash means anything from three drops up; but dashes have potent flavor or they wouldn't be dashes, so it's important to be as accurate as possible. Thus, if you're making Sazeracs for sixteen people and you need sixteen times a dash of Pernod, a little calculating will quickly tell you that you need 2 teaspoons of Pernod, and it's best to measure it exactly rather than make a clumsy guess.

> *TEASPOON* Equals $\frac{1}{3}$ tablespoon, or $\frac{1}{6}$ ounce. Use a measuring spoon, not a long-handled bar spoon, which is designed for mixing rather than measuring.

> *TABLESPOON* Equals 3 teaspoons, or $\frac{1}{2}$ ounce.

Pony Equals 1 ounce, or the small end of a double-ended measuring jigger. Also equals the normal capacity of the liqueur glass or the pousse-café glass.

Jigger Equals 1½ ounces. Also called a bar measuring glass, it's the standard measure for mixing individual drinks, though generous hosts use a 2-ounce jigger. Although jiggers are supposed to provide exact measurements, they're sometimes grossly inaccurate, so it's a good idea, if possible, to check any new jigger you buy against a lab measuring glass.

Wineglass Used as a measuring term, it equals 4 ounces, which is the amount of an old-fashioned wineglass filled to the brim. But today wine is generally served in a much larger glass—one-third full to permit the wine to be swirled for releasing its bouquet—though the wineglass as a 4-ounce measure still appears in some drink recipes and in food recipes.

Split or nip Equals 6 to 8 ounces, about the same as a half-pint, or the standard 1-cup measure. One refers to a split of champagne, but the same quantity of stout is called a nip.

Pint Measures 16 ounces, ½ quart, or two standard measuring cups.

Fifth Measures 25.6 ounces, ⅘ quart, ⅕ gallon, or 750 milliliters.

Quart Measures 32 ounces, 2 pints, 4 cups, ¼ gallon. Not to be confused (in Canada and England) with the imperial quart, which equals 38.4 ounces, or (in continental Europe) with the liter, which equals 33.8 ounces. (Most

standard wine and champagne bottles contain 750 milliliters, or 25.6 fluid ounces, the same as a fifth.)

MAGNUM Measures about 52 ounces, or double the size of a
standard champagne bottle.

Hosts still attempting to get the hang of the metric system should start
with an old point of reference, namely the U.S. quart, or 32 ounces. It has
been replaced by the liter, which is slightly larger: 33.8 ounces. The liter is
subdivided into milliliters, of which there are 1,000 in a liter, and they're
shown in Tables 1 and 2 as ml. Here, then, are the new bottle sizes and
their closest corresponding old sizes.

TABLE 1   SPIRITS (SIX SIZES)
(NOW USED FOR STANDARD BOTTLINGS. MANDATED AFTER DECEMBER 31, 1979.)

OLD SIZE	OLD SIZE	NEW SIZE	NEW SIZE
Name	*Fluid Oz.*	*Fluid Oz.*	*Milliliters/Liters*
MINIATURE	1.6	1.7	50ML
HALF PINT	8	6.8	200ML
PINT	16	16.9	500ML
FIFTH	25.6	25.4	750ML
QUART	32	33.8	1 LITER
HALF GALLON	64	59.2	1.75 LITERS

Needless to say, such colorful old containers as the demijohn—a narrow-
necked bottle of either glass or stoneware containing 1 to 10 gallons—are
out. Ditto for the tappit hen (about ⅗ gallon), the jeroboam (about ⅘ gallon), and the rehoboam (about 1⅕ gallons). Travelers to Europe may occasionally notice massive bottles of wine seldom shipped to the United States.
These range from the Methuselah (1⅗ gallons) to the Nebuchadnezzar
(about 4 gallons). Both of these huge dimensions are harder to fabricate in
uniformly exact capacities, although you'll find 4-liter jugs of wine and
"box" wines of 5 liters readily available in most liquor stores.

TABLE 2 WINES (SIX SIZES)

(CONVERSION MUST HAVE BEEN COMPLETED BY 1980
EXCEPT FOR WINES BOTTLED ABROAD BEFORE JANUARY 1, 1979.)

OLD SIZE	OLD SIZE	NEW SIZE	NEW SIZE
Names	*Fluid Oz.*	*Fluid Oz.*	*Milliliters/Liters*
SPLIT	7	6.3	187ML
TENTH	12.8	12.7	375ML
FIFTH	25.6	25.4	750ML
QUART	32	33.8	1 LITER
MAGNUM	51.2	50.7	1.5 LITERS
DOUBLE MAGNUM	102.4	101.4	3 LITERS

DRINK CALCULATORS

As a rule, the drinking curve rises headlong on holidays and weekends and descends at other times. Also, a party around a punch bowl will usually drink at least 50 percent more than a party for which the host laboriously mixes drinks one by one to order. Furthermore, the place where one cracks his bottles often determines the amount of liquid cheer consumed. Liquor is downed at a dockside party in far greater volume than when dispensed from a boat's galley. Ale or beer drinkers cavorting at an outdoor lobster barbecue will kill kegs rather than the bottles of an indoor seafood party.

In estimating how much liquor to buy for any party where mixed drinks are served, you must start out with the specific recipes you have in mind. If, for instance, you plan to serve Brandy Sours, you must decide beforehand whether each drink will have a 1½-ounce or 2-ounce base. If you're serving tall coolers with rum and other spirits, you must go back to the base recipe, check each kind of spirit called for, and then expand it to any number up to infinity. Even when your goal isn't infinity, it's always best in your calculations to err on the side of too much. Certainly, if you're buying for your party the same spirits you'd normally stock in your liquor cabinet, leftover bottles are good liquid assets. And when buying half a dozen or a dozen bottles at a time, you can usually tuck away a noticeable saving under the single-bottle price.

A useful guideline for parties, tested over and over, is simply this: most of the crowd will consume two to three drinks at the usual cocktail hour at sundown, before a buffet, or before a sit-down dinner. After dinner, if you're serving highballs, you can again reasonably estimate two to three drinks per person, depending on how long guests remain after the dinner table has been cleared. At a knock-down, drag-out bachelor or bachelorette party (see sidebar on page 54), the two-to-three formula will expand to four-to-six. At a pretheater party, where everyone wants to keep an especially clear head, the formula may dip to one to two drinks per guest. The drink-calculation guide in Table 3 covers cocktails before dinner or postprandial highballs. If you're serving both, calculate both.

(Note: In the measurements below, the word "fifth" [fifth of a gallon] is used even though the old-fashioned fifth is $\frac{2}{10}$ ounce more than the new metric measurement [750ml] replacing it. Because the word "fifth" is still used in this country, it is indicated below and makes no difference in calculations for party requirements. Liters however may be purchased instead of fifths; often you can save money by purchasing the larger bottles.)

Table 3
Cocktail and Highball Calculator

If you're the host for a party of	As a rule they'll consume	If drinks are 1½ ozs. you'll need at least	if drinks are 2 ozs. you'll need at least
6	12-18 DRINKS	2 FIFTHS	2 FIFTHS
8	16-24 DRINKS	2 FIFTHS	2 FIFTHS
10	20-30 DRINKS	2 FIFTHS	3 FIFTHS
12	24-36 DRINKS	3 FIFTHS	3 FIFTHS
20	40-60 DRINKS	4 FIFTHS	5 FIFTHS
30	60-90 DRINKS	6 FIFTHS	8 FIFTHS

The Bachelor Dinner Party

J UDGMENT DAY DOESN'T NECESSARILY COINCIDE with one's wedding day; it often occurs several nights before the nuptials are celebrated, during the trial by alcohol, the riotous rite identified as the bachelor dinner party. Seldom is a bachelor dinner a do-it-yourself bacchanalia in your own pad, however; it is a pay-it-yourself affair, although sometimes the best man and some of his buddies will pick up the tab. In any case, a private room in a hotel or club is infinitely more practical than your own digs for absorbing the shock of baked Alaskas crashing on the floor, Martinis poured into grand pianos, and champagne glasses sailing at supersonic speed into fireplaces. Those about to give up their bachelorhood should be guided by the following straight steers on the last supper.

Choose a private dining room in a club, hotel, or restaurant, while avoiding the type of men's clubs that have always been inhabited by live corpses. A nonmember of a particular club may often use the club's facilities simply by asking one of his acquaintances who is a member to sponsor him as a guest. Some clubs and all hotels include bedroom facilities, where guests who lose all power of locomotion can be quietly transported and stashed away until their heads resume normal size.

A bachelor dinner, in spite of all the ribbing and riling, should allow trenchermen to get together and enjoy an evening of reminiscences and sociability. Although the party may start with Martinis, switch to beer or wine with the steak, champagne with the dessert, Cognac with the coffee, and resume with champagne, toasting on into the night, the party shouldn't be designed to turn men into human drainpipes.

One way to divert the drinkers to eating is to escort guests vigorously to the table right after the second round of cocktails. Offer the kind of soup guests simply can't ignore: bowls of velvety black-bean soup or baked onion soup au gratin. Beefsteak is the traditional meat course at a bachelor dinner. It can be dressed up as a planked steak surrounded with vegetables, but the most impressive and practical is the thick shell steak, a boneless cut of about six portions, which is sliced before serving. Draw the dinner to a close with a platter of assorted cheeses and salted crackers or, if you have a sweet tooth, with a warm wedge of apple pie topped with cheddar cheese, or vanilla ice cream and warm brandied peaches.

The old custom of toasting the bride by breaking a glass against the fireplace is a symbol—of the love of the bride and groom, which will continue to last until the glass is made whole again, or of the fact that the glass can't possibly be used for any worthier purpose. Remember simply that while marriages are sometimes made in heaven, bachelor dinners require more earthly considerations.

When buying wine for a party, the host should allow 3 ounces for a serving of an aperitif wine, sherry, or port. Red and white table wines, including champagne, are usually poured in 4-ounce portions, assuming that you're using generous 11-ounce tulip glasses or wide-bellied wineglasses. If a single wine is served throughout dinner, count on two or three glasses per person. If several wines are served with individual courses, count on one or two glasses of each wine per person. The wine schedule in Table 4 also applies to champagne or other sparkling wines served during dinner. Whether the bubbly is served before dinner as cocktails or after dinner for toasting, the same guide may be followed.

TABLE 4
APERITIF AND TABLE WINE CALCULATOR

If you're serving predinner aperitif wines, not aperitif cocktails, or if you're serving sherry or port for a party of	Your guests will generally average	You should buy or have on hand ready for serving
6	12-18 DRINKS	2 FIFTHS
8	16-24 DRINKS	2 FIFTHS
10	20-30 DRINKS	2 FIFTHS
12	24-36 DRINKS	3 FIFTHS
20	40-60 DRINKS	4 FIFTHS
30	60-90 DRINKS	6 FIFTHS
When serving a single red or white table wine throughout the meal, and your party consists of	Your guests will generally average	You should buy or have on hand ready for serving
6	12-18 DRINKS	3 FIFTHS
8	16-24 DRINKS	4 FIFTHS
10	20-30 DRINKS	5 FIFTHS
12	24-36 DRINKS	6 FIFTHS
20	40-60 DRINKS	10 FIFTHS
30	60-90 DRINKS	15 FIFTHS

Brandy and liqueurs are in a special category when served straight and not as an ingredient in dessert cocktails, liqueur frappés, etc. The usual serving in a small brandy glass as well as the larger brandy snifter is 1 ounce per person; the same goes for liqueurs served straight. (See Table 5.)

TABLE 5
BRANDY AND LIQUEUR CALCULATOR

When pouring brandy or liqueurs as after-dinner drinks for a party of	Your guests will generally average	You should buy or have on hand ready for serving
6	6-12 DRINKS	1 FIFTH
8	8-16 DRINKS	1 FIFTH
10	10-20 DRINKS	1 FIFTH
12	12-24 DRINKS	1 FIFTH
20	20-40 DRINKS	2 FIFTHS
30	30-60 DRINKS	3 FIFTHS

In estimating carbonated beverages such as club soda, tonic water, ginger ale, or cola drinks, a generous guideline is to allow a liter for every two persons. Thus, a person consuming three Gin and Tonics would usually pour from 12 to 14 ounces for his three drinks. The smaller single-serving bottles of carbonated waters are easy to use when guests are pouring their own drinks at cocktail tables. Larger-size bottles are used when a bartender is doing the honors. If you're the rare individual who still makes your own soda water with soda charges, keep plenty of charges in reserve. The usual charge makes one quart (or liter) of soda.

At an all-beer party—a picnic, barbecue, or steak party—count on an average of at least three bottles of beer, ale, or stout per person. A quarter keg will yield 108 12-ounce glasses; a half keg will yield 180 of the same.

CHAPTER 5

Keep Your Spirits Up

L et's assume you're planning to stock a home bar and you don't as yet own an ounce of the straight stuff. You may remember a time when mixed drinks meant Martinis, Manhattans, and highballs. A host of that period acquiring the rudiments of the *ars bibendi* knew that if he owned gin, whiskey, and vermouth, he had the basic trio for serving the popular mixed drinks of his day. In recent years one single drink, the Vodka Martini, has moved gin to a second-fiddle position. And in less time than it takes to say Margarita or Daiquiri, you realize that tequila and rum are now indispensable for the starting lineup.

It's always a comfortable if not sumptuous feeling to buy your liquor leisurely rather than under the pressure of some sudden emergency at the liquor cabinet. It's good to know that your supply of spirits is varied and ample, and that it's at your elbow for drop-ins as well as for prearranged dinners. But when stocking a bar for the first time or building up your present liquor inventory, don't attempt to range the gamut of the spirit world from anisette to zubrovka; consider rather the tastes of the group that socializes casually with you. Every host soon learns that a special Scotch provides a warm afterglow for some of his comrades and a particular bourbon is preferred by others. If the drinking companions in your neck of the woods have a habitual thirst for Sloe Gin Fizzes, you'll want to have sloe gin on hand even though it isn't mentioned in any of the combinations that follow. If there are those in your crowd who are happy only with Harvey Wallbangers (orange juice, vodka, and Galliano liqueur), you'll need Galliano—and ignore the liquor adviser who tells you that Galliano is only an after-dinner liqueur.

You'll save money on any liquor by buying the large size, 1.75 liters, whenever possible, and if you regularly use a large amount of a specific liquor, the case price is usually more economical than the bottle price. But at the outset, a typical supply might reasonably consist of the following bottled goods (assume the list indicates liters, except for assorted liqueurs and aperitifs, for which a smaller size should suffice). As your spirit world expands, you'll begin to think of diversifying this basic closet with a variety of other potables. If, for example, your basic vodka is American, you may want to add a Finnish or Russian vodka, or one of the imported flavored vodkas. Flavored vodkas offer a refreshing zing and have become increasingly popular recently, with Absolut leading the charge (flavored gins and rums, too, are joining the fray). You may also want to add one of the high-proof English gins, or perhaps a bottle of Holland genever gin. If you started with a light Puerto Rican rum, you may want to enhance your offering with an aged añejo rum or one of the 151-proof rums. Thus your starting repertory might reasonably be expanded to include varieties like these.

WHISKEY Irish

SCOTCH Quality blended or single-malt (unblended)

GIN English, Dutch, Damrak (citrus flavored with a touch of honeysuckle)

VODKA Finnish, Polish, Norwegian, Russian, zubrovka, many-flavored

RUM Bacardi, Virgin Islands, Jamaican, añejo, 151-proof

BRANDY Cognac, Armagnac, apple, German, Greek Metaxa, ouzo

3 VODKA	2 BOURBON
2 BLENDED WHISKEY, U.S.	2 SCOTCH
2 GIN	1 CANADIAN WHISKEY
1 DRY VERMOUTH	2 TEQUILA
1 SWEET VERMOUTH	1 BRANDY, U.S.
2 RUM	1 APERITIF
3 ASSORTED LIQUEURS (FRUIT, COFFEE, CRÈME DE MENTHE, ETC.)	(CAMPARI, DUBONNET, ETC.)

TOTAL COST: ABOUT $300

LIQUEURS From straight flavors like apricot or banana to proprietary brands like Southern Comfort, Wild Turkey, Grand Marnier, Cointreau, Chartreuse, Drambuie, Benedictine, Peter Heering, etc.

APERITIFS Amer Picon, Byrrh, Cinzano, Cynar, Lillet, Punt e Mes

Going still further one might wish to add:

WHISKEY Japanese Suntory

UNAGED BRANDIES—Aquavit, slivovitz, kirschwasser

For the average bar host, about $200 would cover a reasonable selection from the above-mentioned lists.

Having stocked your bar with potables calculated to satisfy the tastes of your most sophisticated guests, you may wonder whether, under any circumstances, you should consider stocking and serving any from the imposing list of bottled premixed cocktails.

Premixed drinks are especially useful if you're hiring a bartender of questionable talent for an evening's work or when, at the end of a long, dusty day, you may not have fresh lemons for your Tom Collins thirst. The bottled gin sours made into tall drinks with ice and club soda will perform well as understudies, while bottled whiskey sours elongated with ice and soda are quickly transformed into Whiskey Collinses. On boat trips, in cramped galley quarters, at wayside picnics and for tailgate parties at football or ski sites, the premixed partymates are most welcome. But the fact is that little labor is saved by using them. If you're serving a bottled Martini, for example, you still have to prechill the glasses, take ice out of the freezer, mix and stir the makings in a shaker, pour them, and adorn each Martini with an olive or a lemon twist.

Nevertheless, effort aside, there are some premixed cocktails that will serve you well. The number of such mixes cramming the shelves in liquor stores has grown from a few standard combos to such specialty items as Mai Tais and Stingers—and a few of them are actually first-rate. Among the best of the lot is the bottled Manhattan, which may be even better than the one you make yourself. When the two ingredients—whiskey and vermouth—not only mingle but marry, as they do in the bottle, the result is as superior to the fresh-made mixture as a curry by the third or fourth day. And no one would presume to fault—or imitate—the excellence of English Pimm's No. 1 Cup, the definitive premixed base for a Gin Sling; or the subtlety of that aristocrat of after-dinner drinks, the B&B, an epicurean admixture of brandy and Benedictine.

But be warned that there are limits to these distillery-born combinations. While manufactured Manhattans, Martinis, Rob Roys, and Black Russians may turn up winners, the great majority of premixes made with fruit juice draw an average-to-poor grade, simply because bottled orange or lemon juice can't begin to match the fresh. Our advice: be as selective about the premixes you purchase as you are about the appropriate occasions to serve them. For most purposes—and people—it's more fitting (and more fun) to do it yourself.

There will be times when your normal bar supply will be temporarily expanded for mass drinking—a big cocktail celebration, holiday blowout, or similar affair for which the number of heads and the possible number of drinks must be estimated. In such cases, the slide rule works like this: a fifth (750ml) of hard liquor will be enough for seventeen 1½-ounce (standard-size) drinks. A liter (formerly quart) will provide twenty-two drinks. At a dinner party, count on two to four jiggers of hard liquor per person, dispensed in either straight or mixed forms. At a bachelor party, allow from three to six jiggers.

Finally, a few sensible reminders: your bar may be a movable one on wheels, a built-in piece of sectional furniture, the shelves above a clothes closet, a tea wagon, or a wicker hamper in the back of your station wagon. Reserve supplies may be stashed away wherever it's convenient—in cellar or attic. But within easy reach, close to your mixing counter, there should be one bottle of each commonly used liquor. Your inventory isn't an old rock collection to be hunted for behind bookshelves, nor is a host normally able to pop fifths Houdini-like out of a silk hat. Keep everything arranged conveniently so that you can find the liquor you're looking for without fumbling or squinting at labels. For big blowouts, punch-bowl, and holiday parties, fill in your stock well in advance of the fest itself. Don't get caught scrounging for replacements at the eleventh hour.

A host may commence many things; he may finish few. But every host at his home-bar base learns that the one thing that always gets finished is liquor. Still, you may now and then find an odd bottle that has reached the aged-in-the-coffin stage. Take such oddments, supplement them with fresh liquors, and turn them into coolers, pitchers, or punches. It's fun to invent them and to make room simultaneously for new liquors that may readily become a going concern.

Introduction to Cocktails

The most overwhelmingly popular of all potables, the open sesame to brunch parties, lunch parties, dinner parties, midnight supper parties, and the next morning's revival parties, the cocktail is undoubtedly America's most noted contribution to the world of bibulous pleasure. The stories concerning the origin of the word cocktail are nearly as many and varied as the mixtures themselves. Among them, the following legends have a life of long vintage.

The word came from the French *coquetel*, once used to describe a mixed drink in the Bordeaux region One of the earliest written references can be traced back to an American magazine in 1806, in which it was stated that the "cocktail is a stimulating liquor, composed of spirits of any kind, sugar, water, and bitters."

Army officers in the South were once served a luscious mixed drink by a lovely Southern belle. Her name? "Octelle, suh!"

A distinguished American general was invited to the court of a Mexican monarch whose daughter appeared with a drink in the royal cup of gold encrusted with rubies. When the obvious question of who would drink first racked all the king's men, the daughter solved the problem very intelligently by drinking the libation herself. The stunning princess's name, of course, was Coctel.

Western horse traders, whose nags weren't worth the price of their pelts, on sale day, fed their horses liquor, which made them cock their tails and come to life with incredible spirit.

New Orleans apothecary Antoine Amedee Peychaud, born in France, would serve his guests a concoction of brandy, water, sugar, and his famous bitters in an eggcup (*cocquetier* in French). The word was subsequently shortened to "cocktay" and, eventually, "cocktail."

Morning tipplers in New Amsterdam, visiting inns for a pick-me-up, would invariably run into Dutch barmaids, who (you guessed it) used the tails of roosters for sweeping away the previous night's litter.

A young Irish lass (this tale by James Fenimore Cooper) not only managed to procure and roast chickens from Tory farmers for her Revolutionary guests but also decorated their drinks with feathers from cocks' tails.

Whether or not these stories are any more real than Paul Bunyan's blue ox, it's clear that the cocktail has long been a part of America's drinking heritage. And even today, Americans remain the foremost masters and idolaters of the cocktail.

Cocktails range from appetite-awakening, bone-dry Martinis to velvety dessert cocktails that serve as a climax to a rich feast. Hosts taking the lead at their own cocktail parties should weigh the counsel in chapter 3, Barmanship. In time, as your cocktail repertoire expands, the ups and downs of the cocktail shaker will become second nature. But even the most polished perfectionists follow certain well-tested guidelines for cocktails, hence the following review of the more important considerations in drink making.

1. Inferior liquors aren't masked in cocktails, and a fine gin will seem even finer in a Martini. The same goes for whiskeys, rums, vodkas, and vermouths.

2. Don't imitate the free-pouring bartenders of public bars. Use standard measures, whether they be teaspoons, jiggers, ounces, cups, or quarts. When you multiply quantities for parties, be mathematically accurate.

3. Ice must be hard, cold, and clean—not weeping. Fresh ice at 0°F or below will produce a much brisker drink than lazy ice turning to water.

4. Though cocktails must be icy cold (proper dilution is part of the art), they shouldn't be watery. Anyone can start shaking cocktails. An artist knows when to stop. Normally 2 to 2½ ounces poured into a cocktail shaker will grow to approximately 4 ounces after proper shaking. Use a 4½-ounce glass, or a 6-ounce glass for larger cocktails.

5. Use the proper glass for each cocktail, and make sure that it's sparkling clean and prechilled, when necessary. The glass should first chill the hand and then the lips; the icy cocktail itself will take care of the rest.

6. You should, of course, use fresh ingredients in your cocktails whenever possible, especially when it comes to fruit juices.

7. Cocktails with fruit juices, eggs, syrups, etc., are usually shaken; those containing only liquor and vermouth are stirred (although one of the most eminent Martini men of modern times, Somerset Maugham, insisted that his Martinis be shaken, à la Bond). The stirred cocktail is clear, the shaken cloudy.

8. Make your own personal recipe changes only with the greatest care, remembering that some cocktails are dominated by a single straight, powerful flavor—the Martini by gin, for instance, or the Negroni by Campari—while others are a medley of flavors: liquors, fortified wines,

juices, bitters, fruits, etc. A fine cocktail of the latter type is always in delicate balance; even its aftertaste leaves a pleasant sense of the tart and the sweet, the strong and the weak. Sometimes adding or subtracting an eighth of a teaspoon will make a noticeable difference. Be creative if you will, but create slowly and deftly. A new drink is always an evolution.

There are indeed thousands of drink recipes available to quench nearly every imaginable kind of thirst—from the simplest and most enduring of standards to wild combinations arising from the libationary imaginations of bartenders around the world—with new ones created every day. To help you get a handle on what might seem like a daunting variety, the following definitions describe some of the more basic types of cocktails and how they're made.

BUCKS Bucks are medium-long drinks—served in tall, 8-ounce glasses—that always contain ginger ale and fresh lemon or lime juice. Traditionally the fruit was squeezed and dropped into the glass. You'll find you get better bucks if the lemon or lime juice is measured into the glass and the drink then garnished with a slice of fruit as its crowning touch.

BUILD In the 1930s and '40s, bartenders didn't have electric blenders. All drinks, therefore, were made, or "built," right in the glass: ice first, followed by alcohol, juice, etc., then stirred with a bar spoon.

COBBLERS Like a fix (see page 67), of which it is a larger version, a cobbler is built in the glass and drunk without club soda, quinine water, or any other sparkling mixer. Though most recipes are designed to fill a 12-ounce glass—including the cracked ice that forms the base of each—they can be extended or abbreviated to fit your own glassware. The cracked ice in a filled glass will usually collapse somewhat when stirred with liquor; an ice refill is then necessary.

COLLINSES Among the oldest and best-known tall summer drinks, collinses always start with liquor, lemon juice, and soda and bear a striking resemblance to fizzes (see page 68). A Tom Collins and a Gin Fizz are for all practical purposes the same drink. A slice of lemon is an accepted garnish. Some bartenders dress up the collins with slices of oranges, cherries, and other bits of fruit, although this practice is frowned upon by veteran benders at the bar.

COOLERS Also similar to the collins, but with allowances for a greater variety of ingredients, coolers are basically tall drinks, usually shaken or blended and served in 12- to 14-ounce glasses. Often garnished to catch the eye and stir the senses, these drinks will chase your summertime blues far away.

DAISIES The daisy, which originated in the mauve decade, is a medium-tall drink served, if possible, in knob glassware, a silver mug, or any vessel that conveys a feeling of sumptuousness. An amalgam of spirits and fruit juice, a daisy is invariably sweetened with a red agent such as grenadine or raspberry syrup and usually topped with a float of some compatible liqueur—a last-minute touch that adds to its subtlety and good humor.

FIXES Fixes are medium-tall drinks in which the ingredients are "fixed" in the glass itself, which is then packed with crushed or finely cracked ice. As with the cobbler, no club soda or other extender is added, and shaking or straining is unnecessary. The simple fix of liquor, sugar, ice, and a slice of lemon is an heirloom from Victorian drinking days. Modern variations make gloriously refreshing summer libations.

FIZZES Fizzes are effervescent cooling agents built on lemon or lime juice and iced club soda. They are usually designed for tall, 14-ounce glasses but can easily be stretched into 16-, 18-, or 20-ounce potables for further appeasement of parched throats.

FLIPS Flips, like pousse-cafés and frappés, prove that good liquids often come in small glasses. A flip is simply a liquor or wine with egg and sugar, shaken to a creamy froth. Flips are rich; too much egg makes them overrich. Thus, for each drink it's best to use a small egg, or one large egg for two flips. A classic Brandy Flip, for instance, is made like this: 2 ounces brandy, 1 small egg, and 1 teaspoon sugar are shaken with plenty of ice, strained into a Delmonico glass, then lightly topped with freshly grated nutmeg. Following the same pattern, standard flips are made by substituting whiskey, gin, rum, applejack, port, sherry, or Madeira for the brandy.

PICK-ME-UPS The ancient Egyptians thought that boiled cabbage would ward off a big head after an all-night drinking session. A ground swallow's beak blended with myrrh was recommended by the Assyrians. In South America, the Warau Indian women took care of their overindulgent males by deftly tying them like mummies in hammocks until their hangovers passed. In Europe and North America, repentant revelers seek out the "hair of the dog": the very thing that caused you to see double may be the shot in the arm that will straighten your sight. For generations, experienced barmen, especially in men's clubs, where hangover victims can be observed and treated at close range, have vouched for the hair-of-the-dog therapy. Naturally, the danger of taking a swig of liquor the morning after is that the stimulus and relief it brings may provide just enough narcosis to set you right back on the rocky road to ruin. Nevertheless, the effect of a small amount of liquor, especially if combined with citrus juice or tomato juice, seems in many cases to have an extremely salutary effect.

RICKEYS The first time you try a rickey, your reaction may be the same kind of shudder you get with the first taste of Campari or Greek olives. But the instant shock of pleasure to a heat-weary body will draw you back again and again. All rickeys are highballs made with lime juice and club soda, with no added sugar.

The word rickey evokes an immediate association with gin. But the Gin Rickey—though it's a justifiably renowned classic among warm-weather coolers—is only one among a multitude of these refreshingly effervescent lime libations. Other rickeys can be made by substituting various liquors for gin. Bourbon, blended whiskey, Canadian whisky, Scotch, apple brandy, vodka, and rum all make interesting and refreshing rickeys.

SANGAREES Sangarees are slightly sweet lowball drinks on the rocks. Unlike an Old-Fashioned, the sangaree contains no bitters. Each drink usually receives a benediction of freshly grated nutmeg, and should be very well stirred to make sure it is properly diluted.

SOURS While a Whiskey Sour is the best known, these shaken, short potables can be made with almost any liquor or liqueur, as long as the drinks include lemon or lime juice and sugar.

THE MARTINI

Over the years, the Martini—that most famous of all cocktail-hour thoroughbreds—has evolved into a drink that is practically all gin with only the faintest hint of vermouth. This preference for drier and drier Martinis (while "dry" usually means less sweet, in reference to Martinis it means less vermouth) has spawned some strange equipment and countless jokes. Some barmen ritualize the exacting vermouth formula with a long Rx dropper; some spray their vermouth from atomizers. Reaching the *reductio ad absurdum*, the fanatical claim they waft the vermouth bottle top over the gin or mutter the word "vermouth" under their breath while stirring their raw concoction in the mixing glass. It would be unfortunate if the use of vermouth in the Martini became extinct, for its bite, however faint, is trenchant. It turns cold gin into a civilized cocktail.

Most top-flight barmen make their Martinis with about ten or twelve parts gin to one part dry vermouth. The drink may be served "up," meaning in a regular stemmed cocktail glass, or on the rocks in an old-fashioned glass. You can drop a twist of lemon peel into the glass or rub the rim with the peel before adding it to the drink. The Martini's most common garnish is an olive, pitted or stuffed. With a cocktail-onion garnish, it turns into a Gibson.

A Martini must be piercingly cold; at its best, both gin and vermouth are prechilled in the refrigerator, well stirred with ice, and poured into a prechilled glass. Energetic stirring with the ice is all-important; the dilution makes the drink both smooth and palatable. Those who merely combine gin and vermouth beforehand and then refrigerate without stirring wind up serving raw slugs to guests who are quickly cargoed and who completely miss the pleasure of a well-made Martini.

Introduction to Cocktails

Although vermouth is the spirited minor ingredient, a bottle opened for pouring and left standing in the liquor cabinet for weeks will lose its bell-ringing zest. To retain as much as possible of the flavor of the aromatic herbs used in making vermouth, store the opened bottle in the refrigerator. It's a good idea for the Martini man to buy his vermouth in pint bottles and make frequent replacements.

Here are several variations on the familiar Martini theme (you'll find more in the Vodka and Gin chapters).

12-to-1 MARTINI
2 oz. gin
1 tsp. dry vermouth

8-to-1 MARTINI
2 oz. gin
¼ oz. dry vermouth

4-to-1 MARTINI
2 oz. gin
½ oz. dry vermouth

GIBSON
As noted, any of the above Martini mixtures garnished with a cocktail onion.

BLENTON
1¼ oz. gin   **1 dash Angostura bitters**
¾ oz. dry vermouth

Stir well with ice. Strain into prechilled cocktail glass. A Martini variation so old that it's new. Total effect on the palate: warming and elevating.

CORDIAL MARTINI
1¼ oz. gin   **¼ oz. Cordial Médoc**
¼ oz. dry vermouth

Stir gin, vermouth, and Cordial Médoc well with ice. Strain into prechilled cocktail glass or over rocks. Twist lemon peel over drink and drop into glass.

FINO MARTINI
2 oz. gin
½ oz. fino sherry

Stir well with ice. Strain into prechilled cocktail glass. Add olive or lemon twist. Serve with a side dish of freshly toasted, salted almonds.

FLYING DUTCHMAN

Curaçao
2 oz. gin
¼ oz. dry vermouth

Into a prechilled cocktail glass, pour enough curaçao so that when the glass is slowly twirled, it will coat the sides. Stir gin and vermouth well with ice. Strain into glass.

GIN AND IT

2 oz. gin
Italian sweet vermouth

Stir gin well with ice. Into a prechilled cocktail glass, pour enough vermouth so that, when the glass is slowly twirled, it will coat the sides. Add the gin. The English drink is often served at room temperature. *The "It" stands for the Italian sweet vermouth. A Gin and French is the same drink, but with French dry vermouth.*

KNICKERBOCKER

2 oz. gin   **⅛ oz. sweet vermouth**
½ oz. dry vermouth

Stir well with ice. Strain into prechilled cocktail glass. Serve without benefit of cherry, olive, or lemon twist. *This version of the Martini appeals to those who like vermouth in both sweet and dry forms.*

MARSALA MARTINI

¾ oz. gin   **¾ oz. dry Marsala**
¾ oz. dry vermouth   **Lemon peel**

Stir gin, vermouth, and Marsala well with ice. Strain into prechilled cocktail glass. Twist lemon peel above drink and drop into glass.

MARTINEZ

2 oz. gin   **½ tsp. maraschino liqueur**
½ oz. dry vermouth   **2 dashes orange bitters**

Stir well with ice. Strain into prechilled cocktail glass. *Martini men with a strain of Spanish in their veins go for this one. Alleged to have been the original Martini.*

MARTINI, HOLLAND STYLE

2 oz. Dutch genever gin   **Lemon peel**
½ oz. dry vermouth

Stir gin and vermouth well with ice. Strain into prechilled cocktail glass. Twist lemon peel above drink and drop into glass.

PAISLEY MARTINI

2¼ oz. gin   **1 tsp. Scotch**
¼ oz. dry vermouth

Stir well with ice. Strain into prechilled cocktail glass. *The flavor of the Scotch in this 9-to-1 Martini is just subtle enough to let the drinker know that something delightfully offbeat is in his glass.*

PERFECT

1½ oz. gin
½ oz. dry vermouth

½ oz. sweet vermouth

Stir well with ice. Strain into prechilled cocktail glass. Add olive or twist of lemon peel if desired. *Modern Martini men would call this an "imperfect" Martini, but "perfect" is its traditional name.*

SWEET MARTINI

2 oz. gin
½ oz. sweet vermouth

Orange peel

Stir gin and vermouth well with ice. Strain into prechilled cocktail glass. Twist orange peel above drink and drop into glass. *While "sweet Martini" sounds like a contradiction in terms, the drink is not only tolerable, but titillating.*

MISTS

A mist is simply straight liquor poured over crushed ice. The normal proportions are 1½ ounces of liquor poured into an 8-ounce tall old-fashioned glass filled with crushed ice. Sometimes a twist of lemon is added. Mists are cousins of frappés, which are sweet liqueurs poured over crushed ice. Actually, the large amount of fine ice in a mist doesn't befog the liquor's intrinsic flavor; the quality of a fine whiskey in a mist will seem more vivid than the same shot bolted straight down. We now draw the veil from ten of the best-known mists.

> *BRANDY MIST* The triumphant flavor of cognac makes the noncognac brandies seem pallid by comparison. (In mixed drinks the story may be different.) Metaxa, the Greek semisweet brandy, creates a velvety, tremulous mist.

> *SCOTCH MIST* Best when made with a full-bodied, twelve-year-old Highland Dew. When it comes to mists, some of the lighter Scotches turn into ordinary fog.

> *VODKA MIST* Ice and vodka emerge as just ice and vodka, nothing more (unless you use one of the stronger flavored vodkas, such as Finlandia Cranberry), but an added dram of dry vermouth (a mere teaspoon or so) and a twist of

lemon turn the mist into an instant Vodka Martini. Zubrovka vodka makes a subtle mist.

KIRSCHWASSER MIST A happy, silvery mist with a hauntingly dry aftertaste of cherries.

BOURBON MIST Either 86 or 100 proof is fine, but more important than proof is to use a quality aged bourbon with a smooth, ripe flavor. Half bourbon and half Southern Comfort creates a heavenly mist.

RYE MIST One of the best ways to appreciate genuine straight rye—cool and refreshing.

BLENDED U.S. WHISKEY MIST As in bourbon, smoothness shows up in the very first sip. A slice of lemon is a pleasant garnish.

CANADIAN MIST Use top-of-the-line Canadian whisky, but increase portion to 1¾ ounces to keep the cool north-country flavor from dissipating too soon.

GIN MIST It's surprising how close a Gin Mist is to the modern Martini. Add a tiny splash of dry vermouth for a Martini Mist. A good way to introduce Dutch genever gin to someone who's never tasted it is via the mist.

RUM MIST The potent flavors of Martinique and Jamaica rums emerge beautifully in mists. Light rum is extremely pleasant with a slice of lime or a small gardenia as garnish. For a more rummy accent, float a teaspoon of 151-proof rum on a light-rum mist.

HIGH
SPIRITS

If the word highball is heard less and less frequently these days, the drink itself is called for more and more often. Drinkers everywhere now ask for Scotch and Soda, Bourbon and Water, Applejack and Ginger Ale, and other happy mixtures suited to their own thirst specifications. Although the high-ball is the easiest drink in the world to define—a small amount of something strong with a larger amount of something weak in a tall glass with ice—it's the one potable for which you seldom see a recipe. As a matter of fact, a host who, in the intimacy of his own digs, strictly follows a highball recipe is inhospitable. It's the one drink guests themselves expect to mix to their own tastes, in the same way that they salt and pepper their food. No two-finger measurements are alike and no two guests will ever say "when" at the same point on the stopwatch. Even at commuter stand-up bars, where whiskey is carefully measured in a standard jigger, the mixer ration may vary depending on the heavy-handedness of any particular bartender on a given day.

But the highball is only one of countless potables in tall glasses. A tall drink at the end of a long, tiring day can do things no short drink can ever hope to do. A wilted worthy need only look at a lofty drink clinking with ice, and miracu-lous changes take place within him. His collar seems to cling less tenaciously. He begins to talk in more relaxed, civilized tones. And then, as the first sip of a tall drink passes over his tongue and throat, like spring water gurgling into a hot arroyo, he feels the unparalleled pleasure of a long-delayed thrill.

One of the obvious virtues of tall mixed drinks is that they never seem to get in the way of food, or vice versa. A man may hesitate to eat a trout *au bleu* while drinking a Manhattan, but he won't hesitate to drink a tall spritzer of Rhine wine and soda before, during, or after the trout. Although wine pundits will be horrified at the thought, tall coolers sup-plant *both* cocktails and wine at many a fine feast. Ounce for ounce, a tall cooler with club soda is actually no stronger than wine. But in the final analysis, tall drinks are made not for debating but for happy guzzling.

In preparing tall drinks, whether they are 8, 12, or 20 ounces, the host should follow this modern code for presenting them.

USE A FINE LIQUOR. The flavor of a poor liquor is actually intensified in a tall drink; you have time to scrutinize it more carefully than when you down it in one gulp. This doesn't mean that you must buy a sixteen-year-old bonded whiskey the next time you serve a round of Whiskey Collinses, but you should seek one of the eminent brands of liquor that are mellow, smooth, and pleasing whether taken straight or in a tall drink.

BE METICULOUS about the quality of the iced club soda or the ginger ale. For a small number of highballers, serve splits of soda or ginger ale. Larger bottles of carbonated waters, except at a party, just stand around going quietly flat unless you and your guests are unusually speedy drinkers.

ADD BUBBLE WATER just before drinks are delivered. For optimum sparkle and so that it retains its fizz as long as possible, pour it against the inside of the tilted glass. Be sure the effervescent water is ice cold.

PLAIN TAP WATER, if used, must be clear and clean, without evidence of rust, lime, iron, chlorination, or other urban evils. Use bottled spring water, if necessary, when your guests decline bubbles.

USE ENOUGH LIQUOR in a tall drink, at least 1½ ounces in an 8-ounce glass and up to 2 ounces or more in 12- to 20-ounce glasses.

USE THIN GLASSWARE with heavy bottoms to avoid the well-known sliding drink.

The Gin and Tonic has not only joined the tall-drink derby but in many circles is way out in front both in summer and winter. Bitter lemon has joined the same fraternity. Though the British Empire has shrunk, British-inspired bubblies have become more and more popular.

Among simple highballs, the Whiskey Highball is the best known. But there's no dogma that interdicts the use of any liquor in a highball, from aquavit to zubrovka. One of the best contemporary highballs is light, dry rum and iced club soda or iced tonic water.

So-called lowballs are actually served in glasses that hold as much as their taller cousins, but which are squat in shape rather than long; old-fashioned-type glasses ranging from 7 to 11 ounces are considered lowballs. Included below are a few recipes for drinks that, while not necessarily all tall, certainly belong in a category all to themselves.

The drink recipes that follow each respective chapter are usually designed for a 4½-ounce short glass when a cocktail glass is indicated; 5 ounces for short old-fashioned glasses; about 8 to 11 ounces when a highball or large old-fashioned glass is called for; and some 12 to 14 ounces for collins and other tall glasses. The parsimonious 3-ounce cocktail glasses are now skeletons in most liquor closets; not only does the larger cocktail provide more sumptuous bliss for guests, but it's also a boon to the host because it means fewer refills and the coveted chance to sit down, drink, and enjoy the revelry.

The following chapters will give you an overview and brief history of the various kinds of wines, beers, liquors, and spirits discussed. As for the drink recipes that follow each chapter: whether old-fashioned or new, vintage or fresh off the vine, whether you're having a quiet dinner party (for anywhere from two to twenty) at home or raising the roof, you're sure to find among some 1,400 cocktails included here the perfect partner for any persuasion, occasion, or otherwise impromptu gathering you may have the pleasure and good fortune to happen upon.

And to get you started on your merry mixologist's way, here are a few cocktails that belong in a category all their own or, rather, defy easy categorization. The only thing these drinks have in common—with those we've already discussed as well as with one another—is their excellence as libations for a long day's night or as party potables.

ALABAMA SLAMMER

1 oz. Southern Comfort
1 oz. amaretto

½ oz. sloe gin
½ oz. lemon juice

Pour into highball glass over rocks. Stir.

AMARETTO BREEZE

1 oz. amaretto
1 oz. Malibu rum

1 oz. Midori
Pineapple juice

Shake amaretto, rum, and Midori well with ice. Top off with pineapple juice. Stir.

AMARETTO COBBLER

1½ oz. gin
2 oz. orange juice
1 oz. lemon juice

½ oz. amaretto
1 slice orange

Fill a 12-oz. glass with finely cracked ice. Add gin, orange juice, lemon juice, and amaretto. Stir well. Add more ice to fill glass almost to rim. Stir. Add orange slice.

APRICOT ANISE FIZZ

1¾ oz. gin
½ oz. apricot-flavored brandy
Iced club soda
¼ oz. anisette
½ oz. lemon juice

½ brandied or fresh apricot
Lemon peel

Shake gin, apricot-flavored brandy, anisette, and lemon juice well with ice. Strain into tall 14-oz. glass half-filled with ice. Fill glass with soda. Stir. Add brandied apricot. Twist lemon peel above drink and drop into glass.

BANANA BREEZE

1½ oz. Midori
1 oz. banana liqueur

1 oz. blue curaçao
3 oz. pineapple juice

Shake well with ice. Strain into highball glass over ice.

BEETLEJUICE

½ oz. vodka
½ oz. Midori
½ oz. blue curaçao
½ oz. raspberry schnapps

½ oz. cranberry juice
Splash Rose's Lime Juice
1 pineapple stick
1 cherry

Shake very well with ice. Strain into tall collins glass over rocks. Garnish with pineapple stick and cherry.

BLACK CHERRY

½ oz. raspberry liqueur
½ oz. coffee liqueur
½ oz. Bailey's Irish Cream
½ oz. vodka

¾ oz. light cream
Club soda
1 maraschino cherry

Shake liqueurs, Bailey's, vodka, and cream well with ice. Pour into tall collins glass. Top off with club soda. Stir gently. Drop in cherry.

BY THE POOL

1 oz. Midori
1 oz. peach schnapps

1 oz. orange juice
1 oz. 7-Up

Shake Midori, schnapps, and orange juice well with ice. Top off with 7-Up. Stir.

CANTELOOP

1 oz. vodka
1 oz. Midori

1 oz. peach schnapps
Club soda

Pour vodka, Midori, and peach schnapps into old-fashioned glass over rocks. Top off with club soda. Stir.

CARTHUSIAN COOLER

1 oz. yellow Chartreuse
1 oz. bourbon

Iced club soda

Put three large ice cubes into a tall 14-oz. glass. Add Chartreuse and bourbon. Fill glass with soda. Stir.

CHARTREUSE COOLER

2 oz. yellow Chartreuse
3 oz. orange juice
1 oz. lemon juice

Iced bitter lemon
1 slice orange

Shake Chartreuse, orange juice, and lemon juice well with ice. Strain into tall 14-oz. glass half-filled with ice. Fill glass with bitter lemon. Add orange slice.

CHERRY COLA

1½ oz. spiced rum
½ oz. amaretto

Cola

Pour rum and amaretto into highball glass over rocks. Top off with cola. Stir.

CLAM-JUICE COCKTAIL

4 oz. clam juice
½ oz. ketchup
½ oz. lemon juice

1 dash Worcestershire sauce
Salt and pepper
Celery salt

Shake clam juice, ketchup, lemon juice, Worcestershire sauce, salt, and pepper well with ice. Strain into prechilled Delmonico glass. Sprinkle with celery salt. *Non-alcoholic but a wonderful bracer.*

COCONUT COOLER

1½ oz. CocoRibe
½ oz. California brandy
1½ oz. papaya nectar

½ oz. lemon juice
1 slice lemon

Shake CocoRibe, brandy, papaya nectar, and lemon juice well with ice. Strain into tall or squat 8-oz. glass. Add ice cubes to fill glass. Stir. Add lemon slice.

COCONUT FIZZ

2 oz. CocoRibe
1 oz. lemon juice
½ slightly beaten egg white

Iced club soda
1 slice lemon

Shake CocoRibe, lemon juice, and egg white extremely well with ice. Strain into tall 12-oz. glass half-filled with ice cubes. Fill with club soda. Stir. Add lemon slice.

COCONUT GROVE

1½ oz. CocoRibe
½ oz. triple sec
½ oz. lime juice

Iced club soda
1 slice lime

Shake CocoRibe, triple sec, and lime juice well with ice. Strain into 8-oz. glass. Add 2 ice cubes. Add soda to fill glass. Stir. Add lime slice.

COCORIBE MILK PUNCH

2 oz. CocoRibe
4 oz. milk

1 small egg
Ground cinnamon

Shake CocoRibe, milk, and egg extremely well with ice. Strain into 10-oz. glass. Sprinkle with cinnamon.

CORDIAL MÉDOC CUP

1 oz. Cordial Médoc
½ oz. cognac
1 oz. lemon juice

½ tsp. sugar
Iced brut champagne
1 slice orange

Shake Cordial Médoc, cognac, lemon juice, and sugar well with ice. Strain into 10-oz. glass with two large ice cubes. Fill glass with champagne. Stir very slightly. Add orange slice. *A tall drink for toasting.*

CRANBERRY COOLER

1 oz. cranberry liqueur
1 oz. California brandy

½ oz. triple sec
Iced tonic water

Fill 14-oz. glass three-quarters with ice. Add cranberry liqueur, brandy, and triple sec. Stir well. Fill glass with tonic water. Stir.

CRANBERRY FIZZ

1 oz. cranberry liqueur
1 oz. vodka
¾ oz. lemon juice
½ egg white

1 tsp. sugar
Iced club soda
1 slice lemon

Shake cranberry liqueur, vodka, lemon juice, egg white, and sugar well with ice. Strain into tall 14-oz. glass half-filled with ice. Fill glass with soda. Stir. Add lemon slice.

CRANBERRY FLIP

1 oz. cranberry liqueur   1 small egg
1 oz. California brandy   Freshly grated nutmeg

Shake cranberry liqueur, brandy, and egg extremely well with ice. Strain into prechilled Delmonico glass. Sprinkle with nutmeg.

CURAÇAO COOLER

1 oz. blue curaçao   Iced orange juice
1 oz. vodka   Lemon peel
½ oz. lime juice   Lime peel
½ oz. lemon juice   Orange peel

Shake curaçao, vodka, lime juice, and lemon juice well with ice. Strain into tall 14-oz. glass. Add two large ice cubes. Fill glass with orange juice. Stir well. Twist each of the peels above the drink and drop into glass. *Cool as the blue-green Caribbean itself.*

DEEP END

1 oz. Cordial Médoc   2 oz. chilled orange juice
½ oz. gin   Iced club soda
2 oz. chilled papaya nectar   ½ slice orange

Pour Cordial Médoc, gin, papaya nectar, and orange juice into tall 14-oz. glass three-quarters filled with ice cubes. Stir well. Add soda to fill glass. Stir. Add orange slice.

EGGNOG FRAMBOISE

4 oz. milk   ½ oz. dark Jamaica rum
1 small egg   2 level tsp. sugar
1 oz. framboise   Freshly grated nutmeg
½ oz. cognac

Shake milk, egg, framboise, cognac, rum, and sugar extremely well with ice. Strain into 10-oz. glass. Sprinkle with nutmeg.

GRAPPA STREGA

1 oz. grappa   ¼ oz. orange juice
1 oz. Strega   Lemon peel
¼ oz. lemon juice

Shake grappa, Strega, lemon juice, and orange juice well with ice. Strain into prechilled cocktail glass. Twist lemon peel above drink and drop into glass.

HONKY TONIC

1 oz. Sciarada   Iced tonic water
1 oz. gin   1 slice lemon
½ oz. lemon juice

Pour Sciarada, gin, and lemon juice into tall 12-oz. glass half-filled with ice cubes. Stir well. Fill with tonic water. Stir. Add lemon slice.

ITALIAN ICES

1 oz. vodka
1 oz. blue curaçao
1 oz. Chambord raspberry liqueur

1 oz. Rose's Lime Juice
3 oz. 7-Up

Shake vodka, curaçao, Chambord, and lime juice well with ice. Strain into collins glass over rocks. Top off with 7-Up.

KIRSCH CUBA LIBRE

1½ oz. kirschwasser
½ lime

Iced cola

Put three large ice cubes into a tall 14-oz. glass. Add kirschwasser. Squeeze lime above drink and drop into glass. Fill with cola. Stir.

LATIN DOG

½ oz. Sciarada
½ oz. Pernod

Chilled grapefruit juice

Fill 8-oz. glass with ice cubes. Add Sciarada, Pernod, and enough grapefruit juice to fill glass. Stir well. *Very pleasant brunch drink.*

NIGHT OF THE IGUANA

½ oz. vodka
½ oz. tequila
½ oz. coffee liqueur

1 oz. Rose's Lime Juice
1 slice lime

Shake very well with ice. Strain into tall collins glass over rocks. Garnish with lime slice.

OSTEND FIZZ

1½ oz. kirschwasser
½ oz. crème de cassis
½ oz. lemon juice

1 tsp. sugar
Iced club soda
1 slice lemon

Shake kirschwasser, crème de cassis, lemon juice, and sugar well with ice. Strain into tall 14-oz. glass half-filled with ice. Fill glass with soda. Stir. Add lemon slice. *Splendid with a summer smorgasbord.*

PEACH PARADISE

1 oz. Midori
1 oz. Malibu rum
1 oz. Peachtree schnapps

2 oz. orange juice
2 oz. pineapple juice

Shake well with ice. Strain into tall collins glass over rocks. Stir.

RED BAIT

1 oz. sloe gin
½ oz. dark Jamaican rum
2 oz. chilled guava nectar

½ oz. lime juice
Iced tonic water
1 slice lime

Pour sloe gin, rum, guava nectar, and lime juice into tall 14-oz. glass three-quarters filled with ice cubes. Stir well. Add tonic water to fill glass. Stir. Add lime slice.

RED DEATH

1 oz. vodka
1 oz. Southern Comfort
1 oz. amaretto
½ oz. sloe gin

½ oz. triple sec
3 oz. orange juice
1 oz. lime juice

Shake very well with ice. Strain into tall collins glass over rocks.

RED DEVIL

1 oz. vodka
1 oz. peach schnapps
1 oz. Southern Comfort
1 oz. sloe gin

1 oz. triple sec
2 oz. orange juice
Splash grenadine

Shake very well with ice. Strain into tall collins glass over rocks.

RED PERIL

1 oz. sloe gin
½ oz. vodka
2 oz. chilled papaya nectar

½ oz. lime juice
Iced club soda
1 slice lime

Pour sloe gin, vodka, papaya nectar, and lime juice into tall 14-oz. glass three-quarters filled with ice cubes. Stir well. Add soda to fill glass. Stir. Add lime slice.

ROYAL FLUSH

1½ oz. Crown Royal
1½ oz. peach schnapps

½ oz. Chambord raspberry liqueur
3 oz. cranberry juice

Shake very well with ice. Strain into tall collins glass over rocks. Or float cranberry juice on top last for a touch of sunset.

SCREAMING BANANA BANSHEE

½ oz. banana liqueur
½ oz. vodka
½ oz. white crème de cacao

1½ oz. light cream
1 cherry

Shake well with ice. Strain into prechilled cocktail glass. Drop in cherry.

SIMPATICO

2 oz. peppermint schnapps
1 oz. white rum

Iced bitter lemon
1 slice lemon

Pour peppermint schnapps and white rum into tall 14-oz. glass three-quarters filled with ice cubes. Stir well. Add bitter lemon to fill glass. Stir. Add lemon slice.

SLOE AND BITTER

1 oz. sloe gin
1 oz. tequila
½ oz. lemon juice

Iced bitter lemon
1 slice lemon

Shake sloe gin, tequila, and lemon juice well with ice. Strain into tall 12-oz. glass three-quarters filled with ice cubes. Fill glass with bitter lemon. Stir. Add lemon slice.

SLOE CRANBERRY COOLER

2½ oz. ice cold sloe gin
6 oz. ice cold cranberry juice

1¼ oz. lemon juice
1 slice lemon

Pour sloe gin, cranberry juice, and lemon juice into tall 14-oz. glass. Add ice cubes to fill glass. Stir well. Add lemon slice.

SLOE DOG

1 oz. sloe gin
½ oz. gin

2 oz. grapefruit juice
1 slice lime

Shake sloe gin, gin, and grapefruit juice well with ice. Strain over rocks in 8-oz. glass. Add lime slice.

SLOE GIN FIZZ

1 oz. sloe gin
1 oz. gin
¾ oz. lemon juice

Iced club soda
1 slice lemon

Shake sloe gin, gin, and lemon juice well with ice. Strain into tall 14-oz. glass half-filled with ice. Fill glass with soda. Stir. Add lemon slice.

SLOW COMFORTABLE SCREW

1 oz. sloe gin
½ oz. Southern Comfort

Orange juice

Pour sloe gin and Southern Comfort into highball glass over rocks. Top off with orange juice. Stir.

SOUTHERN RASPBERRY

¾ oz. framboise
¾ oz. Southern Comfort
½ oz. lemon juice

1 tsp. sugar
Iced club soda
1 slice lemon

Shake framboise, Southern Comfort, lemon juice, and sugar extremely well with ice. Strain over rocks in tall or squat 8-oz. glass. Add splash of soda. Add ice if necessary to fill glass to rim. Stir. Add lemon slice.

STREGA FLIP

1 oz. Strega
1 oz. brandy
½ oz. orange juice
1 tsp. lemon juice

1 small egg
1 tsp. sugar
Grated nutmeg

Shake Strega, brandy, orange juice, lemon juice, egg, and sugar well with ice. Strain into prechilled Delmonico glass. Sprinkle with freshly grated nutmeg.

TALL DUTCH EGGNOG

1½ oz. Advokaat liqueur
1½ oz. light rum
½ oz. 151-proof rum
1 oz. orange juice

6 oz. milk
1 tsp. sugar
½ cup finely cracked ice
Ground cinnamon

Put Advokaat, both kinds of rum, orange juice, milk, sugar, and ice into blender. Blend at high speed 10 seconds. Pour into tall 14-oz. glass. Sprinkle with cinnamon.
The Dutch way to get the New Year rolling as merrily as possible.

TALL HAOLE

2½ oz. CocoRibe
3 oz. orange juice
2 oz. apricot nectar

1 oz. lemon juice
Iced club soda
½ slice orange

Shake CocoRibe, orange juice, apricot nectar, and lemon juice well with ice. Strain into tall 14-oz. glass half-filled with ice cubes. Add soda to fill glass. Stir. Add orange slice.

TALL LIMONE

1 oz. Sciarada
1 oz. gin
½ oz. lemon juice

Iced bitter lemon
1 slice lemon

Pour Sciarada, gin, and lemon juice into a tall 12-oz. glass three-quarters filled with ice cubes. Stir well. Fill glass with bitter lemon. Stir. Add lemon slice.

TALL MIDORI

1 oz. Midori
1 oz. dark Jamaican rum

½ oz. lime juice
Iced tonic water

Pour Midori, rum, and lime juice into a tall 14-oz. glass three-quarters filled with ice cubes. Stir well. Fill with tonic water.

TIDAL WAVE

½ oz. gin
½ oz. light rum
½ oz. vodka
½ oz. peach schnapps

2 oz. orange juice
2 oz. pineapple juice
Splash grenadine
Splash 151-proof rum

Shake very well with ice. Strain into tall collins glass over rocks.

CHAPTER 7

* Wine, Beer, and *
Sake Concoctions *

From the dawn of civilization, humans have created and joyfully imbibed fermented libations such as wine, beer, and sake. Although these classic potations are most often enjoyed on their own or with a meal, the possibilities for savoring wine, beer, and sake don't stop there. A delightful variety of lower-alcohol mixed drinks that stimulate the palate and refresh the senses can be concocted with these pleasurable potions.

Today, wine is no longer the libation poured mostly for the grand bash, the black-tie dinner, or the champagne breakfast; it's something we're taking more and more with our daily bread. If we're the hosts, we offer wine whether we're dishing out spaghetti marinara or sweetbreads *sous cloche*. If we're guests, we recgonize the capable host as one who thoughtfully pairs food and wine to emphasize the virtues of both. And as the happy accompaniment for many a celebration, the champagne toast remains unrivaled in festivity.

As with wine, you can drink too much beer, but you can hardly get tired of it. It's difficult to convey in words the qualities that give gusto to a fine glass of brew, but the key element in all beer, the very soul of its flavor, is the refreshing bite that comes from the hops and which is always damned by non-beer drinkers because it's bitter, as thought that quality were unpalatable. And yet, though you drink it night after night, in fraternity houses, saloons, or penthouses, the first grand gulp always revives the same singular sensation of unparalled goodness.

Sake, now produced in the U.S. as well as its native Japan, has been an integral part of Japanese society for hundreds, if not thousands, of years. Traditionally served straight up and warm, this "rice beer," as it's sometimes called, can also add a versatile twist to any party—to which the recipes we've included here will certainly attest.

WINE COCKTAILS

Wine cocktails are for those who like wine and also enjoy pleasantly odd combinations of cold mixed drinks that help unwind the day and provoke appetites for dinner, but who don't want the fast, sometimes staggering jolt of a Martini or an Old-Fashioned. There are bottled wine cocktails now on the market, but making your own is no formidable task, and the results are extremely pleasant.

The wine cocktails that follow are made from red and white dry table wines, and recipes for port and champagne cocktails are also included. California jug wines are perfect for this kind of bartending. Both red and white wines should be well chilled and served in stemmed wineglasses holding 8 to 10 ounces each, unless otherwise indicated. The kind of wine you use will naturally determine the final results of the mixed drinks: a medium-bodied California mountain Burgundy will become a cocktail with sturdy flavor; a Beaujolais Nouveau used for the same recipe will result in a lighter, fresher-tasting cocktail. Among the whites, any light-bodied dry wine from an Italian Soave to a dry California Chablis will do beautifully.

BASES FILLED

4 oz. chilled dry white wine
½ oz. Cointreau or triple sec
½ oz. Cognac
1 orange peel

Pour wine, Cointreau, and Cognac into large wineglass. Add two ice cubes. Stir well. Twist orange peel above drink and drop into glass.

BERMUDA BLANC

4 oz. chilled dry white wine
½ oz. light rum
1 tsp. Rose's Lime Juice
1 slice lime

Pour wine, rum, and Rose's Lime Juice into large wineglass. Add two ice cubes. Stir well. Add lime slice.

BISHOP

Juice of ¼ lemon	1 tsp. powdered sugar
Juice of ¼ orange	Red wine to fill (Burgundy)

Shake lemon juice, orange juice, and powdered sugar with ice. Strain into tall highball glass. Add two ice cubes and top off with Burgundy. Stir well. Garnish with lemon and orange twist.

BRIGHT BERRY

4 oz. chilled dry red wine	1 tsp. Cognac
½ oz. strawberry liqueur	1 fresh strawberry

Pour wine, strawberry liqueur, and Cognac into large wineglass. Add two ice cubes. Stir well. Add strawberry.

CHABLIS COOLER

½ oz. grenadine	1 oz. vodka
½ oz. lemon juice	Iced Chablis
¼ tsp. vanilla extract	

Sugar-frost a tall 14-oz. glass. Pour grenadine, lemon juice, vanilla extract, and vodka into glass. Stir well. Add three large ice cubes. Fill glass to rim with Chablis. Stir.

CLARET COBBLER

4 oz. dry red wine	½ oz. maraschino liqueur
½ oz. lemon juice	½ slice orange
½ oz. orange juice	½ slice lime

Fill a 12-oz. glass with finely cracked ice. Add wine, lemon juice, orange juice, and maraschino liqueur. Stir well. Add more ice to fill glass to rim. Stir. Garnish with orange and lime slices.

CLARET COCKTAIL

1 oz. dry red wine	¼ oz. lemon juice
1 oz. brandy	½ tsp. anisette
¼ oz. curaçao	Orange peel

Shake wine, brandy, curaçao, lemon juice, and anisette well with ice. Strain into prechilled cocktail glass. Twist orange peel above drink and drop into glass.

CLARET COOLER

4 oz. chilled dry red wine	3 oz. iced club soda
½ oz. brandy	Orange rind, 3 inches long,
1 oz. orange juice	½ inch wide
½ oz. lemon juice	1 slice lemon

Pour wine, brandy, orange juice, lemon juice, and soda into tall 14-oz. glass. Add ice cubes or cracked ice to fill glass. Stir. Place orange rind in drink. Float lemon slice on top.

CLARET RUM COOLER

3 oz. chilled dry red wine
1 oz. light rum
½ oz. kirschwasser
½ oz. Falernum

3 oz. iced club soda
1 slice orange
1 large fresh strawberry

Pour wine, rum, kirschwasser, Falernum, and soda into tall 14-oz. glass. Add ice cubes or cracked ice to fill glass. Stir. Garnish with orange slice and strawberry.

COOL JAZZ

1 oz. dry white wine
¾ oz. banana liqueur

½ oz. lime juice
1 slice banana

Shake wine, banana liqueur, and lime juice well with ice. Strain into cocktail glass. Float banana slice on drink.

CRANBERRY EYE

4 oz. chilled dry red wine
½ oz. cranberry liqueur

½ oz. California brandy
1 slice orange

Pour wine, cranberry liqueur, and brandy into large wineglass. Add two ice cubes. Stir well. Add orange slice.

FRENCH CURVE

4 oz. chilled dry white wine
1 tsp. Pernod
1 tsp. maraschino liqueur

1 slice lemon
½ slice orange

Pour wine, Pernod, and maraschino liqueur into large wineglass. Add two ice cubes. Stir well. Add lemon and orange slices.

HOT SPRINGS COCKTAIL

1½ oz. white wine
1 tablespoon pineapple juice

½ tsp. cherry liqueur
1 dash orange bitters

Shake all ingredients with ice. Strain into cocktail glass.

ITALIAN PERFUME

4 oz. chilled dry white wine
½ oz. Italian brandy

1 tsp. amaretto
1 slice lemon

Pour wine, brandy, and amaretto into large wineglass. Add two ice cubes. Stir well. Add lemon slice.

KIR

3½ oz. ice cold dry white wine
½ oz. ice cold créme de cassis

Pour into prechilled 7- or 8-oz. wide-bellied wineglass. Add an ice cube or two if desired. Proportions may be varied, but the 7-to-1 vin blanc–cassis ratio here (actually a variation of the vermouth cassis) is the most commonly accepted version.

MONK'S WINE

4 oz. chilled dry white wine
1 tsp. green Chartreuse

1 slice lemon

Pour wine and Chartreuse into large wineglass. Add two ice cubes. Stir well. Add lemon slice.

PANAMA COOLER

2 oz. iced Rhine wine
2 oz. iced very dry sherry
1 oz. orange juice
1 tsp. lime juice

½ oz. maraschino liqueur
1 dash Angostura bitters
1 oz. iced club soda
1 slice lemon

Shake Rhine wine, sherry, orange juice, lime juice, maraschino liqueur, and bitters well with ice. Strain into tall 14-oz. glass. Add soda. Fill glass with ice. Stir. Add lemon slice.

PIKE'S PICON

4 oz. chilled dry red wine
½ oz. Amer Picon

1 tsp. grenadine
1 piece orange peel

Pour wine, Amer Picon, and grenadine into large wineglass. Add two ice cubes. Stir well. Twist orange peel above drink and drop into glass.

PINEAPPLE COOLER

2 oz. white wine
2 oz. pineapple juice
½ tsp. powdered sugar

2 oz. seltzer water to fill
1 orange spiral
1 lemon peel

Put white wine, pineapple juice, powdered sugar, and 2 oz. seltzer water in tall collins glass. Stir. Add ice cubes, fill with seltzer water, and stir again. Garnish with lemon twist and orange spiral (end should dangle over edge of glass).

PINK LEMONADE Á LA PLAYBOY

5 oz. chilled rosé wine
2 oz. chilled lemon juice
2 oz. chilled orange juice
½ oz. kirschwasser

2 tsp. sugar
1 slice lemon
1 maraschino cherry

Into tall 14-oz. glass, pour wine, lemon juice, orange juice, kirschwasser, and sugar. Stir well until sugar dissolves. Add two large ice cubes and enough ice cold water (not club soda) to fill glass. Stir. Garnish with lemon slice and cherry.

QUEEN CHARLOTTE

2 oz. red wine
1 oz. grenadine

Lemon-lime soda to fill

Pour red wine and grenadine into tall collins glass over ice cubes. Top off with lemon-lime soda. Stir.

RASPBERRY CLARET CUP

4 oz. dry red wine	1 oz. lemon juice
1 oz. brandy	³⁄₄ oz. raspberry syrup
1 oz. Himbeergeist	Iced club soda
(dry white raspberry brandy)	2 or 3 fresh or frozen whole raspberries

Make sure wine and brandies are ice cold before mixing drink. Put three ice cubes into tall 14-oz. collins glass. Pour wine, brandy, Himbeergeist, raspberry syrup, and lemon juice into glass. Stir until all ingredients are very well blended. Fill glass with soda. Stir slightly. Float raspberries on top.

RED CARPET

1 oz. dry red wine	¹⁄₂ oz. strawberry liqueur
1 oz. Chambery Fraise (strawberry-	Iced club soda
flavored French vermouth)	1 slice lemon

Stir red wine, Chambery Fraise, and strawberry liqueur well with ice. Strain into 6- or 8-oz. wineglass. Add small splash of soda. Stir. Add lemon slice.

RED KIR

4 oz. chilled dry red wine	1 slice lemon
¹⁄₂ oz. crème de cassis	

Pour wine and crème de cassis into large wineglass. Add two ice cubes. Stir well. Add lemon slice.

RED LIGHT

4 oz. chilled dry red wine	¹⁄₂ oz. Cointreau or triple sec
¹⁄₂ oz. Cordial Médoc	1 slice lemon

Pour wine, Cordial Médoc, and Cointreau into large wineglass. Add two ice cubes. Stir well. Add lemon slice.

RED MANHATTAN

1 dash Angostura bitters	4 oz. chilled dry red wine
1 tsp. sugar	¹⁄₂ oz. sweet vermouth
Iced club soda	1 piece orange peel

Pour bitters and sugar into large wineglass. Add a small splash of soda. Stir until sugar dissolves. Add wine and vermouth. Add two ice cubes. Stir well. Twist orange peel above drink and drop into glass.

RHENISH RASPBERRY

¹⁄₄ cup frozen raspberries in syrup,	2 tsp. grenadine
thawed	¹⁄₂ oz. lemon juice
2 oz. Riesling	¹⁄₂ cup crushed ice
1 oz. vodka	Iced club soda

Put raspberries with their syrup, Riesling, vodka, grenadine, lemon juice, and ice into blender. Blend at high speed 10 seconds. Pour into tall 14-oz. glass. Add a splash of soda. Add ice if necessary to fill glass to brim. Stir lightly.

RUBY

2 oz. red wine
½ oz. maraschino liqueur
½ oz. lemon juice

1 dash Angostura bitters
1 slice lemon

Stir wine, maraschino liqueur, lemon juice, and bitters well with ice. Strain into 6- or 8-oz. wineglass. Add lemon slice.

SOFT TOUCH

1½ oz. dry white wine
½ beaten egg white
½ oz. heavy sweet cream

½ oz. lemon juice
1½ tsp. sugar

Shake all ingredients extremely well with ice. Strain into prechilled cocktail glass.

STRAWBERRY BLONDE

3 fresh strawberries
1 oz. strawberry liqueur
6 oz. well-chilled Rhine wine

½ oz. kirschwasser
Iced club soda
1 slice lime

Marinate strawberries in strawberry liqueur for 1 hour. Fasten strawberries onto cocktail spear. Pour Rhine wine, strawberry liqueur, and kirschwasser into tall 14-oz. glass. Add a splash of soda and ice to fill glass. Stir. Add lime slice. Place speared strawberries over rim of glass.

STRAWBERRY VIN BLANC

4 oz. chilled dry white wine,
   Graves if possible
1 oz. strawberry liqueur

Iced club soda
1 slice lemon
1 fresh large strawberry

Pour wine and strawberry liqueur over two ice cubes in tall 12-oz. glass. Stir. Add soda to fill glass. Garnish with lemon slice and strawberry.

SUMMER LIGHT

2 oz. dry vermouth
3 oz. dry white wine

Iced bitter lemon

Pour vermouth and wine into tall 14-oz. glass half-filled with ice cubes. Fill glass with bitter lemon. Stir.

TOKAY FLIP

2½ oz. imported Tokay wine (Tokaji Aszu)
1 tsp. sugar

1 small egg
Nutmeg

Shake Tokay, sugar, and egg well with ice. Strain into prechilled Delmonico glass. Sprinkle with nutmeg. *It may cause another Hungarian revolution to suggest that the magnificent imported Tokay be turned into a flip. Actually, the wine turns into sweet bliss.*

VESUVIO

3 oz. dry white wine
1 tsp. apricot liqueur
1 tsp. amaretto
1 slice cucumber

Stir white wine, apricot liqueur, and amaretto well with ice. Strain into 6- or 8-oz. wineglass. Add cucumber slice.

WHITE-WINE COOLER

6 oz. chilled dry white wine
½ oz. brandy
2 dashes orange bitters
1 tsp. Kümmel (caraway-flavored liqueur)
2 tsp. sugar
½ oz. lemon juice
Iced club soda
Cucumber peel,
    2 inches long, ½ inch wide

Put wine, brandy, bitters, Kümmel, sugar, and lemon juice into tall 14-oz. glass. Stir until sugar dissolves. Add a splash of soda and enough ice to fill glass. Stir. Add cucumber peel.

WINE AND BITTERS

1 tsp. sugar
2 dashes Angostura bitters
Iced club soda
4 oz. chilled dry white wine
1 slice lemon
½ slice orange

Pour sugar, bitters, and a small splash of soda into large wineglass. Stir until sugar dissolves. Add wine and two ice cubes. Stir well. Add lemon and orange slices.

PORT AND MADEIRA COCKTAILS

BRANDIED MADEIRA

1 oz. Madeira
1 oz. brandy
½ oz. dry vermouth
Lemon peel

Stir Madeira, brandy, and vermouth well with ice. Pour over rocks in prechilled old-fashioned glass. Twist lemon peel above drink and drop into glass.

BRANDIED PORT

1 oz. tawny port
1 oz. brandy
½ oz. lemon juice
1 tsp. maraschino liqueur
1 slice orange

Shake port, brandy, lemon juice, and maraschino liqueur well with ice. Strain over rocks into prechilled old-fashioned glass. Add orange slice.

DIABOLO

1½ oz. imported dry white port
1 oz. dry vermouth
½ tsp. lemon juice
Lemon peel

Shake port, vermouth, and lemon juice well with ice. Strain into prechilled cocktail glass. Twist lemon peel above drink and drop into glass.

MADEIRA MINT FLIP

1½ oz. Madeira
1 oz. chocolate-mint liqueur
1 small egg

1 tsp. sugar
Grated nutmeg

Shake Madeira, chocolate-mint liqueur, egg, and sugar well with ice. Strain into prechilled Delmonico glass. Sprinkle with freshly grated nutmeg.

PINKY

2 oz. ruby port
1 oz. strawberry liqueur

½ oz. heavy cream
1 large fresh strawberry

Shake port, strawberry liqueur, and cream well with ice. Strain over rocks into 8-oz. glass. Fasten strawberry on cocktail spear and place over rim of glass.

PORTAMENTO

2 oz. tawny port
1 oz. bourbon
2 dashes Peychaud's or Angostura bitters

½ egg white
1 tsp. lemon juice
1 slice lemon

Shake port, bourbon, bitters, egg white, and lemon juice extremely well with ice. Strain over rocks into 8-oz. old-fashioned glass. Add lemon slice.

PORT AND COGNAC MILK PUNCH

2 oz. white port such as Porto Branco
1½ oz. Cognac
4 oz. (½ measuring cup) milk

1 small egg
Freshly grated nutmeg

Shake port, Cognac, milk, and egg extremely well with ice. Strain into 12-oz. glass. Sprinkle with nutmeg.

PORT ARMS

3 oz. California port
1 oz. California brandy
1 oz. orange juice
½ oz. lemon juice

1 tsp. triple sec
Iced club soda
½ slice orange
1 slice lemon

Shake port, brandy, orange juice, lemon juice, and triple sec well with ice. Strain into tall 14-oz. glass half-filled with ice cubes. Add soda. Stir. Add orange and lemon slices.

PORT CASSIS

2½ oz. chilled white port
   such as Porto Branco
½ oz. crème de cassis

½ oz. lemon juice
Iced club soda
1 slice lemon

Pour port, crème de cassis, and lemon juice over rocks in 8-oz. glass. Stir well. Add splash of soda. Add lemon slice.

PORT COBBLER

4 oz. tawny port
¾ oz. brandy
½ tsp. sugar

Lemon peel
Orange peel
2 large mint leaves

Fill a 12-oz. glass with finely cracked ice. Add port, brandy, and sugar. Stir well. Add more ice to fill glass to rim. Stir. Twist lemon peel and orange peel above drink and drop into glass. Tear mint leaves partially and drop into glass.

PORT COLLINS

2 oz. white port
  such as Porto Branco
1 oz. gin
1 oz. lemon juice

1 tsp. sugar
Iced club soda
1 slice lemon

Shake port, gin, lemon juice, and sugar well with ice. Strain into tall 14-oz. glass half-filled with ice cubes. Add soda. Stir. Add lemon slice.

PORTCULLIS

2 oz. ruby port
1 oz. cherry-flavored brandy
4 oz. cranberry juice cocktail

1 oz. lemon juice
1 slice lemon

Pour port, cherry-flavored brandy, cranberry-juice cocktail, and lemon juice into tall 14-oz. glass half-filled with ice cubes. Stir well. Add ice cubes to fill glass. Stir well. Add lemon slice.

STRAWBERRY WHITE PORT

4 oz. imported white port
Iced tonic water
½ oz. strawberry liqueur

1 slice lemon
1 large fresh strawberry (preferably
  with long stem)

Be sure port is a dry imported wine, such as Sandemans extra-dry Porto Branco. Fill tall 14-oz. glass with ice cubes. Add port. Fill glass to within 1/2 inch of rim with tonic water. Float strawberry liqueur on top by pouring it over the back of a spoon held against the inside of the glass. Place lemon slice so that it rests on top of ice cubes. Place strawberry on lemon slice.

VILLA NOVA

1½ oz. ruby port
1 oz. California or Spanish brandy
Angostura bitters

Iced club soda
Lemon peel

Pour port, brandy, and several dashes bitters over rocks in old-fashioned glass. Stir well. Add splash of soda. Stir. Twist lemon peel above drink and drop into glass.

CHAMPAGNE COCKTAILS

AMERICANA

1 tsp. 100-proof bourbon
1/2 tsp. sugar
1 dash bitters

4 oz. iced brut champagne
1 slice fresh or brandied peach

Stir bourbon, sugar, and bitters in prechilled champagne glass. Add champagne and peach slice.

ARCTIC KISS

2 oz. vodka (Finlandia)
3 oz. champagne

Chill vodka in ice if it's not already in your freezer. Pour into prechilled champagne flute. Fill with champagne.

ARISE MY LOVE

1 tsp. green crème de menthe
6 oz. champagne

Pour crème de menthe into chilled champagne flute. Fill with champagne.

BELLINI

1 oz. peach schnapps
6 oz. champagne

Pour peach schnapps into champagne flute. Fill with champagne.

BLACK VELVET

1 oz. Guinness
3 oz. champagne or sparkling wine

Lemon peel

Pour Guinness carefully into a chilled champagne flute. Add champagne slowly. Garnish with a lemon twist.

CARIBBEAN CHAMPAGNE

1/2 tsp. light rum
1/2 tsp. banana liqueur
1 dash orange bitters

4 oz. iced brut champagne
1 slice banana

Pour rum, banana liqueur, and bitters into prechilled champagne glass. Add champagne. Stir very gently. Add banana slice.

CHAMPAGNE BUCK

1 oz. champagne
** (can even be a day old)**
1/2 oz. gin

Splash cherry brandy
1/2 oz. orange juice, freshly squeezed

Shake ingredients with cracked ice. Strain into chilled cocktail glass. Garnish with an orange twist.

CHAMPAGNE COBBLER

¼ oz. lemon juice
¼ oz. curaçao

Champagne to fill
1 slice orange or pineapple

Pour fresh lemon juice and curaçao into tumbler two-thirds filled with cracked ice. Top with champagne and stir gently. Garnish with slice of orange or pineapple. Serve with straws and a spoon.

CHAMPAGNE FRAISE

½ tsp. strawberry liqueur
½ tsp. kirschwasser

4 oz. iced brut champagne
1 large fresh strawberry

Pour strawberry liqueur and kirschwasser into prechilled champagne glass. Tilt glass so that liqueurs coat bottom and sides of glass. Add champagne. Float strawberry on drink. (Measure ½ tsp. precisely—don't overpour.)

CHAMPAGNE MANHATTAN

1 oz. Canadian whisky
½ oz. sweet vermouth
1 dash bitters

3 oz. iced brut champagne
1 brandied cherry

Stir whisky, vermouth, and bitters well with ice. Strain into prechilled champagne glass. Add champagne and brandied cherry.

CHAMPAGNE NORMANDE

1 tsp. calvados
½ tsp. sugar

1 dash Angostura bitters
4 oz. iced brut champagne

Stir calvados, sugar, and bitters in prechilled champagne glass. Add champagne. Stir very gently.

CHAMPAGNE NOYAUX

½ oz. crème de noyaux
1 tsp. lime juice
1 large toasted almond

4 oz. iced brut champagne
1 slice lime

Stir crème de noyaux and lime juice in prechilled champagne glass. Add almond. Pour champagne into glass. Stir slightly. Float lime slice on top.

CHAMPAGNE OLD-FASHIONED

½ oz. Grand Marnier
½ oz. Forbidden Fruit
1 dash orange bitters

4 oz. iced brut champagne
1 slice lemon

Into prechilled old-fashioned glass, pour liqueurs and bitters. Add champagne. Stir very gently. Launch with lemon slice.

CHAMPAGNE POLONAISE

1 tsp. blackberry liqueur
1½ tsp. Cognac

4 oz. iced brut champagne

Pour blackberry liqueur and Cognac into prechilled, sugar-frosted champagne glass. Add champagne. Stir very gently.

CHARTREUSE CHAMPAGNE

½ tsp. green Chartreuse   4 oz. iced brut champagne
½ tsp. Cognac   Lemon peel

Pour Chartreuse, Cognac, and champagne into prechilled champagne glass. Stir very gently. Twist lemon peel above drink and drop into glass. *Toast the Carthusian order.*

CHERRY CHAMPAGNE

½ oz. iced Peter Heering   ½ pitted fresh cherry
4 oz. iced brut champagne

Pour Peter Heering into stem of prechilled hollow-stemmed champagne glass. Add champagne. Float cherry on drink.

CLASSIC CHAMPAGNE COCKTAIL

½ tsp. sugar   4 oz. iced brut champagne
1 dash Angostura bitters   Lemon peel

Stir sugar and bitters in prechilled champagne glass. Add champagne. Usually, the sparkle of the champagne will blend the ingredients, and little if any stirring is necessary. Twist lemon peel above drink and drop into glass.

CUCUMBER CHAMPAGNE

Cucumber peel   ½ oz. lemon juice
1 oz. Benedictine   8 oz. iced brut champagne

Prechill a 10-oz. Pilsner glass. Wash cucumber, rubbing with a vegetable brush or towel if necessary to remove any waxy coating. Cut a long strip of peel, about ½-inch wide, the entire length of the cucumber. Place in glass. Pour Benedictine and lemon juice into glass. Slowly add champagne. Stir very gently. Let drink set a few minutes for flavors to ripen.

FRENCH FOAM

1 tsp. sugar   1 tsp. kirschwasser
1 dash Angostura bitters   1 split ice cold brut champagne
1 tsp. brandy   Lemon sherbet

Put sugar, bitters, brandy, and kirschwasser into 10-oz. Pilsner glass. Stir with a tall stirring rod until sugar dissolves. Fill glass three-quarters full with champagne. Float a small scoop of sherbet on top. The scoop should contain no more than 2 liquid ounces (a parfait scoop). If such a scoop is not available, use a tablespoon to add the small amount of sherbet.

FRENCH 75

1½ oz. Cognac   2 tsp. sugar
1 oz. lemon juice   Iced brut champagne

Shake Cognac, lemon juice, and sugar well with cracked ice. Strain into 10-oz. glass with two large ice cubes. Fill to rim with champagne. Stir very slightly. *Gin is sometimes substituted for Cognac, making a Champagne Collins out of this tall classic.*

FRENCH 75 COCKTAIL

¼ oz. gin
¼ oz. Cointreau

¼ oz. lemon juice
5 oz. champagne

Shake gin, Cointreau, and lemon juice with cracked ice. Strain into chilled champagne flute. Top with champagne.

GOODNIGHT KISS

1 cube sugar
1 dash Angostura bitters

4 oz. champagne
1 splash Campari

Put sugar cube with one drop of bitters in flute. Add champagne and splash of Campari.

GRAND MIMOSA

½ oz. Grand Marnier
4 oz. champagne

Splash orange juice

Pour Grand Marnier into flute. Fill almost to the top with champagne and top off with fresh orange juice.

KIR ROYALE

½ oz. framboise liqueur

5 oz. champagne

Pour champagne into prechilled champagne flute and add framboise liqueur. Garnish with a twist.

MELBA CHAMPAGNE

½ oz. Himbeergeist
   (raspberry brandy, not liqueur)
4 oz. iced brut champagne

1 fresh or thawed frozen raspberry
Raspberry sherbet, hard-frozen

Pour Himbeergeist into prechilled champagne glass. Add champagne and the raspberry. With a fruit-bailer, scoop out a single small ball of sherbet. Float on champagne.

MIMOSA

½ oz. orange juice

4½ oz. champagne

Pour orange juice over ice in chilled wineglass. Top with champagne and stir gently. Serve immediately.

ORANGE CHAMPAGNE

Peel of ½ orange, in one spiral
2 tsp. curaçao

4 oz. iced brut champagne

Place orange peel in prechilled champagne glass. Add curaçao and champagne. Stir very gently.

PASSION MIMOSA

2 oz. chilled passion fruit juice   **1 strawberry**
Champagne to fill

Pour passion fruit juice into flute. Fill with chilled champagne. Garnish with straw-berry.

PIMM'S ROYALE

1½ oz. Pimm's No. 1   **1 lemon peel**
Champagne to fill   **1 cucumber peel**

Pour Pimm's over ice in large highball glass. Fill with champagne. Garnish with lemon and cucumber peels.

RITZ FIZZ

4 oz. champagne   **1 dash lemon juice**
1 dash blue curaçao   **1 lemon peel**
1 dash amaretto

Pour champagne into chilled flute. Add blue curaçao, amaretto, and lemon juice. Stir. Garnish with lemon twist.

SPARKLING GALLIANO

½ oz. Galliano   **Cucumber peel, 1½ inches long,**
½ tsp. lemon juice   **½ inch wide**
Champagne to fill

Pour Galliano and lemon juice into prechilled champagne glass. Stir. Add champagne and cucumber peel. *Drink to the stars.*

TYPHOON

1 oz. gin   **1 oz. lime juice**
½ oz. anisette   **4 oz. champagne**

Shake all ingredients (except champagne) with ice. Strain into tall, chilled collins glass over ice. Top with champagne and stir gently.*

Please note: there are more recipes that include wine in chapter 16, The Brimming Bowl.

BEER DRINKS

Many an American (and perhaps overly earnest) beer lover, when presented with a bottled beer and asked if they'd like a glass, will reply with a smirk: "No, thanks. It already comes in a glass." Sarcasm aside, they're often right. When the mood hits, there's nothing more refreshing than the simplest of cold brews adorned with nothing more than the bottle it came in. There is another class of beer drinker, however, who might get more bent than a salty pretzel should his favorite brew be offered so crudely. Not only must his beer be poured; it must also flow into the proper prechilled vessel. And so it goes with beer cocktails. Some wouldn't dream of adding anything to the classic formula of barley, hops, malt, and water, but for the more adventurous among you, we offer the following foamy potables.

BEER BUSTER
1½ oz. ice cold 100-proof vodka   **2 dashes Tabasco sauce**
Ice cold beer or ale
Pour vodka, beer, and Tabasco sauce into prechilled tall 14-oz. glass or beer mug. Stir gently. *A drink for those who like to key up with beer rather than with cocktails before dinner; for football fans hoarse from cheering; for those who like a long, cold drink with their bubbling-hot Welsh rabbit; and for cheese connoisseurs with a thirst.*

BLACK & TAN
8 oz. lager beer (Harp)
8 oz. stout beer (Guinness)
Pour lager beer to half-fill pint glass. Using specialized bar spoon or regular table-spoon, slowly pour stout over inverted spoon to fill. This may take some practice, but you should end up with a full pint glass with lager at the bottom and the stout neat-ly separated and floating on top. *A beer Pousse-Café, if you will.*

BOILERMAKER
14 oz. lager beer
1 oz. blended whiskey
Pour beer into pint glass, careful to leave room at the top. Drop in shot glass of whiskey. For a Russian Boilermaker, you got it: substitute ice cold vodka for whiskey. *(Not recommended for those with sensitive front teeth.)*

CHUMBAWUMBA
7 oz. hard cider (Strongbow)   **1 oz. vodka (Smirnoff)**
7 oz. lager beer (Stella Artois)   **1 oz. Scotch (Bells)**
Pour cider and beer into pint glass. Add vodka and Scotch. Stir. *Named after the band in honor of hit drinking song.*

DR. PEPPER
7 oz. lager beer   **1 oz. amaretto**
7 oz. Coca-Cola
Pour beer into prechilled pint glass. Add Coca-Cola. Drop in shot of amaretto.

LAGER & LIME

14½ oz. lager beer
1½ oz. Rose's Lime Juice

Pour beer to nearly fill pint glass. Top off with shot of Rose's Lime Juice. *What Galileo said of wine is perfectly suited to this Toronto favorite: "sunlight trapped in water."*

MONACO

½ oz. grenadine   **3½ oz. 7-Up**
7 oz. lager beer

Pour grenadine, beer, and 7-Up into Pilsner glass over an ice cube or two. Stir gently. *Sweeter than a Shandy, it's a French summer favorite.*

RED EYE

12 oz. lager beer   **Tomato juice to fill**
1 oz. vodka

Pour beer and vodka into pint glass over ice. Top off with tomato juice.

SHANDY

13 oz. lager beer   **1 lemon wedge (optional)**
3 oz. lemonade

Pour beer nearly to fill prechilled pint glass. Add 2 shots of lemonade, or to taste. Garnish with lemon wedge for a summery touch. *Try this classic, light, and refreshing English whistle-wetter with ginger ale or 7-Up, too.*

SNAKEBITE

8 oz. lager beer
8 oz. hard cider

Pour beer and cider into pint glass in equal proportion. *Another English favorite; too many of these and you really will be wondering what bit you.*

SAKE COCKTAILS

Notoriously difficult to classify, this *vin du pays* of Japan is often described as "rice wine" or as a spirit distilled from rice, but it is in fact neither wine nor spirit. And although nearly colorless and quite still, the brewing process by which sake is made comes closest to that of beer. No longer served only with sushi, sake makes for a refreshing change of pace at a summer barbecue. It can also be served up as a truly unique cocktail using one of the recipes offered here.

BLOODY SAKE

3 oz. tomato juice
2 oz. sake
2 tsp. lemon juice

1 dash Tabasco sauce
1 dash Worcestershire sauce
Salt, celery salt, pepper

Pour tomato juice, sake, lemon juice, Tabasco sauce, and Worcestershire sauce into cocktail shaker with ice. Add a sprinkling of salt, celery salt, and pepper. Shake very well. Strain into 8-oz. glass. Add a sprinkling of freshly ground pepper, if desired.

EAST-WEST

2 oz. sake
2 dashes Angostura bitters

Iced cranberry juice cocktail
1 slice lemon

Place three large ice cubes in 8-oz. glass. Add sake and bitters. Fill glass with cranberry juice cocktail. Stir well. Add lemon slice.

HOKKAIDO COCKTAIL

1½ oz. gin
1 oz. sake

½ oz. triple sec

Shake gin, sake, and triple sec with ice. Strain into prechilled cocktail glass.

MOLOKAI

1 oz. sake
1 oz. cranberry liqueur

2 oz. orange juice
1 slice orange

Pour sake, cranberry liqueur, and orange juice into 8-oz. glass. Add ice cubes to fill glass. Stir very well. Add orange slice.

SAKE CASSIS

1 oz. sake
1 oz. vodka
½ oz. crème de cassis

Iced club soda
1 slice lemon

Pour sake, vodka, and crème de cassis over rocks in 10-oz. glass. Stir well. Add a splash of soda. Stir. Add lemon slice.

SAKE SOUR

2 oz. sake
½ oz. lemon juice
1½ oz. orange juice

1 tsp. sugar
½ slice orange

Shake sake, lemon juice, orange juice, and sugar well with ice. Strain into sour glass. Garnish with orange slice.

SAKE STINGER

1 oz. sake
½ oz. white crème de menthe
** or peppermint schnapps**

½ oz. California brandy
Lemon peel

Shake sake, crème de menthe, and brandy well with ice. Strain into cocktail glass. Twist lemon peel above drink and drop into glass.

SAKE SUNRISE

1 oz. sake
1 oz. California brandy

Chilled grapefruit juice
1 tsp. grenadine

Place four ice cubes in squat or tall 10-oz. glass. Add sake, brandy, and enough grapefruit juice to nearly fill glass. Stir well. Pour grenadine on top. Guests stir drink to blend grenadine with other ingredients.

SAKETINI

2 oz. gin
½ oz. sake

Stir well with ice. Strain into prechilled cocktail glass; if desired, an olive or twist of lemon peel may be added. *The Saketini is a reminder that dry vermouth and sake bear an uncanny resemblance to each other.*

SHINTO

2 dashes Angostura bitters
½ tsp. sugar
Iced club soda

1 oz. sake
1 oz. Suntory whisky
1 slice lemon

Pour bitters, sugar, and splash of soda into old-fashioned glass. Stir until sugar dissolves. Add sake, Suntory whisky, and three large ice cubes. Stir well. Add splash of soda. Stir. Garnish with lemon slice.

SURF RIDER

2 oz. sake
1 oz. light rum

3 oz. pineapple juice
Iced bitter lemon soda

Shake sake, rum, and pineapple juice well with ice. Strain into tall 14-oz. glass half-filled with ice cubes. Fill glass with lemon soda.

TOKYO ROSE

1 oz. sake
1 oz. vodka (Grey Goose)

1 oz. Midori melon liqueur
1 cherry

Shake sake, vodka, and Midori with ice. Strain into prechilled cocktail glass. Garnish with cherry.

CHAPTER 8

✳ **Aperitifs** ✳
✳ PREPRANDIAL POTATIONS ✳

Too often in the conviviality of the cocktail hour, drinks are gulped as indifferently as one clinks ice in a highball. But aperitifs, straight or mixed, are never taken for granted. Observe, for example, the Parisian sitting at a favorite café table of an afternoon and partaking of Byrrh, Amer Picon, or Vermouth Cassis with attentive enjoyment, and for whom each day's aperitif is an excitingly different experience. He observes its color, savors its scent, and samples it with a relish one usually associates with newfound pleasures. His senses then undergo the most salutary of metamorphoses: taste buds tingle in anticipation of the evening repast; the local scenery becomes more vivid; and the world becomes a sweeter place.

Even the etymology of "aperitif" evokes its appetite-awakening effects. Though the word is French, it's best understood by going back to its Latin source, *aperio*, meaning "to open, to lay bare." Swallow a jigger of Campari with soda on ice: its unabashed bitterness may cause you to shake your head dubiously over what has been proclaimed a prime libational pleasure, but soon waves of hunger sweep over you, and you can hardly wait for the antipasto tray. The thoughts of the anticipated anchovy fillets, cracked black olives, prosciutto, roasted-pepper salad, and wafer-thin slices of Genoa salami are almost overpowering.

The aperitif's ancient origins are a reminder that the world's first great wines were sharp potations. In 400 B.C., Hippocrates stopped prescribing medicines long enough to conjure up a lusty elixir of wine, resin, and bitter almonds. Pliny, an anti-aperitif man, called the consumption of such concoctions before meals "an outlandish fashion recommended by doctors who are always trying to advertise themselves by some newfangled ideas." Undaunted, adventurous Romans began to create preprandial potations not only from grapes but also from turnips, radishes, asparagus, parsley, thyme, mint, hyssop, and almost anything else that sprang up around the villa. Even seawater was added for tang. Often, grapevines were surrounded by other plants placed close enough to the roots to allow their insinuating essences to seep through the soil and into the fruit before it was plucked. If, now and then, a decidedly toxic plant like wormwood worked its way into a wine, pleasure-seeking Romans didn't hesitate to drink it anyway—as long as it didn't offend their aesthetic sensibilities.

Modern aperitifs, happily, are admixtures of wine, spirits, and as many as forty different kinds of harmless but exotic spices, roots, barks, herbs, buds, and flowers from every corner of the earth. The family is a surprisingly large one with several distinct branches: the wine-based aperitifs (such as Byrrh, Dubonnet, and Punt e Mes); the vermouths (sweet and dry); the distilled aperitifs (Amer Picon, Pernod, pastis, and the like); and such stomach-settling bitters as Dutch Boonekamp.

In American frontier days, pioneers mixed a pint of water with two tablespoons of buffalo gall for a "wholesome and exhilarating drink." Some years later, Kansans refined the formula, combining a mere ounce of wahoo (bark of the winged elm tree, also used for making string and rope) with a quart of whiskey. Somewhat more sophisticated American traditions are observed, along with the European, in the following roster of contemporary wines and liquors used as aperitifs.

AMER PICON A bittersweet French aperitif liqueur of quinine, orange, and gentian, sometimes mixed with ice, soda, and grenadine, and served as an aperitif punch in an 8-ounce glass.

BOONEKAMP BITTERS Dutch-style bitters taken neat before a meal as a stomachic.

BYRRH (PRONOUNCED BEER) A French proprietary aperitif wine with a tangy aftertaste.

CAMPARI An Italian aperitivo, 48 proof, taken with soda and often with a twist of orange peel. Mixed half-and-half with Italian sweet vermouth, you get an Americano; with Italian sweet vermouth and gin, a Negroni.

CHAMBERY FRAISE One of the lightest and most delicately flavored of all French dry vermouths, with a hint of wild strawberries.

CHAMBRAISE Strawberry-flavored French vermouth.

CINZANO This aromatic Italian vermouth is available in both white (Bianco) and red (Rosso) varieties.

CRÈME DE CASSIS Made from black currants, it's actually a liqueur because of its sweetness. In its best-known drink, it's combined with vermouth, ice, and soda as a Vermouth Cassis, or with white wine as a Vin Blanc Cassis.

CYNAR An Italian aperitif liqueur made from artichokes.

DUBONNET A quinine-flavored aperitif wine originally imported from France, now made in the United States, in both red and white types. One or two parts Dubonnet to one part gin and you have a Dubonnet Cocktail.

FERNET BRANCA Of Italian origin, now made in the United States, it combines compatibly with gin or Cognac and vermouth as a predinner cocktail.

FORBIDDEN FRUIT An American liqueur made from the shaddock, a type of grapefruit.

FRENCH KISS A French blend of dry and sweet vermouths.

HERBSAINT Used in cooking as well as cocktails, this locally made anise liquor is often served as a substitute for absinthe in New Orleans, which was banned there in 1912.

KIR GALLIQUE A blend of crème de cassis and white wine—a combination, when mixed to order, also known as a Kir or Vin Blanc Cassis.

LILLET This French red or white aperitif wine has a subtle orange flavor with a subdued bitterness.

MUSCARI A sweet and tart aperitif wine imported from Portugal, with flavors of orange and almond.

OUZO A Middle Eastern high-proof anise liqueur taken before or after dinner.

PASTIS An anise-flavored aperitif liqueur that, like ouzo, turns milky white when mixed with water or poured over ice. It's a favorite of Marseilles fishermen and Riviera jet-setters.

PERNOD A 90-proof, French, anise-flavored aperitif liqueur reminiscent of absinthe. (Absinthe is now banned in the United States and elsewhere, though still available in many parts of Europe. The Pernod name once represented the best and most famous brand of absinthe.) When used in place of vodka in a Screwdriver, the drink becomes a Tiger's Tail.

PINOT DES CHARENTE A French blend of wine from the Cognac region, plus a small amount of Cognac brandy; it may be either white or rosé.

PORT WINE, WHITE In its white version, this consummate Portuguese product, with its full-bodied flavor and bouquet, is immensely popular in France and Belgium as a sundown aperitif; one of its best representatives is Sandeman's Porto Branco.

POSITANO A semidry aperitif vermouth with a pleasant, decisive aftertaste.

PUNT E MES A deep, dark Italian aperitif wine known for its provocative bitterness.

QUINQUINA A French aperitif wine with the subtly bitter taste of quinine.

RAKI A brandy-based, high-proof, anise-flavored aperitif liqueur from the Middle East.

ST.-RAPHAËL A proprietary French aperitif wine noted for its full body and clean flavor.

SHERRY, FINO Bone-dry Spanish sherry, served as an aperitif with or without ice. Even medium-dry sherries are now appearing as appetite sharpeners.

SHOGUN A blend of sake and white wine.

SUZE A dry, 40-proof, French aperitif flavored with orange and gentian.

The Cocktail Supper Party

THE COCKTAIL SUPPER IS BASED ON the theory that it takes more than peanuts to make a party. As a meal, it stands midway between the tidbittery of a mere drinking session and a full-fledged, sit-down dinner. The appetites that always stir wherever drinks are served may be temporarily appeased with hot and cold hors d'oeuvres, but the most satisfying provender the gods can possibly provide is casseroles of chicken, bowls of herbed rice, and beef stew in red wine—the cordial elements of an easy buffet. In planning a cocktail supper, the host or hostess must make sure that the guests are otherwise uncommitted for the evening. The fact that hunger as well as thirst will be exorcised should be clearly spelled out, and the line for winding up the party should not be drawn at any particular time.

At a cocktail supper, let your food be ample, your menu brief. Instead of caravans of rich canapés with more garnishes than you can shake a cocktail spear at, the appetizers should feature a single cold and a single hot hors d'oeuvre of unrivaled goodness. The main dish that follows may be hot or cold, or a seasonable combination of the two. Cold glazed ham, for example, and hot Swedish brown beans form a compatible partnership along with a mushroom-and-asparagus salad with curried mayonnaise. Or a hot beef or veal goulash may be served with hot buttered noodles or with a cold noodle salad and a julienne of radishes, green peppers, and scallions, and a French dressing with Parmesan cheese. Desserts should be the noncooked type, such as strawberries Romanoff or a fresh-fruit compote with kirschwasser, supplemented with a tray of assorted small specialties from the best pastry shop within walking or driving distance.

As for the drinking at a cocktail supper, anything goes. If you want to accompany food with wine, of course you may, but it's not necessary. American devotees of the cocktail will find a Sazerac or a Bourbon Mist quite gratifying with their food as well as before it. Wine-oriented conservatives from the Continent may writhe, but Americans who blissfully drink their 11-to-1 Martinis with the appetizers will be gloriously happy to continue downing them with the meal.

Hosts should also face the fact that at the cocktail hour these days, the most important things aren't necessarily cocktails. They may be highballs, lowballs, or drinks of any variety, from fino sherry to sweet Marsala. An Italian sparkling wine, Prossecco, is perfectly suited to roasted peppers and bread and cheese. Finally, hosts who confidently offer one main dish at a cocktail supper shouldn't hesitate to offer one main drink, perfectly balanced and served, for which they've won their bar spurs.

VERMOUTH An herb-flavored wine fortified with brandy, containing 16 to 19 percent alcohol. May be red, white, or rosé. At one time, French vermouth was light, dry, and almost white, while Italian vermouth was sweet, heavy, and red. Nowadays, both types are produced in Italy, France, South America, and the United States. For mixing purposes, dry vermouth should be light in color with subtle overtones; sweet vermouth should be round in flavor, sweet, but not cloying. But each should be able to stand on its own as a straight iced drink—trenchant, tantalizing, never tiresome.

It should be obvious even from this basic list that the choice of appetite arousers is as diverse as it is diverting. Sipped straight from the bottle or elaborately combined, any of these lively potations will turn on your taste buds with delightful dispatch. To serve an aperitif before the evening's repast makes the truth of Aeschylus's words readily evident: "What is there more kindly than the feeling between host and guest?" Indeed, what better occasion to build around the noble aperitif than a supper party?

APERITIF COCKTAILS

ADONIS
¾ oz. dry vermouth
2 tsp. sweet vermouth
¾ oz. sherry
1 dash orange bitters
Stir vermouths, sherry, and bitters well with ice. Strain into prechilled cocktail glass.

AMERICANO
1¼ oz. Campari
1¼ oz. sweet vermouth
Lemon peel
Club soda (optional)
Stir Campari and sweet vermouth well with ice. Strain into prechilled cocktail glass. Twist lemon peel above drink and drop into glass. If you prefer, a Delmonico or old-fashioned glass may be used instead—with a rock or two and a splash of soda.

AMER PICON COOLER

1½ oz. Amer Picon
1 oz. gin
½ oz. cherry liqueur

½ oz. lemon juice
1 tsp. sugar
Iced club soda

Shake Amer Picon, gin, cherry liqueur, lemon juice, and sugar well with ice. Strain into tall 14-oz. glass half-filled with ice. Add soda. Stir.

ANDALUSIA

1½ oz. very dry sherry
½ oz. Cognac

½ oz. light rum
1 dash Angostura bitters

Stir well with ice. Strain into prechilled cocktail glass.

APPETIZER

¾ oz. Dubonnet
¾ oz. gin

¾ oz. orange juice
3 dashes Angostura bitters

Shake Dubonnet, gin, orange juice, and bitters well with ice. Strain into prechilled cocktail glass.

APPLE BYRRH

1 oz. Calvados (apple brandy)
½ oz. Byrrh
½ oz. dry vermouth

½ tsp. lemon juice
Lemon peel

Shake Calvados, Byrrh, vermouth, and lemon juice well with ice. Strain into prechilled cocktail glass. Twist lemon peel above drink and drop into glass. *Then pass the Gruyère and anchovy canapés.*

APPLE DUBONNET

1 oz. Calvados
1 oz. red Dubonnet

1 slice lemon

Stir Calvados and Dubonnet well with ice. Strain over rocks into prechilled old-fashioned glass. Add lemon slice.

APPLE LILLET

1 oz. Calvados
1 oz. Lillet

1 slice orange

Stir Calvados and Lillet well with ice. Strain over rocks in prechilled old-fashioned glass. Add orange slice. *A perfect drink to kill time while waiting for the hot onion soup.*

BAHIA

1 oz. sherry
1 oz. dry vermouth
2 dashes pastis

1 dash orange bitters
Lemon peel

Stir sherry, vermouth, pastis, and bitters well with ice. Strain into prechilled cocktail glass. Twist lemon peel over drink and drop into glass.

BAMBOO

1 oz. fino sherry
1 oz. dry vermouth

1 dash orange bitters
1 lemon slice

Stir sherry, vermouth, and bitters with ice. Strain into prechilled cocktail glass. Garnish with lemon slice.

BASTARDO

1 oz. dry vermouth
1 oz. sweet vermouth
½ oz. California brandy

2 dashes Angostura bitters
Iced club soda
1 slice lemon

Pour dry vermouth, sweet vermouth, brandy, and bitters over rocks in old-fashioned glass. Stir well. Add splash of soda. Add lemon slice.

BERLENGA

2 oz. white port
¾ oz. gin

1 lemon slice

Stir port and gin with ice. Strain into prechilled cocktail glass. Garnish with lemon slice.

BETSY ROSS

1 oz. port
1 oz. Cognac
1 dash orange liqueur

1 dash Angostura bitters
Lemon peel

Shake port, Cognac, orange liqueur, and bitters with ice. Strain into prechilled cocktail glass. Twist lemon peel over drink and drop into glass.

BITTER-ORANGE COOLER

3 oz. sweet vermouth
2 dashes Angostura bitters
2½ oz. orange juice
½ oz. lemon juice

½ oz. cherry brandy
Orange soda
1 slice orange

Shake vermouth, bitters, orange juice, lemon juice, and cherry brandy well with ice. Strain into tall 14-oz. glass half-filled with ice cubes. Add soda. Stir. Garnish with orange slice.

BITTER PERNOD

1 oz. Pernod
1 oz. vodka
1 oz. lemon juice

Iced bitter lemon
1 slice lemon

Fill tall 14-oz. glass with rocks. Add Pernod, vodka, and lemon juice. Stir very well. Fill with bitter lemon. Add lemon slice.

BITTERSWEET

1¼ oz. sweet vermouth   1 dash orange bitters
1¼ oz. dry vermouth   Orange peel
2 dashes Angostura bitters

Stir both kinds of vermouth and both kinds of bitters well with ice. Strain into prechilled cocktail glass. Twist orange peel above drink and drop into glass. *Salted, shelled pistachios go well with this taste teaser.*

BOB DANDY

1½ oz. Dubonnet
¾ oz. brandy

Stir Dubonnet and brandy well with ice. Strain into cocktail glass over ice.

BUTTERFLY

¾ oz. dry vermouth   ½ oz. red Dubonnet
¾ oz. sweet vermouth   ½ oz. orange juice

Shake everything well with ice. Strain over rocks into prechilled old-fashioned glass. *This combination of orange juice and three fortified wines is extremely light.*

BYRRH BRANDY

¾ oz. Byrrh   ¾ oz. dry vermouth
¾ oz. Cognac

Combine and stir well with ice. Strain into prechilled cocktail glass.

BYRRH CASSIS

1½ oz. Byrrh   1 slice lemon
¼ oz. crème de cassis   Iced club soda (optional)
½ oz. lemon juice

Shake Byrrh, crème de cassis, and lemon juice well with ice. Strain over rocks in prechilled old-fashioned glass. Add lemon slice—and a splash of soda if desired.

BYRRH CASSIS COOLER

2 oz. Byrrh   Iced club soda
½ oz. crème de cassis   1 slice lemon

Fill a tall 14-oz. glass to the rim with ice cubes. Add Byrrh and crème de cassis. Add soda. Stir. Garnish with lemon slice. *Quickens the appetite even though slightly sweet. Nice to hold in your hands when the* blanquette de veau *is simmering in the kitchen.*

BYRRH COCKTAIL

1¼ oz. Byrrh   Lemon peel
1¼ oz. gin

Stir Byrrh and gin well with ice. Strain into prechilled cocktail glass or over rocks in prechilled old-fashioned glass. Twist lemon peel above drink and drop into glass.

CADIZ

¾ oz. amontillado sherry   ½ oz. triple sec
¾ oz. blackberry liqueur   ½ oz. heavy cream
Shake well with ice. Strain over rocks in prechilled old-fashioned glass.

CALIFORNIAN

1½ oz. sweet vermouth   2 oz. orange juice
1 oz. blended U.S. whiskey   1 tsp. orgeat
Combine and shake well with ice. Strain over large ice cube in prechilled old fashioned glass. Be sure the orange juice is freshly squeezed from ripe California navels or Valencias in midseason.

CANADIAN AND CAMPARI

1 oz. Canadian whisky   1 oz. dry vermouth
½ oz. Campari   Lemon peel
Stir whisky, Campari, and vermouth well with ice. Strain into prechilled cocktail glass. Twist lemon peel above drink and drop into glass. *A perfect drink to sip while anticipating the antipasto.*

CARDINAL I

¾ oz. gin   ¾ oz. dry vermouth
¾ oz. Campari   Lemon peel
Stir gin, Campari, and vermouth well with ice. Strain into prechilled cocktail glass. Twist lemon peel above drink and drop into glass. (If you're wondering what a Cardinal II is, just use rum instead of gin.)

COMBO

2½ oz. dry vermouth   ½ tsp. Angostura bitters
½ tsp. curaçao   ½ tsp. sugar
1 tsp. Cognac
Shake everything well with ice. Strain over rocks in prechilled old-fashioned glass. *An elusive, but not illusive, glow is created by this combination of aperitif flavors.*

CORONATION

¾ oz. Dubonnet   ¾ oz. gin
¾ oz. dry vermouth
Stir Dubonnet, dry vermouth, and gin with ice. Strain into prechilled cocktail glass.

CREAMY ORANGE

1 oz. orange juice   ½ oz. heavy cream
1 oz. cream sherry   2 tsp. brandy
Shake well with ice. Strain into prechilled cocktail glass. *A gentle introduction to a brunch omelet.*

CYNAR CALYPSO

1 oz. Cynar
1 oz. light rum
1 oz. pineapple juice

1 oz. lime juice
1 tsp. grenadine

Shake extremely well with ice. Pour into tall or squat 10-oz. glass. Add ice cubes to fill glass. Stir well.

CYNAR SOUR

1 oz. Cynar
1 oz. California brandy
2 oz. orange juice

1 oz. lemon juice
½ slice orange

Shake Cynar, brandy, orange juice, and lemon juice well with ice. Strain into old fashioned glass. Garnish with orange slice.

DANIELLE

1½ oz. sweet vermouth
¾ oz. brandy

1 dash Angostura bitters
1 lemon slice

Shake vermouth, brandy, and bitters with ice. Strain into prechilled cocktail glass. Garnish with lemon slice.

DIPLOMAT

1½ oz. dry vermouth
¾ oz. sweet vermouth

1 tsp. cherry liqueur
1 maraschino cherry

Shake vermouths and liqueur with ice. Strain into prechilled cocktail glass. Garnish with cherry.

DRY SHERRY COLLINS

3 oz. very dry sherry
1 oz. gin
1 oz. lemon juice

1 tsp. sugar, or more to taste
Iced club soda
1 slice lemon

Shake sherry, gin, lemon juice, and sugar well with ice. Strain into 14-oz. glass half-filled with ice cubes. Fill glass with soda. Add lemon slice.

DUBONNET COCKTAIL

1¼ oz. red Dubonnet
1¼ oz. gin

Lemon peel

Stir Dubonnet and gin well with ice. Strain into prechilled cocktail glass. Twist lemon peel above drink and drop into glass.

DUBONNET FIZZ

1 oz. red Dubonnet
1 oz. cherry brandy
1 oz. orange juice
½ oz. lemon juice

1 tsp. kirschwasser
Iced club soda
1 slice lemon
1 fresh or canned pitted black cherry

Shake Dubonnet, cherry brandy, orange juice, lemon juice, and kirschwasser well with ice. Strain into tall 14-oz. glass half-filled with ice. Fill glass with soda. Stir. Add lemon slice and cherry.

EAU-DE-VIE CAMPARI

½ oz. framboise
½ oz. kirschwasser
1 oz. Campari
½ oz. lemon juice

½ tsp. grenadine
Iced club soda
Orange peel

Pour framboise, kirschwasser, Campari, lemon juice, and grenadine into mixing glass with ice. Stir very well. Strain into 8-oz. glass with one or two ice cubes. Add a splash of soda. Stir lightly. Twist orange peel above drink and drop into glass.

FINO

1¼ oz. fino sherry
1½ oz. sweet vermouth

1 slice lemon

Stir sherry and vermouth well with ice. Strain over rocks in prechilled old-fashioned glass. Garnish with lemon slice.

FINO RICKEY

¾ oz. very dry (fino) sherry
¾ oz. gin

¼ large lime
Iced club soda

Put three ice cubes into an 8-oz. glass. Add sherry and gin. Squeeze lime above drink and drop into glass. Add soda. Stir. *Serve with something salty, such as a bowl of assorted stuffed olives or anchovy canapés.*

FIVE O'CLOCK

¾ oz. sweet vermouth
¾ oz. gin

¾ oz. light rum
¾ oz. orange juice

Shake vermouth, gin, rum, and orange juice with ice. Strain into prechilled cocktail glass.

FLORIDIAN

1½ oz. dry vermouth
½ oz. Forbidden Fruit
1 tsp. Falernum

2 oz. grapefruit juice
2 dashes orange bitters
1 slice lime

Shake vermouth, Forbidden Fruit, Falernum, grapefruit juice, and bitters well with ice. Strain over large ice cube in prechilled old-fashioned glass. Garnish with lime slice.

FRAISE FIZZ

1½ oz. gin
1 oz. Chambery Fraise
½ oz. lemon juice
1 tsp. sugar

Iced club soda
Lemon peel
1 large strawberry, sliced in half

Shake gin, Chambery Fraise, lemon juice, and sugar well with ice. Strain into tall 14-oz. glass half-filled with ice. Fill glass with soda. Stir. Twist lemon peel above drink and drop into glass. Add strawberry.

FRENCH PICK-ME-UP

1½ oz. Pernod
1 oz. Cognac
1 small egg
½ oz. lemon juice
2 tsp. sugar
Freshly grated nutmeg

Shake Pernod, Cognac, egg, lemon juice, and sugar extremely well with ice. Strain into 8-oz. glass. Sprinkle with nutmeg. *Fine tranquilizer for the moaning after.*

GASPÉ

2 oz. very dry sherry
1 oz. Canadian whisky
½ oz. Vaklova liqueur
1 piece lemon peel

Stir sherry, whisky, and Vaklova liqueur well with ice. Strain over rocks in 8-oz. glass. Twist lemon peel above drink and drop into glass.

GRANADA

1 oz. very dry (fino) sherry
1 oz. brandy
½ oz. curaçao
Iced tonic water
1 slice orange

Shake sherry, brandy, and curaçao well with ice. Strain into tall 14-oz. glass. Add two large ice cubes. Add tonic water. Stir. Add orange slice.

HIGH POCKET

2 oz. dry vermouth
½ oz. cherry brandy
½ oz. California brandy
½ oz. lemon juice
Iced apricot nectar

Be sure apricot nectar is well chilled beforehand. Shake vermouth, cherry brandy, California brandy, and lemon juice well with ice. Strain into tall 14-oz. glass half-filled with ice cubes. Add apricot nectar to fill glass. Stir.

LILLET COCKTAIL

1½ oz. Lillet
1 oz. gin
Lemon peel

Stir Lillet and gin well with ice. Strain into prechilled cocktail glass. Twist lemon peel above drink and drop into glass.

LILLET NOYAUX

1½ oz. Lillet
1 oz. gin
¼ tsp. crème de noyaux
Orange peel

Stir Lillet, gin, and crème de noyaux well with ice. Strain into prechilled cocktail glass. Twist orange peel above drink and drop into glass. *The scintillating flavor of Lillet is even more pleasant when this drink is poured on the rocks.*

LONG EVENING

¾ oz. dry vermouth
¾ oz. sweet vermouth
2 tsp. brandy
2 dashes Angostura bitters
Soda water to fill
1 lemon slice

Stir vermouths, brandy, and bitters well with ice. Strain into old-fashioned glass over ice. Top off with soda water and garnish with lemon slice.

MANHATTAN MILANO

1 oz. kirschwasser   1 brandied cherry
2 oz. sweet vermouth

Pour kirschwasser and vermouth into mixing glass with ice. Stir very well. Strain into prechilled large cocktail glass. Add cherry. Use regular maraschino cherry if brandied cherries are unavailable.

MUSCARI COOLER

1½ oz. gin   1 tsp. sugar
1 oz. Muscari   Iced club soda
1 oz. lemon juice   1 slice lemon

Shake gin, Muscari, lemon juice, and sugar well with ice. Pour into tall 14-oz. glass half-filled with rocks. Add club soda. Stir. Add lemon slice.

PERNOD AND PEPPERMINT

1 oz. Pernod   Iced club soda
1 oz. peppermint schnapps   1 slice lime
1 oz. lime juice

Fill tall 14-oz. glass with ice cubes. Add Pernod, peppermint schnapps, and lime juice. Stir well. Fill with club soda. Add lime slice.

PERNOD CURAÇAO FRAPPÉ

¾ oz. Pernod   2 tsp. orange juice
¾ oz. curaçao   1 thin slice orange
1 tsp. lemon juice

Stir Pernod, curaçao, lemon juice, and orange juice without ice. Pour over crushed ice in deep-saucer champagne glass. Add orange slice.

PERNOD DRIP

1½ oz. Pernod
1 cube sugar

The first requirement for this drink is an absinthe drip glass. If you don't own a drip glass, you can use a tea strainer over an old-fashioned glass as a substitute. First pour the Pernod into the glass. Place the strainer on the glass. Put the sugar over the drip section on top of the glass. Pack a mound of crushed or finely cracked ice atop the sugar. When the ice has melted, the drip is ready. *Strictly for curio seekers in the spirit world.*

PERNOD FLIP

1 oz. Pernod   1 small egg
½ oz. Cointreau   1 tsp. sugar
2 tsp. lemon juice   Grated nutmeg

Shake Pernod, Cointreau, lemon juice, egg, and sugar well with ice. Strain into prechilled Delmonico glass. Sprinkle with nutmeg.

PERNOD MARTINI

2 oz. gin
½ oz. dry vermouth

⅛ tsp. Pernod

Stir well with ice. Strain into prechilled cocktail glass. *Very nice with an onion-stuffed olive. Some pros pour a soupçon of Pernod into the glass, swirl it around, and then add the rest.*

PICON ON THE ROCKS

1½ oz. Amer Picon
½ oz. lemon juice

Club soda
1 slice lemon

Pour Amer Picon and lemon juice over rocks in prechilled old-fashioned glass. Add a splash of soda. Stir. Garnish with lemon slice.

PICON PUNCH

1½ oz. Amer Picon
¼ tsp. grenadine
Iced club soda

1 tablespoon Cognac
Lemon peel

Pour Amer Picon, grenadine, and splash of soda over rocks into prechilled old-fashioned glass. Stir. Float Cognac on top of drink. Twist lemon peel above drink and drop into glass. *Although Amer Picon is a sweet liqueur, for more than a century the French have sipped it avidly before mealtime. There's just enough bitterness to balance the sweet.*

PLUM APERITIF

1½ oz. dry vermouth
½ oz. Cognac

¼ oz. prunelle (plum liqueur)
1 slice lemon

Stir vermouth, Cognac, and prunelle well with ice. Strain over rocks in prechilled old-fashioned glass. Add lemon slice. *A small jar of fresh beluga caviar will make the mise-en-scène perfect.*

PUNT E LEMON

3 oz. Punt e Mes
Iced bitter lemon

1 wedge old-fashioned-cocktail
orange in syrup

Pour Punt e Mes into tall 12-oz. glass three-quarters filled with ice cubes. Add bitter lemon to almost fill glass. Stir very well. Pierce orange wedge with cocktail spear and rest across top of glass.

PUNT E MES NEGRONI

¾ oz. Punt e Mes
¾ oz. gin

¾ oz. sweet vermouth

Stir well with ice. Strain into prechilled cocktail glass. May be served on the rocks with a twist of lemon or splash of soda or both. *Punt e Mes is one of those Italian aperitifs that cause you first to shudder, then instantly to ask for more.*

RUM APERITIF

1 oz. dry vermouth
1 oz. light rum
1 tsp. dark Jamaican rum

1 tsp. raspberry syrup
½ oz. lemon juice
Lemon peel

Shake vermouth, both kinds of rum, raspberry syrup, and lemon juice well with ice. Strain into prechilled cocktail glass. Twist lemon peel above drink and drop into glass. *This aperitif could just as well be included among the rum cocktails. The effect in either case is the same: a ravenous appetite.*

SANCTUARY

1 oz. red Dubonnet
½ oz. Amer Picon
½ oz. Cointreau

½ oz. lemon juice
1 slice lemon

Shake Dubonnet, Amer Picon, Cointreau, and lemon juice well with ice. Strain over rocks in prechilled old-fashioned glass. Add lemon slice. *Pass the hors d'oeuvres.*

SARASOTA

2 oz. cream sherry
3 oz. papaya nectar
1 oz. light rum

½ oz. lime juice
1 slice lime

Shake sherry, papaya nectar, rum, and lime juice well with ice. Strain into tall 14-oz. glass three-quarters filled with ice cubes. Add lime slice.

SHERRY COBBLER

2½ oz. sherry
1 oz. brandy
½ oz. orange juice

½ tsp. sugar
1 slice cocktail orange in syrup

Fill a 12-oz. glass with finely cracked ice. Add sherry, brandy, orange juice, and sugar. Stir well until sugar dissolves. Add more ice to fill glass to rim. Stir. Garnish with orange slice.

SHERRY GIMLET

2 oz. very dry sherry
1 oz. gin

1 oz. Rose's Lime Juice

Stir sherry, gin, and Rose's Lime Juice well with ice. Strain into 8-oz. glass. Add ice cubes to fill glass. Stir.

SHERRY SOUR

2 oz. very dry sherry
2 tsp. sugar
½ oz. lemon juice

1 oz. orange juice
½ slice orange

Shake sherry, sugar, lemon juice, and orange juice well with ice. Strain into whiskey-sour glass. Garnish with orange slice.

SILVER KIRSCH

1½ oz. Positano
1 oz. kirschwasser
½ oz. lemon juice

½ egg white
1 tsp. sugar
⅓ cup crushed ice

Mix all ingredients in blender for 10 seconds at high speed. Pour into prechilled old-fashioned glass.

SLOE VERMOUTH

1 oz. sloe gin
1 oz. dry vermouth

½ oz. lemon juice

Shake well with ice. Strain into prechilled cocktail glass. *A soft divertissement for a lazy afternoon.*

SOUTHWEST ONE

¾ oz. Campari
¾ oz. vodka

¾ oz. orange juice

Shake well with ice. Strain into prechilled glass. *Named after the London district in which the popular drink originated.*

STRAWBERRY VERMOUTH COOLER

2½ oz. dry vermouth
¼ cup fresh strawberries,
    hulled and sliced
1 oz. gin

2 tsp. strawberry syrup
½ cup crushed ice
Iced club soda
1 slice lemon

Put vermouth, strawberries, gin, strawberry syrup, and ice into blender. Blend 10 to 15 seconds at low speed. Pour into tall 14-oz. glass containing two ice cubes. Add a splash of soda. Stir. Garnish with lemon slice.

SUISSESSE

1½ oz. Pernod
½ oz. anisette

¼ oz. heavy cream
½ egg white

Shake well with ice. Pour into prechilled cocktail glass. *Perfect midnight cocktail that's really more Mediterranean than Swiss.*

SWEPT AWAY

1 oz. Cinzano Rosso
¾ oz. light rum

Pour Cinzano Rosso and light rum into old-fashioned glass over cracked ice.

TALL MUSCARI

1½ oz. Muscari
1 oz. vodka

3 oz. orange juice
Iced tonic water

Pour Muscari, vodka, and orange juice into a tall 14-oz. glass three-quarters filled with ice cubes. Stir well. Fill glass to top with tonic water.

TALL ORDER

3 oz. dry vermouth
4 oz. chilled strawberry nectar

Iced club soda

Pour vermouth and strawberry nectar into tall 14-oz. glass three-quarters filled with ice cubes. Stir very well. Fill glass with soda. Stir gently.

TALL SACK

3 oz. cream sherry
2 oz. apricot nectar
3 oz. orange juice

½ oz. lemon juice
½ slice orange

Shake sherry, apricot nectar, orange juice, and lemon juice well with ice. Strain into tall 14-oz. glass. Add ice cubes to fill glass. Stir. Add orange slice.

TALL SARDINIAN

1 oz. Cynar
1 oz. vodka
2 oz. orange juice

Iced tonic water
1 slice orange

Put 4 large ice cubes into a tall 14-oz. glass. Add Cynar, vodka, and orange juice. Stir well. Fill with tonic water. Add orange slice.

TIGER'S TAIL

4 oz. ice cold fresh orange juice
1 oz. Pernod

1 slice lime

Pour orange juice and Pernod into tall 14-oz. glass. Add cracked ice to fill glass. Stir. Add lime slice. *Magnificent breakfast first course.*

TRIO

¾ oz. dry vermouth
¾ oz. sweet vermouth

¾ oz. gin

Stir well with ice. Strain into prechilled cocktail glass. *A drink for rebels from the dry Martini crowd.*

TROCADERO

1 oz. dry vermouth
1 oz. sweet vermouth
1 dash grenadine

1 dash orange bitters
1 maraschino cherry

Stir vermouths, grenadine, and orange bitters well with ice. Strain into prechilled cocktail glass. Drop in cherry.

VERMOUTH AND GINGER

1 oz. dry vermouth
1 oz. ginger-flavored brandy

Iced ginger ale
1 slice lemon

Pour vermouth and ginger-flavored brandy into an 8-oz. glass with several ice cubes. Stir well. Add ginger ale. Stir. Add lemon slice.

VERMOUTH CASSIS

2½ oz. dry vermouth   **Iced club soda**
½ oz. crème de cassis

Pour vermouth and crème de cassis over one or two rocks in a prechilled old-fashioned glass, a large wineglass, or an 8-oz. highball glass. Stir. Add soda, which the French use to stretch the drink into a long aperitif. *Americans seem to prefer the drink less diluted. A Vin Blanc Cassis is the same drink with dry white wine used instead of vermouth. A slice of lemon may be used as a garnish if desired.*

VERMOUTH COOLER

2 oz. sweet vermouth   **1 tsp. sugar**
1 oz. vodka   **Iced club soda**
½ oz. lemon juice   **1 slice lemon**

Shake vermouth, vodka, lemon juice, and sugar well with ice. Strain into tall 14-oz. glass half-filled with ice. Add soda. Stir. Add lemon slice.

VERMOUTH MARASCHINO

2 oz. dry vermouth   **2 dashes orange bitters**
½ oz. maraschino liqueur   **1 maraschino cherry**
½ oz. lemon juice

Shake vermouth, maraschino liqueur, lemon juice, and bitters well with ice. Strain over large ice cube in prechilled old-fashioned glass. Garnish with cherry.

VERMOUTH SCIARADA

2½ oz. chilled dry vermouth   **1 slice lemon**
½ oz. Sciarada
** (Italian orange-lemon liqueur)**

Pour vermouth and Sciarada over rocks in 8-oz. tall or squat glass. Stir well. Add lemon slice. May also be served in large stemmed wineglass.

VERMOUTH TRIPLE SEC

1 oz. dry vermouth   **2 dashes orange bitters**
½ oz. triple sec   **Lemon peel**
1 oz. gin

Shake vermouth, triple sec, gin, and bitters well with ice. Strain into prechilled cocktail glass. Twist lemon peel above drink and drop into glass.

ZAZA

2 oz. red Dubonnet   **1 slice orange**
1 oz. gin

Stir Dubonnet and gin well with ice. Strain over rocks in prechilled old-fashioned glass. Place the orange slice on the rocks. *Your nose should catch the aroma of the orange before your lips meet the drink. While there are many versions of this Dubonnet cocktail, these are the proportions we like best.*

CHAPTER 9

Whiskey

In the battle of the booze between "white" goods and "brown" goods—that is to say, between white distillates like vodka, gin, tequila, and rum and whiskey (includes domestic bourbons and other blends)—one of the whites has hung up a decisively winning score. Vodka, which holds 25 percent of the total $13 billion American distilled-beverage market, now outsells U.S. straight whiskey, the former lord of the heavies. But when spirit statisticians quit racing their motors and the last ice cube has melted away, 60 percent of our national brown-spirit drinking still consists of whiskey—including bottled-in-bond, Scottish, Canadian, Irish, and Japanese—while vodka holds 50 percent of its respective white category.

What really matters when friends of whiskey touch glasses is not the latest gallonage figures of distilled spirits, but how the battle has affected the kind of whiskey we now pour. Thankfully, many whiskeys aren't what they used to be. One only has to look back at some of the blended whiskeys offered in the 1930s after Repeal, with their unique aftertaste of a dusty stone fence, or some of the more expensive straights that recall raw barrel staves in liquid form to realize how smooth and richly mellow whiskeys have become over the years.

In whiskeydom, there are now two distinct schools of drinkers, at times polarized, at times within friendly distance of each other. First there's the group that wants low-proof whiskeys with balanced, gentle flavors. They idealize lightness, with one firm reservation: they don't want their whiskey to be so gentle that it rolls over and plays dead. When a new federally classified type of whiskey was introduced in 1972, officially designated as "light whiskey," it was hailed as the rising of a new planetary system in the spirit universe. Instead, it turned out to be a small falling meteor. It was distilled at very high proofs where flavor begins to disappear. After aging and cutting to normal proofs, most of the new light whiskeys were very low-pitched in aroma and taste. Some were positively pallid. Only a few brands ever became popular, and these few were good whiskeys even before they joined the "light" category.

In the meantime a rebellious faction has broken away from the light parade, and their spirit philosophy is that they want their whiskey to be truly whiskey-ish, with rousing rather than merely satisfying flavors. Bars and restaurants across the country, in step with this trend, will often stock some fifty varieties of Scotch whiskeys but perhaps only ten of the domestic and foreign blends. As a result, while whiskey sales generally have been dipping year after year, one prominent distillery in the South, Jack Daniel's, not only is bottling more whiskey than in previous years but is hard put to keep up with the demand for its Old Time Tennessee Sour Mash whiskey, a 90-proof specimen of an extremely mellow but deeply flavored spirit. Among Scotch drinkers, an increasing number have picked up the scent of the original and oldest type of Scotch—the single malts, unblended whiskies renowned for their deep, uncompromising flavors.

As a host, it's possible for you to stock the lighter blends and the strapping straights as well as whiskeys in the middle of the spectrum. All of this is to remind you that, as a knowledgeable owner of a liquor cabinet, you can get by with one kind of gin, one kind of vodka, one kind of brandy, and one, maybe two kinds of rum, but you should be able to dispense at least four, and preferably five, different kinds of whiskey: U.S. blended, bourbon, Canadian, Scotch, and Irish. And if your whiskey outlook is liberal, you'll offer two from each class and also consider the smooth Suntory whisky from Japan.

Americans may be puzzled about the uses of aquavit, ouzo, or sake, but when it comes to their own whiskeys, there's no such puzzlement. Most of us know how to serve them in the old ways and are ready and willing to mix them in new ways. From the old colonel with his icy Mint Julep to the young skier with her mug of hot, buttered Bourbon and Ginger, Americans find in their native whiskeys anything from stimulant to solace. When we buy whiskeys, however, we tend to be diehards about the same old brand X we've been buying for years, forgetting that brand Y or Z could not only furnish the pleasure of a newfound potation but could ignite the same gentle flame of surprise that guests find in a new objet d'art on the shelves.

In aspiring to be a judge of good whiskey, don't let color influence your judgment. It has little to do with what we mean by "lightness" in flavor. Some whiskeys receive their tint from the barrels in which they're aged, others—with the outstanding exception of bourbon—from added caramel coloring.

The first step in judging a whiskey is to nose it. If your nose is reasonably sensitive, it's a more accurate and objective instrument for appraising whiskey flavor than the mouth. Pour the whiskey to be sampled into a tulip-shaped glass or a dock glass, which helps to fence in the aroma. Add a little water so that the proof is cut in half—that is, a 90-proof whiskey, for example, is reduced to about 45 proof, the strength that professionals find best for nosing spirits. (Whiskey on the rocks, well stirred, usually drops to half its bottle proof.) Swirl it around the sides of the glass, then hold it to the nostrils for a few seconds and breathe deeply. Repeat the nosing with a second kind of whiskey of the same proof, and note the differences, not necessarily for better or worse but in order to scan the features of the whiskey's flavor, its profile. (Don't repeat the procedure too frequently at one sitting or you may suffer nose fatigue.) In time, with repeated nosings, one develops a flavor memory, so at the first whiff you'll notice the subtle twists of one whiskey's flavor as compared to another's.

Of course, your ultimate objective in appraising whiskey is not merely to judge it but to enjoy it, and that means the pleasure of whiskey in the mouth. An old-fashioned taste test still ritually observed by some whiskey lovers is to pour whiskey into a glass, swirl it around, and empty the glass. A richly flavored whiskey will leave its aroma for several hours, while a more pallid whiskey will fade into nothingness. A somewhat more primitive test is to rub whiskey between the palms of the hands, just as chefs do when testing herbs or other flavoring ingredients. A pungent, heavy aroma will indicate the whiskey's strength of flavor.

The making of whiskey in all countries follows steps that are essentially the same: a mash is made of grain, malt turns it to sugar, yeast turns it to alcohol, heat vaporizes the alcohol, it cools into whiskey, and then it ages in wood. But the subtle variations in the finished product are virtually limitless. The things that make up whiskey flavor, that give it its essence, are called congeners—products other than alcohol that result from distillation. To recruit the pleasant congeners and stave off the poor ones is the real science and sorcery of whiskey making. In a fifth of whiskey there is, all told, only about a teaspoon of congeners, but without them it would be plain alcohol and water.

Some congeners are born in the kind of grain used. Others owe their genes to the yeast's paternity. They must be controlled during the whiskey's stormy adolescence in the big fermenting vats, and in the still they're carefully hoarded by drawing off the liquor at low proofs. By federal regulation, bourbon, the principal whiskey in the United States, must be taken out of the still at 160 proof or less. Actually, most of it is drawn off at considerably lower proofs and is cut to drinking strength later. The higher the proof when the liquor leaves the still, the weaker the flavor. If liquor trickling out of the still goes above 190, much of the gusto of the grain simply disappears. You then have grain neutral spirits, the basis for vodka or gin. It's like a steak cooked rare retaining its magnificent flavor and a steak cooked well done losing its juices. The comparison must be amended, however, because whiskey begins to flash its good stuff only when the congeners become mellow—after aging in the wood, which eliminates the unpleasant and refines the pleasant congeners.

Let us hastily add, however, that you can't judge a whiskey's personality exclusively by age. Some whiskeys mature earlier than others do. Weaker-flavored spirits age more quickly than stronger ones. Whiskey in a large hogshead takes longer to mature than the same whiskey in a small cask because less of it is in contact with the wood. If certain whiskeys are left too long in the wood, for age's sake alone, they sometimes begin to show the "casky" flavor of old age.

Whiskey flavor is coaxed out of a grain mash by either a pot still or a column still. The pot still isn't a yawning soup pot but a huge, onion-shaped metal flask with a blazing fire beneath it and a narrow outlet at the top for trapping and delivering the whiskey vapors into a coil where they're cooled back into a liquid. Some pot stills in Ireland today are monsters holding more than 20,000 gallons (75,700 liters) each. The other, more modern utensil is the column still, a lanky affair three or four stories high in which the alcohol is wheedled out by live steam inside the column rather than by flames beneath it. Column stills are like modern coffeemakers—the slaves of science rather than art—producing a suave, controlled flavor. Pot stills are like old-fashioned enamel coffeepots in which the ground beans have been dumped into the boiling water and swirled around to bring out all the robust coffee essence. Pot stills are generally used for heavy-flavored spirits, column stills for lighter spirits.

Some bourbons today are made, as they were generations ago, in pot stills. Others flow from the column stills. Most of the Scotch and Irish whiskeys exported to this country are now combinations of pot- and column-stilled spirits.

U.S. WHISKEY

The history of American whiskey predates the rebellion of the American colonies against England, and was later marked by another uprising correctly called the Whiskey Rebellion. When Scottish and Irish farmers in western Pennsylvania were told that the rye whiskey they were making would henceforth be taxed, they rose in arms against the government that would penalize them for practicing the Old World art they had brought to the New. This time, however, the rebellion was put down not by a foreign monarch but by President George Washington. Discouraged, small bands of farmers/whiskey-lovers left Pennsylvania and settled in Bourbon County, Kentucky, where they discovered magnificent limestone water, a prime ingredient for whiskey making. The section of northeastern Kentucky called Bourbon honored Louis XVI for his help in freeing the colonies from Britain. Among the most eminent early whiskey makers was the well-known distiller the Reverend Elijah Craig, a Baptist minister.

Good whiskey was always aged in oak barrels, but around the mid-1800s someone discovered that it aged faster and acquired a melodious mellowness when it was kept in charred oak barrels. As legend has it, some distillers found themselves at that time with no available barrels except ones used for transporting salted fish. To get rid of the fishy smell, the insides of the staves were burned, and thus bourbon—something like the whiskey we know today—was born.

For practical purposes, American whiskey production can be grouped into six categories.

STRAIGHT WHISKEY Whiskey distilled at 160 proof or less and aged for at least two years in new, charred-oak barrels; most brands are aged for four years or more. Bourbon is a straight whiskey, concocted from a grain mixture that is at least 51 percent corn; bourbon's counterpart, rye whiskey, is similarly made from a mixture of at least 51 percent rye.

BLENDS OF STRAIGHT WHISKEY Two or more straights united to combine their best features—some for mellowness, some for strength, some for aroma.

BOTTLED-IN-BOND WHISKEY Straight whiskey required to be aged for at least four years (actual age is usually older); recognized by its green rather than red stamp on the bottleneck; produced by a single distillery in one year; bottled at 100 proof; and kept under more or less constant surveillance by Internal Revenue agents. Theoretically it can be a poor whiskey and still be bottled in bond; the revenuers don't care about quality.

LIGHT WHISKEY Whiskey distilled at 161 to 189 proof, a range that results in a lighter flavor and body; it may be aged in used barrels in the same way that Canadian and Scotch whiskies are aged. Much of it is now used as the big component in blended whiskey (see below).

BLENDED WHISKEY A blend of about one-third straight whiskey (regulations say one-fifth is enough) and two-thirds grain neutral spirits or light whiskey (see above); it's often misnamed rye.

TENNESSEE WHISKEY Although it represents only a small part of U.S. whiskey gallonage, this cousin of bourbon, with corn as the leading ingredient, is famed for its luscious mellowness, brought about by slow filtering through a special charcoal of Tennessee maple. Jack Daniel and George Dickel are Tennessee's emissaries to the world of fine spirits.

Like a stubborn, gate-crashing ghost, the word *rye* keeps weaving in and out of bars and drinking parties when what's really meant is blended whiskey. Actually, though once dominant, less than 1 percent of the whiskey wetting American throats today is straight rye. In the finer liquor stores you may still find a distinguished old bottling of straight rye, but that is decidedly the exception. To be sure, rye, the grain, is used in many American whiskeys as a minor ingredient along with other grains such as wheat and barley, but to call for rye in a bar today is as illogical as asking for an onion stew when you really want beef, on the grounds that onions are used for seasoning purposes.

At the end of World War II, three out of four jiggers of whiskey were the neutral-flavored blended whiskey. Shortly thereafter, bourbon drinkers began to cut their traditional 100-proof liquors down to 86. Many of them started to spin out lighter flavors. But it was still bourbon, made from the seraphic oils of the corn—its new, easier flavor as perfectly burnished as ever. Bourbon sales blasted off and eclipsed blended whiskey.

The terms *sweet mash* and *sour mash* can stand clarification. First of all, there's absolutely nothing sour-tasting in a sour-mash whiskey. The "sour" refers to a step in the fermentation process and not the end product—whiskey. A sour-mash whiskey is produced when the liquid grain mixture, or mash (also called beer), contains some spent beer from a previous run of whiskey, usually about 25 percent. Like the base or starter used to make sourdough bread, it's the kind of leftover that makes for controlled fermentation and up- rather than downgrades the new batch. Most straight whiskeys nowadays are made by the sour-mash method during a three-day fermenting period. When whiskeys are made this way, you don't normally see the term "sour mash" on the label. If, however, you see the phrase "old-time," "old-fashioned," or "genuine sour mash" on the label, it indicates that the mash used for that whiskey contained at least 50 percent spent beer, the fermenting period was at least four days, and the resulting flavor was indeed unique. In the mouth, a sweet-mash whiskey is light in flavor and a sour mash is medium-bodied, while an "old-time," "old-fashioned," or "genuine" sour mash is the heaviest in flavor.

SCOTCH
WHISKY

When Bobbie Burns, liquordom's Scottish laureate, said, "O whisky, soul o' play and pranks/Accept a bardie's gratefu' thanks," he was talking about the primitive, high-voltage spirits of his day, a dose fit for doughty laird and rough peasant alike. It was all pot-stilled, and became known as a "self" whisky because it had barley's single, strong flavor unmixed with any other grain. Barley is to the flavor of Scotch as corn is to the flavor of bourbon.

Beginners tasting Scotch for the first time are often puzzled if not dismayed by what some consider its oddly medicinal flavor. The taste of Scotch is due not only to barley but to the fact that the barley is smoked before it's crushed and fermented into a mash. At one time, only peat was used for smoking, and different Scotches were described as having more or less of the peat reek. Nowadays, coal is used as the first step in smoking, and later peat—which is expensive—is burned to give the grain its characteristic Scotch aroma. In some distilleries, fans are used to blow the peat smoke over the grain for a more rapid infusion.

But if it were only the barley and the peat that made Scotch, Scotch could theoretically be made anywhere. Efforts were made to make "Scotch" in other countries, using barley and imported peat, and they were disasters.

Even when using imported water taken from Scotland's highland streams, the results could not be duplicated, which proves that you can import everything that goes into Scotch except the weather: the highland dew and sunshine, as well as the winds, the wet, and the cold that surround Scotch during its long sleep in the casks. Fortunately, all of the elements that go into Scotch can be found bottled at your nearest liquor store.

The modern Scotch that the English, Americans, and other non-Scots drink is an amalgam of two kinds of spirits. The first is the modern grain whiskey, made mostly of corn, a small amount of barley, and sometimes rye and oats. It flows out of tall column stills, and in flavor is as light as thistle-down, but doesn't become the Scotch we know until it's first aged and later fortified with the old-time "self" whisky, also known as single-malt or malt whiskey.

Note that the Scots spell their whisky without an *e*, the absence of which is usually attributed to the alleged Scottish parsimony. Because the Canadians and Japanese also spell their whisky without an *e*, the theory must go down the drain, although Scottish whisky drinkers love to encourage foreign legends of Scottish tightfistedness. "It's guid," an old maltster boasted to me. "It gives us individuality."

But young American drinkers who taste Scotch for the first time don't have to be told that it's a breed apart from the American whiskey they've known. It's such a long jump that many of them are torn between what they think they should like and what they actually do like. Eventually, after they taste different Scotches under different circumstances, many of them find themselves in tune with the great Highland fling.

Blended Scotches coming into the United States are blends not of one heavy malt whiskey with one light grain, but of as many as a dozen heavies with a dozen lights. Some imported Scotch blends are now 80 percent light grain whiskey and 20 percent heavy malt whiskey; the average is perhaps 60 and 40. (Those who keep an assortment of Scotches in their liquor cabinet sometimes assume that most of the light Scotches are now leveled out to a common plateau where one light Scotch doesn't differ noticeably from another. It's a mistaken conclusion, and the host who tastes one light versus another at the same sipping session will discover that any Scotch, no matter how light, shows its own strong profile. The malt still dominates the whiskey in the same way that onions dominate an onion soup—you can use one, two, or three cups of onions in the same pot; it will still emerge as onion soup and not a colorless consommé.) Whatever the relative amounts of heavies and lights, the breeding and crossbreeding of these whiskies is a process so refined and complex that it can rightly be called a Scottish art. And what's amazing is that year after year, Scottish shippers, some of whom blend their whiskey but don't own a distillery, can turn out a spirit that seldom varies, as purebred in flavor as bottles of vintage wine from the same grapes on the same hillside of the same château.

Before World War II, almost all Scotches coming to these shores were at least eight years old. U.S. law says they must be a minimum of four years old, i.e., the youngest of the blend must be four years old. Now they're running between five and seven years, even though many labels indicate no age at all. If you're in a mood for taste exploration, try the same brand of Scotch in an eight- and a twelve-year-old version. The satiny smoothness of the older Scotch is roamin' in the gloamin' at its best. Now and then a label will read "Liqueur Scotch Whisky." It's not a sweet liqueur in the literal sense, but indicates an older Scotch, which the shipper presents as a gilt-edged potation.

At liquor stores, you can choose from any of the four great clans of Scotch being imported.

> BLENDS TWELVE YEARS AND OLDER These are the prestige Scotches, such as Chivas Regal, Johnny Walker Black Label, etc., renowned for their luscious mellowness and subtle balance of malt and grain whiskies.

> BLENDS UP TO EIGHT YEARS OF AGE Most of them are 86 proof, but a few 80-proof specimens are in the pack. Caveat emptor: the reduced proof means not only that alcohol has been taken away but that Scotch whisky itself has been removed and water added. If no age is printed on

the label, you can assume it's between five and seven years, because the youngest of the blend must be four years old by U.S. regulations. Included in this largest of the categories are all well-known labels like Cutty Sark, J&B, Dewar's, Black & White, Teacher's, White Horse, etc.

BLENDS BOTTLED IN THE UNITED STATES To reduce the high duty imposed on bottled-in-Scotland whiskies, these are imported in bulk and bottled here, saving about 15 percent in duty, shipping costs, etc. They are typified by such brands as Passport, Old Smuggler, etc.

SINGLE MALTS These are the traditional and original type of Scotches, made from malted barley alone, pot-stilled, and the product of one distillery. They are the cream of the Scotch sippin' whiskies.

An increasing number of Americans have been finding their whiskey hobby in the single malts. Twenty years ago single malts were virtually unknown in the United States except in some of the crusty men's clubs— and even there they were considered an odd dram to be sipped on a rare occasion, certainly not an everyday drink. Today single malts are on liquor shelves everywhere. American visitors to Scotland, sampling the single malts, soon learn that their spectrum of flavors is immense, ranging from the light Highland malts to the extremely heavy, peaty malts of Campbeltown, which Scots say "go down singing hymns."

All of the single malts are notably self-assertive. They are the least mixable of whiskies, not only because of their smoky overtones but because their subtlety is instantly annulled by such mixers as ginger ale, lemon juice, or vermouth. (Scotches—the blended variety—can, of course, be used in dozens of mixed drinks.) Once you're at home with the somewhat complex flavors of single malts, you may want to take them with an ice cube or two, or a little water rather than soda. In Scotland, single-malt connoisseurs insist that the best possible water for adding to their whiskies is the same spring water that was used in distilling the whiskey itself. Avoid at any cost a noticeably chlorinated tap water. Like Cognac, a single malt is a magnificent after-dinner drink served in a brandy snifter or a tulip-shaped wineglass in which the spirits can be swirled, nosed, and intimately appreciated.

Over the past fifteen years, the quality of many single malts has become much more consistent thanks to modern instrumentation used in malting, distilling, and vatting. The best-selling single malt in the world is Glenfiddich. It's distinguished not only by its three-sided bottle but also by its haunting, dry aftertaste and gentle peatiness. Scots sometimes call it sweet—not sweet in the sugary sense, but sweet in the sense that it carries the kind of aroma you remember for its amiability and graciousness. Another well-known malt whiskey is Smith's The Glenlivet. The article "The" is allowed only with this one brand to distinguish it from other Scotches—at least twenty-three—that have the name Glenlivet hyphenated in their brand names, provoking the Scottish to ironically refer to Glen Livet as the longest glen in Scotland. The Glenlivet is renowned for its deep, mellow flavor and subtle, subdued peatiness. Another single malt, less well known in this country but nonetheless available, is Bruichladdich, which has only a trace of peatiness and an opulently rich flavor.

CANADIAN WHISKY

If, in spelling *whisky*, the Scot in the Canadian seems to have taken charge, in distilling it the French Canadian is obviously the creative force, for Canada turns out the world's lightest, most delicate of spirits, a marvelous balance of corn, rye, and barley. While every bottle of Canadian whisky seems to reflect the icy clarity of the Arctic, you can depend upon its eventual effect to be as warming as any 86-proof potable in the world.

Just how Canadian distillers achieve their subtle flavor balance are both the secret and the fine art of the distillers themselves. Unlike the U.S. Bureau of Tobacco, Alcohol, and Firearms, which regulates the minimum amount of corn that goes into bourbon, the maximum proof beyond which it can't be distilled, and the kind of barrels (only new charred oak) in which the bourbon must be aged, Canadian excisemen follow a policy of laissez-faire when it comes to whiskey making. As long as they collect their taxes, they don't see any reason for insisting that more corn or less rye or more barley and less wheat are necessary to make their whiskey truly Canadian.

We do know that Canada is the second-best customer for used American cooperage (Scotland is the number one consumer), yet we also know that they use some new barrels, too. But what American distillers can never duplicate are the local waters and the special Canadian weather conditions of cloudiness, sunshine, heat, cold, and humidity in which Canadian whiskies mellow during their approximately six years in the wood. Throughout their aging process, the whiskies evaporate in the barrels, leaving headspace at the top. Canadian whisky makers normally replace this headspace with newer whiskies; therefore all Canadian whiskies are sold as blends.

If Scotch malts are the least mixable of whiskies, Canadian whiskies are probably the most mixable. It would be hard to create a better Whiskey Sour, for example, than one made with Canadian spirits. The same goes for a Whiskey Collins. A Manhattan is usually made with a rich U.S. blended rye whiskey or a bourbon. But if you prefer a dry Manhattan made with dry vermouth, then Canadian whisky is your best bet. For liquor to take along when traveling, for tailgate parties, or for any occasion at the journey's end when you want a bracer-upper, Canadian whisky is perfect taken as a straight shot or with any impromptu mixers on hand. Finally, for gift giving, when you don't know the specific hoisting habits of the person for whom the gift is intended, Canadian whisky has a special aura that makes it universally pleasing.

IRISH WHISKEY

In sharp contrast to the light Canadian spirits are Ireland's hearty whiskeys. After a few sturdy drams, amateur whiskey genealogists often trace Irish whiskey to its first maker, Patrick, patron saint of Ireland. When literal-minded whiskey historians insist that Saint Patrick in the fifth century was a brewer of beer rather than a distiller of whiskey, the Irish aren't in the least bit rattled. They simply point out that whiskey is only distilled beer, just as brandy is distilled wine; the whole history of distilling, they add, from the ancient Arabs onward is such a barmy tale that Saint Patrick might just as well be credited along with less worthy benefactors.

When impertinent Sassenachs claim that Irish whiskey is like Canadian but more robust, they make a comparison that may be partly true. But this is nevertheless odious to any true Irishman, who can point out that the very word *whiskey* is a derivative of the Gaelic *uisge beatha*, or "water of life." For there's something regal in the flavor of Irish whiskey that sets it apart not only from Canadian but also from any other whiskey in the world. As best described in Holinshed's *Chronicles* in 1577, "Trulie it is a soverigne liquor if it be orderlie taken."

Before World War I, Irish whiskey heavily outsold Scotch in this country. More than four hundred brands were registered in the United States, and in England it was the drink of those who dined en famille at Buckingham Palace. Between the world wars, the canny Scots stepped in with their new, lighter blends and ran away with the foreign-whiskey market in both England and the United States. The Irish, who considered themselves perfectionists in making whiskey—particularly that which they exported—resisted change. In the nineteenth century, when John Jameson's foremen were planning to build a new fence in the courtyard of his Dublin distillery, Jameson objected strongly. "It may change the taste of the whiskey," he warned. But in whiskey making, the perfectionists of one era are all too often the reactionaries of a succeeding one. Over the years, Irish whiskey did change, but only at a drop-by-drop pace.

In 1970, however, it was remodeled noticeably and notably. The difference between the old and the modern is that the previous Irish whiskey was made in old-fashioned pot stills, and the new Irish whiskey, like most of the Scotch coming to this country, is a blend of pot and column stills. Any pot still produces pungent, low-proof, intensely flavored whiskey; a column or continuous still yields high-proof, light, buoyant whiskey.

Don't assume that the new Irish whiskey is simply Scotch in a Gaelic guise. It's an easy assumption to make because both whiskeys are made from barley, but actually the two barley-born whiskeys are worlds apart in taste. Scotch barley is dried over kilns, where the smoke of peat gives it an unforgettably smoky flavor. Irish barley is dried over smokeless anthracite coal. There are other variations, but that distinction alone is enough to make Irish as different from Scotch as a harp is from a haggis.

As far as mixability is concerned, the new Irish whiskeys leave the old ones far behind. The best-known mixture in which Irish whiskey is "orderlie taken" is, of course, Irish Coffee—a drink as good cold as it is hot (see chapter 17, Hot Cheer). Of the standard bar drinks, an Irish Old-Fashioned or an Irish Sour on the rocks bring out the best of the new Irish blends.

JAPANESE WHISKY

It may come as an odd surprise to Americans to discover that one of the best-selling whiskeys in the world is neither a vigorously trumpeted U.S. blend nor one of those renowned Scotches whose name is boundlessly commended to the whole world, but instead a Japanese product—Suntory Old whisky. If you'd never tasted it and you were to sip it blindfolded, you'd swear you were drinking a fine Scotch. At the most recent count, it was being whisked off liquor-store shelves at the rate of some 8 million cases a year—most of it, of course, sipped in Sake-land.

Like Scotch, Japanese whisky is spelled without an *e*. And also like Scotch, its base of peat-smoked barley is fermented, aged, and blended with grain whiskies, the youngest of which is at least four years old. But while it's similar to Scotch generically, it's as different from the old-fashioned single-malt Scotches as a happicoat is from a kilt. While most Scotches are doughty in flavor, Suntory's chief feature is its rare elegance. Its subtly balanced flavor leaves a gentle but vivid aftertaste.

Scotch depends for its character not only on its smoked barley but on the special small clear streams of water flowing through granite in the Highlands. Japanese whiskeymen, realizing they couldn't move Scotland's streams to the Orient (although they once transported a shipload of water as a trial), built their first big distillery in the placid misty valley of Yamazaki, where the famed spring water was originally chosen for a sixteenth-century tearoom nearby. Most Scotches are blends from numerous small distilleries. By contrast,

Suntory whisky is made in two huge distilleries, one of which houses twenty-four monstrous pot stills, the largest malt distillery in the world. Finally, while hundreds of old Scottish malt lovers depend on their noses and their mouths for blending whiskies, the Japanese take advantage not only of their noses and mouths but, as you might expect, of chromatograph-coupled mass spectrometers, nuclear magnetic-resonance analyzers, and electron microscopes. Undoubtedly it's this happy coupling of art and the latest technology that makes Suntory amazingly consistent from one year to the next.

Holding 60 percent of their own domestic whisky market, it's not the fault of Japanese whisky makers that so little of it is seen in American public and private bars. Those who sip it for the first time may cry "Imitation!" but the same response was heard from those who years ago first tasted California Cabernet Sauvignon and sneered that it was a fake Bordeaux. As the California wines gradually came of age, more and more wine drinkers began recognizing the greatness of California wines in their own right. Something of the same response might eventually be expected of consumers of Japanese whisky in the United States.

In Japan, cocktails and mixed drinks aren't popular. The Japanese prefer to drink their whisky mixed merely with water. Served this way, their delicately balanced whisky acts as a perfect counterpoint to the simple but very artful Japanese cuisine.

In the whiskey world, two significant shifts occurred in recent years. Drinking strengths in many cases were lowered from 100 to 86 proof, and some whiskeys that always were 86 proof were in some instances trimmed down to 80—incidentally chopping distillers' costs somewhat while gratifying the popular move toward lightness in potables. The second change is the substantial improvement of U.S. blended whiskey. At one time the best of it was one-third straight whiskey and two-thirds straight white eye—that is, raw white alcohol, just as it came from the still, cut to drinking strength. It's this two-thirds that was radically transformed. Some U.S. whiskeymen, in an effort to turn out the best blended whiskey, began to age all of it. A good blended whiskey such as Seagram's 7 Crown is made up of about seventy-five different spirits, all of them mellowed by years in the wood.

Drinking tastes are always in ferment, and where future whiskey tastes are destined is still any bar philosopher's guess. Many whiskey lovers believe that the worldwide ebb toward lightness has reached a plateau and is rippling to a halt. Increasing sales of single malts and premium blended whiskeys back the point. As a matter of fact, federal regulations that forbid whiskey to be bottled at less than 80 proof automatically bring to a dead end any effort toward further lightening.

But be it heavy in flavor or light, 86 proof or 80, the real proof of any whiskey is in the drinking. And having discovered this, more and more hosts find themselves in felicitous accord with the canny Scot who said, "There's whusky and there's guid whusky, but there's nae bad whusky."

WHISKEY COCKTAILS

AFTER-DINNER MINT

2 oz. Irish whiskey   **1 splash peppermint schnapps**
½ oz. Kahlua

Pour whiskey and Kahlua over ice into cocktail glass. Add splash peppermint schnapps.

ALGONQUIN

1½ oz. blended whiskey   **1 oz. pineapple juice**
1 oz. dry vermouth

Shake whiskey, vermouth, and pineapple juice with ice. Strain into prechilled cocktail glass.

ALLEGHENY

1 oz. bourbon   **¼ oz. lemon juice**
1 oz. dry vermouth   **1 dash Angostura bitters**
¼ oz. blackberry liqueur   **Lemon peel**

Shake bourbon, vermouth, blackberry liqueur, lemon juice, and bitters well with ice. Strain into prechilled cocktail glass. Twist lemon peel above drink and drop into glass.

BLACK HAWK

1 oz. blended whiskey   **½ oz. lemon juice**
1 oz. sloe gin (creamy cap)   **1 maraschino cherry (optional)**

Shake whiskey, sloe gin, and lemon juice well with ice. Strain into prechilled cocktail glass. Garnish with cherry if desired.

BLENDED COMFORT

2 oz. blended whiskey
½ oz. Southern Comfort
¼ cup thawed frozen peaches
½ oz. dry vermouth
1½ oz. lemon juice

1 oz. orange juice
½ cup crushed ice
1 slice lemon
1 slice cocktail orange in syrup

Put whiskey, Southern Comfort, peaches, vermouth, lemon juice, orange juice, and crushed ice into blender. Blend 10 to 15 seconds. Pour into tall 14-oz. glass. Add ice to fill glass. Garnish with lemon and orange slices.

BOSTON SOUR

2 oz. blended whiskey
Juice of ½ lemon
1 tsp. powdered sugar

1 egg white
1 slice lemon
1 cherry

Shake whiskey, lemon juice, powdered sugar, and egg white with cracked ice. Strain into prechilled whiskey-sour glass. Add lemon slice to rim and top with cherry.

BOURBON COLLINS

2 oz. 100-proof bourbon
2 dashes Peychaud's bitters
½ oz. lemon juice

1 tsp. sugar
Iced club soda
1 slice lemon

Shake bourbon, bitters, lemon juice, and sugar well with ice. Strain into tall 14-oz. glass half-filled with ice. Add soda. Stir. Add lemon slice.

BOURBON CREAM

1 oz. bourbon
½ oz. Wild Turkey liqueur

1 oz. heavy sweet cream

Shake well with ice. Strain into prechilled cocktail glass.

BOURBONNAISE

1½ oz. bourbon
½ oz. dry vermouth

¼ oz. crème de cassis
¼ oz. lemon juice

Shake well with ice. Strain over rocks into prechilled old-fashioned glass. *A perfect way to introduce a French* amie *to American bourbon.*

BOURBON-AND-MADEIRA JULEP

1½ oz. bourbon
1½ oz. Madeira or amontillado sherry
¼ oz. lemon juice

Sugar (optional)
1 pineapple stick
4 sprigs mint

Fill double old-fashioned glass with coarsely cracked ice. Add bourbon, Madeira, and lemon juice. Stir well. Add sugar if desired. Add more ice if necessary to fill glass to rim. Garnish with pineapple stick and mint.

BOURBON DAISY

1½ oz. bourbon
½ oz. lemon juice
1 tsp. grenadine
Iced club soda

1 tsp. Southern Comfort
½ slice orange
1 pineapple stick

Shake bourbon, lemon juice, and grenadine well with ice. Strain into tall 8-oz. glass half-filled with ice. Add soda. Stir. Float Southern Comfort on drink. Garnish with orange slice and pineapple stick.

BOURBON MILK PUNCH

2 oz. bourbon
1 tsp. sugar

8 oz. (1 measuring cup) milk
Freshly grated nutmeg

Shake bourbon, sugar, and milk well with ice. Strain into 12-oz. glass. Sprinkle with nutmeg.

BOURBON RUMBO

1 tsp. sugar
1 dash Angostura bitters
Chilled club soda
¾ oz. bourbon

¾ oz. golden rum
½ oz. sweet vermouth
1 slice cocktail orange
     in syrup, drained

Pour sugar, bitters, and a small splash of soda into 8-oz. tall glass. Stir until sugar dissolves. Add bourbon, rum, vermouth, and several ice cubes. Stir well. Add a splash of soda. Stir. Add orange slice.

BOURBON SLOE-GIN FIX

½ tsp. sugar
1 tsp. water
1½ oz. bourbon
½ oz. sloe gin

½ oz. lemon juice
1 slice lemon
1 slice fresh or brandied peach

Dissolve sugar in 1 tsp. water in an 8-oz. glass. Add bourbon, sloe gin, and lemon juice. Fill glass with crushed ice. Stir well. Add more ice to fill glass to rim. Stir. Garnish with lemon and peach slices.

BRIGHTON PUNCH

1 oz. bourbon
1 oz. Cognac
¾ oz. Benedictine
1 oz. orange juice

½ oz. lemon juice
1 oz. iced club soda
½ slice orange
1 slice lemon

Shake bourbon, Cognac, Benedictine, orange juice, and lemon juice well with ice. Strain into tall 14-oz. glass. Add soda and enough ice to fill glass. Stir. Garnish with orange and lemon slices. *An individual punch brewed outside a punch bowl.*

BROOKLYN

1½ oz. Canadian whisky
¾ oz. dry vermouth

2 dashes cherry liqueur
1 maraschino cherry (optional)

Stir whisky, vermouth, and cherry liqueur well with ice. Strain into prechilled cocktail glass. Garnish with cherry if desired. *A brownstone favorite.*

CABLEGRAM

2 oz. blended whiskey
Juice of ½ lemon
1 tsp. powdered sugar
Ginger ale to fill

Put whiskey, lemon juice, and powdered sugar over ice in 8-oz. glass. Stir well. Top off with ginger ale. *Adds a sweet touch to the traditional whiskey highball.*

CALIFORNIA LEMONADE

2 oz. blended whiskey
Juice of 1 lemon
Juice of 1 lime
1 tbsp. powdered sugar
¼ tsp. grenadine
Soda water to fill
Lemon slice
Orange slice
1 cherry

Shake whiskey, lemon and lime juices, sugar, and grenadine well with ice. Strain into tall collins glass over shaved ice. Top off with soda water. Stir. Garnish with slices of orange and lemon. Drop in cherry and serve with a straw. Could also be called a California Collins.

CANADIAN APPLE

1½ oz. Canadian whisky
½ oz. Calvados
¼ oz. lemon juice
1 tsp. sugar
Ground cinnamon
1 slice lemon

Shake whisky, Calvados, lemon juice, sugar, and a spray of cinnamon well with ice. Strain over rocks into prechilled old-fashioned glass. Add lemon slice. *A delight before a holiday dinner of roast turkey or goose.*

CANADIAN BLACKBERRY FIX

1½ oz. Canadian whisky
½ oz. blackberry-flavored brandy
½ tsp. sugar
½ oz. lemon juice
1 slice lemon
1 fresh blackberry if available

Pour whisky, blackberry-flavored brandy, sugar, and lemon juice into tall 8-oz. glass. Stir very well until sugar dissolves. Fill glass with coarsely cracked ice, or ice from an ice-tray chipper, and stir well. Add ice if necessary to fill glass to rim, and stir. Garnish with lemon slice and blackberry.

CANADIAN CHERRY

1½ oz. Canadian whisky
½ oz. Peter Heering or Cherry Karise
¼ oz. lemon juice
¼ oz. orange juice

Shake well with ice. Strain into prechilled sugar-frosted cocktail glass. Glass rim may be moistened with cherry liqueur before dipping into sugar.

CANADIAN COCKTAIL

1½ oz. Canadian whisky
½ oz. lemon juice
¼ oz. curaçao
1 tsp. sugar
2 dashes bitters

Shake well with ice. Strain into prechilled cocktail glass or over rocks into old-fashioned glass.

CANADIAN DAISY

1½ oz. Canadian whisky
½ oz. lemon juice
1 tsp. raspberry syrup
Iced club soda
1 tsp. Metaxa brandy
2 fresh or thawed frozen raspberries

Shake whisky, lemon juice, and raspberry syrup well with ice. Strain into tall 8-oz. glass half-filled with ice. Add soda. Stir. Float Metaxa on drink. Add raspberries.

CANADIAN OLD-FASHIONED

1½ oz. Canadian whisky
2 dashes Angostura bitters
½ tsp. curaçao
½ tsp. lemon juice
Lemon peel
Orange peel

Pour whisky, bitters, curaçao, and lemon juice into prechilled old-fashioned glass. Add rocks. Stir. Twist lemon peel and orange peel above drink and drop into glass. *More suave than the conventional Old-Fashioned made with U.S. blended whiskey.*

CANADIAN PINEAPPLE

1½ oz. Canadian whisky
½ oz. pineapple juice
½ oz. lemon juice
½ tsp. maraschino liqueur
1 pineapple stick

Shake whisky, pineapple juice, lemon juice, and maraschino liqueur well with ice. Strain over rocks into prechilled old-fashioned glass. Add pineapple stick.

CANADIAN STAVE

2 oz. Canadian whisky
1 oz. red Dubonnet
½ egg white
¼ tsp. Angostura bitters
2 tsp. lemon juice
2 dashes Tabasco sauce

Shake all ingredients well with ice. Strain into prechilled old-fashioned glass. Add ice cubes to fill glass. Stir well.

CELTIC COCKTAIL

1½ oz. Scotch
1 oz. Irish whiskey
½ oz. lemon juice
1 dash Angostura bitters

Shake whiskies, lemon juice, and bitters well with ice. Strain into prechilled cocktail glass.

CHAPEL HILL

1½ oz. blended whiskey
½ oz. curaçao
½ oz. lemon juice
1 slice cocktail orange in syrup

Shake whiskey, curaçao, and lemon juice well with ice. Strain over rocks into prechilled old-fashioned glass. Garnish with orange slice. *Pass freshly toasted salted pecans.*

COFFEE EGGNOG

1½ oz. Canadian whisky	½ oz. heavy cream
1 oz. coffee liqueur	1 tsp. sugar
1 small egg	½ tsp. instant coffee
4 oz. milk	Ground coriander seed

Shake whisky, coffee liqueur, egg, milk, cream, sugar, and instant coffee with ice extremely well—about twice the usual mixing time. Strain into tall 14-oz. glass. Sprinkle with coriander.

COLD IRISH

1½ oz. Irish whiskey	Whipped cream
2 tsp. Irish Mist liqueur	Crème de cacao
Iced coffee soda	

Pour whiskey and Irish Mist into tall 14-oz. glass. Add one large ice cube. Fill glass to within 1 inch of top with soda. Stir. Flavor whipped cream with crème de cacao, using ½ oz. crème de cacao for each ½ cup heavy cream used for whipping. Add a large dollop of whipped-cream topping to each drink.

COMMODORE

1¾ oz. blended whiskey	1 tsp. strawberry liqueur
2 tsp. lime juice	1 dash orange bitters
1 tsp. orange juice	

Shake well with ice. Strain into prechilled cocktail glass. *A subtle blend of whiskey and fruit flavors that's appreciated at the end of a lazy Sunday sail.*

COMMONWEALTH

1¾ oz. Canadian whisky	½ oz. Van der Hum liqueur
¼ oz. lemon juice	Tangerine peel or orange peel

Shake whisky, lemon juice, and Van der Hum well with ice. Strain into prechilled sugar-frosted cocktail glass. Twist peel over drink and drop into glass. *Serve before a dinner of grilled lobster tails.*

COOL COLONEL

1½ oz. bourbon	2 tsp. lemon juice
1 oz. Southern Comfort	2 tsp. sugar
3 oz. chilled strong black tea	Iced club soda

Pour bourbon, Southern Comfort, tea, lemon juice, and sugar into tall 14-oz. glass. Stir until sugar dissolves. Add two large ice cubes and a splash of soda. Stir. *Breathe deeply. Tilt head. Bend elbow.*

CRANBERRY SANGAREE

1 oz. cranberry liqueur	Orange peel
1 oz. U.S. blended whiskey	Freshly grated nutmeg

Fill old-fashioned glass with ice cubes. Pour cranberry liqueur and whiskey into glass. Stir well. Sprinkle with nutmeg. Twist orange peel over glass and drop into drink. *Summer or winter, this drink is always in season.*

CRANBOURBON

2 oz. bourbon
1 dash Angostura bitters
1 tsp. sugar

½ oz. lemon juice
Iced cranberry juice cocktail
1 long strip cucumber rind

Shake bourbon, bitters, sugar, and lemon juice well with ice. Strain into 12-oz. glass half-filled with ice cubes. Add cranberry juice cocktail to fill glass. Stir. Place cucumber rind in glass.

CROTON

1¾ oz. bourbon or blended whiskey
¼ oz. cocktail sherry

Lemon peel

Stir whiskey and sherry well with ice. Strain into prechilled cocktail glass. Twist lemon peel above drink and drop into glass. *A patio or terrace cocktail to be served with a bowl of fresh iced shrimp and a tangy cocktail sauce.*

CURRIER

1½ oz. blended whiskey
½ oz. Kümmel
¼ oz. fresh lime juice

¼ oz. Rose's Lime Juice
1 slice lime

Shake whiskey, Kümmel, and both kinds of lime juice well with ice. Strain into prechilled cocktail glass. Add lime slice. *A cocktail to savor between the fox hunt and breakfast.*

DELTA

1½ oz. blended whiskey
½ oz. Southern Comfort
½ oz. lime juice

½ tsp. sugar
½ slice orange
1 slice fresh peach

Shake whiskey, Southern Comfort, lime juice, and sugar well with ice. Strain over rocks into prechilled old-fashioned glass. Garnish with orange and peach slices. *A drink to accompany Gershwin on the hi-fi.*

DIXIELAND TEA

2 oz. blended whiskey
½ oz. amaretto

Iced tea to fill

Shake or stir with ice. Strain into prechilled cocktail glass. Garnish with a lemon wedge.

DOUBLE DERBY

2½ oz. bourbon
2 oz. cold strong black tea
2 oz. claret
1 oz. red-currant syrup

1 oz. orange juice
½ oz. lemon juice
1 slice cocktail orange in syrup

Pour bourbon, tea, claret, red-currant syrup, orange juice, and lemon juice into double old-fashioned glass. Add ice cubes to fill to brim. Stir well. Add orange slice. If red-currant syrup is not available, red-currant jelly to which a teaspoon of hot water has been added may be heated over a low flame and stirred constantly until liquefied.

DOWN YONDER

1 oz. bourbon
½ oz. peppermint schnapps
2 oz. peach nectar

½ oz. lemon juice
1 slice fresh peach

Shake bourbon, peppermint schnapps, peach nectar, and lemon juice well with ice. Strain into 8-oz. glass. Add ice cubes to fill glass. Stir. Fasten peach on cocktail spear and rest on rim of glass.

DRY MANHATTAN COOLER

2 oz. blended whiskey
1 oz. dry vermouth
2 oz. orange juice
½ oz. lemon juice

½ oz. orgeat or orzata
Iced club soda
1 maraschino cherry

Shake whiskey, vermouth, orange juice, lemon juice, and orgeat well with ice. Strain into tall 14-oz. glass. Add a splash of soda and ice to fill glass. Stir. Add cherry.

GLASGOW

1½ oz. Scotch
¾ oz. lemon juice

¼ oz. dry vermouth
¼ oz. orzata

Shake well with ice. Strain into prechilled cocktail glass. *Serve with thin slices of Nova Scotia salmon on hot buttered toast.*

GODFATHER

1¼ oz. Scotch
¾ oz. amaretto

Pour Scotch and amaretto over rocks into old-fashioned glass. *Never drink this cocktail with your back to the door.*

GRAPEFRUIT COOLER

2 oz. blended whiskey
4 oz. unsweetened grapefruit juice
½ oz. red-currant syrup

1 tsp. lemon juice
½ slice orange
½ slice lemon

Shake whiskey, grapefruit juice, red-currant syrup, and lemon juice well with ice. Strain into tall 14-oz. glass. Add ice to fill glass. Stir. Garnish with orange and lemon slices.

HABITANT COCKTAIL

1½ oz. blended Canadian whisky
1 oz. lemon juice
1 tsp. maple-sugar syrup

1 slice orange
1 maraschino cherry

Shake whisky, lemon juice, and syrup well with ice. Strain over rocks in prechilled old-fashioned glass. Garnish with orange slice and cherry.

INDIAN RIVER

1½ oz. blended whiskey
½ oz. unsweetened grapefruit juice

¼ oz. raspberry liqueur
¼ oz. sweet vermouth

Shake well with ice. Strain over rocks into prechilled old-fashioned glass.

IRISH ALEXANDER ON THE ROCKS

¾ oz. blended Irish whiskey
¾ oz. Irish coffee liqueur

¾ oz. heavy cream

Shake all ingredients well with ice. Pour into prechilled old-fashioned glass. Add ice cubes to fill glass to rim. Stir.

IRISH ALMOND

1½ oz. blended Irish whiskey
½ oz. orange juice
½ oz. lemon juice

2 tsp. orgeat or orzata
1 tsp. toasted almond slices

Shake whiskey, orange juice, lemon juice, and orgeat well with ice. Strain into prechilled whiskey-sour glass. Sprinkle almond slices on top. (To toast almonds, place sliced almonds in shallow pan in oven preheated to 350°F. Bake 8 to 10 minutes or until medium brown, stirring occasionally. Sprinkle with salt. Cool.)

IRISH-CANADIAN SANGAREE

1¼ oz. Canadian whisky
½ oz. Irish Mist liqueur
1 tsp. orange juice

1 tsp. lemon juice
Freshly grated nutmeg

Pour whisky, Irish Mist, orange juice, and lemon juice into prechilled old-fashioned glass. Stir. Add ice to rim of glass. Stir. Sprinkle lightly with nutmeg.

IRISH FIX

1 tsp. sugar
2 tsp. water
2 oz. Irish whiskey
½ oz. lemon juice

½ slice orange
½ slice lemon
2 tsp. Irish Mist

Dissolve sugar in 2 tsp. water in an 8-oz. glass. Add whiskey and lemon juice. Fill glass with crushed ice. Stir well. Add more ice to fill glass to rim. Stir. Garnish with orange and lemon slices. Float Irish Mist on top.

IRISH MILK-AND-MAPLE PUNCH

2 oz. blended Irish whiskey
8 oz. milk

1 tbsp. maple syrup
Freshly grated nutmeg

Shake whiskey, milk, and maple syrup very well with ice. Strain into tall 14-oz. glass. Sprinkle with nutmeg.

JACKSON SQUARE

1½ oz. bourbon   Iced club soda
½ oz. peppermint schnapps   Lemon peel
3 dashes Peychaud's bitters

Pour bourbon, peppermint schnapps, and bitters over rocks into old-fashioned glass. Stir. Add soda. Stir. Twist lemon peel over drink and drop into glass.

JAPANESE FIZZ

2¼ oz. blended whiskey   Iced club soda
¾ oz. port   Orange peel
½ oz. lemon juice   1 pineapple stick
1 tsp. sugar

Shake whiskey, port, lemon juice, and sugar well with ice. Strain into tall 14-oz. glass half-filled with ice. Fill glass with soda. Stir. Twist orange peel above drink and drop into glass. Add pineapple stick.

JOCOSE JULEP

2½ oz. bourbon   1 oz. lime juice
½ oz. green crème de menthe   Iced club soda
6 mint leaves   3 tall mint sprigs
1 tsp. sugar

Put into blender, without ice, bourbon, crème de menthe, mint leaves, sugar, and lime juice. Blend 10 to 15 seconds or until mint is very finely chopped. Pour into tall 14-oz. glass half-filled with ice. Add soda. Stir. Insert mint sprigs. *Serve to nearest belle.*

KENTUCKY

1½ oz. 86-proof bourbon   ½ oz. pineapple juice
½ oz. lemon juice   1 tsp. maraschino liqueur

Shake well with ice. Strain into prechilled sugar-frosted cocktail glass.

KERRY COOLER

2 oz. Irish whiskey   1 oz. lemon juice
1½ oz. Madeira or sherry   Iced club soda
1 oz. orgeat   1 slice lemon

Into tall 14-oz. glass, pour whiskey, Madeira, orgeat, and lemon juice. Stir well. Add three large ice cubes. Fill glass with soda. Stir. Float lemon slice on top.

KLONDIKE COOLER

Soda water   Lemon peel
½ tsp. powdered sugar   1 orange spiral (horse's neck)
2 oz. blended whiskey

Put 2 oz. soda water and sugar in tall collins class. Stir well. Add ice, whiskey, and soda water to fill. Stir. Twist lemon peel over drink and drop into glass. Dangle horse's neck over rim.

LADIES' NIGHT

1¾ oz. blended whiskey   2 dashes Angostura bitters
½ tsp. anisette   1 pineapple stick

Stir whiskey, anisette, and bitters well with ice. Strain into prechilled cocktail glass. Garnish with pineapple stick.

LAWHILL

1¼ oz. blended whiskey   ¼ tsp. maraschino liqueur
¾ oz. dry vermouth   ½ oz. orange juice
¼ tsp. Pernod   1 dash Angostura bitters

Shake well with ice. Strain into prechilled cocktail glass. *For a superb cocktail to mix beforehand, strain into a Thermos and tote along on a picnic.*

LEPRECHAUN

2 oz. Irish whiskey   Lemon peel
Tonic water to fill

Pour whiskey over ice into old-fashioned glass. Top off with tonic water. Stir gently. Twist lemon peel over drink and drop into glass. *Simply refreshing.*

LYNCHBURG LEMONADE

2 oz. Jack Daniel's   7-Up to fill
1 oz. lemonade   Lemon slice
½ oz. grenadine

Shake Jack Daniel's, lemonade, and grenadine with ice. Strain over ice into tall collins glass. Top off with 7-Up. Garnish with lemon slice. *Best enjoyed on the patio.*

MANHASSET

1½ oz. blended whiskey   ¼ oz. sweet vermouth
½ oz. lemon juice   Lemon peel
¼ oz. dry vermouth

Shake whiskey, lemon juice, and both kinds of vermouth well with ice. Strain into prechilled cocktail glass. Twist lemon peel above drink and drop into glass.

MANHATTAN

In the national drink derby, two or three cocktail generations ago, the Manhattan and the Martini always wound up in a dead heat. At the present time, the Manhattan occupies the second spot. Manhattanites, though typically less demanding than Martini fans, have nevertheless stirred up many spirited variations on the whiskey-vermouth theme. In public pouring houses, the usual Manhattan is made with 1½ ounces of whiskey. At private bars, a more generous allowance of whiskey is likely. Here's what most Manhattanites expect.

1½ to 2 oz. blended whiskey   1 dash bitters (optional)
½ oz. sweet vermouth   1 maraschino cherry

Stir whiskey, vermouth, and bitters well with ice. Strain into prechilled cocktail glass. Add cherry.

DRY MANHATTAN Use dry instead of sweet vermouth; a twist of lemon peel or an olive may be substituted for the cherry.

BOURBON MANHATTAN Use 86- or 100-proof bourbon instead of blended whiskey; if 100-proof bourbon is used, a little extra stirring is in order.

CANADIAN MANHATTAN Use Canadian instead of U.S. blended whiskey; don't over-stir, or the delicate flavor of the Canadian spirits will become pallid.

MUSCARI MANHATTAN Use Muscari (an aperitif wine) instead of vermouth.

MAY COCKTAIL
1½ oz. blended whiskey   **Chilled May wine to fill**
¼ oz. kirschwasser   **1 slice lemon**
¼ oz. strawberry liqueur

Shake whiskey, kirschwasser, and strawberry liqueur well with ice. Strain into pre-chilled old-fashioned glass with a large ice cube. Fill glass with May wine. Stir. Garnish with lemon slice.

MINT JULEP
12 mint leaves on stem,   **2 tsp. water**
**   plus 6 mint leaves on stem for garnish**   **2½ oz. 86- or 100-proof bourbon**
1 tsp. sugar

Tear 12 mint leaves partially while leaving them on stem. Place in tall 12-oz. glass or silver julep mug with sugar and water. Muddle or stir until sugar is completely dissolved. Fill glass with finely cracked ice. Add bourbon. Stir. Ice will dissolve partially. Add more ice to fill glass to rim, again stirring. Tear 6 mint leaves partially to release aroma, and insert into ice with leaves on top. Serve with or without straw.

MINT JULEP, DRY, PARTY STYLE (Makes 8 drinks)
1 pint finely chopped mint leaves   **8 sprigs mint**
1 quart bourbon

Steep mint leaves in bourbon for 1 hour at room temperature. Fill 8 tall 14-oz. glasses with finely cracked ice. Strain bourbon and pour into glasses, allowing 4 oz. minted bourbon per glass. Stir. Add more ice to fill glass to rim. Tear a few leaves of each of the mint sprigs and fit a sprig into each glass. If your party is late getting started, store prepared juleps in freezer. *A few sips of this unsweetened julep should turn the longest of hot summer days into the coolest.*

MISTY IRISH

1 oz. blended Irish whiskey
½ oz. Irish Mist liqueur
1 oz. orange juice
½ oz. lemon juice

1 tsp. sugar
½ cup crushed ice
1 brandied cherry

Pour whiskey, Irish Mist, orange juice, lemon juice, sugar, and ice into blender. Blend at high speed 10 seconds. Pour into old-fashioned glass. Add ice cubes to fill glass to rim. Add brandied cherry.

MONTE CARLO

1½ oz. bourbon
¾ oz. Benedictine

1 dash Angostura bitters

Stir bourbon, Benedictine, and bitters well with ice. Strain into prechilled cocktail glass.

MORNING FIZZ

2 oz. blended whiskey
½ egg white
½ oz. lemon juice

1 tsp. sugar
½ tsp. Pernod
Iced club soda

Shake whiskey, egg white, lemon juice, sugar, and Pernod well with ice. Strain into tall 8-oz. glass. Add a splash of soda and enough ice to fill glass. Stir.

MORNING GLORY FIZZ

2 oz. Scotch
1 tsp. Pernod
½ oz. lemon juice
1 tsp. sugar

½ egg white
1 dash Peychaud's bitters
Iced club soda
1 slice lemon

Shake Scotch, Pernod, lemon juice, sugar, egg white, and bitters well with ice. Strain into tall 14-oz. glass half-filled with ice. Fill glass with soda. Stir. Add lemon slice. *A drink for the elite of the fizz fraternity.*

NEVINS

1½ oz. bourbon
½ oz. grapefruit juice
¼ oz. apricot liqueur

¼ oz. lemon juice
1 dash Angostura bitters

Shake all ingredients well with ice. Strain into prechilled sugar-frosted cocktail glass.

NEW WORLD

1¾ oz. blended whiskey
½ oz. lime juice

1 tsp. grenadine
Lime peel

Shake whiskey, lime juice, and grenadine well with ice. Strain into prechilled cocktail glass. Twist lime peel over drink and drop into glass. *Drink this one while listening to Dvorák before a midnight supper.*

NEW YORKER

1½ oz. blended whiskey
½ oz. lime juice
1 tsp. sugar

¼ tsp. grenadine
Lemon peel
Orange peel

Shake whiskey, lime juice, sugar, and grenadine well with ice. Strain into prechilled sugar-frosted cocktail glass. Twist lemon peel and orange peel over drink and drop into glass. *A fruity terrace cocktail appreciated equally under sun or stars.*

NEW YORK SOUR

2 oz. blended whiskey
½ oz. lemon juice
1 tsp. sugar

Chilled dry red wine to fill
½ slice lemon

Shake whiskey, lemon juice, and sugar well with ice. Strain into prechilled 6-oz. sour glass. Fill glass with dry red wine. Stir. Garnish with lemon slice. *A miniature punch in a sour glass.*

NIGHT SHADE

1½ oz. bourbon
½ oz. sweet vermouth
½ oz. orange juice

¼ tsp. yellow Chartreuse
½ slice orange
½ slice lemon

Shake bourbon, vermouth, orange juice, and Chartreuse well with ice. Strain over rocks into prechilled old-fashioned glass. Add orange and lemon slices. *Pass freshly fried, generously salted shrimp chips.*

NORTHERN LIGHTS

1 oz. light Canadian whisky
1 oz. aquavit
1 dash Angostura bitters
½ tsp. grenadine

Iced club soda
1 slice lemon
½ slice orange

Pour Canadian whisky, aquavit, bitters, and grenadine into old-fashioned glass three-quarters filled with ice cubes. Stir well. Add splash of soda. Add lemon and orange slices.

OLD-FASHIONED

An Old-Fashioned may be made with U.S. blended whiskey, Canadian, Irish, or Scotch. In smart men's clubs, the words garnish *and* garbage *were once synonymous; orange and lemon slices, cherries, cocktail sticks, etc. were considered female diversions for filling a glass with fruit instead of the cocktail itself. Over the years, this attitude has been somewhat mitigated. Generally, however, most men and women appreciate the Old-Fashioned unencumbered by superfluous fruit.*

½ tsp. sugar
1 or 2 dashes Angostura bitters
1 tsp. water

1½ to 2 oz. blended whiskey
Lemon peel

Stir sugar, bitters, and water in prechilled old-fashioned glass until sugar dissolves. Fill glass with ice cubes or large pieces of cracked ice. Add whiskey. Stir well. Twist lemon peel over drink and drop into glass.

ORIENT EXPRESS

1½ oz. Suntory Old whisky
½ oz. sweet vermouth

½ oz. triple sec
Juice of ½ lime

Shake whisky, vermouth, triple sec, and lime juice with ice. Strain into prechilled cocktail glass and enjoy the scenery.

PALMETTO COOLER

2 oz. bourbon
½ oz. apricot liqueur
½ oz. sweet vermouth

3 dashes Angostura bitters
Iced club soda
Fresh mint

Fill a tall 14-oz. glass with ice cubes. Add bourbon, apricot liqueur, vermouth, and bitters. Stir well. Fill glass almost to top with club soda and stir lightly. Place generous bouquet of mint sprigs in glass. Tear a few leaves to release aroma.

PREAKNESS

1½ oz. blended whiskey
¾ oz. sweet vermouth
½ tsp. Benedictine

1 dash Angostura bitters
Lemon peel

Stir whiskey, vermouth, Benedictine, and bitters well with ice. Strain into prechilled cocktail glass. Twist lemon peel over drink and drop into glass. *We'll meet you at the finish line.*

PRESBYTERIAN

1½ oz. rye whiskey
1½ oz. ginger ale

1½ oz. soda water
Lemon peel (optional)

Pour rye, ginger ale, and soda water over ice into 8- or 10-oz. highball glass. Twist lemon over drink and drop into glass, if desired.

PRINCE EDWARD

1¾ oz. Scotch
½ oz. Lillet

¼ oz. Drambuie
1 slice cocktail orange in syrup

Shake Scotch, Lillet, and Drambuie well with ice. Strain over rocks into prechilled old-fashioned glass. Garnish with orange slice.

QUEBEC

1½ oz. Canadian whisky
¼ oz. Amer Picon

¼ oz. maraschino liqueur
½ oz. dry vermouth

Shake well with ice. Strain into prechilled sugar-frosted cocktail glass.

ROB ROY

1½ to 2 oz. Scotch
½ oz. sweet vermouth

1 dash orange bitters (optional)

Stir well with ice. Strain into prechilled cocktail glass. *The Rob Roy is, of course, simply a Scotch Manhattan, and variations in whisky and vermouth proportions may be made to your own drinking taste. A light rather than a smoky Scotch is preferred by most people. A brandied cherry may be added for a special flourish. For a dry Rob Roy, use dry vermouth; add a twist of lemon if desired.*

ROB ROY, HOLIDAY STYLE

½ tsp. Drambuie
2 oz. Scotch
¼ oz. dry vermouth

¼ oz. sweet vermouth
1 maraschino or brandied cherry

Pour Drambuie into a prechilled cocktail glass and swirl to coat bottom and sides of glass. Stir Scotch and both kinds of vermouth well with ice. Strain into glass. Add cherry.

RUSTY NAIL

¾ oz. Scotch
½ oz. Drambuie

Pour over rocks into prechilled old-fashioned glass. Stir.

SAN FRANCISCO

2 oz. rye whiskey
¼ oz. Benedictine

¾ oz. lemon juice
Lemon slice

Shake whiskey, Benedictine, and lemon juice with cracked ice. Strain into prechilled cocktail glass. Garnish with lemon slice.

SANGAREE COMFORT

1 oz. bourbon
1 oz. Southern Comfort
1 tsp. lemon juice
1 tsp. peach-flavored brandy

½ tsp. sugar
Iced club soda
Freshly grated nutmeg

Stir bourbon, Southern Comfort, lemon juice, peach-flavored brandy, and sugar in prechilled old-fashioned glass. Add ice up to rim of glass. Add splash of soda. Stir. Sprinkle lightly with nutmeg.

SAZERAC

¼ tsp. abisante, anesone,
   or any other absinthe substitute
½ tsp. sugar
¼ tsp. bitters (Peychaud's, if possible)

1 tbsp. water
2 oz. blended whiskey or bourbon
Lemon peel

Swirl abisante around in prechilled old-fashioned glass until inside is completely coated. Add sugar, bitters, and 1 tbsp. water. Stir until sugar is dissolved. Add a large ice cube and whiskey. Stir well. Twist lemon peel over drink and drop into glass. *A New Orleans specialty and a magnificent prebrunch drink.*

SAZERAC À LA PLAYBOY

¼ tsp. Pernod

1 small sugar cube

2 dashes Peychaud's bitters

1 dash Angostura bitters

Water

1½ oz. straight rye

Lemon peel

Pour Pernod into prechilled old-fashioned glass and roll glass until inside is entirely coated. Add sugar, both kinds of bitters, and enough cold water to barely cover sugar. Muddle until sugar is completely dissolved. Add rye and a large ice cube. Stir well. Twist lemon peel over drink and drop into glass.

SCOTCH APPLE

1½ oz. Scotch

½ oz. apple brandy

4 oz. apple juice

½ oz. orange juice

½ oz. lemon juice

Orange peel

Lemon peel

Shake Scotch, apple brandy, apple juice, orange juice, and lemon juice well with ice. Strain into tall 12-oz. glass half-filled with ice cubes. Stir well. Add ice if necessary to fill glass to rim. Twist orange and lemon peels above drink and drop into glass.

SCOTCH BUCK

1 oz. Scotch

½ oz. ginger-flavored brandy

Iced ginger beer or ginger ale

½ medium-size lime

Fill a tall 8-oz. glass with ice cubes. Add Scotch and ginger-flavored brandy. Stir well. Add ginger beer to fill glass. Stir. Squeeze lime above drink and drop into glass.

SCOTCH HOLIDAY SOUR

2 oz. light Scotch

1 oz. cherry liqueur

½ oz. sweet vermouth

1 oz. lemon juice

½ egg white

1 slice lemon

Shake Scotch, cherry liqueur, vermouth, lemon juice, and egg white well with ice. Strain into prechilled oversize sour glass or into prechilled old-fashioned glass with a large rock. Garnish with lemon slice.

SCOTCH HORSE'S NECK

Peel of whole lemon, in one spiral

3 oz. Scotch

½ oz. sweet vermouth

½ oz. dry vermouth

Place lemon peel in tall 14-oz. glass with one end of peel overhanging rim. Add Scotch and both kinds of vermouth. Fill glass with cracked ice. Stir. Add more ice if necessary to fill glass. Every Horse's Neck is improved if it ages about 10 minutes before sipping.

SCOTCH ORANGE FIX

1 tsp. sugar

2 tsp. water

3-inch piece orange peel, in one spiral

2 oz. Scotch

½ oz. lemon juice

1 tsp. curaçao

Dissolve sugar in 2 tsp. water in 8-oz. glass. Place orange peel in glass. Add Scotch and lemon juice. Fill glass with crushed ice. Stir well. Add more ice to fill glass to rim. Stir. Float curaçao on drink.

SCOTCH SANGAREE

½ tsp. honey
Iced club soda
2 oz. Scotch

Lemon peel
Freshly grated nutmeg

Stir honey, 1 tbsp. soda, and Scotch in prechilled old-fashioned glass until honey dissolves. Add ice to rim of glass. Add a splash of soda. Stir. Twist lemon peel above drink and drop into glass. Sprinkle lightly with nutmeg.

SCOTCH SOLACE

2½ oz. Scotch
½ oz. honey
½ oz. triple sec

4 oz. milk
1 oz. heavy cream
⅛ tsp. freshly grated orange rind

Pour Scotch, honey, and triple sec into 14-oz. glass. Stir until honey is thoroughly blended. Add milk, cream, and orange rind. Add ice cubes to fill glass to brim. Stir well. *Cold, creamy, and soothing.*

SEABOARD

1 oz. blended whiskey
1 oz. gin
½ oz. lemon juice

1 tsp. sugar
2 sprigs mint

Shake whiskey, gin, lemon juice, and sugar well with ice. Strain over rocks into prechilled old-fashioned glass. Tear several leaves of each mint sprig before dropping into drink.

7 & 7

1½ oz. Seagram's 7 Crown
3 oz. 7-Up

Pour Seagram's over ice into highball glass. Top off with 7-Up. *Classic.*

SHAMROCK

1½ oz. Irish whiskey
½ oz. dry vermouth

1 tsp. green crème de menthe
1 sprig mint

Stir whiskey, vermouth, and crème de menthe with ice. Strain into prechilled cocktail glass. Garnish with mint sprig for luck.

THE SHOOT

1 oz. Scotch
1 oz. dry sherry
1 tsp. lemon juice

1 tsp. orange juice
½ tsp. sugar

Shake well with ice. Strain into prechilled cocktail glass. *Serve before a dinner of roast pheasant or partridge.*

SINGAPORE

1½ oz. Canadian whisky
½ oz. sloe gin
½ oz. Rose's Lime Juice

½ oz. lemon juice
Cucumber peel

Shake whisky, sloe gin, Rose's Lime Juice, and lemon juice well with ice. Strain over rocks into prechilled old-fashioned glass. Add cucumber peel.

SOUTHERN GINGER

1½ oz. 100-proof bourbon
1 oz. ginger ale
¼ oz. lemon juice

½ tsp. ginger-flavored brandy
Lemon peel

Shake bourbon, ginger ale, lemon juice, and brandy well with ice. Strain into prechilled cocktail glass. Twist lemon peel above drink and drop into glass.

STILETTO

1½ oz. blended whiskey
1½ tsp. amaretto

Juice of ½ lemon

Pour whiskey, amaretto, and lemon juice into old-fashioned glass over ice. Stir.

STONE FENCE

1½ oz. bourbon
Chilled apple juice

Pour bourbon and apple juice over rocks in 10-oz. glass. Stir well. Add ice cubes if necessary to fill glass.

STONYBROOK

1½ oz. blended whiskey
½ oz. triple sec
¼ tsp. orzata

½ egg white
Lemon peel
Orange peel

Shake whiskey, triple sec, orzata, and egg white well with ice. Strain into prechilled cocktail glass. Twist lemon peel and orange peel over drink and drop into glass. *A drink to accompany barquettes of deviled crabmeat.*

ST. PATRICK'S DAY

¾ oz. Irish whiskey
¾ oz. green crème de menthe

¾ oz. green Chartreuse
1 dash Angostura bitters

Stir whiskey, crème de menthe, Chartreuse, and bitters well with ice. Strain into prechilled cocktail glass.

TIPPERARY COCKTAIL

¾ oz. Irish whiskey
¾ oz. sweet vermouth

¾ oz. green Chartreuse

Stir whiskey, vermouth, and Chartreuse well with ice. Strain into prechilled cocktail glass.

TORONTO

2 oz. Canadian whisky
¾ oz. Fernet Branca
1 tsp. sugar syrup

1 dash Angostura
bitters

Shake whisky, Fernet Branca, sugar syrup, and bitters well with ice. Strain into prechilled cocktail glass.

TROIS RIVIERS

1½ oz. Canadian whisky
½ oz. red Dubonnet

¼ oz. Cointreau
Orange peel

Shake whisky, Dubonnet, and Cointreau well with ice. Strain into prechilled cocktail glass. Twist orange peel over drink and drop into glass. *Perfect before a midnight collation.*

TWIN HILLS

2 oz. blended whiskey
¼ oz. lemon juice
¼ oz. lime juice
2 tsp. Benedictine

1 tsp. sugar
½ slice lemon
½ slice lime

Shake whiskey, lemon juice, lime juice, Benedictine, and sugar well with ice. Strain into prechilled whiskey-sour glass. Garnish with lemon and lime slices. *An offbeat but very superior sour.*

WARD EIGHT

2 oz. blended U.S. whiskey
  or Canadian whisky
½ oz. lemon juice

1 tsp. sugar
½ tsp. grenadine
1 slice lemon

Shake whiskey, lemon juice, sugar, and grenadine well with ice. Strain into tall 8-oz. glass. Add cracked ice or ice slices to fill glass. Stir. Garnish with lemon slice. *A pleasant tall cocktail that survived Prohibition.*

WHISKEY COBBLER

2½ oz. blended whiskey
¾ oz. lemon juice
½ oz. grapefruit juice

1½ tsp. orgeat or orzata
½ slice orange
1 slice fresh or brandied peach

Fill 12-oz. glass with finely cracked ice. Add whiskey, lemon juice, grapefruit juice, and orgeat. Stir well. Add more ice to fill glass to rim. Stir. Garnish with orange and peach slices.

WHISKEY CURAÇAO FIZZ

2 oz. blended whiskey
½ oz. curaçao
1 tsp. sugar

1 oz. lemon juice
Iced club soda
½ slice orange

Shake whiskey, curaçao, sugar, and lemon juice well with ice. Strain into tall 14-oz. glass half-filled with ice. Fill glass with soda. Stir. Add orange slice.

WHISKEY DAISY

1½ oz. blended whiskey
1 tsp. red-currant syrup
½ oz. lemon juice

Iced club soda
1 tsp. yellow Chartreuse
1 slice lemon

Shake whiskey, red-currant syrup, and lemon juice well with ice. Strain into tall 8-oz. glass half-filled with ice. Add club soda. Stir. Float Chartreuse on drink. Add lemon slice.

WHISKEY MAC

1½ oz. Scotch whisky
1½ oz. Stone's ginger wine

Pour whisky and ginger wine over rocks into 8-oz. glass. Stir. *In Scotland this drink is usually served at room temperature without ice. Americans prefer the chilled version. May also be served with a lemon twist.*

WHISKEY OUZO FIX

1 tsp. sugar
2 tsp. water
2 oz. blended whiskey

½ oz. lemon juice
1 tsp. ouzo
Lemon peel

Dissolve sugar in 2 tsp. water in 8-oz. glass. Add whiskey and lemon juice. Fill glass with crushed ice. Stir well. Add more ice to fill glass to rim. Stir. Float ouzo on top of drink. Twist lemon peel above drink and drop into glass.

WHISKEY RICKEY

1½ oz. blended whiskey
3 oz. soda water

1 lime wedge

Pour whiskey and soda water into highball glass over ice. Squeeze lime wedge over drink and drop into glass.

WHISKEY SOUR

2 oz. blended whiskey
¾ oz. lemon juice
1 tsp. sugar

½ slice lemon
1 maraschino cherry (optional)

Shake whiskey, lemon juice, and sugar well with ice. Strain into prechilled whiskey-sour glass. Garnish with lemon slice and cherry if desired. For a more tart drink, reduce amount of sugar. For a mellower Whiskey Sour, use ½ oz. lemon juice and ¼ oz. orange juice. Sours made with Canadian or Scotch whiskies are pleasing variants.

WHISKEY TODDY, COLD

½ tsp. sugar
2 tsp. water

2 oz. bourbon or blended whiskey
Lemon peel (optional)

Put sugar and water into prechilled old-fashioned glass. Stir until sugar dissolves. Fill glass with ice cubes or large pieces of cracked ice. Add whiskey. Stir well. Twist lemon peel over drink and drop into glass if desired. Must be stinging cold.

CHAPTER 10

* Tequila *

Visitors to Mexico in the 1950s and 1960s described the native hard liquor as somewhat akin to rattlesnake venom with an aftertaste carrying the impact of a thousand blackjacks. There was a measure of truth in what they said. Then, as now, you could go into rough village bars and order what was supposed to be tequila. In many cases it wasn't the tequila made by well-known Mexican distillers but a version turned out by local moonshiners. The powerful white funwater was unaged and uncut, tossed down just as it trickled out of the still. It was instant machismo at the highest possible proof, and gringos naturally associated it with the flavors of Mexican chilies and their explosive effects on the taste buds. Of course at that time Margarita was just a girl's name rather than a mixture of tequila, triple sec, and lime juice.

The tequila now flowing to the United States, much of it aged and most of it bottled at 80 proof (the lowest proof allowed under U.S. federal regulations), bears no more resemblance to the legendary Mexican tarantula juice than Grand Champagne Cognac bears to Prohibition's bathtub gin. Tequila's flavor is derived from a special agave plant grown in a delimited area about a hundred miles in circumference around the town of Tequila, near Guadalajara. The Mexican government keeps a tight hand on the type of plant used and, its harvesting, distillation, and labeling, just as the French government calls the signals on the brandy distilled and aged in or near the town of Cognac in the Charente.

First of all, one should clear up the little semantic matter of the words used to identify Mexico's hard liquor and the desert plant with long sharp leaves from which the liquor is made. Spanish explorers from Columbus on called the plant *maguey*. Later, the Swedish botanist Linnaeus called it *agave*, and this is the word that Statesiders and many Mexicans now use. The liquor derived from the plant is called tequila only if the plant is a certain blue species known as *Agave azul* that flourishes in the special soil and climate near the town of Tequila. If the liquor is made from any other species growing in other parts of Mexico, it is called mescal.

For centuries, Mexicans have tapped the growing agave in the field, and have used the sweet juice to make a beerlike beverage called pulque. Pulque is *not* the base used for distilling tequila, and because the beverage is not suitable for shipping, it's not sold outside of its native habitat.

It takes between eight and twelve years for the agave to ripen to the stage at which it's ready for distillation. But don't worry about the farmers who grow it; in between the wide-spaced rows of agave, they grow corn, alfalfa, and other annual crops while waiting for the agave to reach adulthood. When the plant is ripe, the leaves are lopped off, and the core, looking like a monster pineapple and weighing anywhere from 80 to 400 pounds (36–182kg), is separated from the plant and carried from the fields to the distillery. There it's steam-cooked for nearly three days until the woody pulp tastes something like a sweet potato: its starch has been turned to sugar. To convert the sugar to alcohol, the pulp is chopped and pressed for its juice, which is then mixed with yeast and fermented. Finally it is pot-stilled twice and drawn off at a proof slightly above 100.

What isn't widely known in the States is the fact that most of the tequila we drink nowadays is actually a distillate of two principal ingredients. The first, naturally, is the agave plant, which comprises about 55 percent of the blend. The remaining 45 percent is a distillate of sugar, or what's normally considered a rum base, with an almost neutral flavor. One brand, Herradura, is made from 100 percent agave. The best tequilas, like many whiskeys and vodkas, are now charcoal-filtered, providing additional sauvity. Finally, tequilas coming to the States are now aged anywhere from several months to four years, and this adds to their civilized mellowness.

For most mixed drinks, you'll undoubtedly use the standard white tequila. But if you take tequila straight or on the rocks, you'll probably enjoy the older tequilas, often bearing the word *añejo* on the label and distinguished by their gold color. José Cuervo, for instance, the best-selling tequila in the United States, turns out not only the standard white tequila but also one called gold, aged a year in wood. Its most expensive, designated 1800, is aged three to four years in oak barrels. It's a silky-smooth tequila that one could proudly offer after dinner in a brandy snifter.

Gringos are somewhat startled by some brands of mescal with a fat dead worm at the bottom of the bottle. This isn't just a display of Mexican machismo; rather, it is intended as a symbol of authenticity because the worm—called the *gusano de maguey*—normally grows in the plant, and in Mexico it has a certain fame as a food delicacy, with a seafoodlike flavor akin to snails. The *gusano* doesn't alter the flavor of the mescal; rather, the mescal tunes up the flavor of the *gusano*, according to *gusano* gourmets. At a party, the pickled *gusano* is a showstopper whenever Margaritas or Brave Bulls are being poured.

Though much of it is golden in color, tequila is still listed by many as being in the "white goods" category. But there's no identity crisis whatsoever as far as the flavor of tequila is concerned. Some drinkers, in the futile game of trying to describe it, see in it a resemblance to Dutch genever gin. To others the flavor is somewhat reminiscent of freshly ground peppercorns, and to still others there's a reminder of salt and perhaps sugar. Actually, like any distinguished liquor, tequila asserts its own individuality, and it can't and shouldn't be shoved into a simple descriptive slot. It's one of those acquired tastes, and it not only stands up extremely well but also keeps drawing more and more converts, as tequila sales continue to rise.

Indeed, if tequila sales continue to soar at the present rate, the restricted zone around the town of Tequila may not be able to appease the expanding thirst of tequila drinkers in both Mexico and elsewhere. To meet future needs, the Mexican government has given permission to grow the blue agave in another state, Tamaulipas, where the special climate and soil seem congenial to its healthy growth.

Although tequila has come into wide use as a cocktail base north of the Rio Grande, Mexicans and other tequila purists still toss it down using their famed here's-blowing-the-lid routine. Before hoisting the glass, the aficionado tilts his head back; squints in the direction of the camera, the spotlights, or the sun; and squeezes the freshest lime he can find directly into his mouth—and sometimes actually eats part of the lime. Then he swallows his straight tequila in a lightning chugalug, and finally laps up a dab of salt already placed in the soft fleshy hollow between thumb and first finger. Sometimes the order is reversed, with the salt first and the lime last. But however the ritual is performed, all he's actually bolted down is a straight jigger of liquor with less potency than an American Boilermaker (a shot of whiskey dropped into or followed by beer). As much fun as it is to indulge in such drinking histrionics, tequila is equally enjoyable without lime, salt, or dramatics, served either icy cold or at room temperature, sipped and rolled about in the mouth as though you were tasting a fine bourbon or Scotch.

When Christopher Columbus wrote about the native Mexican drink made from the "marrow of the maguey," he may have been referring to pulque—the fermented juice of the maguey, or the distilled beverage we now know as tequila. Quibblers may argue that the art of distillation was introduced to the New World from the Old, but scholars of potable spirits aren't so sure; some believe that the Mexican Indians may indeed have discovered distillation independently. If they did, tequila was undoubtedly the weapon they used to conquer their Spanish conquerors. As early as the 1700s, Mexicans, in the true spirit of imaginative bartenders, were not only drinking their spirits straight but making countless mixed drinks, including a mixture of mescal, lemon juice, cloves, and nutmeg; another of mescal stirred with honey; and a third of mescal and the juice of the prickly pear.

Today, tequila's camaraderie with anything from tomato juice to tonic water makes it a wonderful prop for imaginative hosts who like to offer their guests Bloody Marias instead of Marys and Tequila instead of Tom Collinses. The best-known mixed drink, the Margarita, sometimes miscarries because of the heavy rim of salt around the glass in which it's served. Actually, salt and tequila are a wonderful compound, just as a light spray of salt on grapefruit or a pinch of salt in hot chocolate acts as a natural flavor pick-me-up. But too much salt is *muy malo*. A sensible way to offer the Margarita is to rub about an inch of the rim of a prechilled cocktail glass with lemon or orange peel and dip that inch in salt. Then make your Margarita, and let the drinker take or leave the salt. Or omit the salt entirely from the glass and offer a small open saltcellar with the drink, permitting the guest to sprinkle as much or as little as desired directly into the glass.

Travelers in Mexico are often introduced to *sangrita*. It's sold as a liquid mix in bottles and looks like the tomato-juice mix for a Bloody Mary. Generally, there's no tomato juice in it—the principal ingredient is orange juice, sweetened and colored red with grenadine, and made piquant with assorted spices, including the hottest Mexican chili peppers. Tequila veterans in Mexico order their tequila straight with a glass of sangrita on the side, and then toss down the sangrita and tequila in alternate gulps. In many Mexican homes, however, a fresh sangrita is made that does include tomato juice, as well as orange juice, onion, and spices. (See the version on page 175.) It joins hands beautifully with tequila taken straight and is delightful with many mixed drinks, one of the most popular of which is the Vampiro, a tall drink of tequila, sangrita, and grapefruit juice (see page 180).

As a mixer in short, medium, or tall drinks, tequila has sumptuous possibilities. Whatever associations the taste of the tequila brings to you and however you choose to drink it, the pleasant afterglow is always *muy* simpatico.

TEQUILA COCKTAILS

ACAPULCO ZOMBIE

1½ oz. tequila
1½ oz. vodka
1½ oz. rum

2 oz. orange juice
2 oz. grapefruit juice
1 dash white crème de menthe

Shake tequila, vodka, rum, and juices well with ice. Strain over rocks into 10-oz. high-ball glass. Top off with dash crème de menthe. Stir gently. *Almost too good to be true.*

ALAMO SPLASH

1½ oz. tequila	½ oz. pineapple juice
1 oz. orange juice	1 splash lemon-lime soda

Stir tequila and juices well with cracked ice. Strain over ice into tall collins glass. Top off with soda splash. *You can forget the beach when you've got the Alamo.*

APRICOT AND TEQUILA SOUR

1½ oz. tequila	½ oz. lemon juice
¾ oz. apricot liqueur	

Shake well with ice. Strain into cocktail glass or over rocks into 8-oz. glass.

ARIZONA SUNRISE

1½ oz. tequila	1 splash grenadine
½ oz. Rose's Lime Juice	1 orange slice
4 oz. orange juice	1 maraschino cherry

Shake tequila, Rose's Lime Juice, and orange juice well with ice. Splash grenadine over ice into 8-oz. highball glass and allow to settle. Strain shaker contents over grenadine. Garnish with orange slice on rim and drop in cherry. *Delightful to sip and pretty to look at.*

ARIZONA SUNSET

1½ oz. tequila	1 splash crème de noyaux
1 oz. triple sec	1 orange slice
½ oz. Rose's Lime Juice	1 lime slice
4 oz. orange juice	

Shake tequila, triple sec, Rose's Lime Juice, and orange juice well with ice. Splash crème de noyaux over ice into 8-oz. highball glass and allow to settle. Strain shaker contents over crème de noyaux. Garnish with orange and lime slices. *A wonderful way to end a day.*

BLOODY MARIA

1½ oz. tequila	1 dash Tabasco sauce
2 oz. ice cold tomato juice	1 dash celery salt
1 tsp. lemon juice	1 slice lemon

Pour tequila, tomato juice, lemon juice, Tabasco, and celery salt into prechilled old-fashioned glass. Add rocks or ice slices to fill glass. Stir very well. Add lemon slice. *Viva Maria!*

BLUE MARGARITA

1½ oz. tequila	1 lime wedge
1 oz. blue curaçao	Coarse salt to taste
1 oz. lime juice	

Shake tequila, blue curaçao, and lime juice well with ice. Rub outside rim of deep-saucer champagne glass with juice from lime wedge. Dip outside rim in salt. Strain shaker contents over ice into salt-rimmed glass.

BORDER CROSSING

1½ oz. tequila
½ oz. cranberry liqueur
½ oz. lime juice
1 tsp. sugar
1 slice lime

Shake tequila, cranberry liqueur, lime juice, and sugar well with ice. Strain over rocks into 8-oz. highball glass. Add lime slice.

BRAVE BULL

1 oz. tequila
1 oz. Kahlua
1 piece lemon peel

Pour tequila and Kahlua over rocks into old-fashioned glass. Stir well. Add ice if necessary to fill glass. Twist lemon peel over drink and drop into glass.

BUNNY BONANZA

1½ oz. tequila
1 oz. apple brandy
½ oz. lemon juice
1 tsp. sugar
½ tsp. curaçao
1 slice lemon

Shake tequila, apple brandy, lemon juice, sugar, and curaçao well with ice. Strain into prechilled old-fashioned glass. Add ice to fill glass. Garnish with lemon slice.

BUTTAFUOCO

2 oz. tequila
½ oz. Galliano
½ oz. cherry liqueur
½ oz. lemon juice
Club soda to fill
1 maraschino cherry

Shake tequila, Galliano, cherry liqueur, and lemon juice well with cracked ice. Strain into 8-oz. highball glass over ice. Top off with club soda. Stir. Garnish with cherry. *Fuhgeddaboutit!*

CABALLO

6 oz. ice cold grapefruit juice
1½ oz. tequila
1 oz. amaretto

Pour into tall 14-oz. glass three-quarters filled with ice cubes. Stir well. Add ice cubes if necessary to fill glass to rim. Stir.

CACTUS JUICE

2 oz. tequila
2 oz. lemon juice
2 tsp. triple sec
2 tsp. Drambuie
½ tsp. superfine sugar
1 dash Angostura bitters

Shake well with ice. Strain into prechilled cocktail glass.

CADILLAC MARGARITA

2 oz. tequila (Sauza)
¾ oz. Grand Marnier
1¼ oz Rose's Lime Juice
1 lime wedge
Salt to taste
1 lime slice

Shake tequila, Grand Marnier, and Rose's Lime Juice well with ice. Rub outside rim of deep-saucer champagne glass with lime wedge and dip in salt. Strain contents of shaker into salt-rimmed glass. Garnish with lime slice.

CALIFORNIA DREAMING

2 oz. tequila
1 oz. sweet vermouth
½ oz. dry vermouth
1 maraschino cherry

Stir well with ice. Strain into prechilled cocktail glass. Garnish with cherry. *Feel the glow.*

CHAPALA

1½ oz. tequila
½ oz. orange juice
½ oz. lemon juice
1 dash orange flower water
2 tsp. grenadine
1 slice orange

Shake tequila, orange juice, lemon juice, orange flower water, and grenadine well with ice. Strain over rocks in prechilled old-fashioned glass. Add orange slice.

CHICO

1 oz. tequila
1 oz. blackberry-flavored brandy
½ oz. lemon juice
1 tsp. sugar
Iced club soda
1 slice lemon

Shake tequila, blackberry-flavored brandy, lemon juice, and sugar well with ice. Strain into tall 14-oz. glass half-filled with ice cubes. Add club soda to fill glass. Stir. Add lemon slice.

CHIHUAHUA

1½ oz. tequila
3 oz. grapefruit juice

Pour tequila over ice into cocktail glass. Top off with grapefruit juice. *More bite than a Greyhound.*

CINCO DE MAYO

2½ oz. añejo tequila
1 oz. Rose's Lime Juice
1 splash grenadine

Shake well with lots of ice. Strain into prechilled cocktail glass. *Muy bueno!*

COCONUT TEQUILA

1½ oz. tequila
½ oz. lemon juice
1 tsp. maraschino liqueur
½ cup crushed ice

Put all ingredients into blender. Blend 20 seconds at low speed. Pour into prechilled deep-saucer champagne glass. *Perfect before a Polynesian brunch.*

COMPADRE

1½ oz. tequila
1 tsp. grenadine
½ tsp. maraschino liqueur
2 dashes orange bitters

Stir tequila, grenadine, liqueur, and orange bitters well with ice. Strain into prechilled cocktail glass. *Makes friends wherever it's poured.*

CUERNAVACA COLLINS

1 oz. tequila
1 oz. gin
1 oz. lime juice

2 tsp. sugar
Iced club soda
1 slice lime

Shake tequila, gin, lime juice, and sugar well with ice. Strain into tall 14-oz. glass half-filled with ice cubes. Add soda to fill glass. Stir lightly. Add lime slice.

FREDDY FUDPUCKER

2 oz. tequila
4 oz. orange juice

1 slice lime

Pour tequila and orange juice over ice into 8-oz. highball glass. Pour Galliano slowly over inverted spoon to float on top of drink.

FROZEN BLACKBERRY TEQUILA

1½ oz. tequila
1 oz. blackberry liqueur
½ oz. lemon juice

⅓ cup crushed ice
1 slice lemon

Put tequila, blackberry liqueur, lemon juice, and crushed ice into blender. Blend 10 to 15 seconds at low speed. Pour into prechilled old-fashioned glass. Add rocks to fill glass. Add lemon slice.

FROZEN MATADOR

1½ oz. tequila
2 oz. pineapple juice
½ oz. lime juice

⅓ cup crushed ice
1 pineapple stick

Put tequila, pineapple juice, lime juice, and crushed ice into blender. Blend at low speed 10 to 15 seconds. Pour into prechilled deep-saucer champagne glass. Add pineapple stick. Or pour over rocks into old-fashioned glass; add ice cubes to fill glass; garnish with pineapple stick.

FROZEN SUNSET

1½ oz. tequila
½ oz. lime juice
½ oz. grenadine

½ cup crushed ice
1 slice lime

Put tequila, lime juice, grenadine, and crushed ice into blender. Blend at low speed 10 to 15 seconds. Pour into prechilled old-fashioned glass. Add ice slices or cubes to fill glass. Garnish with lime slice.

GRINGO

1½ oz. tequila
4 oz. Clamato juice
1 tsp. ketchup
1 tsp. lemon juice

½ tsp. horseradish
Tabasco sauce
Worcestershire sauce
Freshly ground black pepper

Pour tequila, Clamato, ketchup, lemon juice, and horseradish into cocktail shaker. Add a dash or two each of Tabasco and Worcestershire. Shake very well with ice. Strain into old-fashioned glass. Sprinkle with ground black pepper.

HOT PANTS

1½ oz. tequila   1 tbsp. grapefruit juice
½ oz. peppermint schnapps   1 tsp. powdered sugar

Shake well with ice. Strain into prechilled old-fashioned glass. (Salt rim optional.)

JACK BLACK MARGARITA

1½ oz. tequila   4 oz. lime juice
½ oz. triple sec   1 lime slice
½ oz. Chambord raspberry liqueur

Shake well with ice. Strain into 8-oz. highball glass over cracked ice. Garnish with lime slice. *Pucker up!*

MARGARITA

1½ oz. tequila   ½ oz. lemon or lime juice
½ oz. Cointreau, triple sec, or curaçao

Shake well with ice. Strain into prechilled salt-rimmed cocktail glass. To prepare glass, rub rim with outside of lemon peel; then dip into salt and shake off excess. Although traditionally the glass for a Margarita is salt-rimmed, it may also be sugar-rimmed. A twist of lime or lemon peel may be added if desired.

MARGARITAVILLE

2 oz. gold tequila (Cuervo 1800)   ½ oz. triple sec
½ oz. tequila (Cuervo white)   1 splash orange curaçao
1¼ oz. Rose's Lime Juice   3 lime wedges

Shake tequilas, Rose's Lime Juice, triple sec, curaçao, and juice squeezed from 2 lime wedges well with ice. Rub outside rim of deep-saucer champagne glass with juice from squeezed lime wedge. Salt only rim outside of glass. Strain shaker contents over cracked ice into glass. Squeeze juice from remaining lime wedge into glass. Can be made in similar fashion using a blender, perhaps the frozen version that songwriter and Margarita aficionado Jimmy Buffet might prefer.

MEXICANA

1½ oz. tequila   1 tbsp. pineapple juice
1 oz. lemon juice   1 tsp. grenadine

Shake well with ice. Strain into prechilled cocktail glass.

MEXICAN CLOVER CLUB

1½ oz. tequila   ½ oz. heavy sweet cream
¾ oz. lemon juice   ½ slightly beaten egg white

½ oz. grenadine

Shake all ingredients extremely very well with ice. Strain into prechilled cocktail glass.

MEXICAN CONNECTION

1 oz. Amer Picon   **Chilled orange juice**
1 oz. tequila

Place two large ice cubes in 8-oz. glass. Add Amer Picon and tequila. Stir well. Add orange juice to fill glass. Stir.

MEXICAN MADRAS

1 oz. gold tequila   **1 dash lime juice**
3 oz. cranberry juice   **1 orange slice**
½ oz. fresh orange juice

Shake well with ice. Strain into prechilled old-fashioned glass. Garnish with orange slice.

MEXICAN MILK PUNCH

1 oz. tequila   **1 small egg**
1 oz. dark rum   **2 tsp. sugar**
4 oz. milk   **Freshly ground nutmeg**
1 oz. heavy cream

Shake all ingredients except nutmeg extremely well with ice. Strain into tall 12-oz. glass. Sprinkle with nutmeg.

MEXICAN MULE

1½ oz. tequila   **½ lime**
Iced ginger beer

Place three large ice cubes in tall 12-oz. glass or 12-oz. mug. Add tequila. Fill glass with ginger beer. Stir. Squeeze lime over drink and drop into glass.

MEXICO PACIFICO

1½ oz. tequila   **⅓ cup crushed ice**
½ oz. lime juice   **1 slice lime**
1 oz. passion fruit syrup

Put tequila, lime juice, passion fruit syrup, and crushed ice into blender. Blend 10 to 15 seconds at low speed. Pour into prechilled deep-saucer champagne glass. Add lime slice. *Exotico!*

MIA VIDA

1 oz. tequila   **½ oz. heavy cream**
½ oz. Kahlua   **Chocolate bar, semisweet**
½ oz. crème de cacao

Shake tequila, Kahlua, crème de cacao, and cream well with ice. Strain into prechilled large cocktail glass. Grate chocolate over large holes of metal grater and sprinkle on drink.

MINT TEQUILA

1½ oz. tequila
6 large mint leaves
½ oz. lemon juice

1 tsp. sugar
½ cup crushed ice

Blend all ingredients at low speed for 15 to 20 seconds. Pour into prechilled old-fashioned glass. Add a rock or two to fill glass to rim. *Lively and minty.*

MONTEZUMA

1½ oz. tequila
1 oz. Madeira

1 egg yolk
½ cup crushed ice

Blend all ingredients at low speed for 10 to 15 seconds. Pour into prechilled champagne flute.

NORTE AMERICANO

1½ oz. tequila
½ oz. very dry sherry
   (manzanilla if possible)

Olive or lemon peel

Stir tequila and sherry very well with ice. Strain into prechilled cocktail glass or over rocks. Add olive, or twist lemon peel over drink and drop into glass.

NUENAS TARDES

1½ oz. tequila
5 oz. chilled apple juice

1 oz. lemon juice
1 slice lemon

Pour tequila, apple juice, and lemon juice into tall 12-oz. glass. Add ice cubes to fill glass. Stir well. Add lemon slice.

NUMERO UNO

1 oz. tequila
1 oz. amaretto

1 oz. heavy cream
Ground cinnamon

Shake well with ice. Strain into large cocktail glass. Sprinkle with cinnamon.

PETROLEO

1½ oz. tequila
½ oz. lemon juice

½ tsp. Maggi sauce
1 slice lemon

Shake tequila, lemon juice, and Maggi sauce well with ice. Strain over rocks in old-fashioned glass. Stir well. Add lemon slice.

PINK TEQUILA

1½ oz. tequila
1 oz. dry vermouth

1 dash grenadine

Shake well with ice. Strain into prechilled cocktail glass.

PRADO

1½ oz. tequila
¾ oz. lime juice
½ egg white
½ oz. maraschino liqueur

1 tsp. grenadine
½ slice lemon
1 maraschino cherry

Shake tequila, lime juice, egg white, maraschino liqueur, and grenadine well with ice. Strain into prechilled whiskey-sour glass. Add lemon slice and cherry.

RANCHO CONTENTO

1½ oz. tequila
4 oz. orange juice
¼ oz. dry vermouth

¼ oz. sweet vermouth
1 slice orange

Shake tequila, orange juice, and both kinds of vermouth well with ice. Strain into 10-oz. glass. Add two large ice cubes and orange slice.

ROSITA

1 oz. tequila
½ oz. dry vermouth
½ oz. sweet vermouth

1 oz. Campari
Lemon peel

Stir well with ice. Strain into old-fashioned glass over cracked ice. Twist lemon peel above drink and drop into glass. *Bittersweet heaven.*

SANGRITA (Makes 2¼ cups)

12 oz. tomato juice
4 oz. orange juice
2 oz. lime juice

2 tbsp. diced onion
¼ tsp. salt
1 small hot chili pepper

Blend all ingredients at high speed for 10 seconds. Chill several hours and stir well before serving. Sangrita is a Mexican nonalcoholic drink that is served with tequila, each in a separate glass; guests sip sangrita and tequila alternately. To make a Bloody Mary–type drink, combine 4 oz. sangrita and a jigger of tequila, shake well, and serve on rocks.

SANTA FE

1½ oz. tequila (Cuervo or Sauza)
½ oz. triple sec

7-Up to fill
1 lime wedge

Pour tequila and triple sec over ice into highball glass. Top off with 7-Up. Garnish with lime wedge. *Southwest smooth.*

SEÑOR STINGER

1½ oz. tequila
¾ oz. peppermint schnapps

Shake extremely well with ice. Strain into prechilled cocktail glass. Serve glass of ice water on the side, or pour Stinger over cracked ice in deep-saucer champagne glass. For a somewhat sweeter drink, use white crème de menthe instead of peppermint schnapps.

SEX IN THE DESERT

1 oz. tequila
1 oz. triple sec
1 oz. grenadine
½ oz. Rose's Lime Juice
½ oz. cranberry juice (or cocktail)

Shake well with ice. Strain into prechilled cocktail glass. *Sunscreen definitely not optional.*

SILK STOCKINGS

1½ oz. tequila
1½ oz. light cream
1 oz. crème de cacao
1 dash grenadine
1 dash cinnamon

Shake tequila, light cream, crème de cacao, and grenadine very well with ice. Strain into prechilled cocktail glass. Sprinkle with cinnamon. *Sweet and smooth as, well, silk.*

SLOE TEQUILA

1 oz. tequila
½ oz. sloe gin
½ oz. lime juice
½ cup crushed ice
Cucumber peel

Put tequila, sloe gin, lime juice, and ice into blender. Blend 10 to 15 seconds at low speed. Pour into prechilled old-fashioned glass. Add cucumber peel and fill glass with cubed or cracked ice.

SOUTH OF THE BORDER

1½ oz. tequila
¾ oz. Tìa Maria
Juice of ½ lime
1 lime slice

Shake well with ice. Strain into prechilled sour glass. Garnish with lime slice.

STRAWBERRY MARGARITA

1 oz. tequila
½ oz. strawberry schnapps
½ oz. triple sec
1 oz. lemon juice
1 lemon wedge
Sugar
Fresh strawberries

Shake tequila, schnapps, triple sec, and lemon juice well with ice. Rub outside rim of deep-saucer champagne glass with lemon wedge and dip rim in sugar. Strain contents of shaker into sugar-rimmed glass. Garnish with fresh strawberries. *Sweet and sassy.*

SUNRISE

1½ oz. tequila
½ oz. lime juice
4 oz. chilled orange juice
1 tsp. grenadine
Lime wedge

Pour tequila, lime juice, and orange juice over rocks in squat or tall 8-oz. glass. There should be enough rocks to fill glass to rim. Stir well. Pour grenadine on top and let guest stir Sunrise, or stir grenadine with other ingredients before serving. Fasten wedge of lime to glass. Grenadine up to ½ oz. (3 tsp.) may be used, but drink tends to become cloying. Slice of lime may be used instead of wedge. Crème de cassis may be used in place of grenadine.

SUNRISE ANISE

1½ oz. tequila
½ oz. anise

4 oz. chilled orange juice
1 tsp. grenadine

Pour tequila, anise, and orange juice over rocks in 8-oz. glass. Stir well. Pour grenadine on top and let guests stir it when served. For a somewhat snappier Sunrise, use Pernod instead of anise.

TALL MARGARITA

1½ oz. tequila
½ oz. Cointreau or triple sec
¾ oz. lemon juice

Iced bitter lemon
1 slice lemon

Shake tequila, Cointreau, and lemon juice well with ice. Strain into 12-oz. glass three-quarters filled with ice cubes. Fill glass with bitter lemon. Stir. Add lemon slice. *This drink has legs.*

TALL SUNRISE

2 oz. tequila
½ oz. lime juice
½ oz. curaçao

1 tsp. crème de cassis
Iced club soda
1 slice lime

Shake tequila, lime juice, curaçao, and crème de cassis well with ice. Strain into tall 14-oz. glass half-filled with ice. Fill glass with soda. Stir. Garnish with lime slice. *One to contemplate while waiting for the hot chili.*

TEQUILA CANYON

1½ oz. tequila
½ oz. triple sec
4 oz. cranberry juice

½ oz. pineapple juice
½ oz. orange juice
1 pineapple stick

Pour tequila, triple sec, and cranberry juice over ice into collins glass. Stir. Top off with pineapple and orange juices. Garnish with pineapple stick.

TEQUILA COOLER

1½ oz. tequila
2 oz. Stone's ginger wine
2 oz. orange juice
½ oz. lime juice

Iced tonic water
1 slice lime
½ slice orange

Pour tequila, ginger wine, orange juice, and lime juice into tall 14-oz. glass three-quarters filled with ice cubes. Stir very well. Add tonic water to fill glass. Add lime and orange slices.

TEQUILA DUBONNET

1 oz. tequila
1 oz. red Dubonnet

1 slice lemon

Pour tequila and Dubonnet into prechilled old-fashioned glass. Add cubed or cracked ice to fill glass. Stir. Garnish with lemon slice.

TEQUILA FIZZ

2 oz. tequila
1½ oz. lemon juice
2 tsp. sugar
2 dashes Angostura bitters

1 small egg
Iced club soda
Salt

Shake tequila, lemon juice, sugar, bitters, and egg well with ice. Strain into tall 14-oz. glass half-filled with ice. Fill glass with soda. Stir. Sprinkle very lightly with salt.

TEQUILA FRESA

1½ oz. tequila
¾ oz. strawberry liqueur
½ oz. lime juice

½ tsp. orange bitters
1 slice lime
1 fresh strawberry

Shake tequila, strawberry liqueur, lime juice, and bitters well with ice. Strain over rocks in old-fashioned glass. Add lime slice and strawberry.

TEQUILA FROZEN SCREWDRIVER

1½ oz. tequila
3 oz. iced orange juice

⅓ cup crushed ice
1 slice orange

Put tequila, orange juice, and crushed ice into blender. Blend at low speed for 10 to 15 seconds. Pour into prechilled old-fashioned glass. Add orange slice.

TEQUILA GIMLET

2 oz. tequila
1 oz. lemon juice

½ oz. Rose's Lime Juice

Shake well with ice. Strain into prechilled cocktail glass.

TEQUILA GUAYABA

1½ oz. tequila
½ oz. guava syrup
½ oz. orange juice

½ oz. lime juice
Orange peel

Shake tequila, guava syrup, orange juice, and lime juice well with ice. Pour into prechilled old-fashioned glass. Add a rock or two to fill glass. Twist orange peel above drink and drop into glass. *Pass the guacamole.*

TEQUILA MANHATTAN

2 oz. tequila
1 oz. sweet vermouth
1 dash Rose's Lime Juice

1 slice orange
1 cherry

Shake tequila, vermouth, and Rose's Lime Juice well with ice. Strain over ice into old-fashioned glass. Garnish with orange slice and cherry.

TEQUILA MIEL

1½ oz. tequila
½ oz. honey liqueur

4 oz. grapefruit juice

Shake well with ice. Strain over rocks in squat or tall 10-oz. glass.

TEQUILA OLD-FASHIONED

½ tsp. sugar
2 dashes Angostura bitters
1 tsp. water
1½ oz. tequila

Iced club soda
Lemon peel
1 pineapple stick

Stir sugar, bitters, and water in prechilled old-fashioned glass until sugar is dissolved. Add tequila. Add rocks or cracked ice to glass. Stir well. Add a splash of soda and stir. Twist lemon peel above drink and drop into glass. Garnish with pineapple stick.

TEQUILA RICKEY

1½ oz. tequila
¼ large lime
Iced club soda

Salt
1 sliced cocktail orange in syrup

Put three ice cubes into an 8-oz. glass. Add tequila. Squeeze lime above drink and drop into glass. Add soda. Stir. Sprinkle lightly with salt. Fasten orange slice to cocktail spear. Munch it before or after each swallow.

TEQUILA SOUR

2 oz. tequila
½ oz. lemon juice
1 tsp. sugar

½ slice lemon
1 maraschino cherry

Shake tequila, lemon juice, and sugar well with ice. Strain into prechilled whiskey-sour glass. Add lemon slice and cherry.

TEQUILA SUNSET

1½ oz. tequila
1½ oz. blackberry brandy

4 oz. orange juice, or to fill
1 cherry

Pour tequila and blackberry brandy over ice into 10-oz. highball glass. Top with orange juice. Stir well. Drop in cherry and serve with straw.

TEQUINI

1½ to 2 oz. tequila
½ oz. dry vermouth

Lemon peel
1 cocktail olive (optional)

Stir tequila and vermouth well with ice. Strain into prechilled cocktail glass. Twist lemon peel above drink and drop into glass. Olive may be added for a salty accent. *A Mexican Martini.*

T.K.O.

1¼ oz. tequila
1¼ oz. Kahlua

1¼ oz. ouzo

Shake well with ice. Strain into cocktail glass over ice. *The name says it all.*

TOREADOR

1½ oz. tequila   1 tbsp. light cream
½ oz. crème de cacao

Shake very well with ice. Strain into prechilled cocktail glass. For a rich touch, top with whipped cream and sprinkle with cocoa powder.

VAMPIRO

1½ oz. tequila   3½ oz. grapefruit juice
3 oz. sangrita   ¼ tsp. lime juice

Shake well with ice. Strain into tall 12-oz. glass. Add ice cubes to fill glass to rim. Stir. *The reigning queen of tall tequila drinks in Guadalajara.*

VIVA PONCHO

1½ oz. tequila   1 tsp. sugar
Juice of 1 lemon   Lemon wedge

Shake tequila, lemon juice, and sugar with ice. Rub rim of old-fashioned glass with lemon wedge and dip in sugar. Strain over ice into sugar-rimmed glass.

VOLUPTUOSO

1 oz. tequila   1 cup crushed ice
1½ oz. banana liqueur   1 tsp. sugar
⅓ cup sliced ripe banana   ½ oz. lemon juice

Blend ingredients for 10 seconds at high speed. Pour into tall 12-oz. glass.

WHITE BULL

1½ oz. tequila   1 oz. light cream
1½ oz. Kahlua

Shake very well with ice. Strain into old-fashioned glass over ice.

WILD THING

1½ oz. tequila   1 oz. club soda, or to fill
1 oz. cranberry juice   1 slice lime
½ oz. lime juice

Pour over ice into old-fashioned glass. Garnish with lime slice.

YUCATÁN TONIC

1½ oz. tequila   ½ lime
½ oz. crème de cassis   Iced tonic water

Fill a tall 10-oz. glass with ice cubes. Add tequila and crème de cassis. Stir well. Squeeze lime over drink and drop into glass. Stir. Fill with tonic water.

CHAPTER 11

* And a
Botfle of Rum *

One of rum's most memorable qualities is that it never lets you forget where it comes from. Bourbon, Scotch, or gin drinkers don't necessarily think of corn-covered prairie lands, peat bogs, or verdant groves of juniper shrubs while imbibing their pet potations. But as soon as the first drop of rum is poured, tropical touches inevitably begin to appear: plump mangoes, passion fruit, ripe papayas, green limes, cool coconut milk, and pineapples as heavy and musky as the jungle itself. Even without such exotic embellishments, there's something in the sheer aroma and brandylike smoothness of distilled sugarcane that spurs every mixmaster's imagination.

While making rum is an art, the secret of which is well guarded by the few who hold it, the basic steps in the process can be described simply. First of all, remember that rum is a by-product of sugar. Sugarcane is crushed, it turns to cane juice, and in a small number of distilleries this original juice is used to make rum. Most rum, however, is made from molasses. The sugarcane juice is boiled down; part of the rummish stew turns to crystallized sugar and is removed. The rest, the "mother liquor," or molasses, is first fermented, then distilled. In the big rum distilleries, the molasses is fermented by special strains of yeast developed for specific rums and kept alive by lab technicians who hover over their yeast dynasty like guardian angels, believing it's the inscrutable secret that makes their rum different from all other rums.

All rums are aged. The youngest blend of the prominent rums from Puerto Rico must, by law, be aged at least a year. Most of them are somewhat older. One would assume that the clear—or white—rums were younger than those with a yellow tint, called golden. Actually, in some cases, the difference is merely the addition of caramel coloring. Some of the better-known rums don't attempt to attract the buyer with color but with age, plainly indicated on the label. Ronrico, for example, is four years old. Bacardi Añejo is six years old. Other rare rums from some of the Caribbean islands are aged up to ten years or more, and some rank in flavor with the finest of velvety old brandies. In the aging warehouses of Don Q Puerto Rican rums, the casks are handled in a solera system, whereby a cask is never completely emptied. Part of the old rum always remains to mingle with the new in such proportions that the new merges with the old and takes on its best features.

At least three-fourths of the yo-ho-ho sold in the States is Puerto Rican, a light, dry spirit in favor with contemporary freebooters. An oligarchy of Puerto Rican distillers takes more pride in their rum formulas than a Kentucky colonel takes in his bed of mint leaves. Warehouses in which the rum is kept for aging are patrolled day and night by armed government guards. The lock to each warehouse contains two keyholes, one for the owner and one for the government guard, so that neither can tamper with the sleeping golden distillate. And the government, in cooperation with the University of Puerto Rico, carries on a research program to keep every drop of rum that leaves the island of the highest quality.

Most of the white rum naturally finds its way into Daiquiris, Rum Sours, Rum Martinis, and similar drinks. The rums with more flavor accent, the true golden rums, are the mainstays of Rum and Coke, Rum Collins, and other drinks where a distinct but not overpowering rum aftertaste is desirable. The sturdy, heavy-bodied rums with pungent flavors—typified by Jamaican rums—may in a few cases be taken straight, but are more likely to find their eventual homes in a Piña Colada, Planter's Punch, winter punch bowl, and mixed tropical drinks combined with lighter rums. And if you're really looking for added zing, try some of the new flavored rums, fresh on the market. Taking a cue from the smashing success of flavored vodkas, Bacardi currently offers a very popular Limon variety, with

Bacardi O (orange-flavored) well on the way. Whaler's rums, introduced relatively recently, are also showing great appeal among the flavored-rum crowd. Finally, 151-proof rums are offered by many major distilleries. Rums of this strength have not only almost twice as much alcohol as the 80-proof rums but almost twice as much flavor concentrated in the bottle. At one time the best-known representative of this particular form of kill-devil was the Demerara rum from British Guyana, designed primarily to thaw the frozen veins of Canadian lumberjacks. Today, 151-proof rums serve more urbane needs—their high proof makes them perfect accents for any dessert from baba au rhum to crêpes flambé. In mixed drinks, the 151-proof rums, in small quantities, add a piquant note of concentrated rumminess. A bottle belongs in every man's rum library.

The personality of every rum, no matter how old it may be, depends on its birthplace. The following guide may be helpful in making your selections.

> *PUERTO RICAN RUM* At least three-fourths of the rum sold in the States is Puerto Rican—the prototype of lightness and dryness. Because the Puerto Rican government lays down the law controlling rum standards, all Puerto Rican rums—even the aged ones—are remarkably consistent in quality from one year to the next. Flavors range from the very gently flavored white or silver labels to the more mellow golden rums and on to the six-year or older añejo rums.

> *VIRGIN ISLANDS RUM* Although also in the light, dry class, its flavor is slightly more reminiscent of molasses. Some of it seems to lack sufficient aging. Because some brands are shipped in bulk and bottled in the United States, prices are generally lower than Puerto Rican rums.

> *DOMINICAN RUM* Ron Bermudez, distilled by a firm more than 125 years old, is in the light, dry class.

BARBADOS RUM Intermediate in flavor and color, Barbados rum is known for its soft finish and gentle aftertaste.

CUBAN RUM Because normal trade relations do not now exist between Cuba and the States, no rum is imported, but visitors returning from Cuba usually bring back some of the famed rum from the island. Cuba was the original home of Bacardi—the daddy of light rums, now made in Puerto Rico and elsewhere and the third best-selling hard liquor in the United States. Cuban rums have a light, dry, but luscious flavor with just a trace of sweetness. If and when relations are resumed, the Cuban rums will no doubt flow rapidly to the United States.

U.S. RUM Among the rums made on the U.S. mainland are Bardenay, Jenkins Silver, La Conga, New Orleans (N.O.) Extra Premium Rum, and Tropic Bay; most are of intermediate flavor, well suited for hot winter grogs.

DEMERARA RUM Rum from Guyana, named after the Demerara River and its large sugar fields, is intermediate to heavy in flavor and color; much of it is made from a combination of pot-stilled and column-stilled spirits; widely known in the States is the 151-proof variety.

HAITIAN RUM Although there are a number of rum distilleries in Haiti, the best-known brand in the United States is the famed Barbancourt rum, in the three-star and special-reserve five-star varieties, both 86 proof. The latter, an intermediate-bodied rum, is a magnificent brandylike but mellow rum.

MARTINIQUE RUM There are nearly fifty distilleries in the French colony, producing rums that range from white to dark.

The most eminent brand in the States is Rum Saint James. It is a well-aged, heavy-bodied rum bottled at 94 proof, and has been the darling of rum-sipping connoisseurs for years.

JAMAICAN RUM At one time all Jamaican rum was known for its extremely heavy, pungent flavor. It was all made in pot stills from a mash fermented over a period of three weeks using only the wild yeast of the air. Today, yeast cultures are used, and rums are made from a combination of pot stills and modern column stills. Colors range from a pure white rum to extremely dark ones. In spite of these recent variations, the best-known Jamaican rums imported to this country are the traditional heavy-bodied types. Myers's rum and Appleton Punch rum, although both only 80 proof, are still the sturdy, heavy-bodied, pungent rums indispensable to Planter's Punch and to those fans who like their rum really rummy with a lingering aftertaste. Other freebooters who want not only pungency but also power can select Lemon Hart at 86 proof.

TRINIDAD RUM Trinidad, best known in the States for its Angostura bitters, produces an intermediate-bodied rum veering to the light side, represented by Fernandes Crystal White Rum.

BATAVIAN ARAK This pungent dry rum distilled and aged on the island of Java is seen very little in the United States, although now and then a bottle is obtainable in specialty liquor stores. Its offbeat, far-from-gentle flavor is due to special molasses, local water, and the addition of Japanese rice in the fermenting vats.

An Urban Luau

S TAGING AN INDOOR LUAU IS AS EASY AS POI. Even being sky-high in an apartment can have some built-in blessings: guests don't have to scour about for volcanic rocks, ti leaves, and palm fronds, and you don't have to dig a pit to roast the traditional whole suckling pig. Instead, just ask a butcher to wrap up his juiciest pork-loin roasts, which you can start sizzling on an indoor rotisserie. If naught but the entire pig on a platter will suffice, you can order one from a professional catering service.

Don't get hung up adorning your pad with fishnets and colored-glass globes. Concentrate on laying out a properly Polynesian bar and buffet, which is, after all, where the action is. Begin by visiting your friendly florist. She won't be able to duplicate all four thousand varieties of hibiscus growing on Oahu, but she can supply you with quantities of lush greenery. Tell her the size of your luau table and ask for enough flat ferns to cover it. Order one or two centerpieces of short-stemmed flowers (long-stemmed beauties are quite acceptable as buffet decorations, but at a sit-down feast they invariably create a junglelike atmosphere that inhibits cross-table conversation.) Scatter fruit among the flowers and fronds:

pineapples cut lengthwise, with the meat removed, sliced, and returned to the shells; stalks of yellow and red bananas, grapes, citrus fruits, and mangoes—all make for delicious tropical tidbits that can also serve as decorations. Set the stage as well with plenty of condiments such as chutneys, some mild, others peppery hot. As sideshows, include chopped hard-boiled eggs and chives, tomatoes with basil, cucumbers in yogurt and dill, sliced bananas sprinkled with lime juice and brown sugar, and green salad with avocado and papaya chunks. Tiny morsels of browned coconut meat, called Coco Bits, taste great with coconut-milk or curry dishes.

The potable to proffer at any luau is rum. A stock of light, dark, and 151-proof rum will be the base for rum cocktails, as well as many of the tall coolers. For a special after-dinner tipple, try a sweet Polynesian change of pace such as a pineapple and crème de menthe frappé: fill saucer champagne glasses three-quarters full with finely crushed ice and pour in a shot of undiluted frozen pineapple juice. Stir it in the glass, then add an ounce of green crème de menthe.

The key to a luau feast is neither pig nor poi but *hoomanawanui*, which means "take it easy." Let the party choose its own speed. A luau isn't an organized affair that requires careful supervision by the host. Allow your guests to hang loose. Imagine your pad is an island in the Caribbean, with gentle tropical breezes cooling air and spirit alike. If you've done your planning well, the night can virtually run itself. As you and your guests dream and dance after dinner, you'll find that a luau never really seems to end but slowly drifts off into the moonlight.

Whether one chooses light or heavily flavored rums is sometimes a matter of the age of the drinker. Just as white wines are a pleasant introduction to Bacchus, while the more complex red wines appeal to older drinkers, so the dry white rum via a fruity Mai Tai or a Frozen Banana Daiquiri seems to make its best impression on rum drinkers in the bloom of youth. As one gets older, rums with greater age and more intricate flavors, best savored in a leisurely way, seem more felicitous.

Any young guy or gal today who has learned to wet their lips with something other than water knows that rum has a peculiarly persuasive effect. Whiskey makes you stop arguing. Beer soothes you. Gin disarms you. But rum cajoles. No one has described the effect better than William James when he philosophized about alcohol: "It is in fact the great exciter of the Yes function in man. It brings its votary from the chill periphery of things to the radiant core. It makes him for the moment one with the truth."

RUM
COCKTAILS

ACAPULCO

1½ oz. light rum
½ oz. lime juice
¼ oz. triple sec

½ egg white
½ tsp. sugar
2 fresh mint leaves

Shake rum, lime juice, triple sec, egg white, and sugar well with ice. Strain into prechilled cocktail glass. Tear each mint leaf partially and drop into glass.

ALLA SALUTE!

1½ oz. light rum
1 oz. Sciarada
½ oz. lime juice

3 oz. pineapple juice
Iced club soda
1 slice lime

Pour rum, Sciarada, lime juice, and pineapple juice into tall 12-oz. glass filled with rocks. Stir well. Add soda to fill glass. Stir. Add lime slice.

ALOHA

1 oz. light rum
½ oz. Midori liqueur
½ oz. lime juice

½ oz. dry vermouth
1-inch cube papaya

Shake rum, Midori liqueur, lime juice, and vermouth well with ice. Strain over rocks in 8-oz. glass. Fasten papaya on cocktail spear and place over rim of glass.

APRICOT LADY

1½ oz. light rum
1 oz. apricot-flavored brandy
½ oz. lime juice
½ tsp. curaçao
½ egg white
½ cup crushed ice
½ slice orange

Put rum, apricot-flavored brandy, lime juice, curaçao, egg white, and ice into blender. Blend 15 seconds at low speed. Pour into prechilled old-fashioned glass. Add ice cubes or ice slices to fill glass to rim. Place orange slice on top.

APRICOT PIE

1 oz. light rum
1 oz. sweet vermouth
½ tsp. apricot-flavored brandy
½ tsp. lemon juice
¼ tsp. grenadine
Orange peel

Shake rum, vermouth, apricot-flavored brandy, lemon juice, and grenadine well with ice. Strain into prechilled cocktail glass. Twist orange peel above drink and drop into glass.

BACARDI COCKTAIL

1½ oz. light or golden Bacardi rum
½ oz. lime juice
1 tsp. grenadine

Shake well with ice. Strain into prechilled cocktail glass or over rocks into a prechilled old-fashioned glass. *The proprietary name Bacardi, a rum originally distilled in Cuba but now made in Puerto Rico and other Spanish-speaking lands, has long been the title of this classic rum cocktail.*

BACARDI STINGER

1½ oz. amaretto
1½ oz. Bacardi 151
3 oz. Coke

Pour amaretto and 151-proof rum over ice into 8-oz. highball glass. Top off with Coke. Stir. *Packs a wallop.*

BAHAMA MAMA

½ oz. dark rum
½ oz. coconut liqueur (CocoRibe)
¼ oz. coffee liqueur
¼ oz. 151-proof rum
Juice of ½ lemon
4 oz. pineapple juice
1 pineapple stick

Shake well and pour over ice into tall collins glass. Garnish with pineapple stick.

BAHAMA MAMA SUNRISE

1 oz. dark rum (Myers's)
1 oz. spiced rum (Captain Morgan's)
4 oz. orange juice
2 oz. pineapple juice
½ oz. grenadine
1 maraschino cherry

Pour both rums and both juices over ice into collins glass. Stir. Float grenadine on top. Drop in cherry.

BANANA DAIQUIRI

1½ oz. light rum
½ oz. lime juice
1 oz. orange juice
1 oz. banana liqueur
⅓ cup finely crushed ice

Mix all ingredients in blender at high speed for 10 seconds. Pour into 6-oz. saucer champagne glass or outsize cocktail glass.

BANANA MANGO

1½ oz. light rum
¼ oz. banana liqueur
½ oz. mango nectar
½ oz. lime juice
1 slice fresh mango

Shake rum, banana liqueur, mango nectar, and lime juice well with ice. Strain over rocks in prechilled old-fashioned glass. Add mango slice.

BANANA RUM FRAPPÉ

½ oz. light rum
½ oz. banana liqueur
½ oz. orange juice

Stir without ice. Pour over crushed ice in deep-saucer champagne glass. *A cool postscript for an Asian dinner.*

BARBADOS PLANTER'S PUNCH

2 oz. Barbados Mount Gay rum
½ oz. heavy dark rum
1 oz. lime juice
2 tsp. sugar
3 dashes Angostura bitters
Freshly ground nutmeg
1 slice lime

Shake both kinds of rum, lime juice, sugar, and bitters well with ice. Strain into tall 12-oz. glass three-quarters filled with coarsely cracked ice. Stir well. Add ice if necessary to fill glass to rim. Sprinkle with nutmeg. Add lime slice.

BATTERING RAM

1 oz. light rum
1 oz. dark Jamaican rum
4 oz. orange juice
½ oz. Wild Turkey liqueur
½ oz. lime juice
Iced tonic water
1 slice lime

Shake light rum, dark rum, orange juice, Wild Turkey liqueur, and lime juice well with ice. Strain into tall 14-oz. glass half-filled with ice cubes. Fill glass with tonic water. Stir. Add lime slice.

BEACHCOMBER

1½ oz. light rum
½ oz. lime juice
½ oz. triple sec
¼ tsp. maraschino liqueur

Shake well with ice. Strain into prechilled sugar-rimmed cocktail glass.

BEACHCOMBER'S GOLD

1½ oz. light rum
½ oz. dry vermouth

½ oz. sweet vermouth

Stir well with ice. Strain into prechilled deep-saucer champagne glass. Add cracked ice or ice slices to fill glass. The same mixture of rum and sweet and dry vermouths is also known as the Rum Perfect, usually served in a regular cocktail glass without added ice. Either way, it's delightful.

BEE'S KNEES

1½ oz. light rum
¾ oz. orange juice
½ oz. lime juice

1 tsp. sugar
2 dashes orange bitters
Orange peel

Shake rum, orange juice, lime juice, sugar, and bitters well with ice. Strain into prechilled cocktail glass. Twist orange peel above drink and drop into glass. *A speakeasy heirloom whose orange accent is most mellow.*

BELFRY BAT

1 oz. dark Jamaican rum
1 oz. Sciarada
2 oz. papaya nectar

2 dashes Angostura bitters
Iced club soda
1 slice lemon

Pour rum, Sciarada, papaya nectar, and bitters into tall 14-oz. glass three-quarters filled with ice cubes. Stir well. Add club soda to fill glass. Stir. Add lemon slice.

BELIZE PUNCH

1½ oz. light rum
½ oz. dark rum
½ oz. orange liqueur
½ oz. Rose's Lime Juice

½ oz. cream of coconut
2 splashes grenadine
3 oz. pineapple juice

Shake well with ice. Strain into collins glass over rocks.

BETWEEN THE SHEETS

¾ oz. light rum
¾ oz. California brandy

¾ oz. Cointreau
½ oz. lemon juice

Shake well with ice. Strain into prechilled cocktail glass. *An exhilarating variation on the Rum Sidecar, also known as the Boston Sidecar.*

BITTER BANANA COOLER

1½ oz. light rum
¼ cup sliced banana
¼ cup pineapple juice
½ oz. lime juice

2 dashes Peychaud's bitters
½ cup crushed ice
Iced bitter lemon soda

Put rum, sliced banana, pineapple juice, lime juice, bitters, and crushed ice into blender. Blend for 10 to 15 seconds at high speed. Pour into tall 14-oz. glass. Let foamy cap of drink settle somewhat. Add two ice cubes. Fill glass with bitter lemon soda. *A tall drink in the Frozen Daiquiri tradition.*

BITTER PLANTER'S PUNCH

2 oz. golden rum
1 tsp. sugar
1 tsp. grenadine

½ oz. lemon juice
Iced bitter lemon soda
1 slice lemon

Shake rum, sugar, grenadine, and lemon juice extremely well with ice. Strain into tall 14-oz. glass three-quarters filled with ice cubes. Stir well. Fill glass with bitter lemon soda. Stir lightly. Add lemon slice.

BLACKBEARD

1½ oz. spiced rum (Captain Morgan's)
1½ oz. root beer schnapps

Ice cold cola drink to fill

Pour spiced rum and root beer schnapps over ice into cocktail glass. Top off with cola drink.

BLACK DEVIL

2 oz. light rum
½ oz. dry vermouth

1 black olive

Stir rum and vermouth well with ice. Strain into prechilled cocktail glass. Add black olive.

BLUEBERRY RUM FIZZ

2½ oz. light rum
1 tsp. triple sec
½ oz. blueberry syrup
¾ oz. lemon juice

Iced club soda
1 slice lemon
3 large fresh blueberries

Shake rum, triple sec, blueberry syrup, and lemon juice well with ice. Strain into tall 14-oz. glass half-filled with ice. Fill glass with soda. Stir. Add lemon slice and blueberries.

BLUE HAWAIIAN

1½ oz. light rum
1½ oz. blue curaçao
3 oz. pineapple juice

1 oz. cream of coconut
1 pineapple stick
1 cherry

Shake rum, blue curaçao, pineapple juice, and cream of coconut very well with cracked ice. Pour into tall collins glass. Garnish with pineapple stick and cherry. Can also be served frozen from a blender; just add ⅓ cup ice and blend at high speed for 10 to 15 seconds.

BMW

1½ oz. Bailey's Irish Cream
1½ oz. Malibu rum

1½ oz. whiskey

Shake very well with cracked ice. Strain into prechilled old-fashioned glass. *Gentlemen, start your engines....*

BOLERO

1½ oz. light rum
¾ oz. apple brandy

¼ tsp. sweet vermouth
Lemon peel

Stir rum, apple brandy, and vermouth well with ice. Strain into prechilled sugar-frosted cocktail glass. Twist lemon peel above drink and drop into glass.

BOLO

1½ oz. light rum
½ oz. lemon juice
½ oz. orange juice

½ tsp. sugar
½ slice lemon

Shake rum, lemon juice, orange juice, and sugar well with ice. Strain into prechilled cocktail glass or prechilled whiskey-sour glass. Garnish with lemon slice.

BORINQUEN

1½ oz. light rum
½ oz. passion fruit syrup
¾ oz. lime juice

½ oz. orange juice
1 tsp. 151-proof rum
½ cup crushed ice

Blend all ingredients at low speed for 10 seconds. Pour into prechilled double old-fashioned glass. Add ice cubes or cracked ice to fill glass. Garnish with gardenia if available.

BRASS MONKEY

½ oz. rum
½ oz. vodka

3 oz. orange juice

Stir rum, vodka, and orange juice with ice. Strain into prechilled old-fashioned glass.

BUSHRANGER

1 oz. light rum
1 oz. red Dubonnet

2 dashes Angostura bitters
Lemon peel

Shake rum, Dubonnet, and bitters well with ice. Strain into prechilled cocktail glass. Twist lemon peel above drink and drop into glass.

CALM VOYAGE

½ oz. light rum
½ oz. Galliano or Roiano
½ oz. passion fruit syrup

2 tsp. lemon juice
½ egg white
⅓ cup crushed ice

Blend all ingredients at low speed for 10 to 15 seconds. Pour into prechilled deep-saucer champagne glass. *Mendelssohn is a good accompaniment on this trip.*

CALYPSO COOLER

2½ oz. light rum
1 oz. frozen concentrated pineapple juice,
    thawed but not diluted
½ oz. lime juice

1 tsp. sugar
Iced club soda
1 thin slice fresh pineapple
1 slice lime

Shake rum, pineapple juice, lime juice, and sugar well with ice. Strain into tall 14-oz. glass. Add a splash of soda and enough ice to fill glass. Stir. Garnish with pineapple and lime slices.

CARDINAL COCKTAIL II

2 oz. light rum
¼ oz. orzata
1 tsp. grenadine

¼ oz. triple sec
1 oz. lime juice
1 slice lime

Shake rum, orzata, grenadine, triple sec, and lime juice well with ice. Strain into prechilled old-fashioned glass. Add ice cubes to bring liquid to rim. Garnish with lime slice.

CARIB

1 oz. light rum
1 oz. gin
½ oz. lime juice

1 tsp. sugar
1 slice orange

Shake rum, gin, lime juice, and sugar well with ice. Strain over rocks in prechilled old-fashioned glass. Garnish with orange slice.

CARIBBEAN COFFEE

1 oz. light rum
½ oz. crème de cacao
6 oz. cold, strong coffee, sweetened to taste

1 oz. heavy sweet cream
Dollop of whipped cream

Pour rum, crème de cacao, and coffee into tall 12-oz. glass three-quarters filled with ice cubes. Add heavy cream. Stir well. Add dollop of whipped cream.

CARIBBEAN MULE

1½ oz. light rum
½ oz. dark Jamaican rum
½ oz. lime juice
¼ oz. triple sec

¼ oz. maraschino liqueur
Iced ginger beer or ginger ale
1 slice lime
1 sprig mint

Shake both kinds of rum, lime juice, triple sec, and maraschino liqueur well with ice. Strain into tall 12-oz. glass half-filled with ice cubes. Add ginger beer to almost fill glass. Stir lightly. Garnish with lime slice and mint.

CARIBBEAN PUNCH

1½ oz. light rum
1 oz. dark rum
¾ oz. banana liqueur

1½ oz. pineapple juice
Juice of ½ lime
1½ oz. orange juice

Shake well with ice. Strain into collins glass over rocks.

CARIBBEAN SLING

2 oz. light rum
½ oz. lime juice
½ oz. lemon juice
½ oz. triple sec

1 tsp. sugar
Iced club soda
1 piece cucumber rind ½ inch wide,
** 4 inches long**

Shake rum, lime juice, lemon juice, triple sec, and sugar very well with ice. Strain into tall 14-oz. glass half-filled with ice cubes. Stir well. Add soda to fill glass. Place cucumber rind in glass.

CASABLANCA

2 oz. golden rum
1 dash Angostura bitters
1 tsp. lime juice
¼ tsp. curaçao
¼ tsp. maraschino liqueur

Shake well with ice. Strain into prechilled cocktail glass.

CHERRY DAIQUIRI

1½ oz. light rum
½ oz. lime juice
½ oz. tart cherry liqueur
¼ tsp. kirschwasser
Lime peel

Shake rum, lime juice, cherry liqueur, and kirschwasser well with ice. Strain into prechilled cocktail glass. Twist lime peel over drink and drop into glass.

CHERRY PLANTER'S PUNCH

1 oz. kirschwasser
½ oz. dark Jamaican rum
½ oz. lime juice
2 dashes Angostura bitters
1 tsp. sugar
Freshly grated nutmeg
1 slice lime
½ slice orange

Shake kirschwasser, rum, lime juice, bitters, and sugar extremely well with ice. Strain over rocks into 8-oz. glass. Add ice if necessary to fill glass to rim. Stir well. Sprinkle with nutmeg. Garnish with lime and orange slices.

CHERRY RUM

1¼ oz. light rum
¾ oz. cherry liqueur
½ oz. heavy cream
⅓ cup crushed ice

Blend all ingredients at low speed for 10 to 15 seconds. Pour into deep-saucer champagne glass.

CHERRY RUM COBBLER

1½ oz. light rum
1 oz. cherry-flavored brandy
½ tsp. sugar
½ oz. lemon juice
1 slice lemon
1 maraschino stem cherry

Fill a tall 12-oz. glass with coarsely cracked ice. (Ice from a "chipper" tray is good for this drink.) Add rum, cherry-flavored brandy, sugar, and lemon juice. Stir very well until sugar dissolves. Add ice if necessary to fill glass to rim. Stir. Add lemon slice and cherry.

CHERRY RUM COLA

1½ oz. golden rum
¾ oz. Peter Heering liqueur
1 tsp. lemon juice
Iced cola
1 slice lemon

Fill a 12-oz. glass three-quarters full with ice cubes. Add rum, Peter Heering liqueur, and lemon juice. Stir very well. Add cola to fill glass to rim. Add lemon slice.

CHERRY RUM FIX

1 tsp. sugar
2 tsp. water
1½ oz. light rum
½ oz. Peter Heering or Cherry Karise

½ oz. lemon juice
1 slice lemon
1 brandied cherry

Dissolve sugar in 2 tsp. water in an 8-oz. glass. Add rum, Peter Heering, and lemon juice. Fill glass with crushed ice. Stir well. Add more ice to fill glass to rim. Stir. Garnish with lemon slice and cherry.

CHINA

2 oz. golden rum
¼ tsp. grenadine
¼ tsp. passion fruit syrup

1 tsp. curaçao
1 dash Angostura bitters

Shake well with ice. Pour into prechilled cocktail glass. *A slightly sweet drink but not a dessert cocktail; one to set the mood for a roast-duck dinner.*

CHOCOLATE ECLAIR

2 oz. (¼ measuring cup) chocolate
   ice cream
1 oz. Choclair

1 tbsp. semisweet chocolate shavings
1½ oz. milk
½ oz. light rum

Pour chocolate ice cream, Choclair, light rum, and milk into blender. Blend at high speed for 10 seconds. Pour over rocks into 8-oz. glass. Stir well. Sprinkle chocolate shavings on top.

CHOCOLATE RUM

1 oz. light rum
½ oz. white crème de cacao
½ oz. white crème de menthe

½ oz. heavy cream
1 tsp. 151-proof rum

Shake light rum, crème de cacao, crème de menthe, and cream well with ice. Strain into prechilled cocktail glass. Float 151-proof rum on top.

CHOCOLATIER

2 oz. (¼ measuring cup) chocolate
   ice cream
1 oz. dark Jamaican rum

½ oz. crème de cacao
1½ oz. milk
1 tbsp. semisweet chocolate shavings

Pour chocolate ice cream, rum, crème de cacao, and milk into blender. Blend at high speed for 10 seconds. Pour over rocks into 8-oz. glass. Stir well. Sprinkle chocolate shavings on top.

COCONUT COOLER IN SHELL

1 coconut	1½ oz. light rum
½ cup crushed ice	1 oz. heavy cream
1 oz. canned cream of coconut	

Remove end of coconut opposite coconut eyes. The best procedure is to hold the base of the coconut firmly in the left hand. With a very heavy French knife or cleaver, chop top off by striking coconut with sharp, diagonal blows. Several whacks may be necessary. Avoid spilling coconut juice if possible. Pour out coconut juice and reserve. Into blender, pour ¼ cup coconut juice, ice, cream of coconut, rum, and cream. Blend at high speed for 10 seconds. Pour into coconut shell. Place coconut shell in large dish surrounded with finely crushed ice. There will usually be enough juice from one coconut for three or four drinks. Reserve drinks may be made up beforehand, poured into a pitcher, and stored in the refrigerator. Coconut shells may then be refilled when necessary. *Byron once said that nothing calmed the spirit as much as rum and true religion. The balmy beneficence of the preceding recipe will bear out that astute poet to the fullest.*

COFFEE MILK PUNCH

1 oz. coffee liqueur	5 oz. milk
1 oz. dark Jamaican rum	½ oz. heavy sweet cream
1 small egg	Freshly grated nutmeg
1 tsp. sugar	

Pour all ingredients except nutmeg into cocktail shaker with ice. Shake extremely well to blend egg with other ingredients. Strain into 12-oz. glass. Sprinkle with nutmeg.

COFFEE RUM COOLER

1½ oz. dark Jamaican rum	Iced club soda
1 oz. coffee liqueur	1 slice lime
½ oz. lime juice	

Shake rum, coffee liqueur, and lime juice well with ice. Strain into tall 14-oz. glass three-quarters filled with ice. Fill glass with club soda. Stir. Add lime slice.

COLUMBIA

1½ oz. light rum	½ oz. lemon juice
½ oz. strawberry syrup	1 tsp. kirschwasser

Shake well with ice. Strain into prechilled sugar-frosted cocktail glass. The kirschwasser, though small in proportion, comes through vividly.

CONCH SHELL

4 oz. light rum	
½ oz. lime juice	

Shake well with ice. Strain over rocks in prechilled double old-fashioned glass.

CONTINENTAL

1¾ oz. light rum	½ tsp. sugar
½ oz. lime juice	½ tsp. green crème de menthe

Shake well with ice. Strain into prechilled cocktail glass. *Enjoy this light bracer before a seafood dinner.*

COOL GUANABANA

Grenadine
Superfine sugar
1½ oz. light rum
½ oz. dark Jamaican rum

½ oz. lime juice
4 oz. iced guanabana nectar
1 slice lime

Dip rim of tall 14-oz. glass into grenadine and then into superfine sugar to frost rim. Fill glass with ice cubes. Add both kinds of rum, lime juice, and guanabana nectar. (Guanabana nectar—made from the pulp of the soursop—is available in gourmet shops and in those featuring Puerto Rican foods.) Stir well. Cut lime slice halfway to center and fasten to rim of glass.

CORKSCREW

1½ oz. light rum
½ oz. dry vermouth

½ oz. peach liqueur
1 slice lime

Shake rum, vermouth, and peach liqueur well with ice. Strain into prechilled cocktail glass. Add lime slice.

CRANBERRY RUM PUNCH

1 oz. light rum
1 oz. dark Jamaican rum
4 oz. chilled cranberry juice

2 oz. orange juice
½ oz. lemon juice
1 slice lemon

Shake light rum, dark Jamaican rum, cranberry juice, orange juice, and lemon juice well with ice. Strain into tall 14-oz. glass three-quarters filled with ice cubes. Stir. Add lemon slice.

CREOLE

1½ oz. light rum
1 dash Tabasco sauce
1 tsp. lemon juice

Iced beef bouillon
    or consommé (undiluted)
Salt and pepper

Put two large ice cubes into prechilled old-fashioned glass. Add rum, Tabasco, and lemon juice. Stir well. Fill glass with beef bouillon. Sprinkle with salt and pepper. Stir again. *A pleasant pick-me-up or prebrunch cocktail.*

CUBA LIBRE

2 oz. golden rum
½ lime

Iced cola drink

Half-fill a tall 14-oz. glass with coarsely chopped ice or ice cubes. Add rum. Squeeze lime above drink and drop into glass. Fill with cola. Stir well. Heavier rums such as Jamaican or Martinique may be used in place of golden rum or may be mixed half-and-half with it. A tsp. of 151-proof rum may be floated on top of drink for a rummy bite.

CUBA LIBRE COCKTAIL

1 oz. light rum
½ oz. 151-proof rum
½ oz. cola drink

½ oz. lime juice
½ tsp. sugar
Lime peel

Shake both kinds of rum, cola drink, lime juice, and sugar well with ice. Strain into prechilled cocktail glass. Twist lime peel over drink and drop into glass. *Not to be confused with the Cube Libre (above), a tall rum-cola drink, distinguished by a lime-wedge garnish, that's somewhat slower in its liberating effects.*

CUBAN COCKTAIL

2 oz. light rum
Juice of ½ lime

½ tsp. powdered sugar

Shake well with ice. Strain into prechilled cocktail glass.

CULROSS

1½ oz. golden rum
½ oz. Lillet

1 tsp. apricot-flavored brandy
1 tsp. lime juice

Shake well with ice. Strain into prechilled cocktail glass as a straight-up drink or over rocks into a prechilled old-fashioned glass. Equally satisfying either way.

DAIQUIRI

2 oz. light rum
½ oz. lime juice

½ tsp. sugar

Shake well with ice. Pour into prechilled sugar-frosted cocktail glass or over rocks in an old-fashioned glass. Sugar may be increased if a sweeter Daiquiri is desired.

DARK & STORMY

3 oz. dark rum (Gosling's)
8 oz. ginger beer

Pour rum and ginger beer over ice into 13-oz. hurricane glass. Stir gently.

DERBY DAIQUIRI

1½ oz. light rum
½ oz. lime juice
1 oz. orange juice

½ oz. simple syrup
⅓ cup crushed ice

Blend all ingredients for 10 to15 seconds at low speed. Pour into prechilled oversize cocktail glass or deep-saucer champagne glass.

DERBY RUM FIX

1 tsp. sugar
2 tsp. water
2 oz. light rum
½ oz. lime juice

1 oz. orange juice
1 slice cocktail orange in syrup
1 maraschino cherry

Dissolve sugar in 2 tsp. water in an 8-oz. glass. Add rum, lime juice, and orange juice. Fill glass with crushed ice. Stir well. Add ice to fill glass to rim. Stir. Garnish with orange slice and cherry.

DEVIL'S TAIL

1½ oz. golden rum
1 oz. vodka
½ oz. lime juice
¼ oz. grenadine

¼ oz. apricot liqueur
⅓ cup crushed ice
Lime peel

Blend rum, vodka, lime juice, grenadine, apricot liqueur, and ice at low speed for 10 to 15 seconds. Pour into prechilled deep-saucer champagne glass. Twist lime peel over drink and drop into glass. *Powerfully pleasant rather than pugnacious.*

DRACULA

1½ oz. light rum
2 dashes Angostura bitters
½ tsp. grenadine

4 oz. cranberry juice cocktail
1 oz. lemon juice

Shake well with ice. Strain into 14-oz. glass. Add ice cubes to fill glass to rim. Stir.

ELEPHANT'S EYE

1 oz. dark Jamaican rum
1 oz. sweet vermouth
½ oz. triple sec

½ oz. lime juice
Iced tonic water
1 slice lime

Shake rum, sweet vermouth, triple sec, and lime juice well with ice. Strain into tall 14-oz. glass half-filled with ice cubes. Add tonic water to fill glass. Stir. Add lime slice.

EL PRESIDENTE

1½ oz. golden rum
½ oz. dry vermouth
1 tsp. dark Jamaican rum

1 tsp. curaçao
2 tsp. lime juice
¼ tsp. grenadine

Shake well with ice. Strain into prechilled cocktail glass. *Hail to the chief.*

EMERALD CITY

1½ oz. Malibu rum
1 oz. Midori
1 oz. blue curaçao

½ oz. Rose's Lime Juice
7-Up

Shake rum, Midori, curaçao, and Rose's Lime Juice well with ice. Strain into collins glass over rocks. Top off with 7-Up. Stir.

FERN GULLY

1 oz. dark Jamaican rum
1 oz. light rum
½ oz. cream of coconut
½ oz. lime juice

2 tsp. orange juice
1 tsp. orzata
⅓ cup crushed ice

Blend all ingredients for 10 to 15 seconds at low speed. Pour into prechilled deep-saucer champagne glass. *More rummy than the usual Frozen Daiquiri, but delicious.*

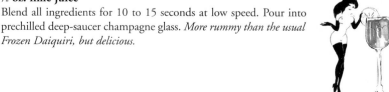

FERN GULLY FIZZ

1 oz. dark Jamaican rum
1 oz. light rum
1 oz. pineapple juice
¾ oz. lime juice

1 tsp. sugar
Iced club soda
1 slice or chunk fresh pineapple
1 slice lime

Shake both kinds of rum, pineapple juice, lime juice, and sugar well with ice. Strain into tall 14-oz. glass half-filled with ice. Fill glass with soda. Stir. Garnish with pineapple and lime slices.

FORT LAUDERDALE

1½ oz. golden rum
½ oz. sweet vermouth
¼ oz. orange juice

¼ oz. lime juice
1 slice cocktail orange in syrup

Shake rum, vermouth, orange juice, and lime juice well with ice. Strain over rocks into prechilled old-fashioned glass. Add orange slice.

FRENCH COLONIAL

1½ oz. golden rum
½ oz. crème de cassis
½ oz. Cointreau or triple sec

½ oz. lemon juice
Iced tonic water
1 slice lemon

Shake rum, crème de cassis, Cointreau, and lemon juice well with ice. Strain into tall 14-oz. glass three-quarters filled with ice cubes. Add tonic water. Stir. Add lemon slice.

FROSTY DAWN COCKTAIL

1½ oz. light rum
1 oz. orange juice

½ oz. Falernum
¼ oz. maraschino liqueur

Shake well with ice. Strain over rocks into prechilled old-fashioned glass.

FROZEN APPLE DAIQUIRI

1½ oz. light rum
½ oz. apple juice
½ oz. lemon juice

⅓ cup crushed ice
1 tsp. sugar
1 apple wedge, with skin

Blend rum, apple juice, lemon juice, crushed ice, and sugar for 10 to 15 seconds at low speed. Pour into prechilled deep-saucer champagne glass. Add apple wedge.

FROZEN BANANA DAIQUIRI

1½ oz. light rum
½ oz. lime juice
½ medium-size, very ripe
   banana, sliced

½ cup finely crushed ice
1 to 2 tsp. sugar, to taste

Mix all ingredients in blender at low speed for 10 to 15 seconds. Pour into 6-oz. saucer champagne glass or outsize cocktail glass.

FROZEN BERKELEY

1½ oz. light rum
½ oz. California brandy
½ oz. passion fruit syrup

½ oz. lemon juice
⅓ cup crushed ice

Blend all ingredients for 10 to 15 seconds at low speed. Pour into deep-saucer champagne glass.

FROZEN DAIQUIRI

1½ to 2 oz. light rum
½ oz. lime juice

½ to 1 tsp. sugar
½ cup crushed ice

Blend all ingredients at low speed for 10 to 15 seconds. Pour into deep-saucer champagne glass. May be served with a small straw. The drink can be made rummier by floating a tsp. of 151-proof rum on top of the Daiquiri in the glass, or it can be made with golden rum or any of the heavier-bodied rums, such as Jamaican, Barbados, or Martinique.

FROZEN GUAVA DAIQUIRI

1½ oz. light rum
1 oz. guava nectar (not syrup)
½ oz. lime juice

1 tsp. banana liqueur
⅓ cup crushed ice

Blend all ingredients for 10 to 15 seconds at low speed. Pour into prechilled deep-saucer champagne glass.

FROZEN GUAVA-ORANGE DAIQUIRI

1½ oz. light rum
¾ oz. guava syrup
½ oz. lime juice

½ oz. orange juice
⅓ cup crushed ice

Blend all ingredients for 10 to 15 seconds at low speed. Pour into prechilled deep-saucer champagne glass.

FROZEN MINT DAIQUIRI

2 oz. light rum
½ oz. lime juice
½ cup crushed ice

6 large mint leaves
1 tsp. sugar

Blend all ingredients for 20 seconds at low speed. Pour into deep-saucer champagne glass. *Perfect prelude to a lamb-chop dinner.*

FROZEN PASSION FRUIT DAIQUIRI

1½ oz. light rum
½ oz. passion fruit syrup
½ oz. lime juice

½ oz. orange juice
¼ oz. lemon juice
⅓ cup crushed ice

Blend all ingredients at low speed for 10 to 15 seconds. Pour into deep-saucer champagne glass.

FROZEN PEACH DAIQUIRI

1½ oz. light rum
½ oz. lime juice
¼ cup frozen sliced peaches, thawed
½ oz. syrup from frozen peaches
⅓ cup crushed ice

Blend all ingredients at low speed for 10 to 15 seconds. Pour into deep-saucer champagne glass. You'll find the rich flavor of the frozen peaches and their syrup peachier than the fresh fruit for this drink.

FROZEN PINEAPPLE DAIQUIRI

1½ oz. light rum
½ oz. lime juice
⅓ cup crushed ice
½ tsp. sugar
4 canned pineapple chunks, drained

Blend all ingredients for 10 to 15 seconds at low speed. Pour into deep-saucer champagne glass. The canned pineapple is actually better than the fresh for this fruity cocktail.

FROZEN SESAME DAIQUIRI

1½ oz. rum
½ oz. sesame-seed syrup (ajonjoli)
½ oz. lime juice
½ oz. dry vermouth
½ oz. orange juice
⅓ cup crushed ice

Blend all ingredients for 10 to 15 seconds at low speed. Pour into deep-saucer champagne glass.

FROZEN SOURSOP DAIQUIRI

1½ oz. light rum
¼ oz. dark Jamaican rum
1 oz. guanabana (soursop) nectar
¼ oz. lime juice
¼ cup sliced banana
⅓ cup crushed ice

Blend all ingredients for 10 to 15 seconds at low speed. Pour into deep-saucer champagne glass. The delicious soursop is now available in the United States as a canned nectar.

FULL MOON FEVER

1½ oz. spiced rum
½ oz. light rum
½ oz. Malibu rum
½ oz. Midori
1 oz. Rose's Lime Juice
3 oz. pineapple juice

Shake well with ice. Strain into collins glass over rocks. Add ice to fill glass if necessary.

FUZZY COMFORT

1½ oz. light rum
½ oz. sloe gin
½ oz. Southern Comfort
½ oz. peach schnapps
4 oz. orange juice

Pour rum, sloe gin, Southern Comfort, and peach schnapps over ice into tall collins glass. Stir. Top off with orange juice and stir gently.

GAUGUIN

2 oz. light rum
½ oz. passion fruit syrup
½ oz. lemon juice
¼ oz. lime juice
⅓ cup crushed ice
1 maraschino cherry

Blend rum, passion fruit syrup, lemon juice, lime juice, and crushed ice at low speed for 10 to 15 seconds. Pour into deep-saucer champagne glass. Add cherry.

GEORGIA RUM COOLER

2½ oz. light rum
1 tsp. salted peanuts
½ oz. lemon juice
1 tsp. grenadine
1 tsp. Falernum
½ cup crushed ice
Iced club soda
Ground cinnamon

Blend rum, peanuts, lemon juice, grenadine, Falernum, and crushed ice at high speed for 30 seconds. Pour into tall 14-oz. glass. Let froth on drink settle. Add two ice cubes and a splash of soda. Stir. Sprinkle lightly with cinnamon. *Pass the platter of cold country ham sliced paper-thin.*

GINGER SPICE

1½ oz. spiced rum
3 oz. ginger ale

Pour spiced rum over ice into highball glass. Top with ginger ale. *And everything's nice.*

GOLDEN GATE

¾ oz. light rum
¾ oz. gin
1 tsp. 151-proof rum
½ oz. lemon juice
½ oz. crème de cacao
½ tsp. Falernum
1 slice orange

Shake light rum, gin, 151-proof rum, lemon juice, crème de cacao, and Falernum well with ice. Strain over rocks in a prechilled old-fashioned glass. Add orange slice. *Leaves a rich afterglow.*

GOOD WILL CAPE

1½ oz. light rum
1 oz. apricot brandy
½ oz. orange juice
½ oz. lime juice
2 dashes orange bitters
1 orange slice

Shake rum, brandy, juices, and bitters well with ice. Strain into prechilled cocktail glass. Garnish with orange slice and share the good vibrations.

GUANABANA

1½ oz. light rum
1 oz. guanabana (soursop) nectar
1 tsp. lime juice

Shake well with ice. Strain into prechilled cocktail glass. Drink must be served ice cold.

GUANABANA COOLER

2 oz. light rum
4 oz. chilled guanabana nectar
1 oz. chilled orange juice
1 tsp. lime juice

Club soda to fill
½ slice orange
1 slice lime

Pour rum, guanabana nectar, and orange and lime juice into tall 14-oz. glass three-quarters filled with ice cubes. Stir well. Add soda to fill glass to rim. Add orange and lime slices.

GUAVA COOLER

1½ oz. rum
1½ oz. guava nectar
½ tsp. sugar
½ oz. maraschino liqueur

½ oz. lemon juice
½ oz. pineapple juice
Iced club soda
½ slice lemon

Shake rum, guava nectar, sugar, maraschino liqueur, lemon juice, and pineapple juice well with ice. Strain into tall 14-oz. glass half-filled with ice. Add soda. Stir. Garnish with lemon slice. *Wonderful cooler before or with a jambalaya feast.*

HAVANA COCKTAIL

1½ oz. light rum
1½ oz. pineapple juice

2 tsp. lemon juice

Shake well with ice. Strain into prechilled cocktail glass. *Light up a fat cigar.*

HAWAIIAN DAISY

1½ oz. light rum
½ oz. pineapple juice
1 tsp. lime juice
1 tsp. grenadine

Iced club soda
1 tsp. 151-proof rum
1 papaya chunk in syrup

Shake light rum, pineapple juice, lime juice, and grenadine well with ice. Strain into tall 8-oz. glass half-filled with ice. Add soda. Stir. Float 151-proof rum on drink. Add papaya chunk.

HEMINGWAY DAIQUIRI

1½ oz. light rum
1 oz. maraschino liqueur

½ oz. lime juice
½ oz. grapefruit juice

Shake well with ice. Strain into prechilled cocktail glass. *A farewell to worries.*

HORSE & JOCKEY

1½ oz. añejo rum
1 oz. Southern Comfort

½ oz. sweet vermouth
2 dashes Angostura bitters

Stir well with ice. Strain into prechilled cocktail glass. *Perfect for a day at the races.*

HUMMER

1½ oz. light rum
1½ oz. coffee liqueur

2 scoops vanilla ice cream
½ cup cracked ice

Blend all ingredients at low speed for 10 to 15 seconds. Pour into tall highball glass.

HURRICANE

1 oz. light rum
1 oz. golden rum
½ oz. passion fruit syrup
2 tsp. lime juice

Shake well with ice. Strain into prechilled cocktail glass. Quantities may be doubled and drink poured over rocks into a coconut shell or double old-fashioned glass.

ICED RUM COFFEE

1½ oz. light rum
1 tsp. dark Jamaican rum
6 oz. iced double-strength coffee
Sugar
2 tbsp. sweetened whipped cream

Pour rums and coffee into tall 14-oz. glass. Add ice to fill glass. Add sugar to taste. Top with whipped cream.

ICED RUM TEA

1½ oz. light rum
½ oz. 151-proof rum
6 oz. iced strong black tea
1 tsp. sugar
1 tsp. Falernum
1 tsp. lemon juice
1 slice lemon
2 large mint
leaves

Pour rums, tea, sugar, Falernum, and lemon juice into tall 14-oz. glass. Add ice to fill glass. Stir. Garnish with lemon slice and mint leaves partially torn. To prevent tea from clouding, let cool to room temperature before combining with ice.

ICE PALACE

1½ oz. light rum
1 oz. Galliano
1 oz. apricot brandy
2 oz. pineapple juice
½ oz. lemon juice
1 orange slice

Shake rum, Galliano, apricot brandy, and juices well with ice. Strain into tall collins glass over ice. Garnish with orange slice.

INDEPENDENCE SWIZZLE

2 oz. dark Trinidad rum
3 dashes Angostura bitters
1 tsp. honey
1 tsp. sugar
½ oz. lime juice
1 slice lime

In tall 14-oz. glass, stir rum, bitters, honey, sugar, and lime juice until honey is blended with other ingredients. Add finely cracked ice to fill glass. Twirl with a swizzle stick if you have one, or stir and churn with a bar spoon or tall iced-tea spoon. As drink is stirred, ice will melt. Add more ice as necessary to fill glass to rim, swizzling or stirring until ice and liquids reach top of glass. Add lime slice. *A drink shared to celebrate the independence of Trinidad and Tobago.*

ISLE OF THE BLESSED COCONUT

1½ oz. light rum
½ oz. cream of coconut
½ oz. lime juice
¼ oz. lemon juice
¼ oz. orange juice
½ tsp. sugar
⅓ cup crushed ice

Blend all ingredients at low speed for 10 to 15 seconds. Pour into deep-saucer champagne glass. *Serve with a bowl of toasted coconut slices.*

JADE

1¾ oz. golden rum
½ tsp. green crème de menthe
½ tsp. curaçao
1½ tsp. lime juice
1 tsp. sugar
1 slice lime

Shake rum, crème de menthe, curaçao, lime juice, and sugar well with ice. Strain into prechilled cocktail glass. Add lime slice. *Minty, but not overpowering.*

JAMAICAN ELEGANCE

1½ oz. golden Jamaican rum
½ oz. brandy
½ oz. pineapple juice
1 oz. lime juice
1 tsp. simple syrup or rock-candy syrup
1 slice lime

Shake rum, brandy, pineapple juice, lime juice, and syrup well with ice. Strain into prechilled tall 14-oz. glass. Add ice to fill glass. Add lime slice.

JAMAICAN GINGER

1½ oz. light rum
½ oz. dark Jamaican rum
½ oz. 151-proof rum
½ oz. Falernum
½ oz. lime juice
Iced ginger beer
½ slice pineapple in crème de menthe
1 cube preserved ginger in syrup

Shake the three kinds of rum, Falernum, and lime juice well with ice. Strain into tall 14-oz. glass half-filled with ice. Fill glass with ginger beer. Stir. Garnish with pineapple and ginger.

LA SEVILLA

1½ oz. light rum
1½ oz. port
Juice of ½ lemon
1 tsp. powdered sugar
1 egg white
Soda water to fill

Shake rum, port, lemon juice, powdered sugar, and egg white very well with ice. Strain into tall highball glass over ice. Top off with soda water.

LEEWARD

1½ oz. light rum
½ oz. Calvados
½ oz. sweet vermouth
Lemon peel

Shake rum, Calvados, and vermouth well with ice. Strain over rocks into prechilled old-fashioned glass. Twist lemon peel above drink and drop into glass. *Pass the anchovy canapés sprinkled with chopped hard-boiled egg.*

LEMON RUM COOLER

2 oz. light rum
1 tsp. 151-proof rum
2 oz. pineapple juice
½ oz. lemon juice

½ oz. Falernum
Iced bitter lemon soda
1 slice lemon

Shake both kinds of rum, pineapple juice, lemon juice, and Falernum well with ice. Strain into tall 14-oz. glass. Add two ice cubes. Fill glass with bitter lemon soda. Add lemon slice.

LORD AND LADY

1½ oz. dark rum
1½ oz. Tia Maria

Pour rum and Tia Maria into old-fashioned glass over ice. Stir.

MADAM ROSA

1½ oz. light rum
½ oz. cherry-flavored brandy
2 oz. orange juice

½ oz. lime juice
Iced tonic water

Shake rum, cherry-flavored brandy, orange juice, and lime juice well with ice. Strain into tall 12-oz. glass. Add two large ice cubes. Fill with tonic water. Stir.

MAESTRO

1½ oz. añejo rum
1 oz. cream sherry
1 oz. lime juice

4 oz. ginger ale
Lemon peel

Shake añejo rum, cream sherry, and lime juice well with ice. Strain into collins glass over ice. Top with ginger ale. Twist lemon peel above drink and drop into glass. *Bravo!*

MAI TAI

3 oz. light rum
½ oz. lime juice
¼ tsp. triple sec
¼ tsp. orzata

½ tsp. sugar
1 slice lime
1 sprig mint
1 pineapple stick

Shake rum, lime juice, triple sec, orzata, and sugar well with ice. Strain into prechilled double old-fashioned glass. Add enough cracked ice or ice cubes to fill glass. Tear one or two mint leaves partially to release flavor. Garnish with lime slice, mint sprig, and pineapple stick.

MALIBU BAY BREEZE

1½ oz. Malibu rum
2 oz. cranberry juice

2 oz. pineapple juice

Pour rum into highball glass over ice. Top with cranberry juice and pineapple juice. Stir.

MANDEVILLE

1½ oz. light rum
1 oz. dark Jamaican rum
¾ oz. lemon juice
1 tsp. Pernod

½ oz. cola drink
¼ tsp. grenadine
1 slice orange

Shake both kinds of rum, lemon juice, Pernod, cola drink, and grenadine well with ice. Strain over rocks into prechilled old-fashioned glass. Add orange slice.

MARY PICKFORD

1½ oz. light rum
1 oz. pineapple juice
½ tsp. maraschino liqueur

½ tsp. grenadine
1 maraschino cherry

Shake well with ice. Strain into prechilled cocktail glass. Drop in cherry.

MÉNAGE À TROIS

1½ oz. dark rum
1 oz. triple sec

1 oz. light cream

Shake very well with ice. Strain into prechilled cocktail glass. *Bring a friend.*

MOBILE MULE

2 oz. light rum
½ lime

Iced ginger beer

Pour rum into tall 12- or 14-oz. glass or copper mug with ice cubes or cracked ice. Squeeze lime above drink and drop into glass. Fill with ginger beer. Stir. *A variation on the vodka-inspired Moscow Mule.*

MOCHA COOLER

6 oz. cold, strong, freshly brewed coffee
1 oz. light rum
½ oz. Galliano

1 tsp. sugar or more to taste
Heavy cream

Pour coffee, rum, Galliano, and sugar into tall 12-oz. glass. Stir well until sugar dissolves. Add ice to nearly fill glass and stir well again. Float heavy cream on top by pouring it over the back of a spoon so that cream flows to rim of glass.

MONKEY WRENCH

1½ oz. light rum
3 oz. grapefruit juice

1 dash Angostura bitters

Shake well with ice. Strain into prechilled old-fashioned glass over ice.

MUMSICLE

1½ oz. dark rum
1½ oz. bourbon

1 dash Angostura bitters
1 maraschino cherry

Stir rum, bourbon, and bitters well with ice. Strain into prechilled cocktail glass. Garnish with maraschino cherry.

MUSKMELON

1½ oz. light rum
¼ cup sliced ripe cantaloupe meat
⅓ cup crushed ice
½ tsp. sugar

½ oz. orange juice
½ oz. lime juice
1 cube cantaloupe on cocktail spear

Put rum, sliced cantaloupe, ice, sugar, orange juice, and lime juice into blender. Blend at low speed for 10 to 15 seconds. Pour into prechilled old-fashioned glass. Add ice cubes or ice slices, if necessary, to fill glass to rim. Garnish with cantaloupe cube.

MUTINY

1½ oz. dark rum
½ oz. red Dubonnet

2 dashes Angostura bitters
1 maraschino cherry

Stir rum, Dubonnet, and bitters well with ice. Strain into prechilled cocktail glass. Garnish with maraschino cherry.

NAVY GROG

1 oz. dark Jamaican rum
½ oz. light rum
½ oz. lime juice
½ oz. orange juice
½ oz. pineapple juice

½ oz. guava nectar
¼ oz. Falernum
½ cup crushed ice
4 large mint leaves

Put both kinds of rum, lime juice, orange juice, pineapple juice, guava nectar, Falernum, and crushed ice into blender. Blend at low speed for 15 seconds. Pour into double old-fashioned glass. Add ice to fill glass to rim. Tear mint leaves partially and float on drink. Serve with straw.

NEVADA

1½ oz. light rum
1 oz. grapefruit juice
1 oz. lime juice

2 tsp. superfine sugar
1 dash Angostura bitters

Shake well with ice. Strain into prechilled cocktail glass. *You may never want to leave Las Vegas again.*

NEW ORLEANS BUCK

1½ oz. light rum
½ oz. lime juice
½ oz. orange juice

2 dashes Peychaud's bitters
Iced ginger ale
1 slice lime

Shake rum, lime juice, orange juice, and bitters well with ice. Strain into 8-oz. glass half-filled with ice. Add ginger ale. Stir. Add lime slice.

OCHO RIOS

1½ oz. Jamaican rum
1 oz. guava nectar
½ oz. heavy cream

½ oz. lime juice
½ tsp. sugar
⅓ cup crushed ice

Blend all ingredients at low speed for 10 to 15 seconds. Pour into prechilled deep-saucer champagne glass. *A creamy, rummy drink recommended after a spearfishing expedition.*

OLD-FASHIONED RUM AND MUSCARI

1 oz. light rum
1 oz. Muscari
Angostura bitters

Iced club soda
Lemon peel

Pour rum, Muscari, and 2 or 3 dashes Angostura bitters into old-fashioned glass. Fill glass with rocks. Stir well. Add splash of soda. Twist lemon peel over drink and drop into glass.

ORANGE COLADA

4 oz. orange juice
1 oz. light rum
1 oz. dark Jamaican rum
1 tbsp. Coconut Snow (a powdered coconut mixture)

1 tsp. sugar
1 cup crushed ice

Pour all ingredients into blender. Blend at high speed for 10 seconds. Pour into tall 14-oz. glass. Add one or two ice cubes if necessary to fill glass. To make a piña colada, substitute pineapple juice for the orange.

ORANGE COOLER IN SHELL

1 extra-large California orange
1 oz. 151-proof rum
½ oz. curaçao

½ oz. lime juice
1 tsp. sugar
1 slice cocktail orange in syrup

Cut a cap off top of orange about ½ inch from top. With a sharp grapefruit knife, gouge out the orange flesh, leaving orange shell intact. Squeeze enough juice from the flesh to make 1½ oz. Shake orange juice, rum, curaçao, lime juice, and sugar well with ice. Strain into orange shell. Place orange shell in a bowl or soup dish about 7 inches in diameter. Pack finely crushed ice around orange. Fasten orange slice onto cocktail spear and place across orange cup. Serve with a short colored straw. *A show-off concoction for drink hobbyists and rum specialists.*

PAGO PAGO

1½ oz. golden rum
½ oz. fresh lime juice
½ tsp. green Chartreuse

¼ tsp. white crème de cacao
½ oz. pineapple juice

Shake well with ice. Strain into prechilled cocktail glass. *Pineapple comes through beautifully.*

PASSION FRUIT COOLER

4 oz. passion fruit nectar (not syrup)
1½ oz. light rum
1 oz. gin

½ oz. lemon juice
1 oz. orange juice
2 sprigs mint

Shake passion-fruit nectar, rum, gin, lemon juice, and orange juice well with ice. Strain into tall 14-oz. glass. Add enough coarsely cracked ice or ice cubes to fill glass. Decorate with mint after partially tearing several leaves to release fragrance.

PENSACOLA

1½ oz. light rum
½ oz. guava nectar
½ oz. orange juice

½ oz. lemon juice
⅓ cup crushed ice

Blend all ingredients for 10 to 15 seconds at low speed. Pour into deep-saucer champagne glass.

PIÑA COLADA

1½ oz. light rum
2 oz. pineapple juice
1 oz. cream of coconut

⅓ cup cracked ice
1 pineapple stick
1 cherry

Put rum, pineapple juice, cream of coconut, and ice into blender. Blend at high speed for 10 to 15 seconds. Pour into tall collins glass. Garnish with pineapple and cherry.

PINK CREOLE

1½ oz. golden rum
½ oz. lime juice
1 tsp. heavy cream

1 tsp. grenadine
1 black cherry, soaked in rum

Shake rum, lime juice, cream, and grenadine well with ice. Strain into prechilled cocktail glass. Add rum-soaked cherry.

PINK RUM AND TONIC

2½ oz. light rum
½ oz. lime juice
1 tsp. grenadine

Iced tonic water
1 slice lime

Shake rum, lime juice, and grenadine well with ice. Strain into tall 14-oz. glass half-filled with ice. Add tonic water. Stir. Add lime slice. *Curiously refreshing yo-ho-ho.*

PINK VERANDA

1 oz. golden rum
½ oz. heavy Jamaican rum
1½ oz. cranberry juice

½ oz. lime juice
1 tsp. sugar
½ egg white

Shake well with ice. Strain into prechilled old-fashioned glass. Add ice slices or ice cubes if necessary to fill glass to rim.

PLANTER'S PUNCH

1½ oz. dark Jamaican rum
3 oz. orange juice
½ oz. lemon juice
1 tsp. sugar

¼ tsp. grenadine
1 slice lemon
1 slice orange

Shake rum, orange juice, lemon juice, sugar, and grenadine well with ice. Strain over rocks into tall 10-oz. glass. Stir well. Add ice if necessary to fill glass. Garnish with orange and lemon slices.

PLANTER'S PUNCH WITH FALERNUM

2 oz. dark Jamaican rum	½ oz. lime juice
1 dash Angostura bitters	Iced club soda
½ oz. Falernum	1 slice orange
1 tsp. sugar	1 maraschino cherry

Shake rum, bitters, Falernum, sugar, and lime juice extremely well with ice. Strain into tall 14-oz. glass three-quarters filled with ice cubes. Stir. Add club soda to fill glass. Garnish with orange slice and cherry.

PLAYBOY COOLER

1¼ oz. golden Jamaican rum	2 tsp. lemon juice
1¼ oz. Jamaican coffee liqueur	Cola drink
3 oz. pineapple juice	1 slice pineapple

Shake rum, coffee liqueur, pineapple juice, and lemon juice well with ice. Strain into prechilled tall 14-oz. glass. Add ice to fill glass to 1 inch from top. Add cola. Garnish with pineapple slice.

POLYNESIA

1½ oz. light rum	½ egg white
1 oz. passion fruit syrup	⅓ cup crushed ice
¼ oz. lime juice	

Blend all ingredients for 10 to 15 seconds at low speed. Pour into prechilled deep-saucer champagne glass.

POLYNESIAN PARADISE

1½ oz. golden rum	½ oz. sweet vermouth
1 tsp. brown sugar	¼ oz. triple sec
¾ oz. lime juice	⅓ cup crushed ice

Blend all ingredients at low speed for 10 to 15 seconds. Pour into prechilled deep-saucer champagne glass. *Paradise found.*

PONCE DE LEÓN

1½ oz. light rum	½ oz. mango nectar
½ oz. grapefruit juice	1 tsp. lemon juice

Shake well with ice. Strain into prechilled sugar-frosted cocktail glass.

PORT ANTONIO

1 oz. golden rum	½ oz. coffee liqueur
½ oz. dark Jamaican rum	1 tsp. Falernum
½ oz. lime juice	1 slice lime

Shake both kinds of rum, lime juice, coffee liqueur, and Falernum well with ice. Strain over rocks into prechilled old-fashioned glass. Add lime slice.

 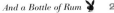

PORT MARIA

1½ oz. light rum   1 tsp. Falernum
¾ oz. pineapple juice   Grated nutmeg
½ oz. lemon juice

Shake rum, pineapple juice, lemon juice, and Falernum well with ice. Strain into prechilled cocktail glass. Sprinkle nutmeg on top.

PUERTO RICAN PINK LADY

1¾ oz. golden rum   1 tsp. grenadine
¾ oz. lemon juice   ⅓ cup crushed ice
½ egg white

Blend all ingredients at low speed for 10 to 15 seconds. Pour into sugar-rimmed deep-saucer champagne glass.

QUADRUPLE PINEAPPLE *(Makes 4 single or 2 double drinks)*

1 large chilled pineapple   3 oz. orange juice
½ cup pineapple sherbet   1½ oz. lime juice
6 oz. light rum   ½ oz. maraschino liqueur

The pineapple should measure at least 7 inches from base to top of fruit, not including stem. Cut a cap off pineapple about ½ inch from top. To remove meat from pineapple, cut a deep circle around edge of pineapple about ½ inch from rim, leaving a large cylinder of fruit, which must then be gouged out. A sharp boning knife is a good instrument for the job. Cut wedges of fruit loose by slicing diagonally toward rim of fruit. Use a grapefruit knife or large potato cutter to remove small pieces of fruit. Do not pierce shell of fruit or it will leak. The cavity of the pineapple should be large enough to hold 2 measuring cups of liquid. Test it for size. Cut hard core of fruit away and discard it. Cut enough tender pineapple meat to make ½ cup fruit in small dice. Into well of blender, put the ½ cup diced pineapple, sherbet, rum, orange juice, lime juice, and maraschino liqueur. Blend 5 seconds. Pour into pineapple shell. Place pineapple in deep dish or bowl surrounded with finely crushed ice. Place two or four colored straws in drink, allowing for two or four pineapple sippers. A second round may be prepared beforehand from the same pineapple and blended just before refilling pineapple. *An elaborate production, beloved by rum barons.*

ROSE HALL

1 oz. dark Jamaican rum   1 tsp. lime juice
1 oz. orange juice   1 slice lime
½ oz. banana liqueur

Shake rum, orange juice, banana liqueur, and lime juice well with ice. Strain over rocks into old-fashioned glass. Add lime slice.

RUM AND COCONUT COOLER

2½ oz. light rum   Iced club soda
1 oz. cream of coconut   1 slice lemon
½ oz. lemon juice   1 maraschino cherry

Shake rum, cream of coconut, and lemon juice well with ice. Strain into tall 14-oz. glass half-filled with ice. Add a splash of soda. Garnish with lemon slice and cherry.

RUM AND PINEAPPLE COOLER

2½ oz. light rum
2 oz. pineapple juice
½ oz. lemon juice
1 tsp. 151-proof rum
1 tsp. sugar

1 dash Angostura bitters
Iced club soda
1 pineapple chunk
1 papaya chunk in syrup

Shake light rum, pineapple juice, lemon juice, 151-proof rum, sugar, and bitters well with ice. Strain into tall 14-oz. glass. Add a splash of soda and enough ice to fill glass. Garnish with pineapple and papaya chunks fastened onto a cocktail spear.

RUM AND SHERRY

1½ oz. light rum
¾ oz. sherry

1 maraschino cherry

Stir rum and sherry well with ice. Strain into prechilled cocktail glass. Add cherry. The felicitous blend of rum and sherry may be made with very dry cocktail sherry, medium amontillado, or rich cream sherry to meet your own choice of dryness or sweetness. All are delightful.

RUM BUCK

1½ oz. light rum
½ oz. lime juice
Iced ginger ale

1 slice lime
Toasted slivered almonds

Shake rum and lime juice well with ice. Strain into 8-oz. glass half-filled with ice. Add ginger ale. Stir. Add lime slice and about a tsp. of almonds.

RUM CASSIS

1 oz. light-bodied rum
1 oz. dry white wine or dry vermouth
2 tsp. crème de cassis

Chilled club soda
1 slice lime

Pour rum, wine, and crème de cassis over rocks into 8-oz. tall glass or old-fashioned glass. Stir well. Add a splash of soda. Stir lightly. Add lime slice.

RUM CITRUS COOLER

2 oz. light rum
1 oz. orange juice
½ oz. lime juice
½ oz. Cointreau

1 tsp. sugar
Iced 7-Up
1 slice lime
½ slice lemon

Shake rum, orange juice, lime juice, Cointreau, and sugar well with ice. Strain into tall 14-oz. glass half-filled with ice. Add 7-Up. Stir. Garnish with lime and lemon slices. *Solace or celebration after eighteen holes on the fairway.*

RUM COCONUT FIZZ

2¼ oz. light rum	Iced club soda
½ oz. cream of coconut	1 slice lime
½ oz. lime juice	

Shake rum, cream of coconut, and lime juice well with ice. Strain into tall 14-oz. glass half-filled with ice. Fill glass with soda. Stir. Add lime slice. *Sip while the teriyaki is browning over the charcoal.*

RUM CURAÇAO COOLER

1 oz. dark Jamaican rum	Iced club soda
1 oz. curaçao	1 slice lime
½ oz. lime juice	½ slice orange

Shake rum, curaçao, and lime juice with ice. Strain into tall 14-oz. glass. Add a splash of soda and ice to fill glass. Garnish with lime and orange slices.

RUM DUBONNET

1½ oz. light rum	1 tsp. lime juice
¾ oz. red Dubonnet	Lime peel

Shake rum, Dubonnet, and lime juice well with ice. Strain into prechilled cocktail glass. Twist lime peel over drink and drop into glass.

RUM EGGNOG

2 oz. dark rum	1 egg yolk
6 oz. milk	Nutmeg to taste
1 tsp. powdered sugar	

Shake rum, milk, sugar, and egg yolk very well with ice. Strain over rocks into collins glass. Sprinkle freshly ground nutmeg on top.

RUM GIMLET

2 oz. light rum	1 lime wedge
1 oz. Rose's Lime Juice	

Stir rum and Rose's Lime Juice well with ice. Strain into prechilled cocktail glass. Garnish with lime wedge.

RUM MARTINI

2½ oz. light rum	Lemon peel
1½ tsp. dry vermouth	

Stir rum and vermouth with ice. Strain into prechilled cocktail glass. Twist lemon peel over drink and drop into glass.

RUM MILK PUNCH

2 oz. light rum	1 tsp. powdered sugar
1 cup milk	Nutmeg to taste

Shake rum, milk, and sugar very well with ice. Strain into collins glass over a couple of ice cubes. Sprinkle freshly ground nutmeg on top to taste.

RUM OLD-FASHIONED

½ tsp. sugar
1 or 2 dashes Angostura bitters
1 tsp. water
2 oz. light, golden, or dark Jamaican rum

Lime peel
1 tsp. 151-proof rum

Mix sugar, bitters, and water in old-fashioned glass until sugar is completely dissolved. Add two ice cubes or several pieces of cracked ice. Add 2 oz. Jamaican rum. Stir well. Twist lime peel over drink and drop into glass. Float 151-proof rum on top.

RUM PINEAPPLE FIZZ

2 oz. golden rum
½ oz. 151-proof rum
⅓ cup fresh pineapple, small dice
½ egg white
2 tsp. sugar

½ oz. lemon juice
½ oz. lime juice
½ cup crushed ice
Iced club soda
1 slice lime

Put both kinds of rum, pineapple, egg white, sugar, lemon juice, lime juice, and ice into blender. Blend at low speed for 10 to 15 seconds. Pour into tall 14-oz. glass. Add ice cubes to almost fill glass. Add a splash of soda and lime slice.

RUM RICKEY

1½ oz. light or dark rum
3 oz. club soda

Lemon peel

Pour rum into cocktail glass over ice cubes. Top off with club soda. Stir. Twist lemon peel over drink and drop into glass.

RUM ROYALE

1 oz. light rum
2 oz. Sauternes
1½ oz. lemon juice
2 oz. pineapple juice

1 tsp. sugar
1 dash Peychaud's bitters
1 cube pineapple
1 maraschino cherry

Shake rum, Sauternes, lemon juice, pineapple juice, sugar, and bitters well with ice. Strain into prechilled tall 14-oz. glass. Add ice to fill glass. Affix pineapple cube and cherry to cocktail spear and rest on rim of glass.

RUM SAZERAC

1 sugar cube
1 dash Angostura bitters
2 oz. light rum

1 oz. Pernod
Water to fill

Soak sugar cube in Angostura bitters and muddle in old-fashioned glass. Pour rum over ice. Add Pernod and top off with water. Stir gently.

RUM SCREWDRIVER

1½ oz. light rum
3 oz. cold fresh orange juice

1 slice orange

Put rum and orange juice (without ice) into blender. Blend for 10 to 15 seconds at low speed. Pour over rocks into old-fashioned glass. Garnish with orange slice. *A perfect brunch beginner.*

RUM SIDECAR

1½ oz. golden rum
½ oz. Cointreau or triple sec
½ oz. lemon juice
¼ oz. dark Jamaican rum

Shake golden rum, Cointreau, and lemon juice well with ice. Strain into prechilled cocktail glass or into old-fashioned glass over rocks. Float dark rum on top.

RUM SOUR

2 oz. light or golden rum
½ oz. lemon juice
1 tsp. orange juice
1 tsp. rock-candy syrup or sugar
½ slice orange

Shake rum, lemon juice, orange juice, and syrup or sugar well with ice. Strain into prechilled whiskey-sour glass. Add orange slice. A teaspoon of 151-proof rum may be floated on top for a more rummish accent. For a heavier-bodied but richly mellow Rum Sour, use dark Jamaican rum.

SAGUENAY

1 oz. light rum
1 oz. dry vermouth
1 tsp. lemon juice
2 tsp. crème de cassis

Shake well with ice. Strain over rocks into old-fashioned glass. Add a splash of club soda if desired.

SAN JUAN

1½ oz. light rum
1 oz. grapefruit juice
1 tsp. cream of coconut
2 tsp. lime juice
⅓ cup crushed ice
2 tsp. 151-proof rum

Put 1½ oz. light rum, grapefruit juice, cream of coconut, lime juice, and ice into blender. Blend at low speed for 10 to 15 seconds. Pour into deep-saucer champagne glass. Float 151-proof rum on top.

SAN JUAN SLING

¾ oz. light rum
¾ oz. cherry liqueur
¾ oz. Benedictine
½ oz. lime juice
Iced club soda
Lime peel

Shake rum, cherry liqueur, Benedictine, and lime juice well with ice. Strain into tall 14-oz. glass half-filled with ice. Add soda. Twist lime peel over drink and drop into glass.

SANTIAGO

1¾ oz. light rum
1 oz. grenadine
Juice of 1 lime
½ tsp. powdered sugar
1 slice orange

Shake very well with ice. Strain into prechilled cocktail glass. Add ice to fill glass if necessary. Garnish with orange slice.

SCORPION

2 oz. light rum	½ oz. orzata
2 oz. orange juice	½ cup crushed ice
½ oz. lemon juice	1 slice orange
1 oz. California brandy	

Put rum, orange juice, lemon juice, brandy, orzata, and ice into blender. Blend at low speed for 10 to 15 seconds. Pour into double old-fashioned glass with enough ice cubes to fill glass to rim. Add orange slice.

SEPTEMBER MORN

1½ oz. light rum	1 tsp. grenadine
½ oz. lime juice	½ egg white

Shake well with ice. Strain into prechilled sugar-frosted cocktail glass. Glass rim may be moistened with grenadine before dipping into sugar.

SESAME

1½ oz. light rum	½ oz. sesame-seed syrup (ajonjoli)
½ oz. lime juice	

Shake well with ice. Strain into prechilled cocktail glass. Sesame is a versatile seed. It's available in syrup form in stores featuring Caribbean products. *A rummy and offbeat drink.*

SHARK'S TOOTH

1½ oz. golden rum	¼ oz. sloe gin
¼ oz. lemon juice	1 dash Angostura bitters
¼ oz. passion fruit syrup	Orange peel
¼ oz. sweet vermouth	1 maraschino cherry

Shake rum, lemon juice, passion fruit syrup, vermouth, sloe gin, and bitters well with ice. Strain into prechilled sugar-frosted cocktail glass. Twist orange peel over drink and drop into glass. Add cherry.

SHAW PARK

1 oz. golden rum	¼ oz. apricot liqueur
½ oz. Cointreau or triple sec	½ oz. lime juice

Shake well with ice. Strain into prechilled cocktail glass or pour over rocks.

SHOO-IN

½ oz. dark Jamaican rum	½ oz. maraschino liqueur
1 oz. light rum	2 oz. chilled grapefruit juice
1 oz. California brandy	2 oz. chilled pineapple juice

Pour all ingredients into tall 14-oz. glass half-filled with ice cubes. Stir well. Add ice cubes if necessary to fill glass. Stir.

SHORE LEAVE

1 oz. light rum	Iced tonic water
1 oz. sloe gin	1 slice lime
½ oz. lime juice	

Shake rum, sloe gin, and lime juice well with ice. Strain into tall 12-oz. glass three-quarters filled with ice cubes. Fill glass with tonic water. Stir. Add lime slice.

SOUTHERN BANANA COMFORT

1 oz. golden rum	⅓ oz. lime juice
1 oz. Southern Comfort	1 tsp. sugar
¼ cup sliced banana	⅓ cup crushed ice

Blend all ingredients at low speed for 10 to 15 seconds. Pour into saucer champagne glass. *The best possible way to usher in a platter of fried or barbecued chicken.*

ST. AUGUSTINE

1½ oz. light rum	1 tsp. Cointreau
1 oz. grapefruit juice	Lemon peel

Shake rum, grapefruit juice, and Cointreau well with ice. Strain into prechilled sugar-frosted cocktail glass. Twist lemon peel over drink and drop into glass. *Perfect before a pompano dinner.*

ST. CROIX COOLER

Peel of ½ large orange	2½ oz. orange juice
2 oz. light rum	1½ oz. lemon juice
½ oz. dark Jamaican rum	1 dash orange flower water
1 oz. brandy	Iced club soda
1 tbsp. brown sugar	

Cut orange peel from stem end in one continuing spiral about ½ inch wide. Place peel in tall 14-oz. glass, permitting one end to overhang rim. Shake both kinds of rum, brandy, brown sugar, orange juice, lemon juice, and orange flower water well with ice. Strain into glass. Fill glass to rim with coarsely cracked ice or ice cubes. Add a splash of soda. Stir. *A rich tropical cooler that will easily outlast two ordinary cocktails.*

STRATOSPHERE

1 oz. rum	½ oz. lemon juice
½ oz. California brandy	1 tsp. sugar
¼ oz. tart cherry liqueur	

Shake well with ice. Strain into prechilled cocktail glass. *Pleasant to drink around a cheese fondue.*

STRAWBERRY FROZEN DAIQUIRI

1½ oz. light rum	1 tsp. sugar
½ oz. lime juice	½ oz. heavy cream
½ tsp. maraschino liqueur	⅓ cup crushed ice
¼ cup thawed frozen strawberries in syrup	

Whirl all ingredients in blender at high speed for 10 seconds. Pour into deep-saucer champagne glass or old-fashioned glass.

STRAWBERRY RUM FLIP

1 oz. strawberry liqueur
1 oz. light rum
1 tsp. lemon juice

1 small egg
1 tsp. sugar
Ground nutmeg

Shake strawberry liqueur, rum, lemon juice, egg, and sugar well with ice. Strain into prechilled Delmonico glass. Sprinkle with freshly ground nutmeg.

TAHITI CLUB

2 oz. golden rum
½ oz. lime juice
½ oz. pineapple juice

1 tsp. maraschino liqueur
1 slice orange

Shake rum, lime juice, pineapple juice, and maraschino liqueur well with ice. Strain into prechilled old-fashioned glass. Add cracked ice or ice cubes to fill glass. Add orange slice.

TALL ISLANDER

2 oz. light rum
3 oz. pineapple juice
1 oz. lime juice
1 tsp. dark Jamaican rum

1 tsp. sugar syrup
Iced club soda
1 slice lime

Shake light rum, pineapple juice, lime juice, dark rum, and syrup well with ice. Strain into tall 14-oz. glass. Add a splash of soda and enough ice to fill glass. Stir. Add lime slice. *Equally at home in a high-rise or down among the sheltering palms.*

SHANGHAI COCKTAIL

1½ oz. light rum
1 oz. anisette

1 tsp. grenadine
Juice of ½ lemon

Shake well with ice. Strain into prechilled cocktail glass.

TIE ME TO THE BEDPOST

1½ oz. Malibu rum
½ oz. Midori liqueur

½ oz. Absolut Citron
½ oz. Rose's Lime Juice

Shake well with ice. Strain into prechilled whiskey-sour glass. *Silk sash optional.*

TORRIDORA COCKTAIL

1½ oz. light rum
½ oz. coffee liqueur

¼ oz. heavy cream
1 tsp. 151-proof rum

Shake light rum, coffee liqueur, and cream well with ice. Strain into prechilled cocktail glass. Float 151-proof rum on top. *In the Caribbean, the dinner hour commences rather late, about nine o'clock in the evening. By this time, the sweetness of the cocktail hour will have passed on, and one will be left with a rummy repose and a fine appetite.*

TRADE WINDS

2 oz. golden rum
½ oz. lime juice
½ oz. plum brandy

1½ tsp. sugar
⅓ cup crushed ice

Blend all ingredients at low speed for 10 to 15 seconds. Pour into prechilled deep-saucer champagne glass. *Potent with plum flavor, but not a scalp raiser.*

TSUNAMI

1½ oz. spiced rum (Captain Morgan's)
½ oz. Malibu rum
½ oz. dark rum (Myers's)

4 oz. pineapple juice
Splash grenadine

Pour rums over ice into tall collins glass. Add pineapple juice. Stir. Float grenadine on top.

UNISPHERE

1½ oz. golden rum
1 tsp. grenadine
½ oz. lime juice

½ tsp. Benedictine
½ tsp. Pernod

Shake well with ice. Strain into prechilled cocktail glass. Small amounts of the liqueurs come through beautifully without overpowering the flavor.

WATERMELON COOLER

½ cup diced watermelon, sans seeds
2¼ oz. light rum
½ oz. lime juice
¼ oz. maraschino liqueur

1 tsp. sugar
½ cup crushed ice
1 slice lime

Put watermelon, rum, lime juice, maraschino liqueur, sugar, and ice into blender. Blend for 10 to 15 seconds at low speed. Pour into tall 14-oz. glass. When foam subsides, add ice to fill glass. Stir. Add lime slice.

ZOMBIE

1½ oz. dark rum
1½ oz. light rum
½ oz. apricot brandy
1 oz. pineapple juice

1 oz. orange juice
1 oz. lemon juice
½ oz. Bacardi 151
1 pineapple stick

Shake rums, apricot brandy, and juices very well with ice. Pour into tall 13-oz. glass. Float 151-proof rum on top. Garnish with pineapple stick. *You'll sleep well tonight.*

CHAPTER 12

* Vodka *

Vodka's amazing success (for years it's been outselling any other spirit in the United States) is no longer news, but what is incredible is that it reached the top of the liquor heap despite all the false witnesses who originally baptized it in this country and springboarded it with phony descriptions. Foremost of the misleaders was the U.S. government, which issued Standards of Identity that distillers must follow both when they make vodka and when they later describe it in their advertising. With well-intended but somewhat fuddled reasoning, the government declared that vodka (a Russian word meaning "little water") cannot be sold as vodka unless it is free from "distinctive character, aroma, taste, or color."

Now nothing that passes over the taste buds (including water) is free from taste. To demonstrate how false the injunction is, pour orange juice into two glasses, add a jigger of vodka to one of them, and ask one or any number of tasters to note the difference if any. Unless the tasters' taste buds are completely paralyzed, they consistently spot the Screwdriver from the plain orange juice. Vodka obviously has considerably less taste than whiskey, brandy, rum, or ouzo, but when added to any other potable—from beef bouillon to branch water—it distinctly modifies the flavor of that to which it is added.

"Free from aroma"? Take two tulip-shaped glasses. Pour water into one and vodka into the other. Submit them for nosing to anyone present—a sober judge, a nondrinker, or whom you will. Notice the instant jolt as the glass with vodka is sniffed.

"Free from character"? If, by character, you mean something that confers distinctiveness, then all vodkas should be exactly alike. How far from the facts that this parts company can easily be shown by simply tasting two or three different vodkas side by side. You'll notice that while they're all from the same breed, small but notable differences stand out. You'll notice deviations in smoothness, graininess, or traces of sweetness, and in some vodkas you may even detect flavors mildly reminiscent of various herbs and spices.

As vodka drinking continues to mount, old myths continue to dissolve. The claim that vodka is undetectable on the breath is seldom touted anymore. Drink too much vodka and your breath unfortunately will proclaim that there's a full cargo aboard. The old fable about vodka's abnormal potency—a handful of people still compare it to bottled dynamite—is also rapidly disappearing as drinkers realize that 80-proof or 100-proof vodka is no more of a stiff glass than 80- or 100-proof whiskey. In fact, the next morning, vodka seems to leave fewer cranberry eyes and somewhat smaller heads than other liquors.

When a distiller makes vodka, the goal is to make "pure" ethyl alcohol, which will later be cut to drinking strength by adding water. By "pure" the distiller means as free as possible from congeners, the substances that give flavor to whiskey, rum, brandy, etc. Vodka makers have several ways of eliminating congeners. The first is to distill vodka at the highest possible proof, always above 190. It must be distilled with such artful care that only the smoothest fraction of spirits is accepted; the balance of the run is rejected or redistilled. It may be distilled several times, i.e., rectified in order to eliminate traces of residual congeners. Often the vodka is filtered through charcoal for further purification, and the kind and amount of charcoal is important. Sometimes vodka is agitated by special devices for flavor elimination. Finally it's put through filter pads. These finishing processes are a fine art indeed, and the subtle differences between vodkas are the result of the sensitive skill with which these final steps are handled.

Vodkas are usually made from grain. One of the more notable exceptions is Turkish Izmira vodka made from white beets, which give it a subtle distinction. Stories of vodka made from potatoes were true to a limited extent in

Europe. During World War II, middle-European moonshiners made vodka from potato peelings because potatoes were desperately needed for food. Theoretically you can distill vodka from any fermented mash, but large distillers use corn, wheat, rye, and other grains normally used in whiskey.

Because the quality of the water used to make vodka is important, advertisers naturally stress this component. Finnish vodka, for instance, is made from Ice Age water. Extremely deep wells, the importer says, tap a moraine formation left by glaciers eons ago. Another vodka from Denmark is, the producer says, made from glacial ice collected from a Greenland ice cap. \

Since many vodka advertisers can no longer beard each other on the raw ingredients, some of them resort to boasting of their conspicuously high prices. For several years, Russian vodka was the most expensive sold in this country. Now, importers who handle vodka from the People's Republic of China might claim that theirs would put an even deeper dent in your pocketbook.

Liquor stores carry many brands of vodka prominently marked as "Flavored Vodka." The best of the flavored vodkas come from Europe and are highly useful for party purposes. Perhaps among the best known is zubrovka, a vodka from Poland with a yellowish-greenish cast. In the bottle you will see several blades of an herb popularly known as buffalo grass. Zubrovka is somewhat sweetish—although by no means a liqueur—and is best appreciated served straight and bitingly cold. Another is the Scandinavian aquavit, flavored with caraway, dill, and other herbs and spices.

From Russia there are a number of vodkas with unique and fascinating flavors. They should be sipped rather than killed, bottoms-up. These scintillating vodkas include:

PERTSOVKA Pepper-flavored

STARKA Aged vodka with a brandylike flavor (also made in Poland)

OKHOTNICHYA Herb-flavored

The Brunch Party

O F ALL FORMULAS CONCOCTED TO CAST OFF the post-Saturday-night pall, none is more likely to recapture the previous night's camaraderie and smooth the rumpled features of the late-rising night owl quicker than a festive early-afternoon array of good food and drink. There are winter brunches before a blazing log fire, spring brunches for inaugurating the new cabin cruiser, summer after-tennis fêtes held at courtside, and autumn brunches offered either indoors or on your terrace, to mention just a few of the species and subspecies.

Although your agenda may be scheduled for a noonish kickoff, the whole day's docket should be as flexible as possible. A bon voyage brunch, for instance, before a plane flight may be given on the midmorning or mid-afternoon of departure. And brunchers who love the pleasant preamble of a jog, a swim, a short drive, or just the indulgence of breathing in the cool morning zephyrs before brunchtime are entitled to the privilege of eating when they're hungry and drinking when they're dry—in either order.

One of the first duties of the brunchmaster is to set a sumptuous table, and the first step toward that end is to acquire tableware that's vivid and inviting. A single glass of orange juice or a Screwdriver is a somewhat humdrum sight, but the same drinks become munificent and inviting when they're served from deep glass pitchers resting in an iced champagne bucket. Highly burnished Sheffield platters and coffee sets, once of interest mainly to antiquarians, can be sought after as modern graces of the brunch table. At an alfresco brunch, a hibachi or a portable charcoaler with a smoker top is perfect for conquering early-afternoon appetites. Scrambled eggs should arrive on imposing platters or nestled in warm chafing dishes.

One of the most auspicious sights at any brunch table is a commodious bread basket piled high with warm quick breads. If you have access to a French baker, you can garner fresh brioches, the richest and silkiest of soft rolls, flaky croissants so tender they seem to float away when you sample them, long salt sticks, and crisp club rolls. For an Italian twist, procure a panettone, a huge, billowy mound of a yeast cake with raisins and candied fruit. For partisans of Americana there are blueberry muffins, corn muffins, and pecan buns. All quick breads require no more toil than brief baking or warming in the oven. And the best coffee in the world will taste even better if you own an electric grinder and use it just before brewing.

Sunday brunches start with pick-me-ups that have the effect of alternately stimulating and soothing; the usual Screwdrivers with vodka may be varied with rum, sherry, or Pernod. And be sure to lay in a stock of after-brunch liqueurs—especially a fine coffee liqueur with a float of heavy cream, served ice cold. We know of no potion that so gently makes the clock stand still.

Other flavored vodkas currently available, just to name a few, include:

ABSOLUT MANDARIN Tropical fruit–flavored

HANGAR ONE MANDARIN BLOSSOM TANGERINE Citrus fruit–flavored

STOLICHNAYA PERSIK Peach-flavored

STOLICHNAYA VANILLA Vanilla-flavored

SOOMSKAYA RIABINOVAYA Ashberry-flavored

WYBOROWA PINEAPPLE Hints of tropical fruit and mocha

The art of flavoring your own vodka or using vodka as a base for home-made liqueurs is accomplished easily enough, and bartenders have been doing it for years. To make pepper-flavored vodka, it is necessary to steep slightly crushed peppercorns (whole black or white pepper) in vodka for only three or four days, and then strain the spirits through cheesecloth or filter paper. The more peppercorns used, the more pungent the flavor. About 2 tablespoons to a pint of vodka give it a resounding zing. For Kümmel liqueur, steep 2 table-spoons kümmel (pounded in a mortar), ½ teaspoon crushed coriander seeds, ¼ cup sugar syrup, and a 2-inch piece of orange rind in a pint of vodka for about two weeks, then strain. Star anise can be used in the same way for anise liqueur. To make tea vodka, place two tea bags in 4 ounces of vodka for sev-eral hours. It may be sweetened if desired. Apricots, cherries, and other fruits can be employed for your own imaginative combinations.

Because of its vivacious and seemingly endless versatility, vodka gives the inventive host unbridled rein to concoct new drinks indefinitely. When the spirit world was suddenly stirred up by Screwdrivers nearly thirty years ago, it wasn't a question of loving vodka less but of loving orange juice more. Then someone discovered a magnificent combination in vodka and ginger beer: the Moscow Mule. Shortly thereafter, longshoremen who liked to follow their straight whiskey with a beer chaser (the Boilermaker) found that vodka could be poured right into the foamy suds of their beer mugs and the results were a liquid joyride. It was a time when hosts were discovering the brunch as the right meal at the right time of the weekend for easy entertaining, and they stretched out their hands to their guests with such vodka drinks as Bloody Marys, Bullshots, and Salty Dogs. Vodka has since thrown down the gauntlet to gin in the Vodka Martini, the Vodka and Tonic, and the Vodka Gimlet. The Black Russian (vodka and Kahlua liqueur) has a foamy cousin in the Black Cossack (vodka and Guinness Stout).

Finally there's the Russian and Scandinavian rite of a skoal with neat vodka, upending the glass in a single swallow. A good deal of high-go macho is involved in the custom. If repeated too frequently within too short a time span, both toaster and toastee will, as light is swallowed up by darkness, simply flicker out in the here's-looking-at-you routine. The best defense is to follow every skoal by a spoonful of caviar on toast, an anchovy canapé, a chunk of cheese, or any other hors d'oeuvre capable of delaying action. If the bottoms-up routine is repeated during the meal, it's wise to busy yourself playing a good knife and fork as assiduously as possible.

If you, as the host, are planning to offer vodka in this manner, use pony glasses, holding no more than 1 ounce. Fill each glass no more than three-quarters full. Serve your vodka icy cold, preferably enrobed in ice. As the *arbiter bibendi*, be sure to keep the water goblets full, and drink unto others as you would have them drink unto you.

VODKA COCKTAILS

AQUAVIT FIZZ

2½ oz. aquavit
½ oz. lemon juice
1 tsp. sugar
½ egg white

1 tsp. Peter Heering or Cherry Karise
Iced club soda
Lemon peel
1 brandied cherry

Shake aquavit, lemon juice, sugar, egg white, and Peter Heering well with ice. Strain into tall 14-oz. glass half-filled with ice. Fill glass with soda. Stir. Twist lemon peel above drink and drop into glass. Add brandied cherry.

AQUAVIT RICKEY

1½ oz. aquavit   ¼ large lime
1 tsp. extra-dry Kümmel   Iced club soda

Put three ice cubes into an 8-oz. glass. Add aquavit and Kümmel. Squeeze lime above drink and drop into glass. Add soda. Stir.

AQUEDUCT

1½ oz. vodka   ½ oz. lime juice
¼ oz. curaçao   Orange peel
¼ oz. apricot liqueur

Shake vodka, curaçao, apricot liqueur, and lime juice well with ice. Strain into prechilled cocktail glass. Twist orange peel above drink and drop into glass. *Make book on this drink without any qualms.*

BEACH SUNDAY

1½ oz. peach-flavored vodka   3 oz. cranberry juice
1 oz. Chambord raspberry liqueur Juice of ½ lime

Stir well with ice. Strain into prechilled cocktail glass.

BELLINI MARTINI

2 oz. vodka   1½ oz. peach schnapps
1½ oz. peach nectar   Lemon peel

Shake vodka, peach nectar, and peach schnapps with ice. Strain into chilled cocktail glass. Twist lemon peel over drink and drop into glass.

BERLIN MARTINI

2 oz. vodka (Smirnoff)   ½ oz. Sambuca
1½ oz. schnapps   1 blackberry

Shake vodka, schnapps, and Sambuca with ice. Strain into chilled cocktail glass. Garnish with blackberry.

BERRY ME IN THE SAND

1½ oz. triple berry vodka (Red Tassel)   2 oz. orange juice
½ oz. triple sec

Stir well with ice. Strain into chilled cocktail glass.

BITTER LEMON BRACER

2 oz. vodka   1-inch piece orange peel
2 oz. orange juice   1-inch piece lemon peel
½ oz. lemon juice   1 slice orange
Iced bitter lemon

Fill 14-oz. glass with ice cubes. Add vodka, orange juice, and lemon juice. Fill with bitter lemon and stir very well. Twist orange and lemon peels over drink and drop into glass. Cut orange slice and fasten onto rim of glass. For a drier bracer, use tonic water instead of bitter lemon.

BLACK RUSSIAN

1½ oz. vodka
¾ oz. Kahlua coffee liqueur

Shake well with ice. Strain over rocks into prechilled old-fashioned glass. *Serve at poolside during the cocktail hour or by candlelight at the witching hour.*

BLOODY MARY

1½ oz. vodka
3 oz. tomato juice
½ oz. lemon juice
1 tsp. ketchup

1 dash Worcestershire sauce
1 dash celery salt
1 dash Tabasco sauce

Shake all ingredients well with ice. Strain into tall or squat 8-oz. glass.

BUCKEYE MARTINI

2¼ oz. vodka
¼ oz. dry vermouth

1 large ripe black olive

Stir vodka and vermouth well with ice. Strain into prechilled cocktail glass. Add olive.

BULLSHOT

4 oz. beef bouillon
1½ oz. vodka

1 tsp. lemon juice
1 dash Tabasco sauce

Pour ingredients over rocks into squat 10-oz. glass. Stir well. Add ice if necessary to fill glass. Sprinkle, if desired, with freshly ground pepper.

BUNNY MOTHER

1¼ oz. vodka
1 oz. orange juice
1 oz. lemon juice
1 tsp. sugar

¼ oz. grenadine
¼ oz. Cointreau
½ slice orange
1 maraschino cherry

Shake vodka, orange juice, lemon juice, sugar, and grenadine well with ice. Strain into prechilled 12-oz. mug. Add coarsely cracked ice to fill mug to <1/2> inch from top. Float Cointreau on top. Garnish with orange slice and cherry.

CARAWAY FLIP

1½ oz. aquavit
½ oz. lemon juice
½ oz. orange juice

1 small egg
2 tsp. sugar
Freshly ground nutmeg

Shake aquavit, lemon juice, orange juice, egg, and sugar extremely well with ice. Strain into 6-oz. glass. Sprinkle with nutmeg.

CARIBBEAN MARTINI

1½ oz. vanilla-flavored vodka
¾ oz. Malibu rum

1 splash pineapple juice

Shake well with ice. Strain into prechilled cocktail or martini glass.

CHERRY ISLE

1 oz. aquavit	Iced tonic water
1 oz. Peter Heering liqueur	1 slice lime

Pour aquavit and Peter Heering into 10-oz. glass half-filled with rocks. Stir well. Add tonic water. Stir. Add lime slice.

CHERRY VODKA

1¼ oz. 100-proof vodka	½ oz. Peter Heering or Cherry Karise
½ oz. lime juice	

Shake well with ice until the shaker is almost too cold to hold. Strain into prechilled cocktail glass.

CHIQUITA

1½ oz. vodka	½ oz. lime juice
½ oz. banana liqueur	1 tsp. sugar
¼ cup sliced ripe banana	¼ cup finely crushed ice

Put all ingredients into blender. Blend at low speed for 15 seconds. Pour into deep-saucer champagne glass.

CHOCOLATE BLACK RUSSIAN

2 oz. (¼ cup) chocolate ice cream	½ oz. vodka
1 oz. Kahlua	1½ oz. milk

Pour all ingredients into blender. Blend at high speed for 10 seconds. Pour over rocks into 8-oz. glass. Stir well.

COEXISTENCE COLLINS

2 oz. vodka	Iced club soda
½ oz. lemon juice	Cucumber peel, 2 inches long,
1 tsp. sugar	½ inch wide
1 tsp. Kümmel	Lemon peel

Shake vodka, lemon juice, sugar, and Kümmel well with ice. Strain into tall 14-oz. glass half-filled with ice. Add soda. Stir. Add cucumber peel. Twist lemon peel above drink and drop into glass.

COFFEE COOLER

4 oz. cold coffee	1 oz. coffee liqueur
1½ oz. vodka	1 tsp. sugar
1 oz. heavy cream	1 small dip coffee ice cream

Shake coffee, vodka, cream, coffee liqueur, and sugar well with ice. Strain into tall 14-oz. glass. Add ice cream. *A sweet cooler that serves as both iced coffee and dessert in one glass.*

COSMOPOLITAN

1¼ oz. vodka, plain or citron
¼ oz. lime juice

¼ oz. Cointreau or Triple Sec
1 slice lime

Shake vodka, lime juice, and Cointreau or Triple Sec well with ice. Strain into pre-chilled martini glass. Garnish with lime slice. *A sophisticated concoction that packs a wallop.*

CREAMY SCREWDRIVER

6 oz. orange juice
2 oz. vodka
1 small egg yolk or ½ large yolk,
   lightly beaten

¾ cup finely cracked ice
1 tsp. sugar

Put all ingredients into well of blender. Blend for about 20 seconds. Pour over two or three ice cubes into tall 14-oz. glass. Add more ice cubes if necessary to fill glass.

CYNAR SCREWDRIVER

1 oz. Cynar
1 oz. vodka

4½ oz. ice cold orange juice

Shake ingredients well with ice. Strain into prechilled tall or squat 10-oz. glass.

DULCET

1 oz. vodka
½ oz. curaçao
½ oz. anisette

½ oz. apricot liqueur
1 tsp. lemon juice
½ brandied apricot

Shake vodka, curaçao, anisette, apricot liqueur, and lemon juice well with ice. Strain over cracked ice or rocks in prechilled old-fashioned glass. Add brandied apricot.

FLYING GRASSHOPPER

1 oz. vodka
½ oz. green crème de menthe

½ oz. white crème de cacao

Stir well with ice. Strain into prechilled cocktail glass. *More potent and less rich than the plain Grasshopper.*

FROZEN APPLE

1½ oz. vodka
¼ oz. Calvados or applejack
½ oz. lime juice

¼ cup diced fresh apple
¼ cup finely crushed ice
½ tsp. sugar

Put all ingredients into blender. Blend at low speed for 15 seconds. Pour into deep-saucer champagne glass. *A north-country version of the Frozen Daiquiri.*

FROZEN AQUAVIT

1½ oz. aquavit
½ oz. lime juice
½ egg white

½ cup crushed ice
1 tsp. sugar
1 tsp. kirschwasser

Put all ingredients into blender. Blend at low speed for 10 to 15 seconds. Pour into prechilled deep-saucer champagne glass.

GALWAY GRAY

1½ oz. vodka
1 oz. white crème de cacao
1 oz. Cointreau
½ oz. lime juice
1 oz. light cream

Stir vodka, crème de cacao, Cointreau, and lime juice well with ice. Strain into prechilled cocktail glass. Float cream on top.

GREAT DANE

1½ oz. aquavit
¼ oz. dry vermouth
1 oz. sweet vermouth
2 cocktail onions

Stir aquavit, dry vermouth, and sweet vermouth well with ice. Strain into prechilled cocktail glass with onions, or serve on rocks.

GYPSY

2 oz. vodka
½ oz. Benedictine
1 tsp. lemon juice
1 tsp. orange juice
1 slice orange

Shake vodka, Benedictine, lemon juice, and orange juice well with ice. Strain over rocks into prechilled old-fashioned glass. Add orange slice.

HARVEY WALLBANGER

1½ oz. vodka
4½ oz. ice cold orange juice
¾ oz. Galliano

Put three large ice cubes into tall or squat 10-oz. glass. Add vodka and orange juice. Stir well. Float Galliano on top. Or shake vodka, orange juice, and Galliano with ice and strain into glass; add ice cubes to fill glass; stir.

HOLLYWOOD NIGHTS

1½ oz. vodka
1½ oz. Chambord raspberry liqueur
1 oz. triple sec
1 oz. Rose's Lime Juice

Stir well with ice. Strain into prechilled old-fashioned glass.

KREMLIN COLONEL

2 oz. vodka
½ oz. lime juice
1 tsp. sugar
2 large fresh mint leaves

Shake vodka, lime juice, and sugar well with ice. Strain into prechilled cocktail glass. Tear each mint leaf in half to release aroma and drop into glass.

KRETCHMA

1 oz. vodka
1 oz. crème de cacao
½ oz. lemon juice
½ tsp. grenadine

Shake well with ice. Strain into prechilled cocktail glass. *Serve to friends with a deep addiction to chocolate.*

LORENZO

1 oz. vodka
1 oz. Tuaca liqueur

½ oz. lime juice

Shake well with ice. Moisten rim of glass with Tuaca and dip into sugar. Strain into prechilled sugar-frosted cocktail glass. *One sip of this and you'll understand why Lorenzo de'Medici was called Il Magnifico.*

MANGO COOLER

3 oz. ice cold mango nectar
1½ oz. vodka
½ oz. ice cold lemon juice
1½ oz. ice-cold orange juice

½ oz. Cointreau
1 slice orange
1 slice mango, if in season

Into tall 14-oz. glass, pour mango nectar, vodka, lemon juice, orange juice, and Cointreau. Add ice to fill glass. Garnish with orange and mango slices. *A fruity libation to serve before an Asian or Polynesian menu.*

MARY KÜMMEL

3 oz. tomato juice
1 oz. Kümmel
1 oz. vodka
1 tbsp. lemon juice

1 dash Tabasco sauce
1 dash Worcestershire sauce
Salt, celery salt, pepper

Pour tomato juice, Kümmel, vodka, lemon juice, Tabasco sauce, and Worcestershire sauce into cocktail shaker with ice. Add a sprinkling of salt, celery salt, and pepper. Shake very well. Strain into 8-oz. glass. Add a sprinkling of freshly ground pepper if desired.

MIDNIGHT SUN

1½ oz. aquavit
½ oz. unsweetened grapefruit juice
½ oz. lemon juice

1 tsp. sugar
½ tsp. grenadine
½ slice orange

Shake aquavit, grapefruit juice, lemon juice, sugar, and grenadine well with ice. Strain into prechilled whiskey-sour glass. Add orange slice. *Keep herring tidbits within reach.*

MOSCOW MULE

1½ to 2 oz. vodka (Smirnoff)
½ lime

Iced ginger beer

Pour vodka into tall 12- or 14-oz. glass or copper mug with ice cubes or cracked ice. Squeeze lime above drink and drop into glass. Fill with ginger beer. Stir. *A variation on the Moscow Mule includes a long spiral of lemon peel in the mug.*

NECTARINE COOLER

2 oz. vodka
3 oz. iced orange juice
¼ cup cold sliced ripe nectarine
1 tsp. sugar

⅓ cup crushed ice
Iced club soda
1 slice fresh nectarine
1 slice lemon

Put vodka, orange juice, nectarine, sugar, and crushed ice into blender. Blend at low speed for 15 to 20 seconds. Pour into tall 14-oz. glass. Add a splash of soda and enough ice to fill glass. Stir. Garnish with nectarine and lemon slices.

PEACH BUCK

1¼ oz. vodka
2 tsp. peach-flavored brandy
½ oz. lemon juice

Iced ginger ale
1 slice lemon
1 slice fresh or brandied peach

Shake vodka, peach-flavored brandy, and lemon juice well with ice. Strain into 8-oz. glass half-filled with ice. Add ginger ale. Stir. Garnish with lemon and peach slices.

PEARL HARBOR

1½ oz. vodka
½ oz. Midori

3 oz. pineapple juice

Pour vodka, Midori, and pineapple juice into old-fashioned glass over rocks. Stir.

PINK LEMONADE

1½ oz. Absolut Citron
1½ oz. Chambord raspberry liqueur

1 oz. Rose's Lime Juice

Shake well with ice. Strain into prechilled old-fashioned glass.

POLYNESIAN PICK-ME-UP

½ cup pineapple juice
1½ oz. vodka
½ tsp. curry powder
½ tsp. lemon juice

1 tbsp. heavy cream
2 dashes Tabasco sauce
½ cup crushed ice
Cayenne pepper

Put pineapple juice, vodka, curry powder, lemon juice, cream, Tabasco sauce, and crushed ice into blender. Blend for 10 seconds at high speed. Pour into prechilled old-fashioned glass. Dust very lightly with cayenne.

RED APPLE

1 oz. 100-proof vodka
1 oz. apple juice
½ oz. lemon juice

½ tsp. grenadine
1 dash orange bitters

Shake well with ice. Strain into prechilled cocktail glass. *Not to be confused with a Vodka and Apple Juice, a lowball rather than a cocktail.*

RED DANE

1½ oz. aquavit
2 oz. cranberry juice cocktail
½ oz. lime juice

1 tsp. sugar
1 slice lemon

Shake aquavit, cranberry juice cocktail, lime juice, and sugar well with ice. Strain into 8-oz. glass over rocks. Stir. Add lemon slice.

ROCK-AND-RYE COOLER

1½ oz. vodka
1 oz. rock and rye
½ oz. lime juice

Iced bitter lemon soda
1 slice lime

Shake vodka, rock and rye, and lime juice well with ice. Strain into tall 14-oz. glass half-filled with ice. Add bitter lemon soda. Stir. Garnish with lime slice.

ROCOCO

1½ oz. cherry vodka　　　　　　　　1 oz. orange juice
½ oz. triple sec

Shake well with ice. Strain into prechilled cocktail glass.

RUDDY MARY

1½ oz. aquavit　　　　　　　　½ egg yolk
½ cup tomato juice　　　　　　¼ oz. lemon juice
1 tbsp. heavy cream　　　　　　¼ oz. ketchup
1 dash Tabasco sauce　　　　　　½ cup crushed ice

Put all ingredients into blender. Blend at high speed for 20 seconds. Pour into old-fashioned glass. When foam settles, add ice to fill glass to rim.

RUSSIAN BEAR

1 oz. vodka　　　　　　　　½ oz. heavy cream
½ oz. crème de cacao

Shake well with ice. Strain into prechilled cocktail glass.

RUSSIAN CARAMEL

1 oz. vodka　　　　　　　　1 oz. heavy cream
1 oz. Caramella　　　　　　Freshly grated nutmeg

Shake vodka, Caramella, and cream well with ice. Strain into large cocktail glass. Sprinkle nutmeg on top.

RUSSIAN COFFEE

¾ oz. vodka　　　　　　　　¾ oz. heavy cream
¾ oz. coffee liqueur　　　　⅓ cup crushed ice

Blend all ingredients at low speed for 10 to 15 seconds. Pour into prechilled deep-saucer champagne glass.

RUSSIAN ESPRESSO

1½ oz. vodka　　　　　　　　½ tsp. lemon juice
½ oz. espresso-coffee liqueur　　Lemon peel

Pour vodka, coffee liqueur, and lemon juice over rocks into prechilled old-fashioned glass. Stir well. Twist lemon peel above drink and drop into glass. *A coexistence cocktail.*

SALTY DOG

1½ oz. vodka　　　　　　　　1 tsp. lemon juice
3 oz. unsweetened grapefruit juice　Salt

Pour vodka, grapefruit juice, and lemon juice over rocks into old-fashioned glass. Sprinkle with salt or salt rim. Stir. *Sans salt, call it a Greyhound.*

SCREWDRIVER

1½ oz. vodka
4½ oz. ice cold orange juice,
 freshly squeezed

1 tsp. lemon juice (optional)

Shake extremely well with ice or pour into blender and blend with ice at high speed for 5 seconds. Strain into prechilled tall or squat 10-oz. glass. Lemon juice gives the Screwdriver an extra twist.

SCREWDRIVER WITH SHERRY

½ cup orange juice
2 oz. oloroso sherry

1 oz. vodka
½ cup crushed ice

Put all ingredients into blender. Blend for 20 seconds. Pour into double old-fashioned or tall 14-oz. glass. Add ice cubes to fill glass. *An outsize Screwdriver especially suited for the brunchboard.*

SEA ROVER

1½ oz. aquavit
½ oz. strawberry liqueur

½ oz. lime juice
1 piece lime peel

Shake aquavit, strawberry liqueur, and lime juice well with ice. Strain into prechilled cocktail glass. Twist lime peel above drink and drop into glass.

SILVERADO

1½ oz. vodka
1½ oz. Campari

1 oz. orange juice

Pour vodka, Campari, and orange juice over ice into old-fashioned glass. Stir well.

SKIFFLE

1½ oz. Absolut Vodka
1½ oz. banana-flavored liqueur

3 oz. fruit punch

Stir well with ice. Strain into highball glass over rocks.

SKI JUMPER

1½ oz. aquavit
1 tsp. Kümmel liqueur
1 tsp. lemon juice

Iced bitter lemon
1 slice lemon

Pour aquavit, Kümmel, and lemon juice into tall or squat 10-oz. glass three-quarters filled with ice cubes. Stir well. Fill glass with bitter lemon. Stir. Add lemon slice.

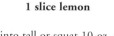

SLOE SWEDE

1½ oz. aquavit	¾ oz. lemon juice
½ oz. sloe gin	Iced club soda
½ slightly beaten egg white	1 slice lemon
1 tsp. sugar	

Shake aquavit, sloe gin, egg white, sugar, and lemon juice extremely well with ice. Strain into tall 14-oz. glass three-quarters filled with ice cubes. Stir well. Add soda to fill glass. Stir. Add lemon slice.

SMITH AND WESSON

1 oz. vodka	1 oz. light cream
1 oz. Kahlua	Club soda

Pour vodka, Kahlua, and cream into old-fashioned glass over rocks. Top off with club soda. Stir.

SOVIET

1½ oz. vodka	½ oz. dry vermouth
½ oz. amontillado sherry	Lemon peel

Stir vodka, sherry, and vermouth well with ice. Strain over rocks into prechilled old-fashioned glass. Twist lemon peel above drink and drop into glass. *Liquid tranquilizer.*

SVETLANA

1½ oz. 100-proof vodka	¼ oz. orange juice
½ oz. sweet vermouth	Orange peel
¼ oz. kirschwasser	

Shake vodka, vermouth, kirschwasser, and orange juice well with ice. Strain into prechilled cocktail glass. Twist orange peel above drink and drop into glass. Serve bitingly cold. *No nyets will be heard.*

SWEDISH SIDECAR

1 oz. aquavit	½ oz. lemon juice
½ oz. Cointreau or triple sec	½ oz. orange juice

Shake aquavit, Cointreau, lemon juice, and orange juice well with ice. Strain into prechilled sugar-frosted cocktail glass.

TALL BLONDE

1 oz. aquavit	Iced bitter lemon
½ oz. apricot liqueur	1 slice lemon

Pour aquavit and apricot liqueur into tall 12-oz. glass three-quarters filled with ice cubes. Stir well. Add iced bitter lemon to fill glass. Stir. Add lemon slice.

TOVARICH

1½ oz. vodka	½ oz. lime juice
½ oz. Kümmel	Lime peel

Shake vodka, Kümmel, and lime juice well with ice. Strain into prechilled cocktail glass. Twist lime peel above drink and drop into glass.

VODKA FRAISE

¾ oz. vodka
¾ oz. light rum
½ oz. strawberry liqueur

½ oz. lime juice
½ tsp. grenadine
½ large fresh strawberry

Shake vodka, rum, strawberry liqueur, lime juice, and grenadine well with ice. Strain into prechilled sugar-frosted cocktail glass. Drop strawberry on top.

VODKA GIMLET

2 oz. vodka
½ oz. Rose's Lime Juice

Stir well with ice. Strain into prechilled cocktail glass.

VODKA GRAND MARNIER

1½ oz. vodka
½ oz. Grand Marnier

½ oz. lime juice
1 slice orange

Shake vodka, Grand Marnier, and lime juice well with ice. Strain over rocks into prechilled old-fashioned glass. Garnish with orange slice.

VODKA MARTINI

2 oz. vodka
¼ oz. dry vermouth

Lemon peel or olive, to taste

Stir well with ice. Strain into prechilled cocktail glass or serve over rocks. Garnish with twist of lemon peel or olive. *Lacks the zip of the gin-based Martini, but it's a wonderful midday solace for vodka partisans.*

VODKA OLD-FASHIONED

½ tsp. sugar
2 dashes Angostura bitters
1 tsp. water

2 oz. vodka
Lemon peel

Dissolve sugar with bitters and water in old-fashioned glass. Add vodka. Fill glass to rim with cubes, slices, or coarsely cracked pieces of ice. Stir very well. Twist lemon peel above drink and drop into glass.

VODKA SOUR

1¾ oz. vodka
¾ oz. lemon juice
1 tsp. sugar

1 slice lemon
1 maraschino cherry

Shake vodka, lemon juice, and sugar well with ice. Strain into prechilled whiskey-sour glass. Garnish with lemon slice and cherry.

VODKA STINGER

1½ oz. vodka
½ oz. white crème de menthe

Shake extremely well with ice. Pour into prechilled cocktail glass. Drink must be served extremely cold. *May be either pre- or postprandial. Or both.*

WARSAW

1½ oz. vodka
½ oz. blackberry liqueur
½ oz. dry vermouth

1 tsp. lemon juice
Lemon peel

Shake vodka, blackberry liqueur, vermouth, and lemon juice well with ice. Strain into prechilled cocktail glass. Twist lemon peel above drink and drop into glass.

WINDEX

1½ oz. vodka
1 oz. triple sec

1 oz. blue curaçao

Stir well with ice. Strain into prechilled cocktail glass.

CHAPTER 13

Gin

The next time someone asks, "Who was Sylvius?" be prepared with the answer: he was the inventor of gin. Sylvius's proper name was Franciscus de la Boë. he was a professor of medicine at the Dutch University of Leiden, and the pure lab alcohol that Dr. Sylvius distilled with the oil of juniper berries was intended as a blood cleanser to be sold in apothecaries rather than taverns. This was during the seventeenth century, when drinking most distilled liquors snapped the neck and left a lingering ball of fire in the throat. The professor's comparatively smooth and inexpensive nostrum soon not only cleansed the blood of countless native Hollanders but also juiced up the minds and bodies of English soldiers campaigning in the Lowlands. Englishmen brought the new Dutch formula back to their cold, foggy isle, and a mass warming of an entire nation took place over the next several centuries.

Beginning in England with the reign of William of Orange, gin drinking became a mark of the highest patriotism. The number of amateur gin makers mushroomed until eventually every fourth house in London was a gin shop; English workmen were even paid a share of their wages in gin. In the late nineteenth century, the elaborate gilded and mirrored Victorian gin palaces came into being and gin rose to a peak of glamour, reaching its apex with the introduction to England of the American cocktail. Not even Prohibition's bathtub gin, generations later, nor the runaway rise of vodka could cause gin to fall again.

All dry gins made in England or the United States are created almost equal. They start out as neutral spirits made from grain. These spirits, which form the base of gin, are close to but not quite like vodka. They're later redistilled in the presence of juniper berries and about ten to fifteen other forms of flavor sorcery, such as coriander, bitter almonds, cardamom, cassia (cinnamon) bark, angelica, and lemon and orange peel. It's this second flavoring step that reveals the gin maker's art and accounts for most of the differences in gins.

Deepest-flavored of all is the imported Dutch gin called genever or Hollands. (The English word *gin* is a contraction of the Dutch *genever*, which means "juniper.") Holland gin makers use fresh juniper berries, chopped and added right to the fermenting mash before distillation takes place, and they distill their gins at rather low proofs. This technique imparts an odd, impressive flavor that is so assertive that Hollands is seldom used in a mixed drink; it's always taken bitingly cold and neat. While the first gulp is always somewhat surprising to Americans, it leaves a rich aftertaste much like an old eau-de-vie. As with Germany's Steinhäger gin—which is very similar to it in flavor—genever is sold in stone crocks.

English gins differ from one another just as American gins do. When the gin maker uses spices, he becomes something of a cook. The spices he uses vary in flavor potency from season to season, so too much of this or a little less of that can make a perceptible difference. You can almost bet that two gin makers with the same formula, like two chefs working with the same recipe, will come up with two different products. The gin gap between England and America, although not as wide as it used to be, is still there. The main differences between English and American gins are these.

- •English gins cost about one-third more because of duties, shipping charges, handling, etc., and because of the fact that many of them are 94 proof against an American high of 90 proof.

- •The starting spirits of English gins, before they're flavored with juniper, are distilled at about 180 proof, 10 proof less than their American counterparts. It's a small difference but just enough to make the English base flavor more pronounced.

- English starting spirits contain less corn and more barley than their American counterparts, which also makes for eventual flavor differences.

- English water differs from American, and this affects both the alcoholic base for gin and the water used to later cut the gin to bottle proof.

In both Great Britain and the United States some gins are now distilled under vacuum, permitting the flavors of the spices to be liberated at low temperatures rather than the pugnaciously high ones of normal stills, which sometimes cause flavors to be rough. Other gins are flavored not by immersing the botanicals right in the still but by passing the final alcohol vapors, as they come from the still, through a separate chamber, called a gin head, where the juniper and other spices convey a pleasant subtlety to the spirits before they're condensed. How "ginny" a gin you select—how vividly flavored—is a matter of personal taste.

At least ten different gins in the United States carry the phrase "London Dry." The phrase is meaningless, although at one time in England, when sweet gin was widely sold, it could have been significant. Today it may evoke some geographical fascination but has nothing whatever to do with London itself. Most English gin makers, in fact, seem to avoid the phrase.

Whatever the manner in which they're flavored, both American and English gins are considered to be dry. Until recently that meant unsweetened, but virtually all gins today are unsweetened. When one speaks of dry gin these days, they mean one that is more muted in flavor, though not pallid, and above all smooth. Actually, the only nondry gin is English Old Tom, which is made with added sugar as a sweetener and is exported mostly to Asia. There are also a few fruit-flavored gins on the market, but they're not a significant segment of the gin world. And sloe gin isn't gin at all but a liqueur made with the sloe plum of the blackthorn.

In addition to being dry, most gins in Great Britain and America are unaged, but a few in both countries are mellowed in the wood for further blending and flavor development. Although American liquor laws don't permit gin labels to carry any statement of age, these elder statesmen can be recognized by their clear straw color.

Over the centuries, English gin drinkers have created their own terminology, and some of it has spilled across the ocean. "Pink gin," for instance, is simply gin with a dash of Angostura bitters; "Gin and It" is a blend of gin and Italian vermouth; and the Gin Sling, which has been a British standby since General Gordon drank it at the officers' mess in Khartoum, will probably outlast the final expiration of the Empire. This concoction is sold bottled as Pimm's No. 1 Cup.

About the only class of mixed drinks in which you don't find gin are hot grogs, although skiers have been known to sip a hot Gin Toddy now and then after a vigorous run on the slopes. Otherwise, if you're a gin partisan, you can use it in almost any mixed drink in which vodka is normally poured. One of the most delightful cocktails is a Gin Sour on the rocks. The best-known tall gin drink is the Tom Collins, while the perennial lion among short drinks for generations has been the Martini. For some reason—which sociologists might study—a drinker who doesn't mind taking his whiskey or brandy straight will hesitate to honor gin in the same way. The exceptions are Holland gin, or gin that is icy cold. Gin drinkers have been known to keep a bottle at all times in the refrigerator or even the freezer (it won't freeze because of the alcohol) and to take a nip now and then in the same way they'd drink aquavit or other schnapps—neat. All those wags who joke about how little vermouth they use in a Martini—just a drop from an eyedropper or a tiny spritz from an atomizer—are simply gin fans who are too embarrassed to admit that they love gin straight.

Wherever it comes from and whatever company it keeps, Sylvius's venerable and versatile nostrum remains among the best possible medicines for the treatment of the common thirst. It is written that Elijah the Prophet once derived sublime comfort from sitting under a juniper tree. It's not surprising that most people today prefer to take their juniper through the lips in the comfort of an armchair.

GIN COCKTAILS

ABBEY

1½ oz. gin
1 dash orange bitters

Juice of ¼ orange
1 cherry

Shake gin, orange bitters, and orange juice with ice. Strain into prechilled cocktail glass. Drop in cherry.

ALASKA

1½ oz. gin
¾ oz. yellow Chartreuse

2 dashes orange bitters
Lemon peel

Stir well with ice. Strain into prechilled cocktail glass. Twist lemon peel over drink and drop into glass.

ALEXANDER'S SISTER

¾ oz. gin
¾ oz. white or green crème de menthe

¾ oz. heavy cream

Shake well with ice. Strain into prechilled cocktail glass.

ALEXANDER WITH COFFEE

¾ oz. gin
¾ oz. coffee liqueur

¾ oz. heavy cream

Shake well with ice. Strain into prechilled sugar-frosted cocktail glass. Moisten rim of glass with coffee liqueur before dipping into sugar. Especially good with espresso-coffee liqueur. *Like all Alexanders, which are really sweet cocktails, this one is both a pre- and postprandial drink.*

ALEXANDER WITH GIN

¾ oz. gin
¾ oz. crème de cacao

¾ oz. heavy cream

Shake well with ice. Strain into prechilled cocktail glass. (A classic Alexander made with a brandy base instead of gin will be found among brandy cocktails.)

ALEXANDER WITH PRUNELLE

¾ oz. gin
¾ oz. prunelle

¾ oz. cream
Ground cinnamon

Shake gin, prunelle, and cream well with ice. Strain into prechilled cocktail glass. Sprinkle lightly with cinnamon.

ALLIES' COCKTAIL

1 oz. gin
1 oz. dry vermouth

½ tsp. Kümmel

Stir with ice. Strain into prechilled cocktail glass.

ALMOND EYE

1 oz. gin
1 oz. California brandy
½ oz. amaretto

1 oz. lemon juice
1 tsp. grenadine
Iced club soda

Shake gin, brandy, amaretto, lemon juice, and grenadine well with ice. Strain into 8-oz. glass. Add two ice cubes. Add splash of soda. Stir.

ANGLER'S COCKTAIL

1½ oz. gin
3 dashes orange bitters

2 dashes Angostura bitters
1 dash grenadine

Shake well with cracked ice. Strain into old-fashioned glass over rocks.

BAYARD FIZZ

2 oz. gin
½ oz. lemon juice
2 tsp. maraschino liqueur
1 tsp. raspberry syrup

Iced club soda
1 slice lemon
2 fresh or thawed frozen raspberries

Shake gin, lemon juice, maraschino liqueur, and raspberry syrup well with ice. Strain into tall 14-oz. glass half-filled with ice. Fill glass with soda. Stir. Add lemon slice and raspberries.

BELLS OF ST. MARY'S

1½ oz. gin
1 oz. triple sec

1 oz. apricot brandy
2 tsp. lemon juice

Shake well with ice. Strain into prechilled cocktail glass.

BENNETT

1½ oz. gin
½ oz. lime juice
1 tsp. sugar

2 dashes Angostura bitters
Lime peel

Shake gin, lime juice, sugar, and bitters well with ice. Strain into prechilled cocktail glass. Twist lime peel above drink and drop into glass.

BERLINER

1½ oz. gin
¼ oz. dry Kümmel

½ oz. dry vermouth
¼ oz. lemon juice

Shake well with ice. Strain into prechilled cocktail glass. *Best appreciated with freshly made, well-buttered smoked-salmon canapés.*

BERMUDA

¾ oz. brandy
¾ oz. gin
¾ oz. dry vermouth

Club soda
Lemon peel

Pour brandy, gin, and dry vermouth into highball glass over rocks. Top off with club soda. Stir. Twist lemon peel over drink and drop into glass.

BERMUDA ROSE

1½ oz. gin
1½ tsp. apricot brandy
1½ tsp. grenadine

Shake well with ice. Strain into prechilled cocktail glass.

BERNARDO

1½ oz. gin
1 oz. triple sec
2 tsp. lemon juice
2 dashes Angostura bitters
Lemon peel

Shake gin, triple sec, lemon juice, and bitters well with ice. Strain into prechilled cocktail glass. Twist lemon peel over drink and drop into glass.

BIJOU

¾ oz. gin
¾ oz. sweet vermouth
¾ oz. green Chartreuse
1 dash orange bitters
1 cherry

Shake gin, vermouth, Chartreuse, and bitters well with ice. Strain into prechilled cocktail glass. Drop in cherry.

BISCAYNE

1 oz. gin
½ oz. light rum
½ oz. Forbidden Fruit
½ oz. lime juice
1 slice lime

Shake gin, rum, Forbidden Fruit, and lime juice well with ice. Strain over rocks into prechilled old-fashioned glass. Add lime slice.

BISHOP'S COCKTAIL

1 oz. gin
1 oz. Stone's ginger wine
1 slice lemon

Stir gin and ginger wine well with ice. Strain over rocks into old-fashioned glass. Add lemon slice.

BITTER LEMON COOLER

1½ oz. dry vermouth
1 oz. gin
1 tsp. strawberry syrup
1 tsp. lemon juice
Iced bitter lemon soda
Lemon peel

Shake vermouth, gin, strawberry syrup, and lemon juice well with ice. Strain into tall 14-oz. glass containing two large ice cubes. Add bitter lemon soda. Stir. Twist lemon peel above drink and drop into glass.

BLOODHOUND

1 oz. gin
½ oz. dry vermouth
½ oz. sweet vermouth
1 large strawberry

Shake gin and both kinds of vermouth well with ice. Strain into prechilled cocktail glass. Drop strawberry into glass. The best dry vermouth for this one is Chambery Fraise.

BLUEBIRD OF HAPPINESS

1½ oz. gin
½ oz. triple sec
½ oz. blue curaçao
2 dashes Angostura bitters
Lemon peel
1 maraschino cherry

Stir gin, triple sec, and blue curaçao and bitters well with ice. Strain into prechilled cocktail glass. Garnish with lemon peel and cherry.

BLUE DEVIL

1½ oz. gin
½ oz. blue curaçao
½ oz. lemon juice
1 slice lemon

Shake gin, curaçao, and lemon juice well with ice. Strain into prechilled cocktail glass garnished with lemon slice. *A gentle blues chaser.*

BONNIE PRINCE CHARLIE

1¼ oz. gin
½ oz. Lillet
¼ oz. Drambuie

Shake well with ice. Strain into prechilled cocktail glass. *Inspiration for gin drinkers with both French and Scottish blood in their veins.*

BOOMERANG

2 oz. gin
½ oz. dry vermouth
2 dashes Angostura bitters
½ tsp. maraschino liqueur
1 maraschino cherry

Stir gin, vermouth, bitters, and maraschino liqueur well with ice. Strain into prechilled cocktail glass. Drop in cherry.

BOXCAR

1½ oz. gin
1 oz. triple sec
1 tsp. lemon juice
½ tsp. grenadine
1 egg white

Shake well with ice. Strain into prechilled whiskey-sour glass.

BRITTANY

1½ oz. gin
½ oz. Amer Picon
¼ oz. orange juice
¼ oz. lemon juice
Orange peel

Shake gin, Amer Picon, orange juice, and lemon juice well with ice. Strain into prechilled cocktail glass. Twist orange peel above drink and drop into glass.

BRONX

1½ oz. gin
½ oz. orange juice

¼ oz. dry vermouth
¼ oz. sweet vermouth

Shake well with ice. Strain into prechilled cocktail glass. For a drier Bronx, omit sweet vermouth and increase gin to 1¾ oz. *One of the few inventions of the Prohibition era really worth retaining when made with fine gin rather than the notorious bathtub variety.*

BULLDOG

2 oz. gin
Juice of ½ orange

Ginger ale

Pour gin and orange juice over rocks into highball glass. Top off with ginger ale. Stir.

CABARET

1 oz. gin
½ oz. dry Vermouth
½ oz. Benedictine

2 dashes Angostura bitters
1 maraschino cherry

Shake gin, vermouth, Benedictine, and bitters well with ice. Strain into prechilled cocktail glass. Drop in cherry.

CAFÉS DE PARIS

2 oz. gin
½ oz. anisette

1 egg white
1 oz. heavy cream

Shake well with ice. Strain into prechilled whiskey-sour glass. *Ooh la la!*

CAPTAIN COOK

1½ oz. gin
½ oz. maraschino liqueur

1 oz. orange juice

Shake well with ice. Strain into prechilled cocktail glass.

CAPTAIN'S TABLE

1½ oz. gin
1 oz. Campari
1 oz. orange juice

1 tsp. grenadine
Ginger ale
1 maraschino cherry

Shake gin, Campari, orange juice, and grenadine well with ice. Strain into collins glass over rocks. Top off with ginger ale. Stir. Drop in cherry.

CARUSO

1½ oz. gin
1 oz. dry vermouth

1 oz. green crème de menthe

Stir well with ice. Strain into prechilled cocktail glass.

CASINO ROYALE

2 oz. gin
½ oz. lemon juice
1 tsp. maraschino liqueur

1 dash orange bitters
1 egg yolk

Shake well with ice. Strain into prechilled whiskey-sour glass.

CHATHAM

1¼ oz. gin
½ oz. ginger-flavored brandy
¼ oz. lemon juice
1 small piece preserved ginger in syrup

Shake gin, ginger-flavored brandy, and lemon juice well with ice. Strain into prechilled cocktail glass. Garnish with preserved ginger.

CHELSEA HOTEL

1½ oz. gin
½ oz. triple sec
2 tsp. lemon juice

Shake well with ice. Strain into prechilled cocktail glass.

CHERRY COBBLER

1½ oz. gin
½ oz. Peter Heering or Cherry Karise
½ oz. crème de cassis
1 tsp. sugar
½ oz. lemon juice
1 slice lemon
1 maraschino cherry

Fill a 12-oz. glass with finely cracked ice. Add gin, Peter Heering, crème de cassis, sugar, and lemon juice. Stir well until sugar dissolves. Add more ice to fill glass to rim. Stir. Add lemon slice and cherry.

CHERRY SLING

1½ oz. gin
½ oz. cherry liqueur
½ oz. lime juice

Shake well with ice. Strain into prechilled cocktail glass. Use a tart cherry liqueur such as Peter Heering or Cherry Karise for best results.

CLOISTER

1½ oz. gin
½ oz. grapefruit juice
¼ oz. lemon juice
¼ oz. yellow Chartreuse

Shake well with ice. Strain into prechilled cocktail glass. *A contemplative kind of drink, perfect for an autumn sundown.*

CLOVER CLUB

1½ oz. gin
¾ oz. lemon juice
1 tsp. grenadine or raspberry syrup
½ egg white

Shake well with ice. Strain into prechilled cocktail glass.

CLOVER CLUB ROYALE

1½ oz. gin
¾ oz. lemon juice
1 tsp. grenadine or raspberry syrup
½ egg yolk

Shake well with ice. Strain into prechilled cocktail glass. A trifle richer than the Clover Club, this velvety cocktail is even smoother when made with ⅓ cup crushed ice in a blender and poured over the rocks into an old-fashioned glass.

COCONUT GIN

1½ oz. gin
½ oz. lemon juice

¼ **oz. maraschino liqueur**
¼ **oz. cream of coconut**

Cream of coconut, from the can, should be well mixed before using. Shake all ingredients well with ice. Strain into prechilled sugar-frosted cocktail glass. *Sets up a beautiful indoor tropical breeze.*

COLD GIN TODDY

2 oz. gin
½ **tsp. sugar**

Lemon peel

Shake gin and sugar well with plenty of ice and strain into old-fashioned glass filled with large cubes or slices of ice. Twist lemon peel above drink and drop into glass.

COLONIAL COCKTAIL

1½ oz. gin
1 oz. grapefruit juice

1 tsp. maraschino liqueur
1 olive

Shake gin, grapefruit juice, and maraschino liqueur with ice. Strain into prechilled cocktail glass. Garnish with olive.

COPENHAGEN

1 oz. gin
1 oz. aquavit

¼ **oz. dry vermouth**
1 large stuffed olive

Stir gin, aquavit, and vermouth well with ice. Strain into prechilled cocktail glass. Add olive.

CORDIAL MÉDOC

1 oz. gin
½ **oz. Cordial Médoc**

½ **oz. dry vermouth**
¼ **oz. lemon juice**

Shake well with ice. Strain into prechilled cocktail glass. *For a bon-voyage cocktail party before flying to Paris.*

CORDIAL MÉDOC SOUR

1½ oz. gin
½ **oz. Cordial Médoc**

½ **oz. lemon juice**
½ **slice orange**

Shake gin, Cordial Médoc, and lemon juice well with ice. Strain into prechilled whiskey-sour glass. Garnish with orange slice.

CRIMSON SUNSET

2 oz. gin
2 tsp. lemon juice

½ tsp. grenadine
½ oz. tawny port

Shake gin, lemon juice, and grenadine well with ice. Strain into prechilled cocktail glass. Float port on top.

DANISH GIN FIZZ

1½ oz. gin
½ oz. Peter Heering or Cherry Karise
¼ oz. kirschwasser
½ oz. lime juice

1 tsp. sugar
Iced club soda
1 slice lime
1 maraschino cherry

Shake gin, Peter Heering, kirschwasser, lime juice, and sugar well with ice. Strain into tall 14-oz. glass half-filled with ice. Fill glass with soda. Stir. Add lime slice and cherry. *A single round will pave the way for a Danish open-sandwich party.*

DELMONICO COCKTAIL

1 oz. gin
½ oz. brandy
½ oz. sweet vermouth

½ oz. dry vermouth
1 dash Angostura bitters
Lemon peel

Stir gin, brandy, vermouths, and bitters well with ice. Strain into prechilled cocktail glass. Twist lemon peel over drink and drop into glass.

DIAMOND FIZZ

2 oz. gin
Juice of ½ lemon

1 tsp. powdered sugar
Ice cold brut champagne

Shake gin, lemon juice, and powdered sugar well with ice. Strain into highball glass over rocks. Top off with champagne. Stir gently.

DIXIE COCKTAIL

1 oz. gin
½ oz. dry vermouth

1 tbsp. anise
Juice of ¼ orange

Shake with ice. Strain into prechilled cocktail glass.

DRAGONFLY

1½ oz. gin
3 oz. ginger ale

1 lime wedge

Stir with ice. Garnish with lime wedge.

DUNDEE

1 oz. gin
½ oz. Scotch
½ oz. Drambuie

¼ oz. lemon juice
Lemon peel

Shake gin, Scotch, Drambuie, and lemon juice well with ice. Pour over rocks into prechilled old-fashioned glass. Twist lemon peel above drink and drop into glass.

EMERSON

1½ oz. gin | **Juice of ½ lime**
1 oz. sweet vermouth | **1 tsp. maraschino liqueur**

Shake with ice. Strain into prechilled cocktail glass.

ENGLISH MULE

3 oz. ice cold green-ginger wine | **Iced club soda**
1½ oz. gin | **1 piece preserved ginger in syrup**
2½ oz. ice cold orange juice

Put three ice cubes into tall 14-oz. glass. Pour wine, gin, and orange juice into glass. Stir well. Fill glass with soda. Stir slightly. Fasten preserved ginger, well drained, onto cocktail spear. Fit spear into straw in glass.

ENGLISH ROSE

1½ oz. gin | **1 tsp. grenadine**
¾ oz. apricot brandy | **¼ tsp. lemon juice**
¾ oz. dry vermouth | **1 cherry**

Shake gin, brandy, vermouth, grenadine, and lemon juice well with ice. Strain into sugar-frosted deep-saucer champagne glass. Drop in cherry.

EUROPEAN

1 oz. gin | **½ oz. dry vermouth**
½ oz. cream sherry | **½ tsp. Grand Marnier**
½ oz. red Dubonnet | **1 maraschino cherry**

Stir gin, sherry, Dubonnet, vermouth, and Grand Marnier with ice. Strain into old-fashioned glass over rocks. Stir well. Drop in cherry.

FALLEN ANGEL

1½ oz. gin | **1 dash Angostura bitters**
½ tsp. white crème de menthe | **1 cherry**
Juice of ½ lemon

Shake gin, crème de menthe, lemon juice, and bitters well with ice. Strain into prechilled cocktail glass. Drop in cherry.

FIRST BLUSH

1½ oz. gin | **1 tsp. cherry brandy**
½ oz. triple sec | **1 maraschino cherry**
1 oz. lemon juice

Shake well with ice. Strain into prechilled cocktail glass. Drop in cherry.

FLAMINGO COCKTAIL

1½ oz. gin | **Juice of ½ lime**
½ oz. apricot brandy | **1 tsp. grenadine**

Shake well with ice. Strain into prechilled cocktail glass.

FLORIDA

1¼ oz. orange juice
½ oz. gin
¼ oz. kirschwasser

¼ oz. triple sec
1 tsp. lemon juice

Shake well with ice. Strain into prechilled sugar-frosted cocktail glass. *A drink with less hard liquor than citrus juice but always clears up the fog.*

FOGGY DAY

1½ oz. gin
¼ oz. Pernod

Lemon peel
1 slice lemon

Shake gin and Pernod with ice. Strain over rocks into prechilled old-fashioned glass. Rub lemon peel around rim of glass and drop peel into glass. Add lemon slice.

GENEVER COCKTAIL

1½ oz. Dutch genever gin
½ oz. lime juice
½ oz. orange juice

1 tsp. sugar
1 dash Angostura bitters

Shake well with ice. Strain over rocks into prechilled old-fashioned glass. *Odd but very obliging.*

GENOA

¾ oz. gin
¾ oz. grappa
½ oz. Sambuca

½ oz. dry vermouth
1 cocktail olive

Stir gin, grappa, Sambuca, and vermouth well with ice. Strain into prechilled cocktail glass. Add olive.

GENTLEMAN'S CLUB

1½ oz. gin
1 oz. brandy

1 oz. sweet vermouth
1 oz. club soda

Pour gin, brandy, vermouth, and club soda into old-fashioned glass over rocks. Stir well.

GIMLET

2 oz. gin
½ oz. Rose's Lime Juice

Stir extremely well with ice. Strain into prechilled cocktail glass. Long stirring is absolutely essential to present this English classic in its best light. The above formula, 4-to-1, may be made 5-to-1, if desired, by adding ½ oz. gin. Glass may be sugar-frosted by moistening rim with Rose's Lime Juice before dipping into sugar.

GIN AND CAMPARI

1¼ oz. gin
1¼ oz. Campari

Orange peel

Stir gin and Campari well with ice. Strain over rocks into prechilled old-fashioned glass. Twist orange peel above drink and drop into glass. *Savor it in sips.*

GIN AND GINGER COOLER

1 oz. gin
1 oz. ginger-flavored brandy
½ oz. lemon juice
1 tsp. sugar

4 oz. ginger beer or ginger ale
1 slice lemon
1 small chunk preserved ginger
in syrup

Shake gin, ginger-flavored brandy, lemon juice, and sugar well with ice. Strain into tall 12-oz. glass half-filled with ice. Stir. Add ginger beer. Stir. Add ice if necessary to fill glass. Stir. Garnish with lemon slice and preserved ginger.

GIN AND LIME

1½ oz. gin
½ oz. fresh lime juice
½ oz. orange juice

1 tsp. Rose's Lime Juice
Lime peel

Shake gin, fresh lime juice, orange juice, and Rose's Lime Juice well with ice. Strain into prechilled cocktail glass. Twist lime peel above drink and drop into glass.

GIN AND SIN

1½ oz. gin
1 oz. orange juice

1 oz. lemon juice
½ tsp. grenadine

Shake well with ice. Strain into prechilled cocktail glass.

GIN AQUAVIT

1½ oz. gin
½ oz. aquavit
½ oz. lemon juice

1 tsp. sugar
½ egg white
1 tsp. heavy cream

Shake well with ice. Strain into prechilled old-fashioned glass over two or three ice cubes. *A light, foamy drink.*

GIN BRACER

2 oz. gin
½ oz. ketchup
½ oz. lemon juice
1 dash Tabasco sauce

1 dash celery salt
¼ tsp. Worcestershire sauce
1 cup crushed ice

Blend all ingredients at low speed for 15 to 20 seconds. Pour into tall 10-oz. glass. Add ice cubes to fill glass.

GIN BUCK

1½ oz. gin
½ oz. lemon juice

Iced ginger ale
1 slice lemon

Shake gin and lemon juice well with ice. Strain into 8-oz. glass half-filled with ice. Add ginger ale. Stir. Add lemon slice.

GIN CASSIS

1½ oz. gin	½ oz. crème de cassis
½ oz. lemon juice	

Shake well with ice. Strain into prechilled cocktail glass or into prechilled old-fashioned glass with one or two rocks.

GIN COBBLER

1 tsp. powdered sugar	½ cup crushed ice
3 oz. club soda	1 maraschino cherry
2 oz. gin	1 orange slice

In an old-fashioned glass, dissolve the sugar in club soda. Add gin and crushed ice. Stir well. Garnish with cherry and orange slice.

GIN DAIQUIRI

1½ oz. gin	½ oz. lime juice
½ oz. light rum	1 tsp. sugar

Shake well with ice. Strain into prechilled sugar-frosted cocktail glass.

GIN DAISY

1½ oz. gin	Iced club soda
½ oz. lemon juice	1 slice lemon
1½ tsp. raspberry syrup	2 sprigs mint

Shake gin, lemon juice, and raspberry syrup well with ice. Strain into tall 8-oz. glass half-filled with ice. Add soda. Garnish with lemon slice and mint sprigs.

GIN FIZZ

2 oz. gin	Iced club soda
½ oz. lemon juice	1 slice lemon
1 tsp. sugar	

Shake gin, lemon juice, and sugar well with ice. Strain into tall 14-oz. glass half-filled with ice. Fill glass with soda. Stir. Add lemon slice. Brandy, whiskey, rum, or vodka may be used in place of the gin. A 10- or 12-oz. glass may be used instead of the 14-oz., but any diminution in its size only shortens the pleasure of the long, lazy drink implied by a fizz.

GIN MINT FIX

1 tsp. sugar	½ oz. lemon juice
2 tsp. water	1 tsp. white crème de menthe
2 oz. gin	2 large mint leaves

Dissolve sugar in 2 tsp. water in an 8-oz. glass. Add gin, lemon juice, and crème de menthe. Fill glass with crushed ice. Stir well. Add more ice to fill glass to rim. Stir. Tear mint leaves slightly and float on drink.

GIN OLD-FASHIONED

¼ tsp. sugar	1¾ oz. gin
1 or 2 dashes Angostura bitters	Lemon peel

Put sugar and bitters into prechilled old-fashioned glass. Stir until sugar dissolves, adding a tsp. of water if necessary to complete the process. Add gin and two or three ice cubes or large pieces of coarsely cracked ice. Stir well. Twist lemon peel above drink and drop into glass. Old-Fashioneds are frequently garnished with an orange slice, a lemon slice, a pineapple chunk, a cherry, etc., but knowledgeable Old-Fashioned drinkers shun the fruit salad.

GIN SANGAREE

½ tsp. powdered sugar	Club soda to fill
1 tsp. water	1 tbsp. port
2 oz. gin	Nutmeg

Dissolve powdered sugar in water and add gin over rocks. Top off with club soda. Stir. Float port on top. Sprinkle lightly with nutmeg.

GIN SIDECAR

¾ oz. high-proof English gin	¾ oz. lemon juice
¾ oz. triple sec	

Shake well with ice. Strain into prechilled cocktail glass. The gin substitutes for brandy in this version of the classic Sidecar.

GIN SOUR

1½ oz. gin	1 tsp. sugar
½ oz. lemon juice	½ slice orange
¼ oz. orange juice	1 maraschino cherry

Shake gin, lemon juice, orange juice, and sugar well with ice. Strain into prechilled whiskey-sour glass. Garnish with orange slice and cherry.

GIN SOUTHERN

1½ oz. gin	¼ oz. grapefruit juice
½ oz. Southern Comfort	¼ oz. lemon juice

Shake well with ice. Strain into prechilled cocktail glass. *For drinking men and Southern belles who appreciate verandas and magnolia blossoms.*

GIN SWIZZLE

2 oz. gin	1 tsp. sugar
½ tsp. Angostura bitters	Iced club soda
½ oz. lime juice	

Shake gin, bitters, lime juice, and sugar well with ice. Strain into tall 14-oz. glass half-filled with ice. Add soda. Stir. *A patriarchal drink invented when swizzle sticks were smart, but now best handled in a cocktail shaker and tall glass.*

GOLDEN GIN FIZZ

2¼ oz. gin
1 oz. lemon juice
1 egg yolk
2 tsp. sugar

Iced club soda
1 slice lemon
Freshly ground nutmeg (optional)

Shake gin, lemon juice, egg yolk, and sugar well with ice. Strain into tall 14-oz. glass half-filled with ice. Fill glass with soda. Stir. Add lemon slice. Sprinkle with nutmeg if desired.

GOLDEN HORNET

1½ oz. gin
½ oz. amontillado sherry

½ oz. Scotch
Lemon peel

Stir gin and sherry well with ice. Strain over two rocks into prechilled old-fashioned glass. Float Scotch on top. Twist lemon peel over drink and drop into glass.

GRANVILLE

1½ oz. gin
¼ oz. Grand Marnier

¼ oz. Calvados
¼ oz. lemon juice

Shake well with ice. Strain into prechilled cocktail glass.

GREENBACK

1½ oz. gin
1 oz. green crème de menthe

1 oz. lemon juice

Shake well with ice. Strain into old-fashioned glass over rocks.

GREEN DEVIL

1½ oz. gin
½ oz. lime juice

¼ oz. green crème de menthe
2 sprigs mint

Shake gin, lime juice, and crème de menthe well with ice. Strain over two or three rocks into prechilled old-fashioned glass. Tear several mint leaves to release aroma before adding to drink as garnish.

HARLEM COCKTAIL

1½ oz. gin
1 oz. pineapple juice

½ tsp. maraschino liqueur
1 pineapple stick

Shake gin, pineapple juice, and maraschino liqueur with ice. Strain into prechilled cocktail glass. Garnish with pineapple stick.

HAWAIIAN COCKTAIL

2 oz. gin
½ oz. triple sec

1 tbsp. pineapple juice

Shake well with ice. Strain into prechilled cocktail glass.

HONEYDEW COOLER

⅓ cup diced ripe honeydew melon
1½ oz. gin
¼ tsp. Pernod
1 tbsp. heavy cream

¾ oz. lemon juice
½ tsp. sugar
½ cup crushed ice
Iced club soda

Put honeydew, gin, Pernod, cream, lemon juice, sugar, and crushed ice into blender. Blend at low speed for 15 to 20 seconds. Pour into tall 14-oz. glass. When foam settles, add a splash of soda and enough ice to fill glass to rim if necessary.

HORSE'S NECK WITH GIN

Peel of whole lemon
2 oz. gin

½ oz. lemon juice
Iced ginger ale

To peel lemon, start at stem end, using a sharp paring knife, and cut peel about ½ inch wide in a continuous strip until lemon is completely peeled. Place peel in a 14-oz. highball glass so that the top of peel overlaps rim of glass, with the rest spiraling down into glass. Fill glass with coarsely cracked ice. Pour gin and lemon juice into glass. Fill with ginger ale. Stir.

HUDSON BAY

1 oz. gin
½ oz. cherry liqueur
½ oz. orange juice

¼ oz. lime juice
¼ oz. 151-proof rum
1 slice lime

Shake gin, cherry liqueur, orange juice, lime juice, and rum well with ice. Strain into prechilled cocktail glass. Add lime slice. *A winter or summer cocktail with prodigious thawing powers.*

JAMAICA GLOW

1½ oz. gin
½ oz. dry red wine
½ oz. orange juice

1 tsp. dark Jamaican rum
1 slice lime

Shake gin, wine, orange juice, and rum well with ice. Strain into prechilled sugar-frosted cocktail glass. Add lime slice. *This relic of plantation days is still a magnificent reviver for surf riders and scuba divers.*

JASMINE

1½ oz. gin
¼ oz. Cointreau
¼ oz. Campari

¾ oz. lemon juice
Lemon peel

Stir with cracked ice. Strain into prechilled cocktail glass. Twist lemon peel over drink and drop into glass.

JEWEL OF THE NILE

¾ oz. gin
¾ oz. sweet vermouth
¾ oz. green Chartreuse

1 dash orange bitters
1 cherry

Stir gin, vermouth, Chartreuse, and bitters well with ice. Strain into prechilled cocktail glass. Drop in cherry.

JOULOUVILLE

1 oz. gin
½ oz. apple brandy
½ oz. lemon juice

¼ oz. sweet vermouth
¼ tsp. grenadine

Shake well with ice. Strain into prechilled cocktail glass.

KEY COCKTAIL

1½ oz. gin
½ oz. lime juice
¼ oz. dark Jamaican rum

¼ oz. Falernum
1 pineapple stick

Shake gin, lime juice, rum, and Falernum well with ice. Strain into prechilled cocktail glass. Garnish with pineapple stick.

K.G.B.

1½ oz. gin
½ oz. Kirschwasser
2 tsp. apricot brandy

½ oz. lemon juice
½ tsp. superfine sugar
Lemon peel

Shake well with ice. Strain into highball glass over rocks. Twist lemon peel over drink and drop into glass.

LEAP YEAR

2 oz. gin
½ oz. sweet vermouth

½ oz. Grand Marnier
¼ oz. lemon juice

Shake with cracked ice. Strain into prechilled cocktail glass.

LONDON BUCK

2 oz. gin
½ tsp. maraschino liqueur
2 dashes orange bitters

½ tsp. sugar syrup
Lemon peel

Shake well with ice. Strain into prechilled cocktail glass. Twist lemon peel over drink and drop into glass.

LONDON TOWN

1½ oz. gin
½ oz. maraschino liqueur

2 dashes orange bitters

Stir well with ice. Strain into prechilled cocktail glass.

MATINEE

1 oz. gin
½ oz. Sambuca
½ egg white

1 tsp. heavy cream
½ oz. lime juice

Shake all ingredients well with ice. Strain into prechilled cocktail glass. *A comfortable midafternoon cocktail. May also be served as a pick-me-up the morning after with a sprinkling of freshly ground nutmeg.*

MILLION-DOLLAR COCKTAIL

1½ oz. gin
¾ oz. sweet vermouth
2 tsp. pineapple juice

1 tsp. grenadine
1 egg white

Shake well with ice. Strain into prechilled cocktail glass.

MINT COLLINS

2 oz. gin
4 large mint leaves
½ oz. lemon juice
1 tsp. sugar

½ cup crushed ice
Iced club soda
1 slice lemon

Put gin, mint leaves, lemon juice, sugar, and crushed ice into blender. Blend at high speed for 15 seconds or until mint leaves are finely chopped. Pour into tall 14-oz. glass. Add soda to fill glass. Stir. Add lemon slice.

MINTED GIN

1½ oz. gin
½ oz. lemon juice
1 tsp. sugar

1 slice lemon
½ slice orange
2 sprigs fresh mint

Shake gin, lemon juice, and sugar well with ice. Strain into prechilled old-fashioned glass with rocks. Garnish drink with lemon and orange slices. Tear mint leaves before placing on rocks. *A perfect drink for unwinding after eighteen holes on the fairway.*

MOLDAU

1½ oz. gin
½ oz. plum brandy
¼ oz. orange juice

¼ oz. lemon juice
1 brandied cherry

Shake gin, plum brandy, orange juice, and lemon juice well with ice. Strain into prechilled old-fashioned glass with two or three ice cubes. Garnish with brandied cherry.

MONTMARTRE

1½ oz. dry gin
½ oz. sweet vermouth

½ oz. triple sec
1 cherry

Stir well with ice. Strain into prechilled cocktail glass. Drop in cherry.

MONTREAL GIN SOUR

1 oz. gin
1 oz. lemon juice
1 tsp. powdered sugar

½ egg white
1 slice lemon

Shake well with ice. Strain into prechilled whiskey-sour glass. Garnish with lemon slice.

MORRO

1 oz. gin
½ oz. golden rum
½ oz. lime juice

½ oz. pineapple juice
1 tsp. sugar

Shake well with ice. Strain into prechilled sugar-frosted glass. Moisten rim of glass with Falernum before dipping into sugar. *Once tasted, the marriage of gin and rum is one of those unions that no one in his right drinking sense would dream of putting asunder. Fruit juices in this drink help fortify the nuptials.*

NAPOLEON

2 oz. gin
½ tsp. curaçao

½ tsp. Dubonnet

Stir well with ice. Strain into prechilled cocktail glass.

NEGRONI

¾ oz. gin
¾ oz. Campari

¾ oz. sweet vermouth

Stir well with ice. Strain into prechilled cocktail glass. May be served on the rocks with a twist of lemon or splash of soda or both.

NEW ORLEANS GIN FIZZ

2½ oz. gin
1 oz. lemon juice
½ egg white
1 tsp. heavy cream

¼ tsp. orange flower water
2 tsp. sugar
Iced club soda
1 slice lemon

Shake gin, lemon juice, egg white, cream, orange flower water, and sugar well with ice. Strain into tall 14-oz. glass half-filled with ice. Fill glass with soda. Stir. Garnish with lemon slice. *A variation of the Ramos Gin Fizz.*

NORTH POLE

1 oz. gin
½ oz. maraschino liqueur
½ oz. lemon juice

1 egg white
Whipped cream

Shake well with ice. Strain into prechilled cocktail glass. Top with whipped cream.

PALM BEACH

1½ oz. gin
1½ tsp. sweet vermouth

1½ tsp. grapefruit juice

Shake well with ice. Strain into prechilled cocktail glass.

PAPAYA SLING

1½ oz. gin
Juice of 1 lime
1 tbsp. papaya juice

1 dash Angostura bitters
Club soda
1 pineapple stick

Shake gin, lime juice, papaya juice, and bitters well with ice. Strain into collins glass over rocks. Top off with club soda. Stir. Garnish with pineapple stick.

PARISIAN

1 oz. gin
1 oz. dry vermouth

¼ oz. crème de cassis

Shake well with ice. Strain into prechilled cocktail glass.

PARK AVENUE

1½ oz. gin
¾ oz. sweet vermouth

1 tbsp. pineapple juice

Stir well with ice. Strain into prechilled cocktail glass.

PETER PAN

¾ oz. gin
¾ oz. dry vermouth

¾ oz. orange juice
2 dashes Angostura bitters

Shake well with ice. Strain into prechilled cocktail glass.

PETTICOAT JUNCTION

2 oz. gin
½ oz. sweet vermouth

½ oz. Campari
Lemon peel

Stir well with ice. Strain into prechilled cocktail glass. Twist lemon peel over drink and drop into glass.

PICCADILLY

1½ oz. gin
¾ oz. dry vermouth

¼ tsp. anise
¼ tsp. grenadine

Stir well with ice. Strain into prechilled cocktail glass.

PINK PUSSYCAT

1½ oz. gin
3 oz. pineapple juice

1 tsp. cherry brandy

Pour gin and pineapple juice into old-fashioned glass over ice. Stir. Float cherry brandy on top.

POLO COCKTAIL

2 oz. gin
1 tbsp. lemon juice

1 tbsp. orange juice

Shake with ice. Strain into prechilled cocktail glass. Top off with ice if necessary.

OAHU GIN SLING

Lime-rind spiral
2 oz. gin
½ oz. crème de cassis
½ oz. Benedictine

1 oz. lime juice
1 tsp. sugar
Iced club soda

To make lime-rind spiral, cut continuous strip of lime peel from stem end to bottom of fruit. Place peel in tall 14-oz. glass, hooking it onto rim. Shake gin, crème de cassis, Benedictine, lime juice, and sugar well with ice. Strain into glass and add ice cubes until three-quarters full. Fill glass with soda. Stir.

OLD-FASHIONED ARTICHOKE

1 oz. gin	Iced club soda
½ oz. dry vermouth	1 slice lemon
½ oz. Cynar	

Pour gin, vermouth, and Cynar over rocks in old-fashioned glass. Stir well. Add splash of soda. Add lemon slice.

OPAL COCKTAIL

1½ oz. gin	1 tbsp. orange juice
½ oz. triple sec	¼ tbsp. powdered sugar

Shake very well with ice. Strain into prechilled cocktail glass.

ORANGE BLOSSOM

1½ oz. gin	½ slice orange
1 oz. orange juice	

Shake gin and orange juice well with ice. Strain into prechilled sugar-frosted cocktail glass. Glass may be sugar-frosted by moistening rim with orange peel before dipping into sugar. Add orange slice.

ORANGE BLOSSOM FROZEN

1½ oz. gin	2 drops orange flower water
2 oz. orange juice	¼ cup cracked ice
½ oz. curaçao	½ slice orange
½ oz. lemon juice	

Put gin, orange juice, curaçao, lemon juice, orange flower water, and ice into blender. Spin for 5 to 8 seconds. Pour into deep-saucer champagne or old-fashioned glass. Place orange slice on top.

ORANGE BUCK

1½ oz. gin	Iced ginger ale
1 oz. orange juice	1 slice cocktail orange in syrup
½ oz. lemon juice	

Shake gin, orange juice, and lemon juice well with ice. Strain into 8-oz. glass half-filled with ice. Add ginger ale. Stir. Add orange slice.

ORANGE FIZZ

2 oz. gin	1 tsp. sugar
1½ oz. orange juice	2 dashes orange bitters
½ oz. lemon juice	Iced club soda
2 tsp. triple sec	1 slice orange

Shake gin, orange juice, lemon juice, triple sec, sugar, and bitters well with ice. Strain into tall 14-oz. glass half-filled with ice. Fill glass with soda. Stir. Add orange slice.

ORANGE OASIS

1½ oz. gin
½ oz. cherry brandy
3 oz. orange juice

Ginger ale
1 maraschino cherry

Shake gin, cherry brandy, and orange juice with ice. Strain into highball glass over rocks. Top off with ginger ale. Stir. Drop in cherry.

PEACHBLOW FIZZ

2 oz. gin
½ oz. strawberry liqueur
½ oz. lemon juice
½ tsp. sugar

1 tsp. heavy cream
Iced club soda
1 slice lemon
1 large fresh strawberry

Shake gin, strawberry liqueur, lemon juice, sugar, and cream well with ice. Strain into tall 14-oz. glass half-filled with ice. Fill glass with soda. Stir. Garnish with lemon slice and strawberry. *A classic old fizz—as well as a semantic mystery because there's no peach in the recipe—and a joy for parched throats.*

PIMM'S CUP

1½ oz. Pimm's No. 1 Cup
Iced 7-Up or lemon soda

1 slice lemon
Cucumber peel

Pour Pimm's Cup into 8- or 10-oz. glass or Pimm's glass tankard with ice. Fill with 7-Up. Add lemon slice and cucumber peel. Stir. *The old English Gin Sling is bottled as Pimm's No. 1 Cup, made with a gin base and fruit flavors. Other prepared Pimm's Cups are bottled with different liquor bases, but the No. 1 is the best known in the States.*

PIMM'S RANGOON

1½ oz. Pimm's No. 1 Cup
Ginger ale

Lemon peel
Cucumber peel

Pour Pimm's over rocks into tall highball glass. Top off with ginger ale. Stir. Garnish with lemon and cucumber peels.

PINEAPPLE MINT COOLER

2 oz. gin
½ oz. white crème de menthe
3 oz. pineapple juice
1 oz. lemon juice

Iced club soda
1 pineapple stick
1 green cocktail cherry

Shake gin, crème de menthe, pineapple juice, and lemon juice well with ice. Strain into tall 14-oz. glass. Add a splash of soda and enough ice to fill glass. Stir. Garnish with pineapple stick and cherry.

PINK GIN

2 oz. gin
2 dashes Angostura bitters

In Britain, the custom is simply to stir these ingredients at room temperature in a small cocktail glass. For American tastes, it's more pleasant if the gin and bitters are well stirred with ice and then poured into a prechilled glass. *This is one of the drinks that sustained Sir Francis Chichester so beautifully on his long, lonely trip round the world.*

PINK LADY

1½ oz. gin
¼ oz. lime juice
1 tsp. heavy cream

1 tsp. grenadine
½ egg white

Shake well with ice. Strain into prechilled cocktail glass. Glass may be sugar-frosted by moistening rim with grenadine before dipping into sugar.

PIROUETTER

1 oz. gin
½ oz. Grand Marnier
1 oz. orange juice

1 tsp. lemon juice
Orange peel

Shake gin, Grand Marnier, orange juice, and lemon juice well with ice. Strain into prechilled cocktail glass. Twist orange peel above drink and drop into glass.

PISTACHIO LIME COLLINS

1½ oz. gin
1 oz. pistachio liqueur
1 oz. lime juice

3 large ice cubes
Iced club soda
1 slice lime

Pour gin, pistachio liqueur, and lime juice over ice cubes into tall 12-oz. glass. Stir well. Top off with soda. Stir. Add lime slice.

POLISH SIDECAR

¾ oz. gin
¾ oz. Polish or Polish-style
  blackberry liqueur

¾ oz. lemon juice

Shake well with ice. Strain into prechilled cocktail glass. A large fresh blackberry, if available, is a pleasant garnish for this drink.

POMPANO

1 oz. gin
½ oz. dry vermouth
1 oz. grapefruit juice

4 dashes orange bitters
1 slice orange

Shake gin, vermouth, grapefruit juice, and bitters well with ice. Strain over rocks into prechilled old-fashioned glass. Garnish with orange slice. *A perfect cocktail for Florida- or Caribbean-bound vacationers.*

PRINCETON

1¼ oz. gin
¾ oz. dry vermouth

½ oz. lime juice

Shake well with ice. Strain into prechilled cocktail glass. *Like the Bronx cocktail, this is one of very few drinks born in Prohibition days worth retaining. Named for the great seat of learning, which, during the Noble Experiment, distinguished itself even more for its prowess in soaking up bathtub gin.*

QUEEN ELIZABETH

1½ oz. gin
½ oz. dry vermouth

1½ tsp. Benedictine

Stir well with ice. Strain into prechilled cocktail glass. *Raise a toast to long life.*

RACQUET CLUB

2 oz. gin
½ oz. dry vermouth

2 dashes orange bitters

Shake (don't stir) with ice in silver cocktail shaker until shaker is completely frosted. Strain into cocktail glass so cold that it's somewhat uncomfortable to hold.

RAMOS GIN FIZZ

2 oz. gin
1 egg white
½ oz. heavy cream
2 tsp. sugar
½ oz. lemon juice

¼ oz. lime juice
½ tsp. orange flower water
1 cup crushed ice
Iced club soda

Put gin, egg white, cream, sugar, lemon juice, lime juice, orange flower water, and crushed ice into blender. Blend at high speed for 5 seconds. Pour into tall 14-oz. glass. Add enough club soda to fill glass. Stir. *In the old days, no New Orleans bartender would think of serving a Ramos Gin Fizz if the drink hadn't been shaken at least 5 minutes. The electric blender does a better job in 5 seconds.*

RED BARON

1½ oz. gin
½ oz. dry vermouth
½ tsp. sweet vermouth

1½ tsp. triple sec
1 lemon wedge

Stir gin, vermouths, and triple sec well with ice. Strain into prechilled cocktail glass. Garnish with lemon wedge.

RED CLOUD

1½ oz. gin
½ oz. apricot liqueur
½ oz. lemon juice

1 tsp. grenadine
1 dash bitters

Shake well with ice. Strain into prechilled cocktail glass.

RENAISSANCE

½ oz. gin
½ oz. dry sherry

½ oz. heavy cream
Freshly grated nutmeg

Shake gin, sherry, and cream well with ice. Strain into prechilled cocktail glass. Spray with nutmeg. *A drink to savor after a lengthy tour of art galleries.*

RENDEZVOUS

1½ oz. gin
½ oz. kirschwasser

½ oz. Campari
Lemon peel

Shake gin, kirschwasser, and Campari well with ice. Strain into prechilled cocktail glass. Twist lemon peel above drink and drop into glass. *An appetite arouser best sipped while a double-thick fillet is browning over the charcoals.*

ROCKY DANE

1 oz. gin
½ oz. dry vermouth
½ oz. Peter Heering

½ oz. kirschwasser
Lemon peel

Shake gin, vermouth, Peter Heering, and kirschwasser well with ice. Strain over rocks into prechilled old-fashioned glass. Twist lemon peel above drink and drop into glass.

ROCKY GREEN DRAGON

1 oz. gin
¾ oz. green Chartreuse

¾ oz. Cognac

Shake extremely well with ice. Strain over rocks into prechilled old-fashioned glass. *A potent dragon to be slowly sipped, not gulped.*

ROLLS-ROYCE

1½ oz. gin
½ oz. sweet vermouth

½ oz. dry vermouth
1 tsp. Benedictine

Stir well with ice. Strain into prechilled cocktail glass.

ROMAN COOLER

1½ oz. gin
½ oz. Punt e Mes
½ oz. lemon juice

1 tsp. sugar
Iced club soda
Lemon peel

Shake gin, Punt e Mes, lemon juice, and sugar well with ice. Strain into tall 14-oz. glass. Add soda and ice to fill glass. Twist lemon peel above drink and drop into glass.

ROMAN FRULLATI

3 oz. gin
¼ cup diced red apple, with skin
¼ cup diced ripe pear, with skin
¼ cup frozen sliced peaches, thawed

1 oz. maraschino liqueur
1 oz. orzata or orgeat
½ cup crushed ice

Put all ingredients into blender. Blend at high speed for 20 seconds. Pour into tall 14-oz. glass. Add ice if necessary to fill glass to rim.

ROSE

1 oz. gin
½ oz. apricot-flavored brandy
½ oz. dry vermouth

½ oz. lemon juice
1 tsp. grenadine
Lemon peel

Shake gin, apricot-flavored brandy, vermouth, lemon juice, and grenadine well with ice. Strain into prechilled cocktail glass. Twist lemon peel above drink and drop into glass.

ROYAL GIN FIZZ

2¼ oz. gin
1 oz. lemon juice
1 whole egg

2 tsp. sugar
Iced club soda
1 slice lemon

Shake gin, lemon juice, egg, and sugar well with ice. Strain into tall 14-oz. glass half-filled with ice. Fill glass with soda. Stir. Add lemon slice.

RUBY IN THE ROUGH

1½ oz. gin
½ oz. cherry brandy

1 tsp. sweet vermouth

Stir well with ice. Strain into prechilled cocktail glass.

SAN SEBASTIAN

1 oz. gin
¼ oz. rum
½ oz. grapefruit juice

¼ oz. curaçao
½ oz. lemon juice

Shake well with ice. Strain into prechilled cocktail glass. *Recommended for galley bartenders after a lazy Sunday-afternoon sail.*

SAVANNAH

1½ oz. gin
1 dash white crème de cacao

Juice of ½ orange
1 egg white

Shake well with ice. Strain into prechilled cocktail glass.

SEVILLE

1 oz. gin
½ oz. fino sherry
½ oz. orange juice

½ oz. lemon juice
½ tsp. sugar

Shake well with ice. Strain into prechilled sugar-rimmed glass.

SINGAPORE GIN SLING

1½ oz. gin
1 oz. cherry-flavored brandy
1 oz. lime juice

Iced club soda
1 slice lime

Shake gin, cherry-flavored brandy, and lime juice well with ice. Strain into tall 14-oz. glass half-filled with ice cubes. Fill glass with soda. Add lime slice.

SOUTH SIDE

2 oz. gin
½ oz. lemon juice

1 tsp. sugar
2 sprigs fresh mint

Shake gin, lemon juice, and sugar well with ice. Strain into prechilled cocktail glass. Tear several leaves of each mint sprig before adding to drink. *Although not as well known as the Mint Julep, the South Side is a delightful summery cocktail with a delicate mint accent.*

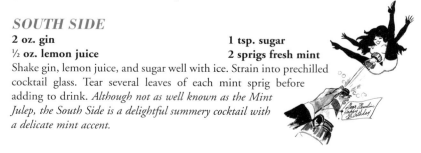

ST. LÔ

1½ oz. gin
½ oz. Calvados

½ oz. lemon juice
1 tsp. sugar

Shake well with ice. Strain into prechilled cocktail glass.

STRAWBERRY CREAM COOLER

1½ oz. gin
1 oz. lemon juice
¼ cup frozen sliced strawberries
(fruit and syrup), thawed

2 tbsp. heavy cream
Iced club soda
1 tsp. sugar

Put gin, lemon juice, strawberries, cream, and sugar into blender. Blend for 10 to 15 seconds at high speed. Pour into tall 14-oz. glass. Add a splash of soda and enough ice to fill glass. Stir.

STRAWBERRY SWIG

1½ oz. gin
½ oz. strawberry liqueur
¼ oz. lime juice

1 dash orange bitters
1 slice lime

Shake gin, strawberry liqueur, lime juice, and bitters well with ice. Strain into prechilled old-fashioned glass over several rocks. Garnish with lime slice.

STREGA SOUR

1½ oz. gin
½ oz. lemon juice

½ oz. Strega
1 slice lemon

Shake gin, lemon juice, and Strega well with ice. Strain into prechilled sugar-frosted cocktail glass. Moisten rim of glass with Strega before dipping into sugar. Garnish with lemon slice.

TANGO

1 oz. gin
½ oz. sweet vermouth
½ oz. dry vermouth

½ tsp. triple sec
1 tbsp. orange juice

Shake well with ice. Strain into prechilled cocktail glass.

TOM COLLINS

2 to 2½ oz. gin
1 to 2 tsp. sugar
½ to 1 oz. lemon juice
Iced club soda

1 slice lemon (optional)
1 slice orange (optional)
1 maraschino cherry (optional)

Shake gin, sugar, and lemon juice well with ice. Strain into tall 14-oz. glass half-filled with ice. Top off with soda. Stir. Add lemon slice and/or orange slice and/or cherry. John Collins takes rye; Joe Collins prefers Scotch. *A Collins was the first cocktail poured after Repeal.*

TURF

1 oz. gin
1 oz. dry vermouth
¼ oz. Pernod

¼ oz. lemon juice
1 slice lemon

Shake gin, vermouth, Pernod, and lemon juice well with ice. Strain over rocks into prechilled old-fashioned glass. Add lemon slice.

TUXEDO

1½ oz. gin
1½ oz. dry vermouth
¼ tsp. maraschino liqueur

¼ tsp. anise
2 dashes orange bitters
1 cherry

Stir well with ice. Strain into prechilled cocktail glass. Drop in cherry.

UNION JACK

1½ oz. gin
¾ oz. sloe gin

½ tsp. grenadine

Shake well with ice. Strain into prechilled cocktail glass.

VERBOTEN

1 oz. gin
½ oz. grapefruit juice
½ oz. lemon juice

½ oz. orange juice
1 tsp. powdered sugar
1 brandied cherry

Shake gin, grapefruit juice, lemon juice, orange juice, and sugar well with ice. Strain into prechilled cocktail glass. Garnish with brandied cherry.

WATERMELON CASSIS

2 oz. gin
1 cup diced watermelon, seeds removed
½ oz. crème de cassis
¾ oz. lemon juice

½ cup crushed ice
Iced club soda
1 slice lemon

Put gin, watermelon, crème de cassis, lemon juice, and crushed ice into blender. Blend at low speed for 10 to 15 seconds. Pour into tall 14-oz. glass. Let drink settle for a few moments. Add two ice cubes and a splash of soda. Add lemon slice.

WEBSTER

1 oz. gin
½ oz. dry vermouth

1½ tsp. apricot brandy
Juice of ½ lime

Shake well with ice. Strain into prechilled cocktail glass.

WHITE ROSE

1¼ oz. gin
½ oz. orange juice
½ oz. lime juice

1 tsp. sugar
½ egg white

Shake well with ice. Strain into prechilled cocktail glass. *There are dozens of different recipes bearing the name White Rose. This balmy concoction is designed for sipping in the vicinity of a glowing fireplace.*

WOODSTOCK

1½ oz. gin
1 oz. lemon juice

¼ oz. maple syrup
1 dash orange bitters

Shake well with ice. Strain into frosty cocktail glass. *A drink from the ski country.*

YELLOW FINGERS

1 oz. gin
1 oz. blackberry brandy

½ oz. banana liqueur
½ oz. heavy cream

Shake well with ice. Strain into prechilled deep-saucer champagne glass.

YOLANDA

½ oz. gin
½ oz. brandy
1 oz. sweet vermouth

½ oz. anisette
1 dash grenadine
Orange peel

Shake well with ice. Strain into prechilled cocktail glass. Twist orange peel over drink and drop into glass.

CHAPTER 14

Brandy
THE EAU-DE-VIE

"Claret is the liquor for boys, port for men; but he who aspires to be a hero must drink brandy." Either Samuel Johnson's classic eighteenth century dictum no longer applies, or the fact that Cognac accounts for 30 percent of total U.S. brandy consumption suggests that heroes have proliferated of late at an unparalleled rate. In any case, Dr. Johnson was on the right track to this extent: brandy taken neat is in itself heroic. There is something about brandy's finesse that caresses the senses and even the palm of your warming hand. The French call it *largeur*, a spreading glow that suffuses the whole body.

Whatever your brandy persuasion, discount the myth that it's necessary to sate your palate with a formal twelve-course dinner before a great brandy can make its presence truly felt. Though it outshines almost any flavor or aroma that has gone before it, it's an impressive finale for even the most informal casserole dinner or buffet supper.

It's a quality achieved simply by distilling wine. Those who passed Chem 101 may recall that alcohol has a lower boiling point than water and that when wine is heated in a still, the vapors rise, leaving the water behind—and then later condense to become the eau-de-vie. The first raw spirits trickling out of medieval European alembics were properly used for treating battle wounds rather than drinking. How they evolved into what we now know as brandy is explained in a number of well-aged, well-blended myths.

One story concerns a Dutch sea captain who had been shipping wine from France to Holland and was rowing in the Charente River near the area that now produces Cognac. He dropped his hat into the water, fished it out, and noticed that it was twice as heavy. As he wrung it out, he thought to himself, "Why not extract the water from the vinous cargo, save a fortune in shipping costs, and then later restore the water to the wine?" The crafty captain arranged to have the wine distilled, only to discover, upon tasting it, a new kind of Dutch courage so stunning that he couldn't possibly think of restoring the water to his *brandewijn* (Dutch for "burnt wine").

Or perhaps you prefer this legend. In England during the sixteenth century, importers often received wine from the same area of France. This wine didn't travel well and was frequently spoiled upon arrival at the English docks. To salvage their investment, they distilled the wine into brandywine, a product that Chaucer had long before identified as the "water of immortality." It was a reasonable name because the powerful distillate, stored in wooden kegs, seemed, unlike wine, to live on and on for years without spoiling.

Italian specialists in drinking mythology easily explain how brandy came to be aged in wood. The way they tell it, an alchemist in the fifteenth century stored his aqua vitae in a cellar barrel. To keep it out of the hands of mercenary soldiers about to plunder his village, he buried the barrel of raw brandy. He died, however, before he could retrieve his trove. Years later, someone discovered the hidden barrel of grappa, half-empty from evaporation, its raw white liquid now infused with a golden color and an indescribably noble flavor. In fact, a large portion of brandy is lost as it evaporates through porous oak barrels during aging; this necessary part of the process is rather romantically called the angel's share.

Indeed, the high drama and lordly legends behind brandy's presumably illustrious origins are easily the grist of tales for a modern-day Chaucer, and would make any admirer of Shakespeare's craft proud. And the perfect venue for such stage worthy stuff? A theater party, but of course!

FLASHBACK

Theater Party

MODERN EPICURES HAVE A PERFECT definition of theater: it's the interlude between the snack beforehand and the supper afterward. The idea of pretheater appeasement rather than a full trencherman's dinner bolted down in time to make the curtain gets a big hand from performers and audiences alike. And for generations, the midnight supper after the show has been one of the most gracious of all ways to entertain.

If your theater party is to be really successful, you'll first pick a play cued to the tastes of your guests. You'll offer them a prologue of cocktails and the kind of food that takes the edge off their hunger but still lets them sit through Ionesco or Beckett with a clear head. Your potables should allow them to roll in the aisles with the play's fun rather than with the aftereffects of five Martinis. And when the show's over, your party will taxi to the armchair comfort of your own hearth, where fine food and wine will help make a bomb tolerable and a superb play bewitching. In the fall and winter, there are all kinds of dialogues for fireplace suppers but none more engaging than the chatter over cast, staging, sets, and story.

While one host can manage this kind of party, there are times when dual hosting works out best. The first producer gets the tickets and is responsible for the early snack and for taxi or limousine service. The second impresario hosts the leisurely after-theater supper and drink. The division of labor needn't follow these specifications to the letter, but it's the one we've found best for intimate theater parties of six to twelve people.

Ironically, the scene of action that hangs up most hosts the first time they stage a two-act theater party isn't the sumptuous supper after the show but the small snack before. Yet the question of how to allay the appetite without overwhelming it can be answered in very practical terms: serve the first course of a dinner.

In planning your after-theater menu, the first rule is not to duplicate the party of the first part. If there were lobster cocktails beforehand, don't serve coquille of seafood to the captive crowd at midnight. Let your supper program fit the changed mood with dishes of substance, but avoid food conversation pieces that try to steal the scene from the show itself. Last-minute preparation, even in your black tie, is perfectly feasible, provided all the behind-the-scenes work has been accomplished beforehand.

Before the theater, those who want light cocktails may elect the Negroni, Vermouth Cassis, or White Wine Cassis. Cocktails on the rocks will appease those who want to make long drinks of short ones. When you return to your apartment after the theater, throw open the full resources of your bar. And for the final program note, what could possibly be better than the warm afterglow of a fine brandy or Cognac?

Cognac

However accidental its beginnings, the method of making and aging brandy has evolved over the centuries into an art of the highest order, an art that achieves its supreme expression in the creation of Cognac. Finest of the brandies, Cognac is as unique as its old home: the countryside astride the Charente and Gironde rivers of which the sleepy town of Cognac is the center. Sixty-four thousand grape growers toil in a land saturated with more sun than any other grape-growing region in France. An odd freak of nature makes the otherwise unfriendly soil—a dour mixture of chalk and pebbles—just about perfect for growing the tart grapes that turn into greenish wine and eventually into aged brandy. Pot stills, kept under government lock and key after the distilling season is over, are identical with those used three centuries ago. Just as important as the grapes and stills is the wood, which comes from the nearby Limousin forest, in which the Cognac is put to sleep. So heady are the vapors around the ancient brandy casks that workmen wear safety belts to keep them from tumbling into the vats. No railroad has ever been permitted to go into the Cognac region. The old distillers fear that a spark might accidentally cause the whole countryside to go up in flames, for during its long hibernation, enough brandy is released as fumes into the air each day to provide Cognac for all of France.

When buying Cognac, it's good to be familiar with the inscriptions and annotations printed on the labels. The phrase "fine champagne Cognac," for example, has no allusion whatever to the bubbly wine produced in an altogether different section of France. The French word *champagne* also means "an open stretch of land," and on a Cognac label it's the tip-off that the grapes used came mainly from two of the finest open sections in the heart of the Cognac region, identified on the map as Grande Champagne and Petite Champagne. (There are five other sections of Cognac, but these are of less importance.) To be labeled "fine champagne," Cognac must contain grapes of which at least 60 percent came from the Grande Champagne. To be labeled "grande fine champagne," the Cognac must have been made from grapes of which 100 percent came from the Grande Champagne heartland.

Stars on Cognac labels, as well as other brandy labels, don't offer much meaningful information to the buyer. You can, for instance, buy a bottle of French brandy with no fewer than five stars on the label for less than ten dollars; it's a good mixing brandy for Sidecars and Brandy Sours, but it's not from the Cognac region and it's completely out of the major-league class. For those interested in myth and mystique, a single star was once used by vintners to signify a good vintage after a poor year. Two stars meant the bottle represented a succession of two good years, and so on. According to one old Cognac tale, the good year was 1811, the "Year of the Comet," which was succeeded by two more wonderful years. Some Cognac houses themselves take credit for having originated the three stars, since stars, like pearls, were symbols of the gems of Cognacland for many years. From a practical standpoint, stars are only the Cognac maker's way of giving a subjective nod to what he considers a better-than-average quality. You're not likely to come across a well-known label with less than three stars. Over the years, such distinguished firms as Hennessy have dropped the stars entirely from their Cognac labels because they consider them meaningless.

A somewhat more meaningful method of coding employs initials. The most common are V.O. (very old) and V.S.O.P. (very superior old pale or particular). The most interesting thing about these initials is that they represent English rather than French designations, obviously coined for the export trade. As with stars, they can't always be taken as a strict code of quality, but bottles marked V.S.O.P. by a particular brandy shipper usually hold finer spirits than a bottling from the same shipper's Cognac without these initials. The V.S.O.P. signet is usually an assurance that the brandy thus marked is largely composed of twenty- to twenty-five-year-old stock. V.V.S.O.P. (very, very superior old pale) signifies stock about forty years old. X.O. (extra old), cordon bleu, and La Reine are also designates of old Cognacs of the finest quality. Sometimes these are called liqueur Cognacs, though they have no relation to sweet liqueurs or cordials.

Interestingly, in a blind tasting of Cognac by professional Cognac tasters, a Cognac marked with three stars was given a higher rating than a

Cognac marked V.S.O.P. by the same distinguished shipper. A great Scotch such as Chivas Regal doesn't need the myth or mystique of stars or initials to tell its story; Cognac makers are beginning to come around to the same sensible viewpoint.

American import laws dispose of the whole question of age very simply. No age is permitted to be printed on a bottle of Cognac, except on a very insignificant number of vintage Cognacs made from grapes of a specific year. The quantity of these vintage Cognacs is so small, and their quality so dubious, that they seldom become a significant item even in a Cognac collector's library. The American ruling is reasonable because the greatest Cognacs are blends of different vineyards, different distilleries, and different years. In mixing their artful blends, the Cognac masters choose one for mellowness, another for virility, another for finesse.

Naturally, a superb Cognac contains more liquid age than youth. One brandy connoisseur, when asked for the perfect age of a Cognac, said it was somewhere between twenty-five and forty. Brandy lovers all agree that waters of immortality beyond the age of fifty begin to slip in quality. Stories about the excellence of a dusty bottle taken from Napoleon's footlocker are only so much romantic nonsense; in the cellars of the old Cognac houses, there may be a cask here and there containing Cognac a hundred years old, but these are museum pieces from which most of the glory has gone with the years. And remember that Cognac ages only in the wood, never in the bottle. When you buy it, therefore, the best advice is to use it. It will never attain a greater quality. And once opened, don't keep it around too long. Frequent uncorking will eventually cause it to lose its original glow.

You may confidently forget all about the stars, initials, and myriad other identification tags when you buy Cognac bearing the labels of the eminent old brandy shippers. Generally speaking, price is one of the better yardsticks. Two others are equally dependable: your nose and mouth. In the last analysis, Cognac can be properly assessed only as it trickles down your throat. You should find yourself not only drinking it but drinking to it as well.

Non-Cognac Grape Brandies

The only other French brandy one can talk about in the same breath as Cognac is Armagnac. Though it's distilled from the same type of grapes grown in the Cognac region, the earth of its home, Gascony, is unlike that of the Cognac area, and the black oak used in making Gascon casks results in a different marriage of wood and spirits. The taste is somewhat harder and more pungent than Cognac, but the brandy of Armagnac is still in the pantheon of great spirits and has immense appeal to the brandy-faithful everywhere.

Marc, a common brandy in France, is distilled from the stems and skins of grapes and has a woody, rustic flavor. Although you aren't likely to find it at your corner liquor store, you'll meet it in many French bistros. Other exported French grape brandies are light-tasting and excellent for mixing purposes.

German brandies from the valley of the Rhine are superb distillates with a faintly sweet perfume, due to the fact that the Rhenish grapes are left on the vine longer than the French variety. While the best-known ambassadors of Spain and Portugal are sherry and port, both countries produce brandies as fortifiers for their wines. Each has its own bouquet and, to many brandy noses, is reminiscent of the national wine. Metaxa, from Greece, the richest-tasting of all brandies, is made from the sweet muscat grape and is a semiliqueur. Greek ouzo, with its pronounced anise flavor, is called a brandy in some quarters but, because of its sweetness, a liqueur in others.

Pisco is a nearly clear 90-proof Peruvian brandy distilled from the muscat or mission grapes of Chile and Peru. It is aged briefly in paraffin-lined containers to keep the brandy from acquiring the color or flavor of the wood. The youthful, high-proof spirit gives you a sensation somewhat akin to a slight earthquake. It usually finds its way into the Peruvian Pisco Sour, a Brandy Sour made with pisco, with a small amount of egg white and a few drops of bitters. First produced in the sixteenth century, "pisco" is derived from the fired clay pots in which the Peruvians stored their spirits.

CALIFORNIA BRANDY

Despite Cognac's monumental prestige in the field of sipping brandies, the fact remains that three out of every four bottles of brandy poured in the United States come from California. In a sense it's as unfair to compare the flavors of the two brandies as it is to compare Scotch with bourbon, although both are whiskeys. The aging process of Cognac transforms the original flavor of the grape into something altogether different. California brandy, after aging, retains the fruity, light flavor of the grape. Like U.S. blended whiskey, it's one of the most mixable of spirits and can be successfully used in any mixed-drink recipe calling for whiskey, from a Manhattan to a Hot Toddy. The prominent California brandies are now aged about four years in the wood and then blended for balanced flavor.

Until 1972 no brandy maker in the world had ever had sufficient cheek to stand his product up against Cognac for comparative tasting. In that year, however, a California brandy was introduced that, to the astonishment of drink experts, hurled a provocative challenge to the French brandymen of the Charente. The newcomer was Christian Brothers X.O. Rare Reserve brandy, made half from eight-year-old pot-stilled brandies and half from column-stilled brandies five to six years old. Only a limited amount of this exceptional brandy is produced each year, and its exquisitely developed aroma (not grapy, unlike typical California brandies), complex flavor, and mellow aftertaste with minimal sweetness make it a really great sipping brandy. Its price may seem extravagant for an American brandy, but it still costs considerably less than any of the well-known Cognacs.

WHITE FRUIT BRANDIES

Great brandies aren't all derived from the meat within a grape's skin. Superb distillations are extracted from other fruits and are generally white, fiery, and unaged in order to preserve their straight fruity essence. Usually not a trace of sugar is apparent. The most noted of these is kirsch (or kirschwasser), a white brandy made of cherries and cherry pits. Crushed plums are used to make quetsch or mirabelle in France and slivovitz in central Europe; the last is an exception to the no-aging rule and develops a light golden aura after six or eight years in the wood. The lush flavor of red raspberries is drawn into framboise in France and Himbeergeist in Germany. Perhaps the most spectacular of the white fruit brandies is Switzerland's pear brandy, which comes with a large whole pear in the bottle. When the pear on the tree is still in its infancy, it is slipped through the neck of the bottle. The bottle is attached to the tree, and the pear blooms and eventually grows to natural size. Later, both bottle and pear are detached from the tree, and the bottle is filled with white pear brandy, which, incidentally, seems to have more of the pear fragrance than the fresh pear itself.

APPLE BRANDY

Long before George Washington wrote to Samuel Laird asking for his apple-brandy recipe, Americans were distilling what we now call applejack. Currently used as a cocktail mixer, it is famed particularly for its role in the Jack Rose cocktail. Its French counterpart, Calvados, is a suave postprandial potation. Applejack, although aged, keeps a vivid perfume of the apple. Calvados retains a subtler hint of the fruit, perhaps because of its longer aging. Vets of World War II who remember the Normandy invasion shouldn't confuse the white lightning surreptitiously made in the cellars of French apple growers with the present-day extremely suave ten-year-old Calvados.

The newest form of liquid apple made in the United States, called blended apple brandy, is a union of aged apple brandy and neutral grain spirits. It's lighter and more satiny than straight apple brandy and, as a mixer in drinks like the Jack Rose or Applejack and Ginger Ale, dances rings around its older version.

APPLE BRANDY COCKTAILS

AMBROSIA

1 oz. applejack	Juice of 1 lemon
1 oz. brandy	Champagne, chilled
1 dash triple sec	

Shake applejack, brandy, triple sec, and lemon juice well with ice. Strain into prechilled deep-saucer glass. Top with champagne. Stir gently.

ANGEL FACE

½ oz. apple brandy	1 oz. gin
½ oz. apricot brandy	

Stir well with cracked ice. Strain into prechilled cocktail glass. *Thank heavens.*

ANTE

1 oz. apple brandy	1 oz. Dubonnet
½ oz. triple sec	

Stir well with cracked ice. Strain into prechilled cocktail glass.

APPLE AND GINGER

1½ oz. applejack	½ oz. lemon juice
¾ oz. ginger-flavored brandy	½ tsp. sugar

Shake well with ice. Strain into prechilled cocktail glass. *A cool alfresco drink.*

APPLE BLOSSOM

1½ oz. applejack	1 tsp. maple syrup
1 oz. apple juice	⅓ cup crushed ice
½ oz. lemon juice	1 slice lemon

Put applejack, apple juice, lemon juice, maple syrup, and crushed ice into blender. Blend at low speed for 10 to 15 seconds. Pour into prechilled deep-saucer champagne glass. Add lemon slice.

APPLE BUCK

1½ oz. applejack	Iced ginger ale
1 tsp. ginger-flavored brandy	1 piece preserved ginger in syrup
½ oz. lemon juice	

Shake applejack, brandy, and lemon juice well with ice. Strain into 8-oz. glass half-filled with ice. Add ginger ale. Stir. Add preserved ginger.

APPLECAR

¾ oz. applejack
¾ oz. Cointreau or curaçao

¾ oz. lemon juice

Shake well with ice. Strain into prechilled cocktail glass. *The apple man's Sidecar.*

APPLE GINGER FIX

½ tsp. sugar
1 tsp. water
1 oz. applejack

1 oz. ginger-flavored brandy
½ oz. lemon juice
1 slice lemon

Dissolve sugar in 1 tsp. water in an 8-oz. glass. Add applejack, ginger-flavored brandy, and lemon juice. Fill glass with crushed ice. Stir well. Add more ice to fill glass to rim. Stir. Garnish with lemon slice.

APPLE GINGER SANGAREE

1½ oz. apple brandy
½ oz. green-ginger wine

1 slice lemon
Freshly grated nutmeg

Pour apple brandy and ginger wine over rocks into old-fashioned glass. Stir. Add lemon slice. Sprinkle lightly with nutmeg.

APPLE GRAND MARNIER

1 oz. Calvados
½ oz. Grand Marnier
½ oz. Cognac

Lemon peel
Orange peel

Stir Calvados, Grand Marnier, and Cognac well with ice. Strain over rocks into prechilled old-fashioned glass. Twist lemon peel and orange peel above drink and drop into glass.

APPLEHAWK

4 oz. applejack
4 oz. unsweetened grapefruit juice

½ tsp. sugar

Shake well with ice. Strain into prechilled cocktail glass.

APPLEJACK COLLINS

2 oz. applejack
1 tsp. sugar
1 oz. lemon juice

2 dashes orange bitters
Iced club soda
1 slice lemon

Shake applejack, sugar, lemon juice, and bitters well with ice. Strain into tall 14-oz. glass half-filled with ice. Add soda. Stir. Add lemon slice.

APPLEJACK DAISY

1½ oz. applejack
½ oz. lime juice
1 tsp. raspberry syrup

Iced club soda
1 tsp. ginger-flavored brandy
1 slice lime

Shake applejack, lime juice, and raspberry syrup well with ice. Strain into tall 8-oz. glass half-filled with ice. Add soda. Stir. Float ginger-flavored brandy on drink. Add lime slice.

APPLEJACK MANHATTAN

1¾ oz. applejack
¾ oz. sweet vermouth

1 dash orange bitters
1 maraschino cherry

Stir applejack, vermouth, and bitters well with ice. Strain into prechilled cocktail glass. Garnish with cherry.

APPLEJACK RABBIT

1½ oz. applejack
½ oz. lemon juice

½ oz. orange juice
1 tsp. maple syrup

Shake well with ice. Strain into prechilled sugar-frosted cocktail glass. *Salted nuts or toasted coconut chips are good companions.*

APPLEJACK SOUR

2 oz. applejack
½ oz. lemon juice

1 tsp. sugar
½ slice lemon

Shake applejack, lemon juice, and sugar well with ice. Strain into prechilled whiskey-sour glass. Add lemon slice.

APPLE KNOCKER

2½ oz. applejack
½ oz. sweet vermouth
3 oz. orange juice

½ oz. lemon juice
1½ tsp. sugar
½ cup crushed ice

Blend all ingredients at high speed for 15 to 20 seconds. Pour into tall 14-oz. glass. Let drink settle a moment. Add ice cubes to fill glass. Stir.

APPLE RUM RICKEY

¾ oz. applejack
¾ oz. light rum
¼ large lime

Iced club soda
Orange peel

Put three ice cubes into an 8-oz. glass. Add applejack and rum. Squeeze lime above drink and drop into glass. Add soda. Stir. Twist orange peel above drink and drop into glass.

APPLE SUISSESSE

Grenadine
Superfine sugar
2 oz. applejack

½ slightly beaten egg white
½ oz. heavy sweet cream
½ cup crushed ice

Dip rim of old-fashioned glass in grenadine, then in superfine sugar to make frosted rim. Place in freezer to chill. Pour applejack, 1 tsp. sugar, egg white, cream, and crushed ice into blender. Blend at high speed for 10 seconds. Pour into prechilled glass.

BARTON SPECIAL

1½ oz. applejack
¼ oz. gin

¼ oz. Scotch

Shake well with ice. Strain into prechilled old-fashioned glass over rocks.

BENTLEY

1½ oz. apple brandy   Lemon peel
1 oz. Dubonnet

Stir well with cracked ice. Strain into prechilled cocktail glass. Twist lemon peel over drink and drop into glass.

BITTER APPLE

2 oz. applejack   Iced club soda
2 dashes Angostura bitters   Lemon peel

Pour applejack and bitters into prechilled old-fashioned glass. Add ice slices or cubes to fill glass. Add a splash of soda. Stir well. Twist lemon peel over drink and drop into glass. *Aromatic, potent, and dry.*

BLENHEIM

1 oz. applejack   1 tsp. grenadine
½ oz. apricot-flavored brandy   1 dash orange bitters
¾ oz. lemon juice

Shake well with ice. Strain into prechilled sugar-frosted cocktail glass.

CALVADOS FIZZ

2 oz. Calvados   1 tsp. heavy cream
½ oz. lemon juice   Iced club soda
1 tsp. sugar   1 slice lime
½ egg white   1 maraschino cherry

Shake Calvados, lemon juice, sugar, egg white, and cream well with ice. Strain into tall 14-oz. glass half-filled with ice. Fill glass with soda. Stir. Add lime slice and cherry. *A fine wintertime fizz while waiting for the roast suckling pig.*

DEMPSEY COCKTAIL

1 oz. apple brandy   1 tsp. anise
1 oz. gin   ½ tsp. grenadine

Stir well with ice. Strain into prechilled cocktail glass.

FROZEN APPLE

1½ oz. applejack   1 tsp. sugar
½ oz. lime juice   ⅓ cup crushed ice
½ egg white

Blend all ingredients at low speed for 10 to 15 seconds. Pour into prechilled deep-saucer champagne glass.

FROZEN APPLE AND BANANA

1½ oz. applejack   ⅓ cup crushed ice
½ oz. banana liqueur   1 slice banana
½ oz. lime juice

Blend applejack, banana liqueur, lime juice, and ice at low speed for 10 to 15 seconds. Pour into prechilled deep-saucer champagne glass. Add banana slice.

FROZEN APPLECART

1½ oz. applejack   ½ oz. lemon juice
¼ cup diced red apple, peeled   1 tsp. sugar
⅓ cup crushed ice

Blend all ingredients at high speed for 10 seconds. Pour into deep-saucer champagne glass or outsize cocktail glass.

HONEYMOON COCKTAIL

¾ oz. apple brandy   1 tsp. triple sec
¾ oz. Benedictine   Juice of ½ lemon

Shake well with ice. Strain into prechilled cocktail glass.

JACK-IN-THE-BOX

1½ oz. apple brandy   1 dash Angostura bitters
1 oz. pineapple juice

Shake well with ice. Strain into prechilled cocktail glass.

JACK ROSE

2 oz. applejack   1 tsp. grenadine
½ oz. lime juice or lemon juice

Shake well with ice. Strain into prechilled cocktail glass. *The classic applejack drink.*

LUMBERJACK

1½ oz. apple brandy   1 dash apricot brandy
1 oz. brandy

Stir well with ice. Strain into prechilled cocktail glass.

MOONLIGHT SERENADE

2 oz. apple brandy   1 tsp. powdered sugar
Juice of 1 lemon

Shake well with ice. Strain into old-fashioned glass over rocks.

POLYNESIAN APPLE

1¼ oz. applejack   ½ oz. California brandy
¾ oz. pineapple juice   1 pineapple stick

Shake applejack, pineapple juice, and brandy well with ice. Strain over rocks into prechilled old-fashioned glass. Add pineapple stick. *A standby cocktail when spareribs are slowly turning on the spit over charcoal.*

PUERTO APPLE

1¼ oz. applejack   1½ tsp. orgeat or orzata
¾ oz. light rum   1 slice lime
½ oz. lime juice

Shake applejack, rum, lime juice, and orgeat well with ice. Strain over rocks into prechilled old-fashioned glass. Add lime slice.

RABBIT'S FOOT

¾ oz. applejack
¾ oz. light rum
½ oz. orange juice
½ oz. lemon juice
¼ oz. grenadine
1 slice orange

Shake applejack, rum, orange juice, lemon juice, and grenadine well with ice. Strain into prechilled old-fashioned glass. Add ice to fill glass. Garnish with orange slice.

SAUCY SUSAN

2 oz. apple brandy
½ tsp. apricot brandy
½ tsp. Pernod

Stir with ice. Strain into prechilled cocktail glass.

SOOTHER

½ oz. apple brandy
½ oz. brandy
½ oz. triple sec
Juice of ½ lemon
1 tsp. powdered sugar

Shake well with ice. Strain into prechilled cocktail glass.

SPICED APPLE FLIP (Makes 2 drinks)

3 oz. applejack
1 egg
1 tbsp. sugar
2 tsp. lemon juice
⅛ tsp. ground cloves
⅛ tsp. ground cinnamon
Freshly grated nutmeg

Shake applejack, egg, sugar, lemon juice, cloves, and cinnamon with ice. Strain into prechilled whiskey-sour glasses. Sprinkle with nutmeg.

STEEPLEJACK

2 oz. apple brandy
2½ oz. iced apple juice
2½ oz. iced club soda
1 tsp. lime juice
1 slice lime

Pour apple brandy, apple juice, soda, and lime juice into tall 14-oz. glass. Add ice to fill glass. Stir. Add lime slice.

BRANDY COCKTAILS

ALABAMA

1¾ oz. brandy
½ oz. lemon juice
1 tsp. curaçao
½ tsp. sugar
Orange peel

Shake brandy, lemon juice, curaçao, and sugar well with ice. Strain into prechilled sugar-frosted cocktail glass. Twist orange peel above drink and drop into glass.

AMERICAN BEAUTY

1½ oz. brandy
½ oz. dry vermouth
¼ tsp. white crème de menthe
1 oz. orange juice
1 tsp. grenadine
½ oz. tawny port

Shake brandy, vermouth, crème de menthe, orange juice, and grenadine well with ice. Strain into prechilled cocktail glass. Float port on top.

APRICOT AND RASPBERRY SOUR

1 oz. apricot-flavored brandy
   or apricot liqueur
½ oz. framboise
   (white raspberry brandy)
½ oz. lemon juice
1 oz. orange juice
Iced club soda
½ slice orange or 1 fresh raspberry
   or maraschino stem cherry

Shake apricot-flavored brandy, framboise, lemon juice, and orange juice well with ice. Strain into whiskey-sour glass. Add splash of soda. Stir. Garnish with orange slice or raspberry.

APRICOT COCKTAIL

1½ oz. apricot brandy
1 tsp. gin
Juice of ¼ lemon
Juice of ¼ orange

Shake well with ice. Strain into prechilled cocktail glass.

APRICOT SOUR

1½ oz. apricot-flavored brandy
   or apricot liqueur
½ oz. lemon juice
1 oz. orange juice
Iced club soda
½ slice orange
1 maraschino stem cherry

Shake apricot-flavored brandy, lemon juice, and orange juice well with ice. Strain into whiskey-sour glass. Add splash of soda. Stir. Garnish with orange slice and cherry.

BALTIMORE BRACER

1½ oz. brandy
1 oz. anisette
1 egg white

Shake well with ice. Strain into prechilled cocktail glass.

B&B COLLINS

2 oz. Cognac
½ oz. lemon juice
1 tsp. sugar
Iced club soda
½ oz. Benedictine
1 slice lemon

Shake Cognac, lemon juice, and sugar well with ice. Strain into tall 14-oz. glass half-filled with ice. Add soda. Stir. Float Benedictine on drink. Add lemon slice. California brandy may be used in place of Cognac.

BAYOU

1¾ oz. brandy
¼ oz. peach liqueur
½ oz. mango nectar

2 tsp. lime juice
1 slice fresh or brandied peach

Shake brandy, peach liqueur, mango nectar, and lime juice well with ice. Strain over rocks into prechilled old-fashioned glass. Garnish with peach slice.

BENGAL

1½ oz. brandy
½ oz. maraschino liqueur
½ oz. triple sec

1 oz. pineapple juice
2 dashes Angostura bitters

Shake well with ice. Strain into prechilled cocktail glass.

BITTER BRANDY AND SHERRY

1 oz. brandy
1 oz. oloroso (cream) sherry
½ oz. cherry liqueur

1 tsp. lemon juice
Iced bitter lemon soda
1 slice lemon

Shake brandy, sherry, cherry liqueur, and lemon juice well with ice. Strain into tall 14-oz. glass with two large ice cubes. Add soda. Stir. Add lemon slice.

BLACK BALTIMORE

2 oz. brandy
1 oz. black Sambuca

1 egg white

Shake well with ice. Strain into prechilled cocktail glass.

BOMBAY

1 oz. brandy
½ oz. dry vermouth
½ oz. sweet vermouth

½ tsp. curaçao
¼ tsp. Pernod
1 slice fresh or canned mango

Shake brandy, both kinds of vermouth, curaçao, and Pernod well with ice. Strain over rocks into prechilled old-fashioned glass. Add mango slice. *Serve before a curry dinner.*

BOSTON COCKTAIL

¾ oz. apricot brandy
¾ oz. gin

1½ tsp. grenadine
Juice of ¼ lemon

Shake well with ice. Strain into prechilled cocktail glass.

BRANDIED APRICOT

1½ oz. brandy
½ oz. apricot-flavored brandy

½ oz. lemon juice
Orange peel

Shake brandy, apricot-flavored brandy, and lemon juice well with ice. Strain into prechilled sugar-frosted cocktail glass. Twist orange peel above drink and drop into glass.

BRANDIED APRICOT FLIP

1 oz. brandy
1 oz. apricot-flavored brandy
1 small egg

1 tsp. sugar
Grated nutmeg

Shake brandy, apricot-flavored brandy, egg, and sugar well with ice. Strain into prechilled Delmonico glass. Sprinkle with freshly grated nutmeg.

BRANDIED BANANA COLLINS

1½ oz. brandy
1 oz. banana liqueur
½ oz. lemon juice

Iced club soda
1 slice lemon
1 slice banana

Shake brandy, banana liqueur, and lemon juice well with ice. Strain into tall 14-oz. glass half-filled with ice. Add soda. Stir. Add lemon and banana slices.

BRANDIED CORDIAL MÉDOC

1½ oz. brandy
½ oz. Cordial Médoc

½ oz. lemon juice
Orange peel

Shake brandy, Cordial Médoc, and lemon juice well with ice. Strain into prechilled cocktail glass. Twist orange peel above drink and drop into glass. Either California brandy or Cognac may be used with good results.

BRANDIED GINGER

1½ oz. brandy
½ oz. ginger-flavored brandy
1 tsp. lime juice

1 tsp. orange juice
1 piece preserved ginger in syrup

Shake brandy, ginger-flavored brandy, lime juice, and orange juice well with ice. Strain over rocks into prechilled old-fashioned glass. Garnish with preserved ginger.

BRANDIED PEACH FIZZ

2 oz. brandy
½ oz. peach-flavored brandy
½ oz. lemon juice
1 tsp. sugar

1 tsp. banana liqueur
Iced club soda
1 slice fresh or brandied peach

Shake brandy, peach-flavored brandy, lemon juice, sugar, and banana liqueur well with ice. Strain into tall 14-oz. glass half-filled with ice. Fill glass with soda. Stir. Garnish with peach slice.

BRANDIED PEACH SLING

1¾ oz. brandy
½ oz. peach-flavored brandy
¾ oz. lemon juice
1 tsp. sugar

Iced club soda
1 slice brandied or thawed
  frozen peach
Lemon peel

Shake brandy, peach-flavored brandy, lemon juice, and sugar well with ice. Strain into tall 14-oz. glass half-filled with ice. Add soda. Stir. Add peach slice. Twist lemon peel above drink and drop into glass.

BRANDTINI

1½ oz. brandy
1 oz. gin
1 tsp. dry vermouth
Lemon peel or cocktail olive

Stir brandy, gin, and vermouth well with ice. Strain into prechilled cocktail glass. Twist lemon peel above drink and drop into glass, or serve with cocktail olive.

BRANDY ALEXANDER

¾ oz. brandy
¾ oz. crème de cacao
¾ oz. heavy cream

Shake well with ice. Strain into prechilled cocktail glass.

BRANDY AND AMER PICON

2 oz. Cognac
½ oz. Amer Picon
Lemon peel
Orange peel

Stir Cognac and Amer Picon well with ice. Strain over rocks into prechilled old-fashioned glass. Twist lemon peel and orange peel above drink and drop into glass.

BRANDY APPLE COOLER

2 oz. brandy
1 oz. light rum
3 oz. apple juice
½ oz. lime juice
1 tsp. dark Jamaican rum
1 slice lime

Shake brandy, light rum, apple juice, and lime juice well with ice. Strain into tall 14-oz. glass. Add ice to fill glass. Stir. Float dark rum on drink. Add lime slice.

BRANDY BERRY FIX

1 tsp. sugar
2 tsp. water
2 oz. brandy
1 tsp. strawberry liqueur
½ oz. lemon juice
1 slice lemon
1 large strawberry

Dissolve sugar in 2 tsp. water in an 8-oz. glass. Add brandy, strawberry liqueur, and lemon juice. Fill glass with crushed ice. Stir well. Add more ice to fill glass to rim. Stir. Garnish with lemon slice and strawberry.

BRANDY BUCK

1½ oz. brandy
1 tsp. crème de menthe
½ oz. lemon juice
Iced ginger ale
Fresh grapes

Shake brandy, crème de menthe, and lemon juice well with ice. Strain into 8-oz. glass half-filled with ice. Add ginger ale. Stir. Add three or four seedless grapes or two large pitted black grapes cut in half.

BRANDY CASSIS

1¾ oz. brandy
½ oz. lemon juice
2 tsp. crème de cassis
Lemon peel

Shake brandy, lemon juice, and crème de cassis well with ice. Strain into prechilled cocktail glass. Twist lemon peel above drink and drop into glass.

BRANDY COBBLER

1½ oz. brandy
½ oz. curaçao
½ oz. lemon juice
1 tsp. sugar
1 tsp. kirschwasser
1 pineapple stick

Fill a 12-oz. glass with finely cracked ice. Add brandy, curaçao, lemon juice, sugar, and kirschwasser. Stir well until sugar is dissolved. Add more ice to fill glass to rim. Stir. Garnish with pineapple stick.

BRANDY CRUSTA

Peel of ½ lemon, in one spiral
2 oz. brandy
½ oz. curaçao
2 tsp. lemon juice
1 dash bitters
1 tsp. maraschino liqueur

Place lemon peel and cracked ice or rocks into prechilled sugar-frosted old-fashioned glass. Shake brandy, curaçao, lemon juice, bitters, and maraschino liqueur well with ice. Strain into glass.

BRANDY FINO

1½ oz. brandy
½ oz. very dry sherry
½ oz. Drambuie
½ slice orange
Lemon peel

Shake brandy, sherry, and Drambuie well with ice. Strain over rocks into prechilled old-fashioned glass. Add orange slice. Twist lemon peel above drink and drop into glass.

BRANDY GUMP

2 oz. brandy
½ oz. lemon juice
½ tsp. grenadine

Shake well with ice. Strain into prechilled cocktail glass. *A good one to relax with after an all-day sail.*

BRANDY MANHATTAN

2 oz. brandy
½ oz. sweet vermouth
1 dash bitters (optional)
1 maraschino cherry

Stir brandy, vermouth, and bitters well with ice. Strain into prechilled cocktail glass. Add cherry. For a dry Brandy Manhattan, use dry instead of sweet vermouth.

BRANDY MELBA

1½ oz. brandy
¼ oz. peach liqueur
¼ oz. raspberry liqueur
½ oz. lemon juice
2 dashes orange bitters
1 slice fresh or
   brandied peach

Shake brandy, peach liqueur, raspberry liqueur, lemon juice, and bitters well with ice. Strain into prechilled cocktail glass. Add peach slice. If raspberry liqueur isn't available, raspberry syrup may be substituted.

BRANDY MINT FIZZ

2 oz. brandy
2 tsp. white crème de menthe
1 tsp. crème de cacao
½ oz. lemon juice

½ tsp. sugar
Iced club soda
2 large fresh mint leaves

Shake brandy, crème de menthe, crème de cacao, lemon juice, and sugar well with ice. Strain into tall 14-oz. glass half-filled with ice. Fill glass with soda. Stir. Tear mint leaves partially and place on top of drink.

BRANDY SANGAREE

½ tsp. sugar
Iced club soda
2 oz. brandy

1 tsp. Madeira
Orange peel
Freshly grated nutmeg

Stir sugar and 1 tbsp. soda in prechilled old-fashioned glass until sugar dissolves. Add brandy and Madeira. Add ice to rim of glass. Stir. Add a splash of soda. Stir. Twist orange peel above drink and drop into glass. Sprinkle lightly with nutmeg.

BRANDY SOUR

2 oz. brandy
½ oz. lemon juice
¼ oz. orange juice

½ to 1 tsp. sugar
½ slice lemon

Shake brandy, lemon juice, orange juice, and sugar well with ice. Strain into prechilled whiskey-sour glass. Add lemon slice. *Softer than a Whiskey Sour.*

BRANDY SWIZZLE

2 oz. brandy
1½ oz. lime juice
1 tsp. superfine sugar

1 dash Angostura bitters
Club soda

Shake brandy, lime juice, sugar, and bitters well with ice. Strain into collins glass over ice. Top off with club soda. Stir.

BULLDOG

1½ oz. cherry brandy
¾ oz. gin

Juice of ½ lime

Shake well with ice. Strain into prechilled cocktail glass.

BULL'S-EYE

1½ oz. brandy
2 oz. hard cider

Ginger ale

Pour brandy and hard cider into highball glass over rocks. Top off with ginger ale. Stir.

BULL'S MILK

1½ oz. brandy
1 oz. light rum
1 cup milk

1 tsp. powdered sugar
Nutmeg and cinnamon to taste

Shake brandy, rum, milk, and powdered sugar well with ice. Strain into collins glass over ice. Sprinkle nutmeg and cinnamon on top.

BUTTONHOLE

½ oz. brandy
½ oz. apricot brandy
½ oz. anise
½ oz. white crème de menthe

Shake well with ice. Strain into prechilled cocktail glass.

CHAMPS ELYSÉES

1½ oz. Cognac
½ oz. yellow Chartreuse
½ oz. lemon juice
1 dash Angostura bitters (optional)

Shake well with ice. Strain over rocks into prechilled old-fashioned glass. Bitters may be omitted for a more pronounced Chartreuse flavor.

CHARLIE CHAPLIN

1 oz. apricot brandy
1 oz. sloe gin
1 oz. lemon juice

Shake well with ice. Strain into old-fashioned glass over rocks.

CHERRY BLOSSOM

1¼ oz. brandy
¾ oz. wild-cherry liqueur
2 tsp. lemon juice
¼ tsp. curaçao
¼ tsp. grenadine

Shake well with ice. Strain into prechilled sugar-frosted cocktail glass. Dip rim of glass into wild-cherry liqueur before dipping into sugar.

CHERRY SLING

2 oz. cherry brandy
Juice of ½ lemon
Lemon peel

Pour brandy and lemon juice into old-fashioned glass over rocks. Stir. Twist lemon peel over drink and drop into glass.

CITY SLICKER

2 oz. brandy
½ oz. triple sec
1 tbsp. lemon juice

Shake well with ice. Strain into prechilled cocktail glass.

CLASSIC

1½ oz. brandy
½ oz. lemon juice
¼ oz. maraschino liqueur
¼ oz. curaçao

Shake well with ice. Strain into prechilled cocktail glass. *Tarter than earlier versions of the Brandy Classic.*

COFFEE FLIP

1 oz. Cognac
1 oz. tawny port
1 small egg
1 tsp. sugar
Grated nutmeg

Shake Cognac, port, egg, and sugar well with ice. Strain into prechilled Delmonico glass. Sprinkle with nutmeg.

COGNAC COUPLING

2 oz. Cognac
1 oz. tawny port
½ oz. Pernod
1 tsp. lemon juice
½ tsp. Peychaud's bitters

Shake well with ice. Strain into prechilled old-fashioned glass. Add ice cubes to fill glass. Stir well.

DAME MELBA

¾ oz. peach-flavored brandy
¾ oz. framboise
½ oz. lemon juice

Shake very well with ice. Strain into sugar-frosted cocktail glass.

DAYDREAM

1½ oz. brandy
¾ oz. triple sec
¼ tsp. anisette

Shake well with ice. Strain into prechilled cocktail glass.

DEAUVILLE

1 oz. brandy
½ oz. lemon juice
½ oz. apple brandy
½ oz. triple sec

Shake well with ice. Strain into prechilled cocktail glass.

DRY COLD DECK

1¾ oz. brandy
½ oz. dry vermouth
¼ oz. white crème de menthe

Shake well with ice. Strain into prechilled cocktail glass. *A sophisticated Stinger.*

EAST INDIA

1½ oz. brandy
1 tsp. Jamaican rum
½ tsp. triple sec
½ tsp. pineapple juice
1 dash Angostura bitters
1 cherry

Shake well with ice. Strain into prechilled cocktail glass. Drop in cherry.

ENGLISH HIGHBALL

¾ oz. brandy
¾ oz. gin
¾ oz. sweet vermouth
Club soda
Lemon peel

Pour brandy, gin, and sweet vermouth into highball glass over rocks. Top off with club soda. Stir. Twist lemon peel over drink and drop into glass.

FANCY BRANDY

2 oz. brandy
¼ tsp. triple sec
¼ tsp. powdered sugar
1 dash Angostura bitters
Lemon peel

Shake well with ice. Strain into prechilled cocktail glass. Twist lemon peel over drink and drop into glass.

FEMINA

1½ oz. brandy
½ oz. Benedictine

½ oz. orange juice
1 slice cocktail orange in syrup

Shake brandy, Benedictine, and orange juice well with ice. Strain over rocks into prechilled old-fashioned glass. Add orange slice. *Not biting in the "sour" tradition, but cool and comforting.*

FJORD

1 oz. brandy
½ oz. aquavit
½ oz. orange juice

½ oz. lime juice
1 tsp. grenadine

Shake well with ice. Strain into prechilled cocktail glass.

FONTAINEBLEAU

1½ oz. brandy
1 oz. anisette

½ oz. dry vermouth

Shake well with ice. Strain into prechilled cocktail glass.

FOXHOUND

1½ oz. brandy
½ oz. cranberry juice
1 tsp. Kümmel

1 tsp. lemon juice
½ slice lemon

Shake brandy, cranberry juice, Kümmel, and lemon juice well with ice. Strain over rocks into prechilled old-fashioned glass. Add lemon slice. *Serve before a dinner of pheasant or partridge.*

FRAMBOISE SOUR

1 oz. framboise
¾ oz. lime juice
2 level tsp. sugar

1 wedge prepared cocktail
  orange in syrup
1 fresh raspberry, if available

Pour framboise, lime juice, and sugar into cocktail shaker with ice. Shake about double the usual time for proper dilution. Pour into prechilled whiskey-sour glass. Garnish with cocktail orange and raspberry.

FROUPE

1¼ oz. brandy
1¼ oz. sweet vermouth

1 tsp. Benedictine

Stir well with ice. Strain into prechilled cocktail glass. *Like a sunset's afterglow.*

FROZEN BRANDY AND PORT

1½ oz. brandy
1 oz. port
1 small egg

1 tsp. powdered sugar
⅓ cup crushed ice
Grated nutmeg

Put brandy, port, egg, sugar, and ice into blender. Blend for 20 seconds at low speed. Pour into prechilled saucer champagne glass. Sprinkle with nutmeg.

FROZEN BRANDY AND RUM

1½ oz. brandy
1 oz. golden rum
½ oz. lemon juice

1 egg yolk
⅓ cup crushed ice
1½ tsp. sugar

Blend all ingredients for 15 to 20 seconds at low speed. Pour into prechilled saucer champagne glass. *Soothing.*

GILROY

¾ oz. cherry brandy
¾ oz. gin
1 tbsp. dry vermouth

Juice of ¼ lemon
1 dash orange bitters

Shake with ice. Strain into prechilled cocktail glass.

GOLD COASTER

1 oz. dry vermouth
1 oz. California brandy
½ oz. lemon juice

2 oz. pineapple juice
1 tsp. maraschino liqueur
1 slice fresh pineapple

Shake vermouth, brandy, lemon juice, pineapple juice, and maraschino liqueur well with ice. Strain into 10-oz. glass. Add ice cubes to fill glass. Stir. Fasten pineapple on cocktail spear and place on rim of glass.

GOLDEN SLIPPER

2 oz. apricot brandy
¾ oz. yellow Chartreuse

1 egg yolk

Stir brandy and Chartreuse well with ice. Strain into prechilled cocktail glass. Float egg yolk on top.

GRAPEFRUIT NOG

½ cup unsweetened grapefruit juice
1 oz. lemon juice
1 tbsp. honey

1½ oz. brandy
1 small egg
½ cup crushed ice

Blend all ingredients for 20 seconds. Pour into double old-fashioned glass or tall 14-oz. glass. Add ice cubes to fill glass.

GREEK BUCK

1½ oz. Metaxa brandy
½ oz. lemon juice
Iced ginger ale

1 tsp. ouzo
1 slice lemon

Shake Metaxa and lemon juice well with ice. Strain into 8-oz. glass half-filled with ice. Add ginger ale. Stir. Float ouzo on top of drink. Add lemon slice.

HARVARD

1½ oz. brandy
½ oz. dry vermouth

1 tsp. grenadine
2 tsp. lemon juice

Shake well with ice. Strain into prechilled cocktail glass. *Drier than earlier versions, but still crimson.*

HILLSBOROUGH

1 oz. California brandy
1 oz. Muscari

½ oz. lemon juice
Lemon peel

Shake brandy, Muscari, and lemon juice well with ice. Strain into cocktail glass. Twist lemon peel above drink and drop into glass.

JAPANESE

2 oz. brandy
¼ oz. orgeat or orzata
¼ oz. lime juice

1 dash Angostura bitters
Lime peel

Shake brandy, orgeat, lime juice, and bitters well with ice. Strain into prechilled cocktail glass. Twist lime peel above drink and drop into glass.

LADY SIDECAR

1 oz. brandy
¼ oz. triple sec

¼ oz. lemon juice
1 oz. orange juice

Shake well with ice. Strain into prechilled cocktail glass.

LADYFINGER

1 oz. cherry brandy
1 oz. gin

½ oz. kirschwasser

Shake well with ice. Strain into prechilled cocktail glass.

LAIT DE VIE

2 oz. Cognac or California brandy
4 oz. milk
½ oz. heavy cream

½ oz. grenadine
Freshly grated nutmeg

Shake Cognac, milk, cream, and grenadine with ice. Strain into tall 14-oz. glass filled with ice cubes. Stir. Sprinkle with nutmeg.

LA JOLLA

1½ oz. brandy
½ oz. banana liqueur

2 tsp. lemon juice
1 tsp. orange juice

Shake well with ice. Strain into prechilled sugar-frosted cocktail glass.

LEAP FROG

¾ oz. apricot brandy
¾ oz. light rum

Juice of ½ lime

Stir well with ice. Strain into prechilled cocktail glass.

LIL' NAUE

1 oz. brandy
½ oz. apricot brandy
½ oz. port

1 tsp. powdered sugar
1 egg yolk
Cinnamon

Shake well with ice. Strain into highball glass over rocks. Sprinkle cinnamon on top.

McBRANDY

1½ oz. brandy
1 oz. apple juice

1 tsp. lemon juice
1 slice lemon

Shake brandy, apple juice, and lemon juice well with ice. Strain into prechilled cocktail glass. Add lemon slice. *Serve before a dinner of roast ham or duck.*

MERRY WIDOW

1¼ oz. cherry brandy
1¼ oz. maraschino liqueur

1 cherry

Stir well with ice. Strain into prechilled cocktail glass. Drop in cherry.

METROPOLITAN

2 oz. brandy
½ oz. sweet vermouth

1 tsp. superfine sugar
1 dash Angostura bitters

Shake well with ice. Strain into prechilled cocktail glass.

MIKADO

1½ oz. brandy
½ oz. triple sec
1 tsp. crème de noyaux

1 tsp. grenadine
1 dash Angostura bitters

Shake well with ice. Strain into old-fashioned glass over rocks.

MISSISSIPPI PLANTER'S PUNCH

1 oz. brandy
½ oz. light rum
½ oz. bourbon

Juice of ½ lemon
1 tsp. powdered sugar
Club soda

Shake brandy, rum, bourbon, lemon juice, and sugar well with ice. Strain into collins glass over rocks. Top off with club soda. Stir.

MONTANA

1½ oz. brandy
1 oz. port

½ oz. dry vermouth

Stir well with ice. Strain into old-fashioned glass over rocks.

NETHERLANDS

1½ oz. brandy
1 oz. triple sec

1 dash Angostura bitters

Pour into old-fashioned glass over rocks. Stir well.

NICKY FINN

1 oz. brandy
1 oz. Cointreau

1 oz. lemon juice
1 dash Pernod

Shake with cracked ice. Strain into prechilled cocktail glass.

ORANGE WAKE-UP

4 oz. cold freshly squeezed orange juice
½ oz. Cognac
½ oz. light rum

½ oz. sweet vermouth
1 slice orange

Pour all liquid ingredients into a squat 8-oz. glass. Add ice cubes to fill glass almost to rim. Stir well. Add orange slice.

OUTRIGGER

1 oz. peach brandy
1 oz. lime-flavored vodka

1 oz. pineapple juice

Shake with ice. Strain into old-fashioned glass over rocks.

PEACH BUNNY

¾ oz. peach brandy
¾ oz. white crème de cacao

¾ oz. light cream

Shake well with ice. Strain into prechilled cocktail glass.

PHOEBE SNOW

1¼ oz. brandy
1¼ oz. red Dubonnet

¼ tsp. Pernod

Shake well with ice. Strain into prechilled cocktail glass.

PICASSO

1½ oz. Cognac
½ oz. red Dubonnet
½ oz. lime juice

1 tsp. sugar
Orange peel

Shake Cognac, Dubonnet, lime juice, and sugar well with ice. Strain into prechilled cocktail glass. Twist orange peel above drink and drop into glass.

PISCO SOUR

1½ oz. pisco brandy
½ oz. lemon juice
1 tbsp. sugar

1 tbsp. egg white
Angostura bitters

Shake pisco, lemon juice, sugar, and egg white well with ice. Strain into prechilled cocktail glass with sugar-frosted rim. Float a few drops bitters on top. May also be poured into small punch cups.

PLUM AND TONIC

¾ oz. mirabelle or quetsch
1 oz. gin
½ oz. lemon juice

Iced tonic water
1 slice lemon

Pour mirabelle, gin, and lemon juice over three large ice cubes in tall 10-oz. glass. Add tonic water to fill glass. Stir lightly. Add lemon slice.

POLONAISE

1½ oz. brandy
½ oz. blackberry liqueur
   or blackberry-flavored brandy

½ oz. very dry sherry
1 tsp. lemon juice
2 dashes orange bitters

Shake well with ice. Strain over rocks into prechilled old-fashioned glass.

POOP DECK

1 oz. brandy
1 oz. port

1 tbsp. blackberry brandy

Shake well with ice. Strain into prechilled cocktail glass.

PRAIRIE OYSTER

1½ oz. Cognac
2 tsp. cider vinegar
½ oz. Worcestershire sauce
1 tsp. ketchup

½ tsp. Angostura bitters
1 egg yolk
Cayenne pepper

Shake Cognac, vinegar, Worcestershire sauce, ketchup, and bitters well with ice. Strain into prechilled old-fashioned glass. Add an ice cube or two to fill glass almost to rim. Place egg yolk on top of drink without breaking it. Sprinkle yolk lightly with cayenne. *This oldest and most stunning of all morning-after drinks should be swallowed in one long, determined gulp. Grit your teeth. Then open your eyes very slowly.*

QUAKER

1½ oz. brandy
½ oz. rum
½ oz. lemon juice

1 tsp. raspberry syrup or grenadine
Lemon peel

Shake brandy, rum, lemon juice, and raspberry syrup well with ice. Strain into prechilled cocktail glass. Twist lemon peel above drink and drop into glass. *Two rounds of these and all will be Friends.*

SANTA FE

1½ oz. brandy
½ oz. grapefruit juice

½ oz. dry vermouth
1 tsp. lemon juice

Shake well with ice. Strain into prechilled sugar-rimmed cocktail glass.

SARATOGA

2 oz. brandy
½ oz. pineapple juice
1 tsp. lemon juice

½ tsp. maraschino liqueur
1 dash Angostura bitters

Shake well with ice. Strain into prechilled cocktail glass.

SCOOTER

1½ oz. brandy　　　　　　　　　1 oz. light cream
1 oz. amaretto

Shake well with cracked ice. Strain into prechilled cocktail glass.

SIDECAR

¾ oz. brandy　　　　　　　　　　¾ oz. lemon juice
¾ oz. Cointreau, curaçao, or triple sec

Shake well with ice. Strain into prechilled cocktail glass. All three ingredients may be varied to suit one's taste. For a strong brandy accent, use 1½ oz. brandy, ½ oz. Cointreau, and ½ oz. lemon juice. *One of the most venerable of traditional cocktails.*

SIR WALTER COCKTAIL

¾ oz. brandy　　　　　　　　　　1 tsp. grenadine
¾ oz. rum　　　　　　　　　　　　1 tsp. lemon juice
1 tsp. triple sec

Shake well with ice. Strain into prechilled cocktail glass.

SLOE BRANDY

2 oz. brandy　　　　　　　　　　1 tsp. lemon juice
½ oz. sloe gin (creamy cap)　　　Lemon peel

Shake brandy, sloe gin, and lemon juice well with ice. Strain into prechilled cocktail glass. Twist lemon peel above drink and drop into glass.

SOUTH PACIFIC

1½ oz. brandy　　　　　　　　　¼ oz. white crème de menthe
½ oz. lemon juice　　　　　　　　1 pineapple stick
¼ oz. crème d'ananas

Shake brandy, lemon juice, crème d'ananas (pineapple liqueur), and crème de menthe well with ice. Strain over rocks into prechilled old-fashioned glass. Garnish with pineapple stick.

STINGER

1¼ oz. brandy
1¼ oz. white crème de menthe

Shake well with ice. Strain into prechilled cocktail glass. For a dry Stinger, increase brandy to 2 oz. and reduce crème de menthe to ½ oz. *May be offered before or after dinner; frequently served with a glass of ice water on the side.*

STIRRUP CUP

1 oz. cherry brandy　　　　　　　Juice of ½ lemon
1 oz. brandy　　　　　　　　　　1 tsp. sugar

Shake well with ice. Strain into old-fashioned glass over rocks.

THIRD RAIL

¾ oz. brandy
¾ oz. apple brandy

¾ oz. light rum
¼ tsp. anise

Shake well with ice. Strain into prechilled cocktail glass.

THUMPER

1¾ oz. brandy
¾ oz. Tuaca liqueur

Lemon peel

Stir brandy and Tuaca well with ice. Strain into prechilled old-fashioned glass. Add ice cubes or ice slices to fill glass. Stir well. Twist lemon peel above drink and drop into glass. *One of Italy's oldest liqueurs shines in this drink.*

TIGER'S MILK

1½ oz. brandy
¾ oz. sloe gin

Lemon peel

Shake well with cracked ice. Strain into prechilled cocktail glass. Twist lemon peel over drink and drop into glass.

VALENCIA

1½ oz. apricot brandy
1 tbsp. orange juice

2 dashes orange bitters

Shake well with ice. Strain into prechilled cocktail glass.

VIA VENETO

1¾ oz. brandy
½ oz. Sambuca
½ egg white

2 tsp. lemon juice
1 tsp. sugar

Shake well with ice. Strain over rocks into prechilled old-fashioned glass. *An engaging patio drink that's a little on the sweet side.*

WASHINGTON COCKTAIL

1½ oz. brandy
¾ oz. vermouth

½ tsp. sugar syrup
2 dashes Angostura bitters

Stir well with ice. Strain into prechilled cocktail glass.

WATERBURY

1½ oz. brandy
½ oz. lime juice
½ egg white

½ tsp. grenadine
½ tsp. powdered sugar

Shake well with ice. Strain into prechilled sugar-frosted cocktail glass.

WIDOW'S KISS

1 oz. brandy
½ oz. yellow Chartreuse

½ oz. Benedictine
1 dash Angostura bitters

Shake well with ice. Strain into prechilled cocktail glass.

YELLOW PLUM

1½ oz. quetsch, mirabelle,
   or slivovitz
½ oz. lemon juice

1 tsp. maraschino liqueur
1 tsp. sugar
½ oz. orange juice

Shake well with ice. Strain into prechilled cocktail glass. *Tart, triumphant, titillating.*

ZEPHYR

1½ oz. brandy
½ tsp. curaçao
½ tsp. pineapple juice

2 dashes maraschino liqueur
2 dashes Angostura bitters
1 maraschino cherry

Shake well with ice. Strain into prechilled cocktail glass. Drop in cherry.

Liqueurs

CORDIALLY SPEAKING

enturies ago, liqueurs weren't just sweet little drams to be sipped around a fireplace but wondrous philters believed capable of conjuring all kinds of supernatural feats. Distillers in those days weren't ordinary moonshiners but alchemists whose cordials, it was claimed, "strengtheneth any weake member of man's body" and kept "evil cogitations coming to minde." A certain sweet potion, it was said, "refreshes the spirits and corroborates the brains" (a wonderful solace for those whose brains occasionally needed corroboration), cured assorted ills, and, above all, restored feeble oldsters to the vigor of their youth.

Professional liqueur makers today see their elixirs playing a role that in one important respect is diametrically opposite to their medieval predecessors. Rather than restoring youth, liqueurs—according to an analysis of modern drinking habits—seem to be opening the buds of youth to the full flower of maturity. As liqueur sales continue to rise (cordials and liqueurs form the best-selling and largest—in terms of sheer diversity—category of spirits), more and more young people are discovering that the easiest way to jump the generation gap is to switch from a Hershey Bar to a pony of chocolate almond liqueur.

Chocolate addicts of all ages, in fact, who once had to confine themselves to crème de cacao can now roam over a field that includes such liqueur combinations as chocolate mint, chocolate banana, chocolate raspberry, and chocolate cherry; Choclair—a combination of chocolate and coconut; as well as imported Sabra from Israel, made of

Liqueurs 🐰 **307**

chocolate and orange; and Verana, a chocolate, orange, and almond combination from Spain.

It's not only the liquid chocolate bar that's humming with new varieties; the whole arena of liqueurs seems to be seething with as many new and old varieties as there are people to sip them. Traditional liqueurs concocted from tender rose petals or flakes of twenty-carat gold are challenged by one from Japan with the refreshing cool flavor of honeydew melon and another from Germany faithfully duplicating the subtle flavor of Darjeeling tea.

While the younger crowd today seems to go for the relatively simple liqueurs with one or two dominant flavors, often downing them ice cold in single shots (which is the reason this particular group has come to be called the "shooter crowd"), the more mature drinkers continue to find pleasure in the great French monastery liqueurs, spirits that are moderately sweet but possess rich, complex flavors. Hosts know that a simple pony of Benedictine, or Benedictine and brandy, will make a routine dinner memorable. Liqueurs like Chartreuse, Benedictine, and Izarra, although no longer in the exclusive hands of monks, are status liqueurs not just because of their price but also because their flavors never seem to become tiresome. Their formulas, naturally, are kept secret, although it's acknowledged that Benedictine is based on twenty-seven herbs and plants; Izarra is made of forty-eight herbs, spices, and flowers; and Chartreuse contains no fewer than 130 ingredients. The macho minority who still think that liqueurs are made for softies should try Yukon Jack, a liqueur with a Canadian-whisky base at 100 proof, or a green Chartreuse at a stunning 110 proof.

Even many of the seemingly simple liqueurs often reveal flavor complexities and bouquets that vary drastically from one label to another. One need only compare Kahlua coffee liqueur from Mexico to an espresso-coffee liqueur from Italy to discover the vast gulf between liqueurs derived from a similar source. Even as presumably simple a liqueur as the blackberry-flavored brandy made by Leroux contains no fewer than seven different kinds of blackberries. Each must be balanced from crop to crop each year and from batch to batch; to make the final blend even more deliciously fruity, a small stream of fresh raspberries, with their soft but lush savor, or rich-scented loganberries may be added as artful supporting flavors.

Liqueurs are infusions, percolations, or distillations made from fantastically complex formulas containing—besides a base of brandy or other spirits and sugar—fruits, flowers, herbs, seeds, spices, roots, bark, and kernels gathered from every corner of the world. Infusion is the same process as making tea. Fresh apricots, for example, are steeped in a tank with spirits till both fruit and spirits are intimately united. Percolation is similar to making coffee. Sloes, for example, are placed in a basket, and spirits from the bottom of the percolator are pumped over them to make sloe gin (which, as noted in chapter 13, isn't a gin at all but a liqueur). For many liqueurs, infusion or percolation is only the first step. After flavor extraction, they're distilled into a subtly flavored final product. Some liqueurs are distillations alone, through a flavor head containing, in the case of curaçao for example, sweet and bitter orange peels. White crème de cacao is made by distillation alone; brown crème de cacao is made using all three forms of legerdemain.

Hosts shopping for liqueurs are often bewildered by the nomenclature on the bottles. In the first place, let it be understood that the words *liqueur* and *cordial* mean exactly the same thing. For many generations, both English and American puritans shunned the word *liqueur*, thinking it would identify them too closely with the hard-liquor set; if a drink was called a "clove cordial" or a "conserve of Cowslips Good Against Melancholie," it was considered perfectly respectable. Early liqueur drinkers in Europe used both words together, *liqueurs cordialis*—meaning liqueurs of the heart—to describe the mellifluous compounds invented by monks and dispensed in monasteries for all whose spiritual comfort was miraculously braced by a small potion of bodily comfort. To add to the confusion, some French liqueurs, in France, are still called digestifs.

Besides the words *liqueur* and *cordial*, the phrase "fruit-flavored brandy" appears on many American products these days. This term also refers to a sweet type of after-dinner drink, but with this basic difference: fruit-flavored brandy must be made with a brandy base, while other liqueurs can be made with a base of any distilled spirit. Also, fruit-flavored brandies are generally somewhat less sweet than liqueurs and crèmes and somewhat higher in proof.

The word *crème* normally means a *liqueur* of special smoothness and with a flavor having pronounced body. The word *liqueur* is all-inclusive, taking in the crèmes, the fruit-flavored brandies, and the cordials. Outstanding Cognacs, rums, and Scotches sometimes bear the word *liqueur* on their labels, but don't be misled: it's a boast of excellence rather than a literal description of the contents, which have no resemblance to a true sweet liqueur.

For hosts who don't have the shelf room to store a wide assortment of liqueurs, the compartmented bottle containing from two to four assorted liqueurs is a convenient asset. If you like to pass a tray of assorted liqueurs with or after coffee, the 16.9-oz. (500ml—formerly a pint) bottles are more easily handled than fifths. If there's a new imported or domestic liqueur that seems intriguing but whose flavor is unknown to you, buy the miniature 50ml size for taste exploration before you invest in a large bottle. If you're starting a liqueur collection from scratch and want to be able to offer a reasonable assortment, a bottle each of a coffee liqueur, an anisette, one of the peppermint family like crème de menthe, and one of the proprietary liqueurs like Chartreuse or Peter Heering would be a good starting collection. Of course, if your own fancy runs to something special, like one of the chocolate liqueurs or one of the orange family, by all means indulge yourself.

Often you'll want to buy a liqueur for use in a mixed drink. On the West Coast, where Margaritas (tequila, triple sec, and lime juice) are almost as popular as Martinis are on the East Coast, a bottle of triple sec or other orange liqueur would be part of your basic bar supply. There are parts of the country where Sloe Gin and Coke as well as Peppermint Schnapps and Soda are favorites and where these liqueurs are always kept on hand for private bashes as well as parties. There are vogues in liqueurs, and in some quarters none is now more glittering than amaretto. A relative unknown years back, it's a liqueur made from either almonds or apricot pits that is now available under at least three dozen labels. For years one of the eminent American liqueurs was Forbidden Fruit, made with a West Indian citrus fruit resembling grapefruit.

Among the more recent in the long parade of liqueurs is After Shock, which packs a spicy wallop along with its intense cinnamon flavor.

At impromptu parties, hosts who dust off the old bottle of anisette just because it happened to have lingered on the shelf for too many years should be advised that any bottle of liqueur, after it's been opened, has a limited shelf life. It won't turn sour like wine or otherwise become a drinking hazard, but its flavor in some cases will go downhill after six months. Low-proof liqueurs like a 40-proof triple sec tend to deteriorate more readily than a liqueur at 80 or 100 proof.

Liqueur cocktails—icy mixtures of liqueurs, fruit juices, and in many cases sweet cream—are a refreshing alternative to heavier, more conventional desserts at the party table. They're easy and exciting, and the number of possible creative combinations add up to what Milton called "a wilderness of sweets."

Here now, from abisante to zitronen, is our lexicon of the principal liqueurs available to Americans.

ABISANTE One of the modern replacements for the now outlawed absinthe. The pale green, anise-flavored liqueur turns opalescent when allowed to drip slowly over ice.

ABSINTHE This anise-flavored liqueur was originally 136 proof and made with wormwood, and it was hard to tell whether the proof or the poison was more shattering. It is now illegal in most countries. The firm of Pernod, which originally made absinthe in France, still turns out a luscious 90-proof liqueur in its own name.

ADVOKAAT An eggnog liqueur, originally from Holland and now concocted in the United States. This 40-proof mixture of grain neutral spirits, egg yolks, and sugar usually goes into holiday tipple, accented with rum or brandy. It comes in a thick type of almost custard consistency as well as a thinner version.

AFRI KOKO A 65-proof liqueur of coconut and chocolate imported from Africa.

AK A 49-proof Japanese plum liqueur.

ALLASCH A sweet, cumin-flavored version of Kümmel, it takes its name from the Latvian town where it originated. The name has since been appropriated by other Kümmel makers and means little now.

ALMOND, CRÈME D' A pink liqueur flavored with almonds and/or fruit pits, similar to crème de noyaux. It's been almost pushed out of the picture by amaretto.

ALMONDRADO A Mexican almond liqueur with a tequila base for extra kick.

AMARETTO The reigning queen of the nut-flavored liqueurs. The original version was made from almonds, though there are other amarettos made with apricot pits. It's also available in such combinations as chocolate amaretto, amaretto and brandy, amaretto and coffee, amaretto and orange, etc.

AMBROSIA A 56-proof liqueur from Canada.

AMER PICON A French aperitif liqueur of quinine, oranges, and gentian, served as an aperitif rather than a postprandial liqueur.

ANISE; ANISETTE; ANESONE Liqueurs flavored with anise seeds, reminiscent of licorice; they're usually white but may be colored red. Although anise is the principal feature of the flavor profile, other spices are used by individual bottlers. Proofs range from the 60s to 100; anesone is usually higher in proof and less sweet than anise.

APPLE-FLAVORED BRANDY An apple liqueur, used in drinks calling for applejack, such as the Jack Rose cocktail. Because the liqueur is already sweet, sugar is omitted from the mixed-drink recipe.

APRICOT-FLAVORED BRANDY A somewhat less sweet version of cream-of-apricot liqueur.

APRICOT LIQUEUR; ABRICOTINE; APRY; CRÈME D'ABRICOTS All are names for the liqueur made from the pulp and pits of apricots. Luscious when drizzled over cracked ice in a champagne glass.

AURUM Italian orange liqueur with overtones of herbs; made with a brandy base.

BAHAI A 50-proof Brazilian coffee liqueur.

BANANA LIQUEUR; CRÈME DE BANANES Buy American labels marked "true fruit flavor," which are known for their fidelity to original banana flavor. Most brands are quite sweet; it may be used in place of the fresh fruit in a Banana Daiquiri.

BENEDICTINE One of the greatest of the monastery liqueurs, made of herbs, roots, and sugar, with a Cognac base. Benedictine started reviving tired monks in 1510. Now a proprietary liqueur, the letters D.O.M. on the label stand for *Deo Optimo Maximo*: "To God, most good, most great." The B&B is brandy and Benedictine, one of the most urbane of after-dinner potions.

Ben Shalom Israeli orange liqueur 64 proof.

Blackberry-flavored brandy Less sweet and usually of higher proof than blackberry liqueur; not to be confused with completely dry Hungarian blackberry brandy.

Blackberry liqueur One of the most successful of the berry liqueurs, usually either 50 or 60 proof as opposed to the 70-proof blackberry-flavored brandy. A superb Blackberry Sour can be made by shaking a jigger of the liqueur with ½ ounce lemon juice and ice—no sugar required.

Black currant liqueur Normally labeled "crème de cassis."

Cacao, crème de Liqueur with a base of cacao (chocolate) and vanilla beans. It is available in both brown and white versions; the latter is always used in Grasshopper cocktails, the former in Alexanders.

Cacao Mit Nuss Crème de cacao with a hazelnut flavor.

Café Benedictine A 60-proof liqueur that's a combination of coffee liqueur and Benedictine.

Café, crème de The French name for coffee liqueur is used by both American and foreign distillers. (See Coffee liqueur.)

Café de love A 53-proof coffee liqueur from Mexico.

Café orange A combination of coffee and orange liqueurs.

Calisay A quinine-flavored liqueur from Spain, of medium sweetness.

CARAMELLA Caramel-and-vanilla flavored liqueur; decidedly sweet.

CASSIS, CRÈME DE A low-proof liqueur made from French black currants. Although sweet, it's used as an aperitif in a Vermouth Cassis or White Wine (Vin Blanc) Cassis.

CERISE, CRÈME DE French name for cherry liqueur.

CHARTREUSE Both the green (110-proof) and yellow (86-proof) varieties have been made by the order of Carthusian monks since 1605. The green, most eminent of all liqueurs, contains 130 herbs. The Carthusian order, twice expelled from France, took the secret formula with them to Spain but couldn't find the precise herbs, and Chartreuse in exile never held up to the one produced on native soil.

CHERI-SUISSE A liqueur flavored with chocolate and cherries; extremely well balanced.

CHERRISTOCK A popular Italian cherry liqueur from the Stock distillery, known for its fresh fruity flavor.

CHERRY-AND-PEACH FLAVORED BRANDY Well-balanced 70-proof flavor duo.

CHERRY BLOSSOM LIQUEUR A Suntory Japanese liqueur; 44 proof, with a very light, cherry flavor.

CHERRY-FLAVORED BRANDY With a higher alcohol content than most cherry liqueurs, this version is sometimes made with wild black cherries.

CHERRY HEERING Also known as Peter Heering; famed Danish cherry liqueur.

CHERRY LIQUEUR Somewhat sweeter than cherry-flavored brandy; often made with both sweet and wild cherries.

CHERRY MARNIER A French cherry liqueur made by the distillers of famed French Grand Marnier, with a hint of almond flavor.

CHERRY ROCHER A French cherry liqueur known for its true fruit flavor.

CHERRY VANILLA U.S. 54-proof liqueur combining cherry and vanilla flavors, with the cherry predominating.

CHERRY WITH RUM German 48-proof cherry liqueur with a rum base.

CHOCLAIR U.S. coconut-and-chocolate liqueur with herbal overtones.

CHOCOCO A Virgin Islands liqueur also combining coconut and chocolate.

CHU YEH CHING CHIEN A clear, 92.9-proof liqueur with sharp herbal flavors from mainland China.

CLARISTINE Spicy herbal American liqueur made by Leroux, which follows the formula once used by the Clarisse nuns of Belgium.

CocoRIBE A combination of coconut and rum in a 60-proof liqueur.

COFFEE-AND-GINGER BRANDY Moderately sweet coffee liqueur livened with ginger flavor.

COFFEE LIQUEUR Comes under many names, including Kahlua from Mexico, Tìa Maria from Jamaica, Espresso from dark-roasted Italian coffee, crème de café, Brazilia, Pasha from Turkey, etc. Any of this large galaxy of liqueurs is delightful served ice cold with heavy sweet cream floating on top.

COFFEE SAMBUCA A combination of coffee liqueur and sambuca; the latter is an Italian liqueur made from the elder bush.

COGNAC AND ORANGE This combination of triple-distilled orange liqueur and French Cognac is made by Leroux in the United States.

COINTREAU An eminent French liqueur made by maceration and double distillation of bitter and sweet orange peels; one of the best-selling of the family of orange liqueurs.

CORDIAL MÉDOC A French liqueur made from a blend of oranges, cherries, brandy, and crème de cacao.

CRANBERRY LIQUEUR U.S. liqueur with the tart-and-sweet flavor of fresh cranberries.

CUARENTA Y TRES The words mean "43" in Spanish, signifying the number of ingredients in this vanilla-accented, mildly herbal, decidedly sweet liqueur.

CURAÇAO A liqueur made of the dried peel of small green oranges grown in the Dutch West Indies, plus spices and sometimes port wine and rum. It may be white, blue, or green, although it is normally orange in color from the maceration of bitter orange peels.

DANZIGER GOLDWASSER see Goldwasser, Danziger.

DELECTA U.S. version of a Benedictine-type liqueur; made from herbs and spices.

DRAMBUIE Originally from a recipe presented by Bonnie Prince Charlie to the Mackinnon family, present guardians of its formula, this liqueur is made from Scotch whisky at least ten years old, heather honey, and herbs, and gets its name from the Gaelic phrase *an dram buidheach*, or "the drink that satisfies."

ESCORIAL A 112-proof German herbal liqueur of a green Chartreuse type.

ENZIAN A Bavarian 80-proof liqueur made from the yellow enzian plant; always served ice cold.

FIOR DI ALPI; FIORE D'ALPE; FLORA DI ALPI; FLORA ALPINE All four spellings refer to an Italian liqueur of herbs and spices. The bottle contains a twig covered with crystallized sugar.

FRAISES, CRÈME DE; FRAISETTE Liqueur of either wild or cultivated strawberries; Dolfi fraise de bois is the most prestigious brand of the wild-strawberry category.

FRAMBOISE, CRÈME DE This raspberry liqueur—not to be confused with framboise, a white, unsweetened raspberry brandy—makes a refreshing summer highball with lemon juice, soda water, and ice. It also takes the place of Melba sauce in a Peach Melba.

FRANGELICO An Italian hazelnut liqueur with flavors of berries and flowers.

GALLIANO A mildly spicy but smooth liqueur from Solaro, Italy, with overtones of anise and vanilla; one of the principal ingredients in the Harvey Wallbanger cocktail.

GEBIRGS ENZIAN A German liqueur with the flavor of gentian root, decidedly on the bitter side; used as a stomachic.

GEORGE M. TIDDY'S CANADIAN LIQUEUR A 72-proof liqueur of medium sweetness with citrus overtones.

GILKA German Kümmel liqueur.

GINGER-FLAVORED BRANDY An infusion of fresh ginger root and brandy, usually taken straight or over crushed ice.

GLAYVA A liqueur with a Scotch whisky base, flavored with honey, anise, and herbs.

GOLDWASSER, DANZIGER; GOLD LIQUEUR Goldwasser is the German version of an aromatic liqueur made since 1598. Gold liqueur is the modern American rendition. It contains specks of gold leaf so light that they leave no sensation in the mouth. The gold is harmless and makes the orange-herbal liqueur a sensational conversation piece as an after-dinner drink. In spite of the price of gold, a bottle of gold liqueur costs less than twenty-five dollars a fifth, perhaps a clue to the amount of gold you ingest with each sip.

GRAND MARNIER Distinguished French orange liqueur with a Cognac base, aged in oak casks; famed not only as an after-dinner liqueur but as an ingredient in haute cuisine desserts.

GRASSHOPPER A green-colored liqueur made of white crème de cacao and green crème de menthe; may be sipped straight or shaken with cream and ice for a Grasshopper cocktail.

GREEN TEA LIQUEUR A Japanese Suntory liqueur; 50 proof, with a velvety, true green-tea flavor.

GRENADINE Normally a nonalcoholic sweetener made of pomegranates, the liqueur is a 25-proof version available in liquor shops, which saves the job of searching for it in supermarkets; used in the Tequila Sunrise cocktail.

HALB UND HALB A mildly bitter German liqueur with citrus accents.

HERBSAINT Another substitute for absinthe, without the harmful wormwood; made in New Orleans.

HONEY LIQUEUR A liqueur usually from central Europe, the first sip of which will remind you of easily flowing honey. It's a natural mixer in Brandy Milk Punch, eggnog, etc.

HUNGARIAN PEAR LIQUEUR A 60-proof liqueur of a fruit usually distilled as a nonsweet eau-de-vie.

IRISH MIST Irish whiskey, honey, and orange make this mellifluous liqueur a delightful after-dinner drink; its subtlety is somewhat lost when used in Irish Coffee.

IZARRA A French herbal liqueur of the Chartreuse type, which includes Armagnac in its base. The green version is 100 proof, the yellow 86 proof.

JÄGERMEISTER German 70-proof liqueur with bitter overtones; made from fifty-six herbs.

KAHLUA Mexican coffee liqueur, richly sweet with vanilla overtones, famed for the Black Russian cocktail.

KIRSCH, CRÈME DE; KIRSCHWASSER LIQUEUR A sweet, white cherry liqueur, not to be confused with the completely dry kirschwasser, a white brandy, or eau-de-vie.

KÜMMEL A caraway-flavored liqueur, usually colorless, varying considerably in sweetness depending on brands; the best continental versions are on the dry side.

LEMONIQUE A liqueur with a zest-of-lemon flavor.

LIQUEUR D'OR Gold-flecked liqueur of the Goldwasser type.

LOCHAN ORA Scotch-based liqueur of medium sweetness and delicate herbal flavors.

MACADAMIA LIQUEUR Of the famed (and delicious) Hawaiian nuts, available in Hawaii but not widely distributed on the U.S. mainland.

MANDARINE An 80-proof liqueur of tangerines with a Cognac base.

MARASCHINO A heavily sweet liqueur of cherry and almond flavors; widely used in fruit compotes and other desserts.

MASTIC; MASTIKHA; MASTIKA A Greek liqueur made from the sap of the mastic shrub; extremely pleasant, high-proof, and on the dry side, but there's very little available in the United States.

MENTHE, CRÈME DE This liqueur made of mint leaves may be white, green, pink, or gold. The small amount of menthol in fresh mint leaves gives it its refreshing coolness. Most versions are heavily sweet, in contrast with peppermint schnapps (see page 324).

MIDORI A Japanese liqueur with the flavor of honeydew melon.

MOKA, CRÈME DE Coffee liqueur.

NOISETTE A liqueur of hazelnuts usually combined with herbal flavors.

NOYAUX, CRÈME DE; CRÈME DE NOYA Pink liqueur made with the stones of such fruits as plums, cherries, peaches, and apricots, producing a predominantly almond flavor.

O-CHA Japanese green-tea liqueur with a bitter aftertaste—the perfect finale for an Asian dinner.

OJE A colorless, anise-flavored Spanish liqueur. There are some high-proof bottlings in both sweet and dry varieties.

Ouzo A high-proof Greek aperitif liqueur, somewhat on the dry side; similar to the French pastis with its anise base and usually mixed with ice water, in which it turns milky white.

Parfait Amour Although the words *parfait amour* mean "perfect love," liqueur makers have never agreed on the formula for perfection. One kind is made of lemon, citron, and coriander; another is made of anisette, vanilla, and orange; a third is produced from flowers, including violets. The only constant for this versatile liqueur is its purple color.

Pasha Richly flavored, spicy coffee liqueur from Turkey, vividly reminiscent of Turkish coffee itself.

Passion Fruit Liqueur A Hawaiian product with the intriguing tart flavor of fresh passion fruit, reminiscent of peach or mango.

Pastis; Pastis de Marseille An aniselike liqueur used as both an aperitif and a thirst quencher; makes an immensely refreshing on-the-rocks drink. The best-known brands in North America are the 90-proof Ricard and Pernod.

Peach-flavored Brandy Of higher alcohol content than and not as sweet as peach liqueur.

Peach Liqueur Made from an infusion of whole fruit, sometimes fresh, or fresh and dried mixed, with brandy or neutral spirits as a base. It is an essential, though small, ingredient in Fish-House Punch.

Peanut Lolita America's sweetheart nut liqueur, launched during the term of our first peanut-farmer president.

PEAR LIQUEUR A 60-proof liqueur from Hungary, with the hard-to-capture flavor of fresh pears.

PEPPERMINT GET A very popular French mint liqueur; heavily sweet, 60 proof, noted for mint-flavor fidelity.

PEPPERMINT SCHNAPPS Mint liqueur of a higher alcoholic content and less sweet than crème de menthe; often taken on the rocks or with soda and ice.

PETER HEERING Also known as Cherry Heering; a famed 49-proof Danish liqueur with a vivid, tart, natural cherry flavor.

PIMENTO DRAM Jamaican rum liqueur with peppery, spicy overtones.

PINEAPPLE LIQUEUR; LICOR DE PINE; CRÈME D'ANANAS Liqueur from the Caribbean or Hawaii, with a straight, uncomplicated pineapple flavor.

PISTACHIO LIQUEUR; PISTASHA Medium-sweet green liqueur with the flavor of pistachio nuts.

PONCHE Heavily sweet liqueur with pronounced sherry-brandy taste and raisin overtones.

PRUNELLA; CRÈME DE PRUNELLE Liqueur with the predominant flavor of small tart plums, sometimes blended with prunes and sometimes with figs and vanilla.

RAKI High-proof, anise-flavored liqueur from the Middle East, similar to ouzo.

RASPAIL French herbal liqueur of the Benedictine type.

RASPBERRY LIQUEUR; FRAMBOISE Liqueur made from fresh or wild raspberries.

RATAFIA A general term for aperitif liqueurs from France, made of assorted fruits and fruit pits.

ROCK AND RUM The same as rock and rye except with a rum base; superb in Milk Punch.

ROCK AND RYE Rye whiskey, rock-candy syrup, and fruit juices, with slices of fruit in the bottle. Another type contains crystallized sugar without fruit. This old-fashioned winter solace is a natural for hot drinks in mugs.

ROIANO An amber Italian liqueur with the flavor of anise and vanilla.

RON COCO A 60-proof liqueur of rum and coconut.

ROSE, CRÈME DE A liqueur with vanilla, spices, and the aroma of rose petals. An enchanting end for a shish-kebab party.

ROSOLIO Similar to crème de rose but not as sweet; flavored with spices and orange blossom water.

RUMONA A 63-proof liqueur from Jamaica, with a rum base and flavors reminiscent of coffee and chocolate.

SABRA A chocolate-orange liqueur from Israel.

SAMBUCA Italian liqueur made from the sambuca plant whose fruit is close to anise in flavor; usually served with a few coffee beans for munching. Caffé Sambuca combines coffee and Sambuca liqueurs.

SCIARADA Italian 80-proof liqueur with the color of lime and the flavors of orange and lemon, which manage to be both subdued and lively at the same time.

SLOE GIN This red liqueur, made from sloes (the fruit of the blackthorn bush), is not a gin at all, though juniper berries are sometimes used in its manufacture. It is probably called gin after the European holiday drinks made of gin, crushed sloe, and sugar. Some types, as indicated on the label, will produce a creamy head when shaken with ice.

SOUTHERN COMFORT A famed American liqueur of whiskey base and peaches; excellent as a mixer in tall and short drinks. Its 100 proof adds to its comforting qualities.

STRAWBERRY LIQUEUR Called fraise or fraise de bois (wild strawberries) if imported. Look for a bottle that says "true fruit" flavor; usually low proof.

STREGA LIQUORE Pale yellow Italian liqueur of the monastery type, subtly blended with numerous herbs and spices of which no single one has a predominant flavor.

SWEDISH PUNSCH Also known as caloric punsch, it's popular in Scandinavian countries; made of a rum or arrack base, spices, and citrus flavors.

TANGERINE Liqueur of tangerines with a mild herbal flavor.

TEA BREEZE A French, tea-flavored liqueur.

TIA MARIA A medium-sweet, Jamaican coffee liqueur made from noted Blue Mountain coffee and spices.

TIFFIN A German liqueur with the flavor of Darjeeling tea; has a mildly tannic aftertaste.

TILUS A 70-proof liqueur with truffles as one of its ingredients. Call ahead to check availability.

TRAPPASTINE A French herbal liqueur of the Chartreuse type; comes in both green and yellow varieties.

TRIPLE SEC A popular, colorless, orange-flavored liqueur; flavored with orange flower water, orris root, and other fragrances. It's widely used in the United States for Sidecars, Margaritas, etc.

TUACA Subtly flavored, this medium-sweet Italian liqueur is known as "milk brandy" in Tuscany because milk, oddly, is one of its ingredients; made with a brandy base, the primary flavor is citrus.

VAN DER HUM Literally, "What's his name?" An African liqueur flavored with native tangerine peel and spices.

VAN DER MINT Dutch chocolate-mint liqueur.

VERANA Spanish liqueur of chocolate and orange flavors.

VIEILLE CURE A French monastic-type liqueur in both green and yellow types.

VIOLETTE, CRÈME DE; CRÈME DE YVETTE Very sweet purple liqueur made from petals of violets and spices.

VISNOKA Wild-cherry liqueur from central Europe.

WILD TURKEY LIQUEUR An American 80-proof liqueur in which the base flavor—bourbon—clearly dominates the mild, spicy overtones.

WISHNIAK; WISNIOWKA Cherry-flavored liqueur, moderately spiced, from Poland or other Slavic countries.

YUKON JACK 100- and 80-proof liqueur with a Canadian-whisky base; it's moderately sweet and citrus-flavored, with herbal overtones.

YVETTE CRÈME DE; CRÈME DE VIOLETTE Liqueur of extract of violets.

ZAMOURA Liqueur with a predominant flavor of cloves.

ZITRONEN EIS German liqueur whose principal flavor is lemon.

AFTER-DINNER COCKTAILS

On a dinner or late-supper menu, the after-dinner cocktail can take the place of the dessert or supplement it. As a libation, it's frankly sweet and toothsome. It goes perfectly with a platter of cheese and crackers, a bowl of fresh fruit, or both. It graciously replaces pie and ice cream. For the harried host who has neither the time to make nor the energy to shop for a fresh dessert, it's deliverance. Freshly concocted, any of the following are an imaginative way to conclude a brunch, lunch, or dinner.

AFTER-DINNER CHARADE
1 oz. Sciarada
½ oz. peppermint schnapps
½ oz. heavy cream
Shake extremely well with ice. Strain into prechilled cocktail glass.

AMARETTO CREAM
1 oz. amaretto
1 oz. Muscari
½ oz. heavy cream
Shake well with ice. Strain into prechilled cocktail glass or over rocks.

BANSHEE
1 oz. banana liqueur
½ oz. white crème de cacao
1-inch slice ripe banana
½ oz. cream or milk
½ cup crushed ice
Blend all ingredients for 10 seconds. Pour into deep-saucer champagne glass.

BERRIES AND CREAM
1 oz. blackberry-flavored brandy
1 oz. strawberry liqueur
1 oz. nondairy creamer
½ oz. lime juice
Shake well with ice. Strain into prechilled cocktail glass or serve over rocks. Fresh heavy sweet cream may be used, but it tends to curdle when mixed with the lime juice.

BLUE ANGEL
½ oz. blue curaçao
½ oz. parfait amour
½ oz. brandy
½ oz. lemon juice
½ oz. heavy cream
Shake well with ice. Strain into prechilled cocktail glass. *Cool and incredibly smooth.*

CARAMEL COW
2 oz. (¼ cup) vanilla ice cream
1 oz. Caramella
½ oz. crème de cacao
1½ oz. milk
Blend all ingredients at high speed for 10 seconds. Pour over rocks into 8-oz. old-fashioned glass. Stir well.

CARA SPOSA
1 oz. coffee liqueur
1 oz. curaçao
½ oz. heavy cream
⅓ cup crushed ice
Blend all ingredients at low speed for 10 to 15 seconds. Pour into prechilled deep-saucer champagne glass. Although any kind of coffee liqueur may be used in this drink, the espresso-coffee liqueur is especially pleasant.

CHIQUITA PUNCH

1½ oz. banana liqueur
1½ oz. orange juice
1½ oz. cream

¾ oz. grenadine
¾ cup crushed ice

Blend all ingredients at high speed for 10 seconds. Pour into prechilled old-fashioned glass.

CHOCOLATE MINT

2 oz. (¼ cup) chocolate ice cream
1 oz. peppermint schnapps

½ oz. vodka
1½ oz. milk

Blend all ingredients at high speed for 10 seconds. Pour over rocks into 8-oz. glass. Stir well.

COCO AMOR

1 oz. CocoRibe
½ oz. amaretto

½ oz. lemon juice

Shake extremely well with ice. Strain into prechilled cocktail glass with sugar-frosted rim.

COCO BANANA

1 oz. CocoRibe
½ oz. banana liqueur

½ oz. heavy cream

Shake extremely well with ice. Strain into prechilled cocktail glass.

COCONUT MINT

1 oz. CocoRibe
½ oz. peppermint schnapps

½ oz. heavy cream
1 tbsp. chocolate shavings

Shake CocoRibe, peppermint schnapps, and cream extremely well with ice. Strain into prechilled cocktail glass. Float chocolate shavings on drink.

COFFEE CREAM

1 oz. coffee liqueur
1 oz. California brandy

1 oz. heavy cream

Shake well with ice. Strain into large prechilled cocktail glass or over rocks.

COFFEE GRASSHOPPER

¾ oz. coffee liqueur
¾ oz. white crème de menthe

¾ oz. cream

Shake well with ice. Strain into prechilled cocktail glass.

COFFEE ROIANO

1½ oz. Roiano
½ oz. coffee liqueur

½ oz. heavy cream
⅓ cup crushed ice

Blend all ingredients at low speed for 10 to 15 seconds. Pour into prechilled deep-saucer champagne glass. *May be served not only at the end of a meal but at any time of the day.*

COLD TURKEY

1½ oz. cream sherry
½ oz. Wild Turkey liqueur

1 oz. orange juice
1 slice orange

Pour sherry, Wild Turkey liqueur, and orange juice over rocks in 8-oz. glass. Stir well. Add orange slice. *An after-dinner drink that's not too cloying.*

CREAMY CHARADE

1 oz. Sciarada
½ oz. vodka
½ slightly beaten egg white

½ oz. lemon juice
½ oz. heavy sweet cream

Shake all ingredients extremely well with ice. Strain into prechilled large cocktail glass.

FROZEN BANANA MINT

1 oz. banana liqueur
1 oz. peppermint schnapps
⅓ cup sliced ripe banana

¾ cup crushed ice
2 large mint leaves

Put banana liqueur, peppermint schnapps, sliced banana, and crushed ice into blender. Blend at high speed for 10 seconds. Pour into 8-oz. glass. Float mint leaves on drink.

FROZEN BLACK CURRANT

1 oz. crème de cassis
1 oz. pineapple juice
½ oz. brandy

⅓ cup crushed ice
1 slice orange

Put crème de cassis, pineapple juice, brandy, and crushed ice into blender. Blend at low speed for 10 to 15 seconds. Pour into prechilled deep-saucer champagne glass. Add orange slice.

FROZEN COCO BANANA

2 oz. CocoRibe
⅓ cup sliced ripe banana

½ cup crushed ice
½ oz. lemon juice

Whirl all ingredients in blender at high speed for 10 seconds. Pour into deep-saucer champagne glass.

GINGERMAN

2 oz. (½ cup) chocolate ice cream
1 oz. ginger-flavored brandy

½ oz. light rum
½ oz. milk

Blend all ingredients at high speed for 10 seconds. Pour over rocks into 8-oz. glass. Stir well.

GOLD CADILLAC

¾ oz. crème de cacao
¾ oz. Galliano

¾ oz. heavy cream
⅓ cup crushed ice

Blend all ingredients at low speed for 10 to 15 seconds. Pour into prechilled deep-saucer champagne glass. Or omit crushed ice, shake well with ice, and strain into prechilled cocktail glass.

GOLDEN FROG

½ oz. Strega
½ oz. Galliano
½ oz. vodka

½ oz. lemon juice
¾ cup crushed ice

Blend all ingredients at high speed for 10 seconds. Pour into prechilled old-fashioned glass.

GRASSHOPPER

¾ oz. white crème de cacao
¾ oz. green crème de menthe

¾ oz. heavy cream

Shake well with ice. Strain into prechilled cocktail glass.

GRASS SKIRT

1 oz. CocoRibe
½ oz. light rum

1 oz. pineapple juice
½ oz. lime juice

Shake well with ice. Strain into prechilled large cocktail glass with sugar-frosted rim.

IL MAGNIFICO

¾ oz. Tuaca liqueur
¾ oz. curaçao

¾ oz. heavy cream
⅓ cup crushed ice

Blend all ingredients at low speed for 10 to 15 seconds. Pour into prechilled deep-saucer champagne glass. *May be served before, with, or after the espresso.*

KALANI WAI

1 oz. Midori
1 oz. green crème de menthe

1 oz. heavy cream

Shake all ingredients well with ice. Pour into prechilled old-fashioned glass. Add ice cubes to fill glass to rim. Stir.

LADY IN GREEN

1 oz. pistachio liqueur
1 oz. green crème de menthe

½ oz. heavy cream

Shake well with ice. Strain over rocks into 8-oz. glass. Stir.

MAUI

1 oz. Midori
1 oz. Cointreau or triple sec

½ oz. lemon juice

Shake well with ice. Strain into large cocktail glass or serve over rocks.

MOCHA MINT

¾ oz. coffee liqueur
¾ oz. white crème de menthe

¾ oz. crème de cacao

Shake well with ice. Strain into prechilled sugar- and coffee-frosted cocktail glass.

ORACABESSA

1 oz. banana liqueur
½ oz. lemon juice
½ oz. 151-proof rum

1 slice banana
1 slice lemon

Dip banana slice into lemon juice or orange juice to prevent discoloration. Shake banana liqueur, lemon juice, and rum well with ice. Strain over rocks into old-fashioned glass. Add banana and lemon slices.

ORANGE COMFORT

½ oz. Southern Comfort
½ oz. anisette
¾ oz. orange juice

½ oz. lemon juice
1 slice cocktail orange in syrup

Shake Southern Comfort, anisette, orange juice, and lemon juice well with ice. Strain into prechilled cocktail glass. Garnish with orange slice.

ORANGE FLOWER

1 oz. curaçao
½ oz. cherry liqueur
½ oz. orange juice

1 tsp. lemon juice
1 dash orange flower water
⅓ cup crushed ice

Blend all ingredients at low speed for 10 to 15 seconds. Pour into prechilled deep-saucer champagne glass. *Exhilarating finale for a roast goose dinner.*

PARSON WEEMS

2 oz. (¼ cup) chocolate ice cream
½ oz. cherry-flavored brandy
½ oz. maraschino liqueur

½ oz. California brandy
1½ oz. milk

Blend all ingredients at high speed for 10 seconds. Pour over rocks into 8-oz. glass. Stir well.

PAYOFF

2 oz. (¼ cup) vanilla ice cream
¾ oz. amaretto
¾ oz. California brandy

1½ oz. milk
1 tbsp. toasted slivered almonds

Pour vanilla ice cream, amaretto, California brandy, and milk into blender. Blend at high speed for 10 seconds. Pour over rocks into 8-oz. glass. Stir well. Sprinkle almonds on top.

PINK ALMOND

½ oz. crème de noyaux
½ oz. orgeat or orzata
1 oz. blended whiskey
½ oz. kirschwasser
½ oz. lemon juice
1 slice lemon

Shake crème de noyaux, orgeat, whiskey, kirschwasser, and lemon juice well with ice. Strain over rocks into prechilled old-fashioned glass. Add lemon slice.

PINK CARNATION

2 oz. (¼ cup) vanilla ice cream
½ oz. cranberry liqueur
½ oz. cherry-flavored brandy
½ oz. California brandy
1½ oz. milk

Blend all ingredients at high speed for 10 seconds. Pour over rocks into 8-oz. glass. Stir well.

PINK COCONUT

1½ oz. CocoRibe
½ oz. nondairy creamer
½ oz. lime juice
1 tsp. grenadine

Shake all ingredients extremely well with ice. Strain into prechilled cocktail glass.

PINK RIBBON

1 oz. strawberry liqueur
1 oz. triple sec
½ oz. California brandy
½ oz. lemon juice

Shake all ingredients well with ice. Strain into sugar-frosted cocktail glass.

PINK SQUIRREL

1 oz. crème de noyaux
1 oz. white crème de cacao
¾ oz. heavy cream

Shake all ingredients well with ice. Strain into prechilled sugar-frosted cocktail glass. *Pinker and smoother than a Pink Lady.*

PISTACHIO CREAM

2 oz. (¼ cup) vanilla ice cream
1 oz. pistachio liqueur
½ oz. California brandy
1½ oz. milk

Blend all ingredients at high speed for 10 seconds. Pour over rocks into 8-oz. glass. Stir well.

SHERRIED COFFEE

1¼ oz. oloroso sherry
1¼ oz. coffee liqueur
2 tsp. heavy cream

Shake sherry and coffee liqueur well with ice. Strain over rocks into prechilled old-fashioned glass. Float cream on top.

SNIFTER

¾ oz. Galliano
¾ oz. brandy
1 tsp. white crème de menthe
⅓ cup finely crushed ice

Pour liquors into brandy snifter. Add crushed ice. Stir. May be served with or without a straw.

SOUTHERN PEACH

1 oz. Southern Comfort
1 oz. peach liqueur

½ oz. heavy cream
1 slice fresh or brandied peach

Shake Southern Comfort, peach liqueur, and cream well with ice. Strain over rocks or coarsely cracked ice into prechilled old-fashioned glass. Add peach slice. *It's peaches and cream for grown-ups.*

STRAWBERRY KISS

1 oz. strawberry liqueur
½ oz. kirschwasser
½ oz. light rum

½ oz. orange juice
1 tsp. lemon juice
1 large strawberry

Shake strawberry liqueur, kirschwasser, rum, orange juice, and lemon juice well with ice. Strain into prechilled sugar-frosted cocktail glass. Add strawberry.

SWEET OFFERING

1 oz. Caramella
½ oz. crème de cacao

½ oz. light rum
½ oz. lime juice

Shake all ingredients well with ice. Strain into large cocktail glass.

SWEET TALK

1 oz. blackberry-flavored brandy
½ oz. California brandy

½ oz. heavy cream

Shake all ingredients very well with ice. Strain into cocktail glass.

SWEET WILLIAM

¾ oz. pear brandy
¾ oz. apricot liqueur

¾ oz. heavy cream
Ground cinnamon

Shake pear brandy, apricot liqueur, and cream very well with ice. Strain into prechilled cocktail glass. Sprinkle with cinnamon.

FRAPPÉS

Frappés are even more pleasing than ice cream and cake as a finale for a feast. Cool, clean, and rich, they're a mixture of liqueurs poured over finely crushed ice. You can serve them freshly made, but we prefer to swizzle them up beforehand and store them in the freezer until the drinking lamp is lit. When you take them out, you'll find that an ice cap has formed on top of each drink. But the cap will loosen after a minute or two and the drink can be sipped from the rim with or without a short straw.

ALL-WHITE FRAPPÉ

½ oz. anisette
¼ oz. white crème de menthe

½ oz. white crème de cacao
1 tsp. lemon juice

Stir without ice. Pour over crushed ice into deep-saucer champagne glass.

BRANDY APRICOT FRAPPÉ

¾ oz. California brandy
½ oz. apricot flavored brandy

¼ oz. crème de noyaux

Stir without ice. Pour over crushed ice into deep-saucer champagne glass.

CRANBERRY FRAPPÉ

½ oz. cranberry liqueur
½ oz. cherry brandy

½ oz. orange juice

Pour ingredients over crushed ice into deep-saucer champagne glass.

CHARTREUSE COGNAC FRAPPÉ

¾ oz. yellow Chartreuse
¾ oz. Cognac

Stir without ice. Pour over crushed ice into deep-saucer champagne glass.

CHERRY GINGER FRAPPÉ

1 oz. cherry liqueur
¼ oz. kirschwasser
¼ oz. ginger-flavored brandy

1 brandied cherry
1 piece preserved ginger in syrup

Stir cherry liqueur, kirschwasser, and ginger-flavored brandy without ice. Pour over crushed ice into deep-saucer champagne glass. Pierce brandied cherry and preserved ginger with cocktail spear and place over rim of glass.

CHOCOLATE ORANGE FRAPPÉ

¾ oz. white crème de cacao
¾ oz. orange juice

1 tsp. Galliano or Roiano

Stir without ice. Pour over crushed ice into deep-saucer champagne glass.

COFFEE GRAND MARNIER

½ oz. coffee liqueur
½ oz. Grand Marnier

½ oz. orange juice
1 slice orange

Stir coffee liqueur, Grand Marnier, and orange juice without ice. Pour over crushed ice into deep-saucer champagne glass. Add orange slice.

COGNAC MENTHE FRAPPÉ

1 oz. green crème de menthe
½ oz. Cognac

2 large mint leaves

Stir crème de menthe and Cognac without ice. Pour over crushed ice into deep-saucer champagne glass. Tear each mint leaf partially and place on drink.

DUTCH PEAR FRAPPÉ

1¼ oz. pear brandy
¾ oz. Vandermint liqueur
½ oz. heavy cream

½ cup finely crushed ice
Sweetened whipped cream

Pour pear brandy, Vandermint, heavy cream, and ice into blender. Blend at low speed for 20 seconds. Pour into prechilled old-fashioned glass. Add ice cubes if necessary to fill glass to rim. Top with dollop of whipped cream. Prepare this drink just before serving.

GRAND MARNIER QUETSCH

1 oz. Grand Marnier
¼ oz. quetsch

¼ oz. orange juice
1 slice lemon

Stir Grand Marnier, quetsch, and orange juice without ice. Pour over crushed ice into deep-saucer champagne glass. Add lemon slice. Mirabelle or slivovitz may be used in place of quetsch because all are plum brandies.

KÜMMEL BLACKBERRY FRAPPÉ

¾ oz. Kümmel
¾ oz. blackberry liqueur or
  blackberry-flavored brandy

1 tsp. lemon juice

Stir without ice. Pour over crushed ice into deep-saucer champagne glass.

MIXED MOCHA FRAPPÉ

¾ oz. coffee liqueur
¼ oz. white crème de menthe

¼ oz. crème de cacao
¼ oz. triple sec

Sugar-frost rim of deep-saucer champagne glass. Fill with crushed ice. Stir liqueurs without ice and pour over ice into glass.

SAMBUCA COFFEE FRAPPÉ

1 oz. Sambuca
½ oz. coffee liqueur

Roasted coffee beans

Stir the Sambuca and coffee liqueur without ice. Pour over crushed ice into deep-saucer champagne glass. Place the glass on a saucer along with about half a dozen coffee beans to munch while sipping. It's an Italian custom; the more distinguished the guest, the more coffee beans placed alongside his Sambuca.

SHERRIED CORDIAL
MÉDOC FRAPPÉ

1 oz. Cordial Médoc
½ oz. amontillado sherry

Stir without ice. Pour over crushed ice into deep-saucer champagne glass.

SLOE LIME FRAPPÉ

1 oz. sloe gin   **1 slice lime**
½ oz. light rum

Stir sloe gin and light rum without ice. Pour over crushed ice into deep-saucer champagne glass. Add lime slice. Sip without a straw.

SOUTHERN COMFORT STRAWBERRY FRAPPÉ

¾ oz. Southern Comfort   **Orange peel**
¾ oz. strawberry liqueur   **1 slice lemon**

Stir Southern Comfort and strawberry liqueur without ice. Pour over crushed ice into deep-saucer champagne glass. Twist orange peel above drink and drop into glass. Add lemon slice. *Sip on a summer evening under the stars.*

POUSSE-CAFÉ

This showy little drink is one of the oldest bits of nonsense known to bartenders—and needless to say, the number of drinkers who never stop loving nonsense is greater than ever. If not a cocktail by definition, it is for after-dinner imbibing, and thus we include it here.

The Pousse-Café is a series of liqueurs poured into a small, straight-sided pousse-café glass so that each forms a layer. Since the liqueurs are of different weights or densities, the heaviest stays on the bottom, the next heaviest directly above it, and so on. The main problem that bedevils the Pousse-Café specialist is that the densities of liqueurs of the same flavor often vary from one brand to the next. One man's menthe may not rise above another man's parfait amour. Since the density of a liqueur is not indicated on the bottle's label, a certain amount of trial and error may be necessary in building a Pousse-Café. As a general guide remember that frequently, the higher a liqueur's alcohol content, the lower its density. This doesn't apply in all cases, but it's something of an aid. The so-called demi-sec liqueurs are lighter than the sweet crèmes, and U.S. fruit-flavored brandies are lighter than liqueurs. If you're in doubt about a recipe, make an experimental Pousse-Café before the guests arrive, and when you find a formula that works, stick to it for as long as you're using the same brands of liqueurs.

To keep the ingredients from mingling, pour them slowly over the back of a teaspoon, with the tip of the spoon held against the inside of the glass. Pour slowly and steadily, keeping your eye on the liquid as it flows. If you follow this procedure carefully, the layers should stay separate; you may find, in fact, that a liqueur poured in the wrong order will seep down or rise up to its proper level and stay there intact. For a party, you can make a large number of Pousse-Cafés beforehand, and if you place them carefully in the refrigerator, each small rainbow will remain undisturbed until you need it.

A Pousse-Café may be of three, four, or five layers. Each layer needn't be equal, but each should be of a distinctly different color when held at eye level. Nonalcoholic liquids such as syrups and cream may be poured along with the liqueurs or other spirits. Here are twelve Pousse-Café combinations, with the heaviest liquid listed first and the lighter ones in ascending order. To both create and divert conversation, make an assortment with several combinations on the same tray.

1. White crème de cacao, cherry liqueur, Kümmel, and a dab of whipped cream.

2. Green crème de menthe, Galliano, blackberry liqueur, and kirschwasser.

3. Banana liqueur, Peter Heering or Cherry Karise, and Cognac.

4. Peach liqueur, kirsch liqueur (not kirschwasser), and Pernod.

5. Orzata or orgeat, crème de noyaux, curaçao, and sweet cream mixed with enough crème de noyaux to turn cream pink.

6. Passion fruit syrup, green crème de menthe, strawberry liqueur, and ouzo.

7. Grenadine, brown crème de cacao, Drambuie, and sweet cream flavored with crème de menthe.

8. Crème de noyaux, anisette, Tuaca, and a dab of whipped cream.

9. Grenadine, brown crème de cacao, triple sec, and Sciarada.

10. Brown crème de cacao, maraschino liqueur, yellow Chartreuse, and Cognac.

11. Parfait amour, cherry liqueur, anisette, and sweet cream flavored with a small amount of parfait amour.

12. Strawberry liqueur, cream, Cointreau, and Sciarada.

ANYTIME LIQUEUR COCKTAILS

Whether for after work, after dinner, after a day at the beach, or during long afternoons on the patio, you're sure to find among the following a potable to cordially soothe every palate.

ALMOND JOY

1 oz. amaretto
1 oz. white crème de cacao

2 oz. light cream

Shake well with ice. Strain into prechilled cocktail glass.

BANANA MIDORI

1½ oz. Midori
½ oz. banana liqueur
2 oz. lemonade

½ oz. CocoRibe
½ oz. Rose's blue curaçao

Shake well with ice. Strain into highball glass over rocks.

BANANAS AND CREAM

1 oz. Kahlua
1 oz. Bailey's Irish Cream

1 oz. banana liqueur

Shake very well with cracked ice. Strain into prechilled cocktail glass.

BANSHEE

1 oz. crème de bananes
1 oz. crème de cacao

1 oz. light cream

Shake very well with ice. Strain into prechilled cocktail glass.

COFFEE SOUR

1½ oz. coffee liqueur
1 oz. lemon juice

1 tsp. powdered sugar
1 egg white

Shake well with ice. Strain into prechilled whiskey-sour glass.

CREAMSICLE

1½ oz. vanilla liqueur
1½ oz. milk

2 oz. orange juice

Shake well with ice. Strain into prechilled old-fashioned glass.

DUTCH BROWNIE

1 oz. genever gin
1 oz. brandy

½ oz. chocolate liqueur
Splash heavy cream

Pour gin, brandy, and liqueur into old-fashioned glass over rocks. Stir. Float cream on top.

DUTCH VELVET

1 oz. chocolate mint liqueur
1 oz. banana liqueur

2 oz. light cream
1 tsp. semisweet chocolate, shaved

Shake well with ice. Strain into prechilled cocktail glass. Garnish with shaved chocolate.

GOLDEN DREAM

1½ oz. Galliano
1 oz. white crème de cacao
½ oz. triple sec

2 oz. orange juice
2 oz. light cream

Shake very well with ice. Strain into collins glass over rocks.

JOLLY RANCHER

1½ oz. Midori
1 oz. blueberry schnapps
1 oz. Rose's Lime Juice

Splash grenadine
1 cherry

Shake Midori, schnapps, and Rose's Lime Juice well with ice. Strain into old-fashioned glass over rocks. Float grenadine on top. Drop in cherry.

LIFESAVER

1 oz. Midori
1 oz. light rum

2 oz. pineapple juice

Shake well with ice. Pour into prechilled old-fashioned glass.

MELONBALL

1½ oz. Midori
1½ oz. vodka

Pineapple juice

Pour Midori and vodka into highball glass over rocks. Top off with pineapple juice. Stir.

MIDORI SOUR

2 oz. Midori
1 oz. Rose's Lime Juice

1 tsp. powdered sugar
1 lime wedge

Shake well with ice. Strain into prechilled whiskey-sour glass. Garnish with lime wedge.

MUDSLIDE

1 oz. vodka
1 oz. Kahlua

1 oz. Bailey's Irish Cream

Shake well with cracked ice. Strain into prechilled old-fashioned glass. Can also be made frozen in a blender: just add about ¼ cup (2 to 3 scoops) vanilla ice cream. Or blend well with ice and ½ cup milk.

PEACH BOWL

1½ oz. peach schnapps
3 oz. orange juice

Pour into highball glass over rocks. Stir.

PEACHES AND CREAM

1 oz. vanilla vodka
1 oz. peach schnapps

2 oz. milk

Shake very well with ice. Strain into prechilled cocktail glass.

RASPBERRY RICKEY

1½ oz. Himbeergeist
¼ large lime

Iced club soda
3 fresh or thawed frozen raspberries

Put three ice cubes into an 8-oz. glass. Add Himbeergeist. Squeeze lime above drink and drop into glass. Add soda. Stir. Float frozen raspberries on drink or fasten fresh raspberries to cocktail spear as garnish.

SHADY LADY

1 oz. Midori
1 oz. tequila
3 oz. grapefruit juice

1 lime slice
1 cherry

Pour into highball glass over ice. Stir. Garnish with lime slice and cherry.

SHRINERS' COCKTAIL

1½ oz. sloe gin
1½ oz. brandy
½ tsp. sugar syrup

2 dashes Angostura bitters
Lemon peel

Stir well with ice. Strain into prechilled cocktail glass. Twist lemon peel over drink and drop into glass.

SMITH AND KEARNS

1½ oz. Kahlua   Club soda
1 oz. light cream

Pour Kahlua and light cream into highball glass over rocks. Stir well. Top off with club soda.

SOMBRERO

1½ oz. coffee liqueur
1 oz. light cream

Pour coffee liqueur into old-fashioned glass over rocks. Float cream on top.

SWEET CHASTITY

1 oz. Tia Maria   1 oz. Bailey's Irish Cream
1 oz. Frangelico   1 oz. light cream

Shake very well with cracked ice. Strain into prechilled old-fashioned glass.

YELLOW PARROT

1½ oz. yellow Chartreuse   ½ oz. anisette
1½ oz. apricot brandy

Stir well with ice. Strain into prechilled cocktail glass.

CHAPTER 16

✳ The Brimming ✳
Bowl ✳

In the world of entertaining, there is no more delightfully flexible potable than a good punch. This protean party favorite can assume any festive task to which it's put. Made with light Moselle or Rhenish wines, it can beguile your guests with a delicate flavor that rests easily on the tongue. Switch to the heavier-duty brandies and rums, and it can single-handedly catalyze jolly high spirits and flowing conversation.

Nevertheless, for some time the punch bowl was trotted out only at the year-end saturnalia, when it was filled with a hot wassail or a rich whiskey eggnog, emptied a few times, and then stashed away for the next twelve months. But today, more and more hosts are reviving the reigns of the four Georges of England, when men like David Garrick and Samuel Johnson vied with each other all year round to invent newer and stronger punch recipes as they ladled their way through clubs and taverns all over England, and when punch bowls were the center of conviviality at celebrations of everything from weddings to military triumphs.

Now, as then, there are a few punch recipes in which fruit must be marinated in liquors for a day or two, but—happily—those are the exceptions. Generally, an hour or so is all you need for ripening the strong and the weak, the tart and the sweet into a really superior punch. Yet, for all its simplicity, the punch bowl, with its gleaming island of ice in a sea of liquor, turns any affair into a gala occasion. The mere sight of the brimming bowl seems an irresistible enticement to drinkers of all persuasions, be they light, moderate, or heavy.

Punch is made cold in two ways—by prechilling all the ingredients from the brandy to the bitters, and by placing a floating island of ice in the bowl itself to both cool and properly dilute the liquid. There are a few cold punches, such as some of the champagne varieties, that aren't diluted with ice but instead are sometimes girt in a surrounding vessel of crushed ice. These days, it's sometimes difficult to buy a really good-size chunk of the cold stuff. However, in our age of the cube, this is no particular problem; in fact, cubes are faster in their chilling effect. But to serious punchmakers, they are puny craft alongside the traditional icy blockbuster in the punch bowl. You can make your own by simply freezing water in a metal or plastic container, a deep saucepan, or metal mixing bowl. For each gallon of punch, you'll normally need a chunk of ice made with 2 quarts of water. After freezing, dip the sides of the bowl in warm water for a few seconds and the ice will slide free. The top may form a slight peak and reveal a crack or two, but the inverted iceberg will be smooth and should float serenely.

The punch recipes that follow each make approximately a gallon of potables, enough for eight bibulous guests at three rounds apiece.

APPLE EGG BOWL

12 eggs
½ cup sugar
1 quart applejack
3 quarts milk

1½ cups heavy sweet cream
1 tbsp. vanilla extract
Ground cinnamon

Blend eggs and sugar at low speed for 2 minutes. Pour into punch bowl. Gradually add applejack and beat with wire whip until well blended. Stir in milk, cream, and vanilla. Let mixture ripen in refrigerator at least 1 hour for flavors to blend. Stir well before serving. Serve in punch cups. Sprinkle with cinnamon.

APPLE GINGER PUNCH

24 oz. apple brandy,
  either Calvados or applejack
1 quart plus 1 pint ginger beer or ginger ale
2 red apples
2 yellow apples

24 oz. green-ginger wine
2 oz. maraschino liqueur
1 quart pineapple-grapefruit juice
2 oz. kirsch

Chill all ingredients. Pour all liquids except ginger beer over large block of ice in punch bowl. Stir well. Let mixture ripen 1 hour in refrigerator. Cut unpeeled apples into wedgelike slices, discarding cores. Just before serving, pour ginger beer into bowl. Float apple slices on top.

ARTILLERYMEN'S PUNCH

1 quart 86-proof bourbon
9 oz. light rum
4 oz. dark Jamaican rum
6 oz. apricot-flavored brandy

12 oz. lemon juice
24 oz. orange juice
1 quart strong black tea
¼ cup sugar

Pour all ingredients over a large block of ice in punch bowl. Stir well to dissolve sugar. Let mixture ripen 1 hour in refrigerator before serving.

BARBADOS BOWL

8 medium-size ripe bananas
1 cup lime juice
1 cup sugar
1 fifth light rum

8 oz. 151-proof rum
1 quart plus 12 oz. pineapple juice
12 oz. mango nectar
2 limes, sliced

Chill all ingredients except bananas. Cut 6 bananas into thin slices and place in blender with lime juice and sugar. Blend until smooth. Pour over block of ice in punch bowl. Add both kinds of rum, pineapple juice, and mango nectar. Stir well. Let mixture ripen in refrigerator 1 hour before serving. Cut remaining 2 bananas into thin slices. Float banana and lime slices on punch.

BERMUDA BOURBON PUNCH

3 cups boiling water
3 tbsp. jasmine tea leaves
1 fifth bourbon
8 oz. Madeira
8 oz. lemon juice

1½ oz. Pernod
4 oz. Falernum
1 quart plus 1 pint ginger ale
3 lemons, thinly sliced

Pour boiling water over tea leaves. Steep for 5 minutes; strain, cool to room temperature, and chill in refrigerator. Over large block of ice in punch bowl, pour tea, bourbon, Madeira, lemon juice, Pernod, and Falernum. Stir well. Let mixture ripen 1 hour in refrigerator. Add ginger ale and sliced lemons. Add several spiced walnuts (recipe below) to each drink after pouring it into punch cup.

Spiced Walnuts

1 egg white
2 tsp. cold water
½ lb. shelled walnut halves
1 cup sugar

1 tbsp. ground cinnamon
¼ tsp. ground cloves
⅛ tsp. ground nutmeg

Beat egg white until slightly foamy but not stiff. Add the water and mix well. Combine egg white and walnuts in a bowl; stir to coat nuts; drain thoroughly in colander to remove excess egg white. In another bowl, combine sugar, cinnamon, cloves, and nutmeg. Preheat oven to 325°F. Dip walnuts, a few pieces at a time, into sugar mixture (they should be coated thoroughly but should not have thick gobs of sugar adhering to them), place them on a greased baking sheet, and bake for 20 minutes or until medium brown. Remove from baking sheet with spatula, separating them from sugar coating on pan. Cool to room temperature.

BLACK CHERRY RUM PUNCH

1 fifth light rum	4 oz. fresh lime juice
4 oz. 151-proof rum	8 oz. Peter Heering
4 oz. dark Jamaican rum	8 oz. crème de cassis
8 oz. fresh lemon juice	2 limes, thinly sliced
4 oz. fresh orange juice	1 quart club soda
2 16-oz. cans pitted black cherries	
in heavy syrup	

Put all ingredients except soda into punch bowl. Add block of ice. Stir well. Refrigerate 1 hour. Add soda. Stir well.

BRANDY EGGNOG BOWL

12 eggs	3 quarts milk
½ cup sugar	8 oz. heavy cream
1 fifth Cognac or non-Cognac brandy	Ground nutmeg
4 oz. Jamaica rum	

Carefully separate egg yolks from whites. In punch bowl, combine egg yolks and sugar. Beat well with a wire whisk. Gradually add Cognac, rum, milk, and cream. Beat well. Taste. Add more sugar if desired. Place the bowl in the refrigerator for at least 2 hours. Just before serving, beat egg whites in a separate bowl or in mixer, in two batches if necessary, until stiff. Fold whites into punch, that is, do not mix them with a round-the-bowl movement but use the wire whisk in a down-over-up stroke until whites are thoroughly blended. Ladle into cups. Sprinkle with nutmeg.

CAPE COD CRANBERRY PUNCH

2 quarts plus 6 oz. cranberry juice	1 tsp. ground cinnamon
1 quart 100-proof vodka	½ tsp. ground allspice
6 oz. cherry liqueur	¼ tsp. ground nutmeg
1 tbsp. orange flower water	2 limes, thinly sliced
24 oz. orange juice	

Chill all liquid ingredients. Mix cinnamon, allspice, and nutmeg with a small amount of vodka until a smooth, lump-free paste is formed. Pour the paste and all other liquids over large block of ice in punch bowl. Stir well. Refrigerate 1 hour before serving. Float lime slices on top.

CHAMPAGNE BLUES

Peel of 2 lemons	8 oz. lemon juice
1 fifth blue curaçao	4 fifths dry champagne

Chill all ingredients. Cut lemon peel into strips 1½ to 2 inches long and ¼-inch wide. Pour curaçao and lemon juice into glass punch bowl. Stir well. Add champagne and stir lightly. Float lemon peel, yellow side up, in bowl. Do not use ice in bowl. Punch may be surrounded by cracked ice if desired by placing glass bowl in a vessel of larger diameter.

The Galley Party

IT'S HARD TO IMAGINE SURROUNDINGS more felicitous for a party than topside on a boat moored in a quiet cove, the summer stillness broken only by the gentle lapping of Gin and Tonics against frosty tumblers.

The kind of victuals you stow aboard depends for the most part on the length of your cruise and the size of your galley. If you're speedboating from one yacht club to another, of course, you can pick up food and drink wherever you happen to tie up. Slightly longer trips are simply floating picnics. You pack your portable cooler with unsliced rare roast beef, corned beef brisket, or barbecued chickens, fill a deep bowl with German potato salad, stack the fresh rye and pumpernickel, remember the mustard, add the necessary amount of cold lager or picnic coolers to your cargo, and shove off. But for an all-day or weekend cruise, you'll want hot and hefty fare from your own galley. The sailor assigned to the job may have a misgiving or two when he or she lights the ministove, but when the aroma of crisp bacon or hash-brown potatoes or hot clam chowder first rises on deck, all hands will know that the real master of the vessel is stationed below.

Cruising schedules on rivers, lakes, and seas all over the world are alike in one respect: the best-laid schemes can go awry in the face of becalmed waters or ailing engines. Anticipating these normal delays, an experienced commodore sees to it that there are always extra rations in cans. The entire crew will welcome a canned cured ham as readily as a fresh one. Buy the type that requires no refrigeration. Canned Canadian-style bacon—another name for smoked boneless pork loin—is equally good hot or cold, at sea as well as on land. Corned-beef hash or roast-beef hash, both staunch nautical standbys, can go into the frying pan without any additions, although you can enhance them mightily with a few beaten egg yolks, cream or melted butter, and a spray of Worcestershire sauce. And there are days when nothing, not even 151-proof rum, can warm a crew like mugs of hot, thick soup.

Since most cruising for party purposes takes place in warm or comparatively warm climates, tall coolers fit in perfectly with offshore outings. But the gross tonnage of corkscrews, cans, bottles, ice buckets, tongs, racks, and ice picks can sometimes present a formidable obstacle course twixt the seafarer who's drawn the duty as bartender and his wares. To avoid this kind of overstocking, carry one superb and totable potable, premixed on land, needing in some cases only the addition of carbonated waters. If you decide on straight drinks, try to carry no more bottles and glassware than fit into a mounted bar rack. Finally, insulated unbreakable bar glasses conserve ice and are the mainstay of many a waterborne party.

CHAMPAGNE PUNCH WITH KIRSCH

4 fifths iced brut champagne
5 oz. iced oloroso (cream) sherry
5 oz. iced kirsch liqueur
   (not dry kirschwasser)

4 oz. iced lemon juice
16 oz. iced orange juice

Pour all ingredients into prechilled punch bowl. Stir lightly. Bowl may be surrounded by ice in larger bowl, or punch may be made in pitchers surrounded by ice.

CHAMPAGNE PUNCH WITH MARASCHINO

6 oz. maraschino liqueur
6 oz. Cognac
1 tsp. orange bitters

2 oranges, thinly sliced
1 lemon, thinly sliced
4 fifths iced brut champagne

Put maraschino liqueur, Cognac, bitters, and sliced fruit into punch bowl. Let mixture brew about 1 hour in refrigerator. Place large chunk of ice in bowl. Pour champagne over ice. Stir lightly.

CHAMPAGNE SHERBET PUNCH

2 quarts lemon sherbet or
   lemon ice, frozen very hard

5 fifths iced brut champagne
1½ tsp. Angostura bitters

Be sure lemon sherbet has been in the freezer, set at the coldest point, for at least 1 day. Place lemon sherbet in prechilled punch bowl. Pour champagne over sherbet. Add bitters. Stir. Let mixture ripen in refrigerator for about 15 to 20 minutes before serving.

EMERALD BOWL

3 quarts chilled emerald Riesling
⅔ cup California brandy
⅔ cup apricot-flavored brandy

1½ pints chilled apple juice
16 slices cucumber peel, each
   1 inch long, ½ inch wide

Pour Riesling, California brandy, apricot-flavored brandy, and apple juice over large block of ice in punch bowl. Add cucumber peel. Stir. Refrigerate 1 hour.

FISH-HOUSE PUNCH I

1½ cups sugar
1 quart cold water (not carbonated water)
1 fifth Cognac
1 fifth golden rum

1 fifth Jamaican rum
24 oz. lemon juice
6 oz. peach-flavored brandy

A traditionally high-proof punch. Put sugar into punch bowl. Add about 1 cup of the water and stir until sugar is dissolved. Add all other ingredients, including balance of water. Let mixture ripen in refrigerator about 1 hour. Place large chunk of ice in bowl. Ladle punch over ice. Add more cold water if a weaker mixture is desired.

FISH-HOUSE PUNCH II

2 12-oz. pkgs. frozen sliced peaches,
  thawed
1 quart golden rum
1 fifth Cognac

1 pint lemon juice
1 cup sugar
1 quart ice water

Blend peaches for 1 minute at high speed. Pour over large block of ice in punch bowl. Add rum, Cognac, lemon juice, sugar, and water. Stir well to dissolve sugar. Let punch ripen in refrigerator for about 1 hour before serving.

FLORENTINE PUNCH

2 bottles coffee-cream Marsala wine
2 bottles Italian rosé wine
1 fifth plus 8 oz. brandy

4 oz. lemon juice
2 oranges

Chill all ingredients. Pour both kinds of wine, brandy, and lemon juice over large block of ice in punch bowl. Stir well. Refrigerate 1 hour. Cut oranges into thin rounds. Slice in half and float atop punch.

GUAVA MILK PUNCH

2½ quarts milk
1 quart (32 oz.) guava nectar
1 cup light cream
1 pint plus 4 oz. light rum
6 oz. golden rum

3 oz. 151-proof rum
¼ cup sugar
12 1-inch pieces lemon peel
12 1-inch pieces orange peel

Pour all ingredients except lemon and orange peels into punch bowl. Stir very well to dissolve sugar. Add a large block of ice, lemon peel, and orange peel. Place bowl in refrigerator 1 hour to ripen flavors.

INTERPLANETARY PUNCH

1 fifth light rum
4 oz. dark Jamaican rum
12 oz. peppermint schnapps
1 quart mango nectar
12 oz. (1½ cups) heavy sweet cream

1 quart orange juice
8 large sprigs mint
1 large ripe fresh mango, if available
6 thin slices orange

Prechill all ingredients including liquors. Place large block of ice in punch bowl. Add both kinds of rum, peppermint schnapps, mango nectar, cream, and orange juice. Stir very well. Tear mint leaves from stems. Peel and cut mango into small slices. (Canned mango may be used in place of fresh; canned fruit, however, will not float.) Cut orange rounds into quarters. Float mint leaves and fruit on punch. Refrigerate for 1 hour for flavors to ripen.

IRISH APPLE BOWL

20 oz. applejack
20 oz. blended Irish whiskey
10 oz. Rose's Lime Juice

2 large red apples
4 limes, sliced thin
2 quarts plus 1 pint ginger ale

All ingredients, including spirits, should be prechilled. Apples should be cored but not peeled, and cut into ½-inch dice. Pour applejack, whiskey, and lime juice over large block of ice in punch bowl. Add lime slices and apples. Stir well. Let mixture ripen in refrigerator 1 hour. Pour cold ginger ale into bowl. Stir lightly.

MOSELLE BOWL

1 very ripe medium-size pineapple
½ cup sugar
12 oz. Grand Marnier

16 oz. brandy
4 bottles Moselle wine
1 quart large ripe strawberries

Cut ends off pineapple, remove shell and all "eyes," and cut lengthwise into 4 pieces. Cut away hard core from each piece; then cut crosswise into thin pieces. Place pineapple, sugar, Grand Marnier, and brandy in salad bowl or mixing bowl. Marinate, covered, in refrigerator at least 24 hours—48 hours if possible. Pour well-chilled wine into punch bowl with large block of ice. Add pineapple mixture and stir well. Let mixture ripen in bowl <1/2> hour before serving. Cut stems off strawberries. Cut lengthwise in half and float on punch.

MOUNTAIN RED PUNCH

3 quarts chilled California red wine
½ cup amaretto
½ cup California brandy

½ cup cherry-flavored brandy
1 pint ginger ale
2 oz. julienned almonds, toasted

Pour wine, amaretto, California brandy, and cherry-flavored brandy over large block of ice in punch bowl. Refrigerate 1 hour. Add ginger ale. Stir lightly. Float almonds on top. (Note: almonds may be toasted by placing in a shallow pan in moderate oven for about 10 minutes; avoid scorching.)

ORANGE ALMOND BOWL

6 oz. slivered almonds
2 tbsp. melted butter
Salt
18 oz. blended whiskey
12 oz. Danish aquavit

1 quart plus 8 oz. orange juice
8 oz. sweet vermouth
1 tsp. orange bitters
Peel of 2 large California oranges
1½ quarts quinine water

Preheat oven to 375°F. Place almonds in shallow pan or pie plate. Pour butter over almonds, mixing well. Place pan in oven and bake until almonds are medium brown, about 8 to 10 minutes, stirring once during baking. Avoid scorching. Sprinkle with salt. Chill almonds and all other ingredients. Pour whiskey, aquavit, orange juice, vermouth, and bitters over large block of ice in punch bowl. Refrigerate mixture for 1 hour. Cut orange peel into narrow strips about 2 inches long. Pour quinine water into bowl. Stir. Float orange peel and almonds on punch.

PHI BETA BLUEBERRY

1 fifth 100-proof vodka
16 oz. Metaxa brandy
16 oz. bottled blueberry syrup
12 oz. lemon juice

2 quarts club soda
2 lemons, thinly sliced
1 pint cultivated blueberries

Chill all ingredients. Pour vodka, Metaxa, blueberry syrup, and lemon juice over large block of ice in punch bowl. Let mixture ripen in refrigerator 1 hour before serving. Pour club soda into bowl and stir. Float lemon slices and blueberries on punch.

POLYNESIAN PUNCH BOWL

1 fifth light rum
6 oz. cream of coconut
1 quart plus 1 cup pineapple juice
3 cups orange juice
8 oz. sloe gin

5 oz. peppermint schnapps
1 cup lemon juice
12 thin slices very ripe fresh pineapple
12 thin slices orange
1 pint iced club soda

Pour rum, cream of coconut, pineapple juice, orange juice, sloe gin, peppermint schnapps, and lemon juice into punch bowl. Stir well until all ingredients, particularly cream of coconut, are well blended. Add a large block of ice and pineapple and orange slices; place in refrigerator for about 1 hour for flavors to ripen. Add soda. Stir lightly just before serving.

ROSE PUNCH

3 quarts chilled rosé wine
1 cup cranberry liqueur
½ cup California brandy

16 thin slices ripe fresh pineapple
1 quart large ripe strawberries
1 pint iced club soda

Pour wine, cranberry liqueur, and California brandy over large block of ice in punch bowl. Add pineapple slices and strawberries. Refrigerate 1 hour. Add iced club soda. Stir lightly.

RUM CUP WITH WHITE WINE (8 to 10 punch cups)

1 pint plus 4 oz. light rum
10 oz. very dry white wine
1 cup (8 oz.) orange juice
½ cup (4 oz.) lime juice
2 oz. orgeat

2 oz. Falernum
2 oz. triple sec
6 slices lime
6 large sprigs mint

Pour all ingredients except lime slices and mint into 2-quart pitcher. Add lime slices and mint. Chill 1 to 2 hours. Fill pitcher almost to rim with ice cubes. Stir very well. *Pour into punch cups or 6-oz. fruit-juice glasses.*

SANGRIA (6 servings of 6 to 8 oz. each)

1 whole orange
1 fifth light dry red wine
1 ripe Elberta peach, peeled and sliced
6 slices lemon
1½ oz. Cognac

1 oz. triple sec
1 oz. maraschino liqueur
1 tbsp. sugar or more to taste
6 oz. iced club soda

Cut entire peel of orange in a single strip, beginning at stem end and continuing until spiral reaches bottom of fruit. White part should be cut along with outer peel so that orange fruit is exposed. Leave peel attached to orange bottom so that fruit may be suspended in pitcher. Pour wine into glass pitcher. Add peach and lemon slices, Cognac, triple sec, maraschino liqueur, and sugar. Stir to dissolve sugar. Carefully place orange in pitcher, fastening top end of peel over rim. Let mixture marinate at room temperature at least 1 hour. Add soda and 1 tray of ice cubes to pitcher. Stir well.

WHISKEY PUNCH

3 cups orange juice
1 cup lemon juice
1 cup sugar

2 lemons, thinly sliced
2 quarts blended whiskey
1 quart iced club soda

Put fruit juices and sugar into punch bowl. Stir until sugar dissolves. Add lemon slices. Place a large chunk of ice in bowl. Add whiskey. Refrigerate 1 hour. Add club soda. Stir. Additional club soda may be added if desired.

WHITE SANGRIA *(6 servings of 6 to 8 oz. each)*

1 whole orange
1 fifth dry white wine
2 slices lemon
2 slices lime
1 oz. Cognac

2 tbsp. sugar
1 stick cinnamon
8 large strawberries, stems
  removed, halved
6 oz. iced club soda

Cut entire peel of orange, following procedure for Sangria recipe on page 353. Pour wine into glass pitcher. Add lemon and lime slices, Cognac, sugar, cinnamon, and strawberries. Stir to dissolve sugar. Carefully place orange in pitcher, fastening top end of peel over rim. Let mixture marinate at room temperature at least 1 hour. Add soda and 1 tray of ice cubes to pitcher. Stir.

WHITE WINE PUNCH

3 quarts chilled dry white wine
½ cup triple sec
½ cup kirschwasser
½ cup California brandy

8 slices orange
8 slices lemon
1 pint iced club soda

Pour wine, triple sec, kirschwasser, and brandy over large block of ice in punch bowl. Add orange and lemon slices. Place bowl in refrigerator for 1 hour for flavors to blend. Add club soda. Stir lightly.

PICNIC COOLERS

The following nine drinks are planned for serving from the tailgate, whether it's a day in the dunes, at the dockside, or near a shady grove. All nine are designed for picnic jugs. Soda, rocks, etc. should be brought along in insulated containers.

BITTER BOURBON *(Makes 6 drinks)*

7½ oz. bourbon
5 oz. orange juice
1½ oz. peppermint schnapps

1 tsp. Angostura bitters
Iced tonic water

Shake bourbon, orange juice, peppermint schnapps, and bitters well with ice. Strain into prechilled picnic jug. Serve over rocks in 10-oz. glass. Add tonic water.

BLACK CURRANT COOLER (Makes 6 drinks)

9 oz. blended whiskey　　　　**7 oz. orange juice**
3 oz. crème de cassis　　　　**Iced club soda**
7 oz. lemon juice

Combine whiskey, crème de cassis, lemon juice, and orange juice. Do not mix with ice. Chill in refrigerator. Pour into prechilled picnic jug. Serve over rocks in 10-oz. glass. Add splash of soda.

CARTHUSIAN CUP (Makes 6 drinks)

6 oz. chilled orange juice　　　**Iced club soda**
3 oz. chilled yellow Chartreuse　**6 slices orange**
1 fifth iced dry white wine

Pour orange juice and Chartreuse into prechilled picnic jug. Carry iced dry white wine in another insulated container. Pour 1½ oz. orange juice–Chartreuse mixture into 12- oz. glass. Add 4 oz. wine and about 2 oz. soda. Add ice cubes to fill glass. Stir lightly. Add orange slice.

CELTIC CUP (Makes 6 drinks)

9 oz. Scotch　　　　　　　　**1½ oz. lemon juice**
1½ oz. cherry-flavored brandy　**Iced club soda**
1½ oz. sweet vermouth

Shake Scotch, cherry-flavored brandy, vermouth, and lemon juice well with ice. Strain into prechilled picnic jug. Serve over rocks in 10-oz. glass. Add splash of soda.

ICED COFFEE OPORTO (Makes 6 drinks)

12 oz. tawny port　　　　　　**Heavy cream**
6 oz. brandy
24 oz. (1½ pints) strong black coffee,
　sweetened to taste

Combine port, brandy, and coffee, and chill in refrigerator. Do not shake with ice. Pour into prechilled picnic jug. At picnic site, divide among 6 tall 12-oz. glasses, allowing about 7 oz. for each glass. Add ice cubes to fill glasses. Top with cream and stir. *A tall potable that, for some picnickers, takes the place of dessert.*

PEACH CUP WITH CHABLIS (Makes 6 drinks)

10-oz. package frozen peaches in syrup　**1 fifth iced**
2 oz. California brandy　　　　　　　　**Chablis**
3 oz. lemon juice　　　　　　　　　　**Iced club soda**

Be sure you have an outsize picnic jug to hold all ingredients. Thaw peaches slightly. Put peaches together with their syrup, brandy, and lemon juice in blender. Blend until smooth. Pour into prechilled picnic jug. Add Chablis. At picnic site, divide contents of jug among 6 12-oz. highball glasses. Add several ice cubes to each glass. Add soda. Stir lightly.

RUM AND SOURSOP *(Makes 6 drinks)*

9 oz. light rum
6 oz. lime juice
2 7-oz. cans guanabana nectar

Iced club soda
6 slices lime

Combine rum, lime juice, and guanabana nectar (made from the pulp of the sour-sop—a delightful tropical fruit—and available in specialty food shops). Chill in refrigerator, but do not shake with ice. Pour into prechilled picnic jug. At picnic site, pour into tall 10-oz. glasses, allowing about 5 oz. of the chilled mixture for each drink. Add two large ice cubes to each and a splash of soda. Stir. Add lime slice.

RUMBO *(Makes 6 drinks)*

7 oz. golden rum
1½ oz. banana liqueur
3 oz. lime juice

1½ oz. orange juice
1½ oz. guava syrup
6 slices lime

Shake rum, banana liqueur, lime juice, orange juice, and guava syrup well with ice. Strain into prechilled picnic jug. Serve over rocks as a cocktail rather than as a long drink. Garnish with lime slice.

TALL FRENCH GIMLET *(Makes 6 drinks)*

9 oz. gin
1½ oz. Rose's Lime Juice
1½ oz. Amer Picon

1½ tsp. grenadine
Iced tonic water

Shake gin, lime juice, Amer Picon, and grenadine well with ice. Strain into prechilled picnic jug. At picnic site, divide gimlets among 6 10-oz. glasses, allowing about 3 oz. to each glass. Add ice cubes and tonic water. Stir lightly.

CHAPTER 17

Hot Cheer

When hot drinks had to wait on icy weather, the ideal accompaniments for a Hot Toddy party were a raging blizzard and a roaring fireplace. They're still picturesque backdrops, but nowadays any cool evening in the fall or winter is reason enough for filling the cups to the brim with grogs and nogs—and not just at the hearthside. Almost any casual, brisk-weather get-together—a tailgate party at a football or soccer field, a caravan to the ski country—is perfect for tapping the cordial pleasures of the Thermos. And a demitasse cup filled with a blend of warm blackberry liqueur, Cognac, and lemon is the most tranquil joy we can imagine before sinking into an unbroken night's sleep.

Hot drinks should be just warm enough so that the flavors seem to float like the soft clouds on an old silk painting—but not so hot that they burn the lips. Heat them in a saucepan or chafing dish to just short of the boiling point; then turn off the flame and let them cool somewhat before pouring.

One of the oldest bar tools for making drinks hot was the loggerhead—a long iron tool with a cup or ball at one end. In colonial days the cup was used, among other purposes, for melting pitch to be poured upon the crews of attacking naval vessels; those were the days when men at loggerheads weren't kidding around. It's now remembered as a fireplace device for the much more advanced purpose of heating Rum Flips. In time the loggerhead was succeeded by the poker, which serves just as well for those who feel like indulging in a bit of showmanship. Find one that's ash-free—old pokers with the soot of ages upon them aren't nearly as practical as clean ones that have never seen a fireplace—and heat it glowing hot in a normal gas flame. For reviving drinks that have become coolish from standing too long, keep the poker in the flame for at least three minutes before plunging it into the waiting mug.

The recipes that follow require no such fiery baptism (though it may win applause, it won't improve the drinks); nor are they intended to be enjoyed only at a bibbing party. Just as they can be served day or night, indoors or out, in fair weather or foul, they'll be the best of drinking companions with a colorful variety of meals: a warm Danish toddy of aquavit and Peter Heering before a smorgasbord or smørrebrød, a Buttered Bourbon and Ginger before a chafing dish of creamed chicken hash, a Blackberry Demitasse after an urban luau. And of course, any of the recipes below will serve admirably at an après-ski party, where warmth is most welcome.

Several of the recipes in this chapter depart from the usual one-drink formula. The reason: for some hot potations the nature of the ingredients makes the preparation of a single drink impractical. The Blue Blazer, for example, should be prepared for two in order to create a decent blaze. The taste of the Gin and Jerry becomes unpleasantly eggy unless two are made with each egg. The average café brûlot set serves eight, so the Café Diable recipe is for that number. Wherever a recipe makes more than a single drink, it's because careful party- and taste-testing have shown that the number specified is the minimum for best results. But whichever recipes you try, and for however many people, you'll find that all create warm contentment.

APPLE GROG

1½ oz. applejack
1 tbsp. brown sugar
4 oz. water
2 whole allspice

1 stick cinnamon
2-inch strip lemon peel
½ oz. 151-proof rum

Pour applejack, sugar, and water into saucepan. Add allspice and cinnamon. Bring to boiling point but do not boil. Pour into preheated mug. Twist lemon peel above mug and drop into drink. Float rum on top (pour it over the back of a spoon held along the inside of the mug). Set rum aflame. Let it burn for about 30 seconds, then stir to stop flaming. Warn guests not to burn lips on mug (take the first sip with a spoon).

APRICOT TOM AND JERRY

1 egg, separated
Salt
⅛ tsp. ground allspice
⅛ tsp. ground cinnamon
1½ tsp. sugar

1 oz. apricot-flavored brandy
1 oz. blended whiskey
1 oz. milk
1 oz. heavy cream
Freshly grated nutmeg

Beat egg yolk until light. Add a pinch of salt and the allspice, cinnamon, and sugar, blending well. Beat egg white separately in a small, narrow bowl until stiff. Slowly fold yolk into white. Put egg mixture into a 10-oz. Tom and Jerry mug. Heat apricot-flavored brandy, whiskey, milk, and cream until bubbles appear around edge of pan. Do not boil. Pour into mug slowly, stirring as liquid mixture is added. Sprinkle with nutmeg.

BLACKBERRY DEMITASSE

1 oz. blackberry liqueur
   or blackberry-flavored brandy
1 tbsp. blackberry jelly
½ oz. Cognac

½ oz. water
½ tsp. lemon juice
¼ thin slice lemon

Heat blackberry liqueur, jelly, Cognac, water, and lemon juice without boiling. Stir well until jelly is completely dissolved. Pour into demitasse cup. Add lemon slice.

BLUE BLAZER (Makes 2 drinks)

2 tbsp. honey
¼ cup boiling water

6 oz. Irish whiskey or Scotch
Lemon peel

Both nightcap and toast, the Blue Blazer should be served steaming hot and sipped slowly. (To create a decent blaze, it should always be made for two.) For mixing, you need two heavy and rather deep mugs, about 12-oz. capacity. Rinse them with hot or boiling water before mixing the drink. Then pour honey and boiling water into one mug and stir until honey is dissolved. Heat whiskey in a saucepan until it's hot but not boiling. Pour into second mug. Light it. Pour the whiskey—carefully— back and forth between the mugs. The flowing, blue-flaming stream will be best appreciated in a dimly lit room. Since a few drams of the blazing whiskey may spill, it's best to pour it over a large silver or china platter. When flames subside, pour the Blazer into two thick, cut-glass goblets. Twist lemon peel over Blazer and drop into drink. Some bartenders wear asbestos gloves when making a Blue Blazer.

BUTTERED APPLE GROG

1 oz. apple brandy
1 oz. dry vermouth
2 oz. apple juice
2 whole cloves
¼ baked apple, fresh or canned

1 tsp. sweet butter
1 slice lemon
1 tsp. syrup from canned baked
   apple, or sugar to taste
Sugar

Heat apple brandy, vermouth, apple juice, and cloves until hot but not boiling. Into an old-fashioned glass or coffee cup, put baked apple, butter, and lemon slice. Pour apple-brandy mixture into the glass. Add 1 tsp. syrup if canned baked apple is used, or add sugar to taste. Stir until butter dissolves.

An Aprés-Ski Party

FEW THINGS ON THIS EARTH put a more ravenous edge on one's appetite than a bracing, frost-nipped day on the slopes. When the day's skiing is over, Valhalla seems near at hand as the mountain air becomes suffused with the aromas of hot seafood chowder, strong coffee, and steaming Rum Toddies.

There are a number of techniques for hosting a ski feast. You can muster the whole meal ready-made, from Quiche Lorraine to Cognac, using any first-class restaurant or caterer as your commissary, and then transport it intact to your lodge, where the simple chore of reheating is all that's required. Of course, if your lodge's larder and kitchen facilities lend themselves to on-the-scene cookery, you may prefer starting from scratch. Or you can cook a stew or glaze spareribs in your own kitchen beforehand, pack them in wide-mouthed vacuum jugs and insulated picnic bags, then simply unpack when you're ready to serve the hungry snowpeople. If you're a ski host of the one-day-sojourn-to-a-nearby-slope persuasion, you might take along the raw ingredients in your station wagon, drop the tailgate for a buffet table, light the hibachi or gasoline stove, and broil the teriyaki or sauté the steaks to order.

There was a time when buying cooked collations meant a lot of bother. Advance shopping these days requires about as much effort as a trip on a chairlift, and there are certainly lots of options available to help you create a mouth-watering repast. If you have access to a Swedish food shop or café, Swedish meatballs as well as sweet-and-sour baked beans seem especially designed for cold-induced appetites. Neapolitan Italy may not be the ideal habitat for skiing, but any of the small pastas in rich cheese sauce or tomato sauce are perfect for relishing under the open sky after a day on the slopes. For cooking on the station-wagon barbecue, tender meats such as shish kebabs are quickly done over a crackling fire. Turn such foods frequently because the frigid air above the fire cools them quickly.

If all this begins to sound like a summer picnic, it's not coincidental—but you'll soon discover major differences. There are no ants in the winter, for example, and there are some ski stamping grounds where Klondike temperatures cause cutlery, dinner plates, and mugs to become so frost bitten that they can hardly be handled. To avoid such a cold fate, it's wise to protect your dinnerware in an insulated picnic box—the kind that's used in summer to keep things cold. And if you're carrying hot grog, remember that winter drinks are made with boiling water, and the mugs in which they're served make for really tall drinks; consequently, an insulated gallon jug holds just about enough to warm the cockles and soothe the muscles of four to six skiers. To keep the grog hot, you should preheat the jug by pouring boiling water into it and letting it stand for about five minutes before replacing it with your hot potation.

BUTTERED BOURBON AND GINGER

1½ oz. bourbon
1 oz. ginger-flavored brandy
1 tsp. sweet butter

1 cinnamon stick
6 oz. apple juice
Freshly grated nutmeg

Into a 10-oz. mug or silver tankard, pour bourbon and ginger-flavored brandy. Add butter and cinnamon stick to mug. Heat apple juice to boiling point, but do not boil. Pour into mug. Stir until butter dissolves. Sprinkle with freshly grated nutmeg.

CAFÉ DIABLE (Makes 8 demitasse cups)

2½ cups extra-strong fresh black coffee
2 cinnamon sticks, broken in half
8 whole allspice berries
4 whole cardamom seeds,
    removed from shell

Grated rind of ½ orange
5 oz. Cognac
3 oz. Grand Marnier
2 oz. Sambuca
2 tbsp. sugar

In a deep chafing dish or café brûlot set, simmer ½ cup coffee, cinnamon sticks, allspice, cardamom seeds, and orange rind for about 2 or 3 minutes to release spice flavors, stirring constantly. Add Cognac, Grand Marnier, and Sambuca. When liquors are hot, set ablaze. Stir with a long-handled spoon until flames subside. Add balance of coffee and sugar. When Café Diable is hot, ladle or spoon it into demitasse cups.

CRÈME DE CACAO NIGHTCAP (Makes 4 drinks)

¼ cup heavy cream
2 tsp. sugar
1 tbsp. plus 4 oz. crème de cacao
10 oz. milk

2 oz. California brandy
3 tbsp. sugar
Cocoa

Beat cream in small, narrow bowl until whipped. Stir 2 tsp. sugar and 1 tbsp. crème de cacao into whipped cream. Store in refrigerator until needed. Heat milk, 4 oz. crème de cacao, brandy, and 3 tbsp. sugar until hot but not boiling. Pour hot milk mixture into four footed whiskey-sour glasses or small goblets. Spoon whipped cream on top. Put a small quantity of cocoa into a small, fine wire strainer. Shake strainer above each drink, sprinkling lightly with cocoa. Place glass on saucer for serving.

DANISH TODDY

2 whole cloves
2 whole allspice berries
1 cinnamon stick
1 slice orange

2 oz. Peter Heering or Cherry Karise
1 oz. aquavit
½ oz. Kümmel
5 oz. cranberry juice

Put cloves, allspice, cinnamon stick, and orange slice into a 10-oz. mug. Heat Peter Heering, aquavit, Kümmel, and cranberry juice until hot but not boiling. Pour into mug.

GIN AND JERRY (Makes 2 drinks)

4 oz. gin
1 oz. yellow Chartreuse
3 oz. orange juice

1 tsp. sugar
1 egg
Ground cinnamon

Pour gin, Chartreuse, orange juice, and sugar into saucepan. Heat almost to boiling point, but don't boil. Beat egg in narrow bowl with rotary beater until egg is very light and foamy. Slowly, while stirring constantly, pour hot liquid into bowl with egg. Pour into preheated Tom and Jerry mugs or punch cups. Sprinkle lightly with cinnamon.

HOT BUTTERED APPLE

2 oz. applejack
½ oz. Stone's ginger wine
4 oz. water
1 stick cinnamon

2 whole cloves
1 tsp. sugar
1 tsp. sweet butter
Freshly grated nutmeg

Pour applejack, ginger wine, and water into saucepan. Add cinnamon, cloves, and sugar. Stir until sugar dissolves. Bring to boiling point, but do not boil. Pour into preheated mug. Add butter and stir until butter melts. Sprinkle with nutmeg.

HOT BUTTERED IRISH

1½ oz. blended Irish whiskey
½ oz. orange juice
½ oz. lemon juice
4 oz. water
1 tsp. sugar

2 dashes Angostura bitters
2 whole cloves
1 tsp. sweet butter
1 piece lemon peel
Grated fresh nutmeg

Pour whiskey, orange juice, lemon juice, water, sugar, and bitters into saucepan. Add cloves. Heat to boiling point, but do not boil. Pour into preheated mug. Add butter and stir until butter melts. Twist lemon peel over drink and drop into mug. Sprinkle with nutmeg.

HOT BUTTERED RUM

2 whole cloves
2 whole allspice berries
1-inch stick cinnamon
1 tsp. sugar

1½ oz. hot light rum
½ oz. hot dark Jamaican rum
Boiling water
1 tsp. sweet butter

Put the cloves, allspice, stick cinnamon, and sugar into a mug with a tbsp. or two of boiling water. Let the mixture stand 5 minutes. Add the hot rum (both kinds), 2 oz. boiling water, and butter. Stir until butter dissolves. Add more sugar if desired.

HOT COCONUT COFFEE

2 oz. CocoRibe
6 oz. strong, fresh hot coffee

Whipped cream

Pour CocoRibe and coffee into mug. Add dollop of whipped cream. Because of the sweetness of CocoRibe, sugar is usually not necessary in this drink.

HOT COCORIBE ORANGEADE

4 oz. orange juice
2 oz. water
2 oz. CocoRibe

1 stick cinnamon
½ slice orange

Pour orange juice and water into saucepan. Bring to boiling point, but do not boil. Pour into mug. Add CocoRibe. Stir with stick cinnamon, and leave stick cinnamon in mug. Add orange slice.

HOT DRAMBUIE TODDY

2 oz. Drambuie
½ oz. lemon juice
1 slice lemon

1 slice orange
4 oz. boiling water
1 stick cinnamon

Pour Drambuie and lemon juice into preheated mug or punch cup. (To preheat mug, fill with boiling water for about a minute; then discard water.) Add lemon slice, orange slice, and 4 oz. boiling water. Stir with stick cinnamon and leave it in the mug.

HOT EGGNOG

1 egg
1 dash salt
1 tbsp. sugar
¾ cup (6 oz.) hot milk

2 oz. hot Cognac
1 tsp. dark Jamaican rum
Freshly grated nutmeg

Put whole egg and dash of salt into mixing bowl. Beat egg until it is very thick and lemon yellow in color. Add sugar and beat until sugar is blended in. Add hot milk, Cognac, and rum. Stir well. Pour into mug. Sprinkle lightly with a dash of nutmeg.

HOT GRAPEFRUIT MUG

4 oz. unsweetened grapefruit juice
2 oz. orange juice
1½ oz. gin
½ oz. rock and rye

1 tbsp. honey
2 tsp. sweet butter
Freshly ground nutmeg

In saucepan heat grapefruit juice, orange juice, gin, rock and rye, honey, and 1 tsp. butter. Bring to boiling point, but do not boil. Pour into warm 10-oz. mug. Add remaining butter and stir until butter dissolves. Sprinkle lightly with nutmeg.

HOT IRISH AND PORT

1½ oz. blended Irish whiskey
3 oz. tawny port
2 oz. water

1 stick cinnamon
1 slice orange

Pour whiskey, port, and water into saucepan. Heat to boiling point, but do not boil. Pour into mug. Add stick cinnamon and orange slice. Let drink stand about 3 minutes before serving.

HOT PORT FLIP

3 oz. port wine
1 oz. Cognac
1 tsp. sugar
¼ tsp. instant coffee

1 small egg
1 tbsp. heavy cream
Freshly grated nutmeg

Pour wine and Cognac into saucepan. Add sugar. Stir well. Heat but don't boil. Stir in instant coffee. In a narrow bowl, beat egg with rotary beater until egg is very foamy. Stir in cream. Very slowly, while stirring constantly, pour hot liquid into egg mixture. Pour into preheated mug. Sprinkle with nutmeg.

HOT TODDY

1 tsp. sugar
3 whole cloves
1-inch stick cinnamon
1 thin slice lemon

3 oz. boiling water
2 oz. bourbon
Ground nutmeg

Into a heavy mug put the sugar, cloves, stick cinnamon, and lemon slice. Add 1 oz. boiling water. Stir well. Let the mixture stand about 5 minutes. Add bourbon and remaining 2 oz. boiling water. Stir. Sprinkle lightly with nutmeg.

IRISH COFFEE

5 or 6 oz. fresh, hot black coffee
1½ oz. Irish whiskey

1 tsp. sugar
Sweetened whipped cream

Warm an 8-oz. thick goblet or Irish-coffee glass by rinsing it in very hot or boiling water. Pour coffee and whiskey into goblet. Add sugar. Stir until sugar is dissolved. Add a generous dab of whipped cream.

IRISH TEA

1½ oz. blended Irish whiskey
6 oz. freshly brewed hot Irish black tea
3 whole cloves
3 whole allspice berries
1 stick cinnamon

Sugar, to taste (optional)
2 tsp. honey
1 slice lemon
Freshly grated nutmeg

Put whiskey, tea, cloves, allspice, cinnamon, sugar (if desired), and honey into mug. Stir well. Add lemon slice. Sprinkle with grated nutmeg.

JACK AND JERRY (Makes 4 drinks)

2 eggs, separated
2 tbsp. sugar
1 cup milk
1 oz. heavy cream
1 dash salt
¼ tsp. ground cinnamon

⅛ tsp. ground mace
⅛ tsp. ground ginger
8 oz. applejack
1 pint hot milk
Freshly grated nutmeg

Beat egg yolks and sugar in top part of double boiler until well blended. Slowly stir in 1 cup milk, cream, salt, cinnamon, mace, and ginger. Cook over simmering water, stirring constantly with wire whip, until mixture thickens to the consistency of a light sauce. Remove from fire. Beat egg whites until stiff. Slowly stir cooked mixture into beaten egg whites. Divide among 4 preheated mugs. Pour 2 oz. applejack into each mug. Fill mugs with hot milk. Stir. Sprinkle with nutmeg.

KIRSCH NIGHTCAP

3 oz. Stone's ginger wine
4 oz. water
1 oz. kirschwasser
1 stick cinnamon

2 whole cloves
1 tsp. sugar
Lemon peel

Slowly heat ginger wine and water to boiling point but do not boil. Pour into mug. Add kirschwasser, cinnamon, cloves, and sugar. Stir well. Twist lemon peel above drink and drop into mug.

MEXICAN COFFEE

1 oz. Kahlua coffee liqueur
4 oz. fresh, hot black coffee

Ground cinnamon
Sweetened whipped cream

Pour liqueur and coffee into Irish-coffee glass. Sprinkle with cinnamon. Stir. Top with whipped cream.

MULLED CLARET (Makes 8 drinks)

1 cup boiling water
½ cup sugar
1 lemon, sliced
1 orange, sliced

12 whole allspice berries
12 whole cloves
4-inch cinnamon stick
1 fifth dry red wine

In large saucepan combine boiling water, sugar, sliced lemon, sliced orange, allspice, cloves, and cinnamon stick. Bring to a boil. Reduce flame and simmer 5 minutes. Add wine. Bring to boiling point. Do not boil, but simmer 10 minutes. Pour hot mulled wine into thick glasses or mugs. Place a slice of lemon, a slice of orange, and a few whole spices in each glass.

MULLED KÜMMEL

2 oz. Kümmel
1 oz. vodka
½ oz. lemon juice
1 tsp. sugar
5 oz. water

2 tsp. butter
1 stick cinnamon
1 thin slice lemon
½ slice orange
½ oz. aquavit

In saucepan stir Kümmel, vodka, lemon juice, sugar, water, and 1 tsp. butter. Heat to boiling point, but do not boil. Place cinnamon in warm 10-oz. mug. Pour mulled Kümmel into mug and add remaining 1 tsp. butter. Stir until butter dissolves. Add lemon and orange slices. Float aquavit on top.

MULLED MADEIRA AND BOURBON

2½ oz. Madeira
1 oz. bourbon
1 oz. Lillet
¼ tsp. orange bitters
4 oz. water

1 tbsp. brown sugar
1 cinnamon stick
2 whole cloves
½ slice lemon
Orange peel

Heat Madeira, bourbon, Lillet, orange bitters, water, and brown sugar until hot but not boiling. Put cinnamon stick, cloves, and lemon slice into 10-oz. mug or metal tankard. Fill mug with Madeira mixture. Twist orange peel above drink and drop into mug.

MULLED PORT

4 oz. ruby port
1 oz. dark Jamaican rum
4 oz. water
½ oz. lime juice

1 tsp. sugar
2-inch piece orange peel
1 long stick cinnamon

Pour port, rum, water, lime juice, and sugar into saucepan. Stir. Bring to boiling point, but do not boil. Pour into mug. Twist orange peel over mug and drop into drink. Add stick cinnamon.

MULLED SCOTCH

2 oz. hot Scotch
1 oz. hot Drambuie
2 dashes bitters

1 oz. boiling water
1 maraschino cherry
Lemon peel

Into an old-fashioned glass, pour Scotch, Drambuie, bitters, and boiling water. Stir. Add cherry. Twist lemon peel over drink and drop into glass.

MULLED SHERRY

4 oz. amontillado sherry
2 oz. orange juice
½ oz. brandy
½ oz. lemon juice

1 to 2 tsp. sugar
1 tsp. butter
1 stick cinnamon

Heat sherry, orange juice, brandy, and lemon juice in saucepan over low flame until hot. Do not boil. Pour into mug. Add sugar to taste. Add butter. Stir with stick cinnamon until butter melts. Leave stick cinnamon in mug.

PLAYBOY'S HOT BUTTERED RUM

2 oz. dark Jamaican rum
½ tsp. maraschino liqueur
1 oz. lemon juice
1 tsp. sugar

2 tsp. butter
Boiling water
1 slice lemon
Freshly grated nutmeg

Pour rum, maraschino liqueur, and lemon juice into 12-oz. mug. Add sugar and butter. Fill with boiling water. Stir to dissolve butter and sugar. Add lemon slice. Sprinkle nutmeg on top.

ROCK-AND-RYE TODDY

2 oz. rock and rye
2 dashes Angostura bitters
1 slice lemon

3 oz. boiling water
1 cinnamon stick
Freshly grated nutmeg

Pour rock and rye and bitters into old-fashioned glass. Add lemon slice. Add boiling water and cinnamon stick. Stir. Sprinkle with nutmeg.

SCIARADA TEA

1½ oz. Sciarada
1 mug hot black tea

1 slice lemon
1 stick cinnamon

Pour Sciarada into tea. Add lemon slice. Stir with stick cinnamon. *An après-ski warmer.*

SIMMERING PLUM

5 oz. hot black tea
2 oz. plum brandy
  (slivovitz, quetsch, mirabelle)
1 oz. white crème de menthe

1 tsp. sugar or more to taste
½ oz. heavy cream
1 stick cinnamon
Ground coriander

Stir tea, plum brandy, crème de menthe, sugar, and cream in saucepan. Heat to boiling point, but do not boil. Pour into warm 10-oz. mug with stick cinnamon. Stir. Sprinkle coriander on top.

SNOWBERRY

1½ oz. strawberry liqueur
1 oz. vodka
½ oz. rock-candy syrup or simple syrup
1 oz. lemon juice
5 oz. water

½ large strawberry cut in
  half lengthwise
1 thin slice lemon
½ oz. kirschwasser

In saucepan heat strawberry liqueur, vodka, rock-candy syrup, lemon juice, and water to boiling point, but do not boil. Pour into warm 10-oz. mug. Dip strawberry into rock-candy syrup. Float lemon slice, strawberry half, and kirschwasser on drink.

SNOWSHOE

1 oz. aquavit
½ oz. blackberry-flavored brandy
1 mug hot black tea

1 stick cinnamon
Sugar
1 slice lemon

Pour aquavit and blackberry-flavored brandy into tea. Stir with cinnamon stick; leave cinnamon in mug. Add sugar to taste. Add lemon slice.

SNOWPLOW

8 oz. hot chocolate
1 oz. Bailey's Irish Cream
1 oz. Malibu rum

½ oz. crème de cacao
Whipped cream
Ground cinnamon

Mix hot chocolate to taste in large mug and add liquors. Top with whipped cream and sprinkle with cinnamon.

Metric Conversions

LIQUID MEASUREMENTS

IMPERIAL	METRIC
¼ FLUID OUNCE (1½ TSP.)	7 ML
½ FLUID OUNCE (3 TSP.)	15 ML
¾ FLUID OUNCE (4½ TSP.)	22 ML
1 FLUID OUNCE (2 TBSP.)	30 ML
4 FLUID OUNCES (½ CUP)	125 ML
8 FLUID OUNCES (1 CUP)	250 ML
12 FLUID OUNCES (1½ CUPS)	375 ML
16 FLUID OUNCES (2 CUPS)	500 ML

DRY MEASUREMENTS

IMPERIAL	METRIC
¼ TEASPOON	1 ML
½ TEASPOON	2 ML
1 TEASPOON	5 ML
1 TABLESPOON	15 ML
2 TABLESPOONS	25 ML
3 TABLESPOONS	50 ML
¼ CUP	50 ML
⅓ CUP	75 ML
½ CUP	125 ML
⅔ CUP	150 ML
¾ CUP	175 ML
1 CUP	250 ML

MEASURING EQUIVALENTS

1 PINCH = LESS THAN ⅛ TEASPOON (DRY)

1 DASH = 3 DROPS TO ¼ TABLESPOON (LIQUID)

3 TEASPOONS = 1 TABLESPOON = ½ OUNCE

2 TABLESPOONS = 1 OUNCE

4 TABLESPOONS = 2 OUNCES = ¼ CUP

8 TABLESPOONS = 4 OUNCES = ½ CUP

DIMENSIONS

IMPERIAL	METRIC
⅛ INCH	3 MM
¼ INCH	6 MM
½ INCH	1.5 CM
¾ INCH	2 CM
1 INCH	2.5 CM

Index